ADELE

THE BIOGRAPHY
CHAS NEWKEY-BURDEN

JB

JOHN BLAKE

Published by John Blake Publishing Ltd,
3 Bramber Court, 2 Bramber Road,
London W14 9PB, England

www.johnblakebooks.com

www.facebook.com/johnblakebooks 🆕
twitter.com/jblakebooks 🆕

Previously published in hardback in 2013
This edition published in 2015

ISBN: 978 1 78606 021 1

British Library Cataloguing-in-Publication Data:

A catalogue record for this book is available from the British Library.

Design by www.envydesign.co.uk

Printed in Great Britain by CPI Group (UK) Ltd

5 7 9 10 8 6 4

Papers used by John Blake Publishing are natural, recyclable products made from
wood grown in sustainable forests. The manufacturing processes conform to the
environmental regulations of the country of origin.

Every attempt has been made to contact the relevant copyright-holders, but some
were unobtainable. We would be grateful if the appropriate people could contact us.

CONTENTS

INTRODUCTION

A dele worked Sunday shifts at the cafe her auntie ran in Haringey, north London. As the teenager waited tables, the crackly radio announced the countdown of the pop charts. She wondered what it would be like to have her own song in the hit parade. By the time she was 22, she would be at No 1 in charts around the world.

Her influence is immense: she was named the most powerful person in music when she topped the *Guardian*'s Music Power 100 list. To put this in context, the mighty Simon Cowell finished third. Adele has sold millions of albums worldwide, won numerous awards, including Grammys and a Brit, and as a result has deservedly been crowned queen of the music industry – and all just three years after she released her first single. Along the way she has built a fortune of around £20 million.

It is the authenticity and sincerity of her work that appeals: there are no gimmicks but plenty of soul. With firmly autobiographical lyrics that simply yet powerfully and often painfully speak truths about her personal heartaches, she has touched a nerve with music fans. Speaking as a fan herself, Adele expresses distaste at lazy lyricism. 'You know, I hate – I'm actually offended by – literal, easy lyrics that have no thought behind them and are purely written because they rhyme,' she said. Though her higher standards pay off, they come with an emotional price. Remember, for a moment, how songs like 'Someone Like You' can make you feel: the way they make the hairs on the back of your neck stand up, the way they send a shiver of recognition down your spine, the way they can make your eyes fill with tears and your lips tremble. Now imagine how emotionally draining it is to *perform* those songs night after night on tour.

'That's really hard,' Adele said. She has developed coping mechanisms, including thinking about mundane things as she sings – the furniture store Ikea is one such distracting thought. The challenges of live performances of such material are exceeded by the rewards. 'Anything I find difficult is completely thrown in the bin when I see how people respond to my music,' she said. 'I love it when a wife drags her husband to a show and he's standing there like a lemon. You spend the whole night trying to win him over and by the end he's kissing his wife. That's amazing.'

What a fascinating character Adele is: not least due to the contrast between her musical persona and her everyday personality. Despite the heartbreaking sadness of her music,

Adele remains surprisingly happy and content in her real life. Her raucous, cackling laugh is a catchy and regular feature of her positive and loquacious conversations. Far from discovering a gloomy, self-pitying soul, people who have met her often remark that she laughs more than anyone else. It makes her an attractive personality. When she embarked on the difficult, sometimes soul-destroying tour of American radio and television shows that is required of any overseas artist attempting to 'break the States', she so charmed the industry bigwigs there that as well as wanting to promote her music – 'that decision was a no-brainer for us' said one – they also wanted to go for a drink with her and become her friend.

Her takes on everything from fame to her love life are always diverting. She once recalled how a male fan sent her an unsettling 'crispy tissue' in the post. 'Oh, you sent me a crispy tissue,' she said of the offering. 'I'll definitely get in touch with you! Hey, let's get married and have children!'

Her candour is legendary. Asked when she was typically struck with inspiration to write a new song, she said it usually happened as she got up from her bed to spend a penny in the early hours. She was also asked what she would do if a partner called her fat. 'I'd murder him,' she replied. When she discovered she had won a prestigious Grammy award, she had just returned to her seat from the loo. She had not even done her belt up. Audiences frequently laugh at her on-stage humour, including the dirty jokes. 'What do you call a blonde standing on her head?' she once asked. 'A brunette with bad breath.' Too much information? There is always more where that came from. Explaining why she eschews the social-networking micro-blog site Twitter, which so many other musical stars are addicted to, she said, 'I don't want to write, "Oh, I'm on the toilet – last night's dinner was really spicy." That's just gross.'

Though she is confident and forthright, she is also humble and grounded. She does not even accept the description of 'singer' for herself. 'I always say I'm a singing lady, rather than a singer,' she said. 'Singer is a big word for me. My interpretation of a singer is Etta James and Carole King and Aretha Franklin.' When asked what she would have done had she not made it as a singer, she said, 'If I weren't singing, I'd be a cleaner, I love a clean.'

Adele's songs document real-life dramas and heartaches she has endured: both her albums are about painful breakups, and she said her songs for her second album *21* began life as 'drunken diary ramblings'. These are ramblings that have grown to become the soundtrack of our times, much to her surprise. Adele thought she was the only one dealing with those problems. As she began to sing to the world about her emotions, she discovered that millions of others shared her feelings. When she realised that her songs had left those millions feeling less isolated, she was delighted to have created such a virtuous circle. 'It's like my job is done,' she said.

Done successfully, too. Her second album sold more than three million copies and went platinum ten times. She is the first living artist in nearly 50 years to have two Top 5 singles and albums in the charts at the same time. She has topped the charts in 18 countries to date. The girl from London is huge in America, where she has had a No 1 album, performed on leading shows, including *Saturday Night Live*, and won two Grammy awards in 2009. As her sales have soared, her feet have remained grounded. For instance, when she was backstage at the New York television studio for *The Late Show with David Letterman*, someone observed that her dressing room was rather small. Adele was having none of that: 'You don't complain about your dressing room,' she said and when she got home to London, all she wanted to do was sit in the park with her old friends, chatting and drinking cider.

As we shall see, she gets spectacularly, physically nervous before live performances. Once she is on-stage with the microphone in her hand, the anxiety evaporates. 'I feel more at ease performing than when I'm walking down the street,' she said. 'I love entertaining people. It's a huge deal that people pay their hard-earned money, no matter how much or little, to spend an hour of their day to come and watch me. I don't take that responsibility lightly.' At her live performances, there is little emotional barrier between Adele and her fans. You probably love her because you know that – for all her success and fame – she is someone like you.

Here is her remarkable story.

CHAPTER ONE

BABY BLUE

'People think,' said Adele, 'that I popped out of my mother's womb singing "Chasing Pavements".' One should tread carefully when discussing Adele's early years. Do not, for instance, try telling her that she was 'born to perform'. She will have none of that sort of talk. 'Fuck off, no one's born to perform,' she has snapped.

Adele Laurie Blue Adkins cried, rather than sang, as she was born on 5 May 1988 in London. The soundtrack to that year included Bros wondering aloud when they would be famous, Rick Astley vowing to never give you up and Michael Jackson starting with the man in the mirror. Elsewhere, people partied in warehouses while raving to acid house and, in Wembley Stadium, tens of thousands bounced up and down while calling for the release of Nelson Mandela. In years to come, when future celebrities are profiled, Adele's worldwide hits will be used as a cultural benchmark of the times they were born into. People will be proud to have been born as songs like 'Someone Like You' filled the airwaves.

Adele's mother, Penny Adkins, was 18 when she gave birth to her daughter, or '18 and-a-half', as Adele cutely, and more precisely, puts it. Adele was Penny's first and – to date – only child. Not long before she became a mother, Penny had been – lovingly – shown the door by her own mother and father, who were firm believers that their offspring would benefit from being taught self-reliance the hard way. 'That's what we did with all the kids,' said Penny's mother, Doreen. 'They had to make their own way in life.' This was a rule Doreen had for all her offspring and she has seen the results it led to. 'My kids, they all work. The whole family have got jobs. You have got to get on and it hasn't done any of them any harm.' This sense of independence, toughness and ambition has found its way through Penny to Adele.

Doreen has said that she was not shocked when Penny told her she was pregnant. Adele's father Mark Evans and her mother split when Adele was just three years of age. Therefore, Evans was, Adele has said, 'never in the picture'. As we shall see, the extent of his involvement in his daughter's life is a topic of some disagreement. She described her father as 'a really big Welsh guy who works on the ships and stuff'. She does not mourn the lack of a relationship with him. 'It's fine, I don't feel like I'm missing anything,' she said. 'Some people make a big deal about coming from a single-parent family but I know loads of people who grew up without having their dads around.'

Penny, then an art student, had met Evans in a pub in north London in 1987. Evans described his feelings that night as 'love at first sight'. They quickly became an item and within months Penny was pregnant with Adele.

Evans says it was an unplanned pregnancy; both were determined at that stage to make the most of the situation they found themselves in. Evans says that he proposed to his girlfriend around this time. 'I knew I wanted to spend the rest of my life with Penny so I asked her to marry me,' he said. 'She turned me down – she kept saying we were too young to get married.' Although he split with Penny early in Adele's life, Evans claims a slice of credit for his daughter's musical tastes. 'I'd lie on the sofa all night cradling Adele in my arms and listening to my favourite music – Ella Fitzgerald, Louis Armstrong, Bob Dylan and Nina Simone,' he said. 'Night after night I'd play those records. I'm certain that is what shaped Adele's music.' He added that his musical taste and love of blues music certainly influenced part of his daughter's name. 'The music I loved – and still love today – is what gave me the idea for one of her middle names, Blue. I always think of Adele as Blue.' There were moments of tenderness between father and daughter. An early photograph of her shows Evans proudly holding his daughter wearing a pink babygro and red boots. She seems fascinated by the camera. Nowadays, the fascination flows strongly still – but in the opposite direction.

After Evans split with Penny, he moved back to his native Wales. There, he joined a family business, helping his own father John who had acquired the lease for a cafe in Barry Island funfair. It is the same site that is featured on the popular BBC comedy *Gavin & Stacey*. 'I remember she came to stay in the summer after her fourth birthday and she was carrying this little acoustic guitar she'd picked up in a charity shop,' he said. 'She said she was teaching herself how to play it by listening to the blues songs we used to listen to on my record player and then trying to make the same noise.' Each time he saw Adele, Evans noticed that her musical ability had improved dramatically. 'Within a couple of years, she'd started singing along and I remember thinking, when she was seven, my God, Adele's really got it. She's going to be a huge star one day.' A friend of his, who worked as a music producer, also praised Adele's vocal skills when he heard her sing as a child. He felt her voice had great colour and range. He encouraged her to record herself singing the song 'Heart of Glass' by Blondie. As well as her musical skills, Adele was also practising her lyrical ones: she started writing poetry when she was little more than a toddler.

Evans's own family had been shocked to learn of the pregnancy. But they vowed to help look after the child, regardless of the split. Penny and Adele often spent weekends at the family home in Penarth, near Cardiff. Sometimes, said Evans, they would take caravan trips along the Welsh coast during Adele's summer holidays. Her paternal grandfather, in particular, made a real effort to help raise Adele. 'He just loved my mum and because my dad wasn't in her life they completely took her over as their daughter,' recalled Adele fondly.

'I think my dad was Adele's most significant role model,' said Evans. The feeling was mutual: John idolised Adele, his first grandchild. 'They spent a lot of time together, just the two of them,' said Evans. 'Adele would spend much of the summer with my parents and most of that time my dad would be playing with her, talking to her, showing her the sights.' As a result of this, Adele elevated her grandfather in her own imagination.

'I painted him as this Jesus figure in my life,' she said. Interestingly, Amy Winehouse – who attended the same school as Adele and was a huge influence on her music – was also extremely close to a grandparent. In this case it was her grandmother Cynthia, whose death was said to be a factor in Winehouse's downward spiral after 2006.

Adele is extremely keen to recall the sacrifices Penny made for her. 'She fell pregnant with me when she would have been applying for uni, but chose to have me instead,' said Adele. 'She never, ever reminds me of that. I try to remember it.' Her mother has a creative side to her personality, which Adele describes as 'arty'. She works across several projects and areas including as an artist, a furniture maker, an activity organiser for adults with special needs and as a masseuse. Adele and her mother have always been very close: 'Thick as thieves,' says Adele. 'She's the love of my life.' One of the things that made Adele so intensely fond of her mother is that Penny has a great perspective on life. The way her daughter describes her,

Penny could hardly sound less like the sort of pushy mothers that often loom large in the lives of performers who are successful while young. 'She doesn't worry about little things. She's never disappointed even when I know she probably is. You know that parent thing, "I am not angry; I am disappointed." Like a bullet. She's not like that. She's honest and open and so supportive.'

Adele grew up with Penny's new partner as a stepfather, and she quickly grew close to him. She also has a half-brother called Cameron. The half-siblings bonded as if they were full relatives. 'He looks like my twin,' said Adele. 'We're identical, same hair and everything.' To this day, they find many things to unite them. 'It's bizarre growing up in a completely different city but then, when you see each other, it's as if you've spent every day of your lives together,' said Adele. 'Straight away I'm bullying him. Straight away he's like ... "You fuck off"... It's amazing, immediate. He's lovely. Really shy, which is the only difference.' Despite the absence of her father, Adele never felt isolated at all, partly because her mother comes from a large family. 'There are 33 immediate family members on my mum's side alone,' she said. Indeed, she is one of the 14 grandchildren her maternal grandmother boasts.

Many of those relatives are male, so she was never short of unofficial father figures. 'We are all really bolshie,' she added. That trait comes across often in her interviews and her on-stage chatter between tracks. She invariably enjoyed visiting her cousins, many living nearby. In their company, she got to experience for a while the sensation of being in a large family, with all the joys, tribulations and other experiences that implied. Then, when she got back home, she could return to the pleasures of being – effectively – an only child. It was a strangely agreeable state of affairs for her. 'I'd go and see them, always arguing and hating to share, then I'd be back home to my tidy room and unbroken toys and no fighting over my Barbie,' she said. 'It was like I had the best of both worlds.' She was certainly comfortable with being an only child. Whatever she was up to, she was happiest when she could be in control of the process. 'If I was building a castle out of Lego, I'd have to do it myself,' she said.

She has a similar feeling of wanting to control now, when she embarks on songwriting. Indeed, looking back over her life to date she has sometimes wondered whether it is her only-child status that has contributed to her writing ability. As someone who has rarely read a book, she has found herself considering just why she is so gifted with the pen. 'I don't know if it's because I'm an only child, but I was never, ever good at saying how I felt about things,' she said. 'From the age of about five, if I was told off for not sharing or I didn't tidy my room or I spoke back to my mum, I'd always write a note as my apology.' She found that she could express herself much better with a pen in her hand. Indeed, many of the songs that she has since written can be considered letters of heartache and disenchantment, set to music. Her first hit was written in the same circumstances as many of her childhood letters: immediately following a row with her mum.

Initially, though, her dreams for the future were not musical ones. Instead, Adele dreamt of becoming a fashion reporter or a heart surgeon. Her journalistic ambitions again see her mirror Amy Winehouse, who was working in an entertainment reporting agency before musical fame swept her off her feet. The medical route, meanwhile, wouldn't come as a surprise to astrologers. Her birthday means she was born under the star sign of Taurus. Considered one of the most distinctive of star signs, the typical Taurus is expected to be a calm, consistent person who rarely gets stressed or upset by life. Were Adele that level-headed, then her life and emotional feelings would have made for a set of pop songs with minimal drama, as opposed to the gut-wrenching themes she has written about. It is precisely her emotive nature and eventful life that have helped give her music and image so much edge. A Taurus is also expected to have a stubborn nature and here we have a trait it is much easier to identify in our heroine. This is a highly honest star sign, too, which chimes with the outspoken and forthright nature of Adele. In interviews she frequently gives explosive quotes, some of which have got her into trouble and, of course, her on-stage banter is legendary.

The neighbourhood Adele grew up in is a little over six miles north of central London, and lies in the borough of Haringey. Tottenham is a multi-cultural neighbourhood – researchers at the University College London have declared the southern end of it to be the most ethnically diverse area in Britain.

Around 113 different ethnic groups live there, and between them they speak around 193 different languages. It all meant there was a rich, almost heady, variety of sights and sounds round about her.

In 2010, Tottenham had the highest unemployment rate in the capital, and the eighth highest in the UK. There have often been tensions between the police and sections of the local community. These tensions were epitomised during the riots that took place on the Broadwater Farm housing estate in 1985. The trouble was sparked when a popular Afro-Caribbean woman, Cynthia Jarrett, died during a police search of her home. The following day, fighting broke out between police and local youths. This was the first time live fire was used by rioters in Britain. As the violence escalated, a policeman called Keith Blakelock was stabbed to death. Controversy then raged over who had committed the murder, and the three men convicted for the crime were later cleared on appeal. In August 2011, unrest again came to Tottenham, when the death of Mark Duggan in a police operation led to riots and looting which spread from Tottenham across the UK.

Adele supports the local football team, Tottenham Hotspur, and insists that she is not merely another celebrity looking to boost their fame by declaring questionable support for a football club. 'I'm a real Spurs fan,' she said. She is already well on the way to becoming the most famous ever child of Tottenham and is happy enough about this. 'I'm not a fake Tottenham girl, I was born there,' she said proudly.

Among those also born there who have found success and fun in the music industry are rapper and producer Rebel MC, Dave Clark of 1960s band the Dave Clark Five and pop singer Lemar.

For Adele, one of the first singers she admired was Gabrielle, whose full name is Louisa Gabrielle Bobb. Born just a few miles away in Hackney, Gabrielle was discovered after a demo recording of her singing the Tracy Chapman hit 'Fast Car' was circulated. After she was signed up to a recording contract, Gabrielle quickly became a hit artist and a pop icon, thanks to her distinctive eye-patch. Her debut single 'Dreams' topped the charts when Adele was five and quickly became a firm favourite of the Tottenham youngster. By this stage, Adele had already become fascinated by music and, in particular, she was 'obsessed with voices'. She noted the range of emotions that the human voice could express when set to music: 'I used to listen to how the tones would change from angry to excited to joyful to upset.' She was a truly precocious music fan: she understood music both emotionally and intellectually from a very early age.

She was a pretty child: a photograph of her as a four-year-old on Christmas Day shows a well-dressed girl with neck-length fair hair and a cute, slightly nervous expression on her face.

There was always music in the household, even after her father moved out. Adele grew up listening to a more hip, varied and relevant soundtrack than she might have done with an older mum. Penny loved music with the intensity of a teenager well into her twenties. Among her favourite acts were 10,000 Maniacs, the Cure and Jeff Buckley – Penny played their music night and day in the home. Indeed, when Adele was just three years of age, her mother took her to her first concert. They saw the Cure at Finsbury Park. Adele would later record a cover of the band's 'Lovesong'. Penny also allowed her daughter to stay up late on Friday nights, to watch the BBC's live music programme *Later*, presented by the baron of boogie-woogie pianists himself, Jools Holland. Each week, Adele's musical knowledge and tastes swelled. Soon, she could add the likes of Destiny's Child, Lauryn Hill and Mary J Blige to the list of acts she followed.

No wonder Adele quickly grew to love music, not just at an emotional level but an intellectual one as well. Hers was a considered love. 'Cheesy as it sounds, I was sitting in Tottenham, had never left the UK, but felt I could go anywhere in the world and meet another eight-year-old and have something to talk about,' she said. 'I remember noticing that music united people and I loved the feeling of that and found a massive comfort in it. A euphoric feeling, even.' She also found that music could give her an entirely contrasting emotion. The first song that ever made her cry was 'Troy', by Sinead O'Connor. This had long been a favourite song of her mother's. Adele cried when she first heard it and was shocked by how powerfully it moved her. It has a sparse production until towards its climax but it is O'Connor's powerful and emotional delivery that stirs the soul when listening to it. In this regard, it is quite in keeping with the music that Adele would one day make herself.

Little could she have known when she first heard 'Troy' that her own music would one day provoke similar storms of emotions in her own fans. Indeed, she would one day turn many of the millions watching her sing at the Brit awards into blubbering observers shaken by the raw power of her lyrics and her delivery.

However, Adele was not content just to listen to pop songs over and over merely as a fan. She began to sing along with them, particularly Gabrielle's 'Dreams'. Of course, she wasn't alone in that as a youngster, but even then it became clear that Adele had vocal talent. When Penny heard her daughter's voice, she noticed there was something genuinely special about it. Most parents would send a child of that age to bed when they were having friends round for dinner but Penny was too proud of her girl not to show off her already impressive musical ways. She would sometimes arrange for her daughter to give an intimate performance for the guests. More than once she would stand the five-year-old on the dinner table and invite her to sing songs, including 'Dreams'. Adele was never in much doubt about how proud her mother was. 'She just thought I was amazing,' she said. There were other domestic concerts in Adele's bedroom, too. Here, the creative skills of Penny came to the fore. 'My mum's quite arty – she'd get all these lamps and shine them up to make one big spotlight,' said Adele. Penny's friends would cram into the room and sit on the bed to hear the young girl's impressive voice. No wonder Penny was so proud. Later, Adele also sang songs by the Spice Girls on such occasions. The British girl band became a firm favourite from their earliest hits, the lyrics of which made her giggle. '[They were] all sexual innuendos – I love it,' she told *Q*.

The Spice Girls are not a guilty pleasure for Adele. She is proud to be a fan of the Girl Power combo. 'Even though some people think they're uncool, I'll never be ashamed to say I love the Spice Girls because they made me who I am,' she said. 'I'm deadly serious about that. I got into music right in their prime when they were huge.' Her original favourite Spice Girl was Geri, but when the ginger-haired minx left the band Adele turned her affections to Mel B. 'When I was young, I was planning to go to their show at Wembley as Geri, but, just before I went, she left,' she told *Now*. 'I had to go as Mel C and I was never that sporty. I haven't forgiven Geri for that. Geri was my favourite Spice Girl, but she left and broke my heart, so I'm a Scary Spice girl now.' The very fact that the identity of her favourite band member is so important to her shows how much Adele loved the 1990s girl band sensation.

That said, she was not always quite so proud of her Spice Girls fixation as she is now. 'I was a real indie kid,' she told the *Observer*. 'But I'd secretly go home and listen to Celine Dion.' Later in life, she attended one of the Spice Girls reunion shows and felt transported back to her childhood years. 'I loved it!' she said. 'Seeing them was just like being a little kid again.' She also attended a reunion concert of another pop band of her childhood – boy band East 17. 'I used to love them,' she said. Other acts she has name-checked as teenage influences include the Pussycat Dolls and Britney Spears.

Soon Adele was not only listening to such singers but also trying to emulate them in real life. Not for her the miming with a hairbrush in front of the mirror pastime of so many teenage girls; Adele was trying out singing for real and found some willing audiences for her earliest performances.

Penny wasn't well off but she gave her daughter lots of emotional support and encouragement. 'I was one of those kids that was like... "I want to be a ballet dancer" ... "No, a saxophone player" ... "No, a weather girl",' said Adele. 'And my mum would run me to all these classes. She has always said, "Do what you want and, if you're happy, I'm happy."' When Adele asked her mother to buy her a sequin eye-patch like the one sported by her hero Gabrielle, Penny lovingly obliged the request. The accessory did not last long in the child's favour. The day after she received it, Adele was teased about it at school and cast it to one side. In some interviews since, Adele has claimed that she had only ever worn it reluctantly, at the behest of Penny.

There was some of the expected and perfectly normal friction between mother and daughter in Adele's childhood. Although they have always had a strong, close bond, Adele did have moments when she wanted to rebel against her mother. This showed itself partly when it came to Penny's musical tastes, and Adele's reaction to them. 'Even when I was 10 and 11, I knew my mum had brilliant taste in music – I just wasn't ready to embrace it,' she admitted. 'Now they're my favourite artists.'

Of course, many people in their twenties will look back at how they once rebelled against their parents' tastes and ways, and then admit that they have grown to see the merit and wisdom of them.

As for Penny, she paused to wonder, as she listened to the childhood Adele sing, how connected her young daughter was with some of the very adult themes of the music. One day, she heard Adele singing along to the Lauryn Hill song 'Ex-Factor'. Given that her daughter was some years away from becoming a teenager, Penny asked her how many of the song's lyrics – which cover the trauma of a relationship breakup – she really understood. The passion Adele was singing with had sparked Penny's curiosity. 'Do you know what this song is about?' she asked her daughter, who had to admit that she did not. But she *wanted to*.

'I remember having the sleeve notes,' said Adele, 'no one has sleeve notes any more – and reading every lyric and not understanding half of them and just thinking, When am I going to feel like this? When am I going to be able to write and sing like this?'

As for her education, the choice of school would have further influence on her growing passion for music and creativity. Adele stood out at her primary school for one particular reason: she was almost the only white face to be seen in the place. This was not a big deal at all for her. 'I stopped noticing after a while,' she said. Instead of being a problem for Adele, she actually considered this factor a positive one. It meant she got introduced to the finest soul music early in life. 'Through my friend's mum is how I found out about Mary J Blige and the Fugees and stuff like that,' she said. 'I guess, without that, I probably wouldn't be into R&B that wasn't only in the charts.'

What a musical education she was getting in the early years of her life: at home her mother played her indie tunes, she listened to pop on the radio and thanks to her classmates she learned lots about soul music. Her musical knowledge became more refined and she started to listen to the sort of music she would later write and record herself. 'When I was a girl, I loved love songs,' she said. 'And I always loved the ones about horrible relationships. Ones that you could really relate to and made you cry.'

It was only when the family left Tottenham that Adele realised how much the neighbourhood's ethnic mix had suited her. When she was nine, they moved to Brighton where Penny hoped she could better immerse herself in creative ventures. Some children would have loved life in an exciting seaside town like Brighton, but not Adele. 'The people seemed really pretentious and posh, and there were no black people there,' she recalled with disdain. 'I was used to being the only white kid in my class in Tottenham.' She would insist she was never one for the finer points of academia. 'I'm not, and never have been, very academic – it was always music for me,' she said. 'My first school was great but I'd have a kid by now if I hadn't left.'

The family were to return to London, but not before fate intervened cruelly in the life of Adele and her father. A photograph from around this time shows father and daughter looking close and happy. They are sitting at the base of a tree on a warm day, Evans is shirtless and looks in good health. Adele is kitted out in some sporty gear and has her hand resting on her father's knee. Soon, this picture of domestic bliss would give way to a more strained relationship between Adele and her dad. Evans would face a double tragedy in his life, the knock-on effect of which would be an increased estrangement from his daughter. His father John died at the age of 57, having been struck by bowel cancer. In the wake of his loss, Evans split from his new girlfriend. Then came the second blow – his best friend dropped dead after suffering a heart attack. In the face of the bereavements, Evans turned to alcohol for comfort. He has quipped that he made notorious boozer Oliver Reed seem a teetotaller in comparison. 'I barely knew my own name,' he added.

Adele herself was said to be 'utterly distraught' when she learned of her grandfather's passing, but Evans was too upset to help her. 'I was a rotten father at a time when she really needed me,' said Evans. 'I was deeply ashamed of what I'd become and I knew the kindest thing I could do for Adele was to make sure she never saw me in that state ... I was in the darkest place you can imagine. I saw no way out. I didn't really care whether I lived or died.' He found himself asking harsh questions of himself and his relationship with Adele. 'I knew she'd be missing her granddad just as much as I was because they had such a close bond,' he said. 'She adored him ... I was not there for my daughter when I should have been and I have regretted that every second of every day to this moment now.'

Adele has since said that she more or less completely cut off contact with her father around this time. Evans, by contrast, has spoken of more regular meetings with his daughter, sparked by a healing chat they had in London's Camden market after he had kicked the alcohol. What is certain is that Penny and Adele moved from Brighton back to London, but settled this time in the southern half of the capital. Adele was 11 when she and Penny arrived and she started in what she thought was 'a crap comprehensive'. Initially, they settled in Lambeth. Within walking distance of their new home was the sort of multiculturalism that Adele had been familiar with in Tottenham. There were also record stores and concert venues, including the legendary Brixton Academy, which interested her and captured her imagination. Her musical dreams were continuing to grow in intensity, but, while Penny was proud and encouraging of her daughter's creative aspirations, not everyone was quite so positive. Indeed, her hopes and dreams were sometimes dismissed by various adults in her life. 'I had to bear the brunt of negative attitudes from authority figures, such as teachers, who led me to believe that success was unrealistic,' she said.

The musical development continued, as did Adele's dreams. 'I remember when I was ten, I nicked my mum's Lauryn Hill album and listened to it every day after school in my bedroom, sitting on my little sofa bed and hoping to God that one day I'd be a singer,' she said. 'But it was never something I purposely pursued. Me and my friends at the time all had dreams and none of theirs were coming true, so I thought, Why the hell will mine?'

Adele became even more open-minded in her musical tastes, which had grown to encompass more R&B acts and metal bands such as Aerosmith. She was no snob or partisan. As she entered her teenage years, she was ready to explore some of the more mature aisles of the record stores. One day, in the Oxford Street branch of HMV, she saw greatest hits albums from Etta James and Ella Fitzgerald on special offer – 'two for a fiver, in the *jazz section*'. How had such a young girl ended up in, as she emphasised, the *jazz section*? She said, having already got into modern R&B acts, 'from that it was like a natural progression for me to get into the more classic soul artists. Because, while I always knew who Aretha Franklin and Marvin Gaye were – I think they're part of everyone's DNA, really – it was when I first went to the jazz section of HMV in Oxford Street that I became more seriously interested. You know, it's this glass room a bit like your grandparents' room that kids aren't allowed in.'

More candidly, she later added, 'I was 13 or 14 and trying to be cool, only I wasn't really cool at the time as I was pretending to be into Slipknot, Korn and Papa Roach. So there I was in my dog collar and baggy jeans and I saw this CD in the bargain bin. I'd only picked up the CD as I wanted to show my hairdresser the picture so she could do my hair the same.'

She took both CDs home. There they sat on the side,

untouched for some time. It was when she was clearing up her room one day that she rediscovered the abandoned discs, and gave them a try, and, once she did give them a spin, she loved what she heard. 'When I heard the song "Fool That I Am", everything changed for me. I never wanted to be a singer until I heard that.'

The likes of Etta James became out-and-out favourites for Adele. More importantly, they set her on course to explore more jazz and easy-listening music. It was as she listened to these songs, luxuriating in their warm tones, that her own eventual musical quality developed.

With Etta James, it was not only her music that appealed to Adele. She liked, she said, James' 'blonde weave and her catty eyes' and her angry face. When she heard the music, she was struck powerfully by it, 'fell in love – it was like she went in my chest and beat my heart up'. Adele has said of James' singing: 'She was the first time a voice made me stop what I was doing and sit down and listen. It took over my mind and body.'

Etta James was a blues and R&B sensation in the 1950s and 1960s. She is best known musically for the songs 'At Last' and 'I'd Rather Go Blind'. She has endured a torrid personal life which was complicated by her use of heroin. She spent time in a psychiatric hospital and continues to suffer physical health issues. For Adele, the brilliance of James' music outshone all of this. James was just one of the artists that Adele sought to emulate as she taught herself how to sing. 'I taught myself how to sing by listening to Ella Fitzgerald for acrobatics and scales, Etta James for passion and Roberta Flack for control,' she said. Later in life, she would consider naming a dog Ella, after Ms Fitzgerald.

It was not only British record shops that she visited in her teenage years. Adele vividly remembers an exciting holiday to America with her father when she was 15 and she went into a Virgin Records shop in Times Square, New York. As she browsed its aisles, she reflected on how 'amazing' it would be to one day have a record of her own on sale in a foreign country. It seemed an outrageous dream to have at the time – she could hardly even get her head around the prospect of recording a song and that song going on sale in the UK, let alone abroad. By the time she was in her early twenties, not only would she have her albums on sale in America, but she would also be the toast of New York.

Meanwhile, her musical ambitions were given an extra shot by a new television series which kicked off a genre that would dominate for over a decade. As well as being allowed to stay up to watch *Later* with her mother on Friday evenings, Adele was a fan of reality television, including the musical programmes of that genre. One of her favourites was *Pop Idol*, first shown on ITV in 2001. With its memorable panel of judges, including the sharp-tongued Simon Cowell in his first significant public outing, the programme quickly captured the public's imagination. The previous year, viewers had watched *Popstars* produce the pop band Hear'Say. *Pop Idol* took the genre to a whole new level. The fact that a solo artist was the focus gave the search an added intensity and personal dimension. Then there was the pivotal fact that, unlike *Popstars*, this show had a public vote. Rather than just watching a band being formed, the public was invited to phone in and vote for their favourite singer. And the presence of the brooding, blunt-speaking Cowell gave *Pop Idol* an edge. In recent years, Cowell has tempered his frank verdicts. Back in 2001, his judgements were often truly cutting.

Adele loved *Pop Idol* and sat glued to it most weekends. As a girl in her early teens, she was bang inside one of the programme's key demographics. She enjoyed hearing the contestants sing and getting to know their personalities, too. The singer she loved most on *Pop Idol* was the one that went on to win the show – Will Young. The posh, slightly awkward young man from Hungerford in Berkshire was an unlikely winner in some ways. He had a superb voice and the fact he was the only contestant to stand up to Cowell's verdicts sealed his place in the public's affections. In an exciting final which seemed to grip the nation, he beat the more polished but less charismatic Gareth Gates. Adele was delighted. She had picked up the phone to vote for Young many times. She later joked that she had voted 'five thousand times'. An exaggeration, but one that reflects just how much she adored him. Certainly, among the 4.6 million votes that Young received on the final night there was more than one cast by Adele. 'Will Young was my first proper love,' she said. 'I was obsessed.' At school, she found that many of her fellow pupils were divided into fiercely partisan groups: the Young fans and the Gates fans.

The rivalry quickly became quite vicious and Adele found

herself right in the centre of it. She stood up for herself (and, by proxy, for Young) and paid the price for it. 'The Gareth Gates fans were horrible to me and I wasn't having any of it,' she said. 'We had a fight and I was called into the head-teacher's office and sent home. It was serious.' To be sent home from school over an argument about *Pop Idol* – Adele was a passionate fan for sure. Little could she know that in the coming years of her life she would meet Young and appear on the same bill as him, and her own music would become a mainstay of auditioning singers on reality music shows. This is an even bigger triumph than if she had gone from watching the show to winning it herself. She bypassed the whole public auditioning process and became the act that aspiring contestants wanted to emulate.

When she and Penny had first watched *Pop Idol* together, her mother had suggested to Adele that she might like to audition. Adele was not so sure this was a good idea. She had seen how some parents put forward their completely untalented offspring. 'You know you get these parents and they're like, "She's the next Whitney," and then she sings and it's awful,' she said. Also, she had grown tired of the production line of female singer who attempted to copy the Mariah Carey style of vocal delivery but ended up fitting so many notes into one word of lyrics that they would sound like bleating lambs. 'So many people sing like that now and I could do it if I wanted to... but the first time you hear it you're like, "Wow!", and by the fifth time, it's like, "Fuck off, get something new",' said Adele. 'It's more impressive, somehow, if you don't try to impress. Be natural with it. Say it straight.' Therefore, she was not to audition on the second series of *Pop Idol*. That series was won, though, by a big girl with a big voice. Scot Michelle McManus became the somewhat unlikely frontrunner of the second series. With Cowell backing her throughout the competition, she won the public vote.

Adele continued to follow the reality genre, replacing her love of *Pop Idol* with the show that succeeded it, the *X Factor*. 'I'm a super, super fan,' she said. 'I think it's amazing, it's a great opportunity for people as well and it's entertaining – I don't want to go out on a Saturday night and get drunk and take pills with my friends, it's just boring. All them indie kids, they're the ones who are snobby about it, all them indie bands, and stuff, they can kiss my bum.' The lack of musical snobbery inherent in these shows chimes with Adele's down-to-earth heart. The appreciation is mutual: her songs are often attempted by young hopefuls auditioning for the *X Factor* and also *American Idol* in the US. This trend reached its highlight in the 2010 series of the *X Factor*, when popular finalist Rebecca Ferguson sang Adele's version of 'Make You Feel My Love'. Adele was so chuffed and impressed that she wrote Ferguson a letter complimenting her on the performance. However, as we shall see, Adele's songs became so popular at auditions that the show's judges and producers banned them for a while.

The young Adele also loved another celebrity who came to her attention on the small screen. Television presenter Zoë Ball was on the face of it perhaps a slightly unlikely candidate for Adele's affections. Yet, when one hears and considers the reasoning for Adele's admiration, it makes more sense. One can see in the adult Adele the connection she felt with Ball as she watched her on television on Saturday mornings as a kid. 'I used to watch *Live and Kicking* and love her,' said Adele. 'She wasn't even beautiful, she was just brilliant. Real. When she got married and got out of that car in a wedding dress holding a bottle of Jack Daniels, that was it for me. That was how I wanted to be. And I was only little.' The carefree hedonism of Ball was a worthy example for Adele. (And the compliment is in a sense returned by the fact that Ball now spins Adele tracks in her radio slots.) Adele also loved the Saturday-morning television show *CD:UK* and listening to the top 40 chart as it was announced on radio on Sundays.

Another musical hero, who was quite a contrast with Will Young, was The Streets, aka Mike Skinner. The Streets came to widespread attention in 2002 when Adele was 14. The debut album, *Original Pirate Material*, was an attention-grabbing garage affair in which Skinner's sharp observations were delivered in a 'geezer' style. He sang and rapped about the lifestyles of those Brits who lived for the nightclub experience. It sold over a million copies and earned Skinner and his project respect, including from Adele. 'I was so in love with Mike Skinner I wrote him a letter and when I told my friend about it she cussed me so I went and pretended to do the washing up and cried,' she said. From fighting over the posh, cute-faced Will Young to arguing over the more rough-and-ready Skinner, Adele had varied tastes in men as her teenage hormones ran riot.

In her pre-fame years, she had tried a few other ways of earning a living. It is these experiences that have helped form the Adele we love today. She was no pampered creature removed from the ups and downs of the lives of her fans. 'I worked in a cafe for three years with my auntie and cousin. It was really shit pay and long hours but it was the most fun I've ever had,' she said of the job that allowed her to listen to the Top 40 chart countdown as she worked on Sundays. Adele loved a good mooch around the shops as a teenager, so for her next job she thought she would take a job in retail, working on the basis that she would surely enjoy such an environment. It would not turn out to be as interesting as she hoped. 'The worst job I ever had, though, was working for Gap,' she said. 'The money was great but I didn't even end up collecting my pay cheque because I hated it so much. I love high street shops and I thought I'd be on the till or in the changing rooms helping people find their clothes. But all I did was fold jumpers for 12 hours a day. It was so boring I walked out after four days. If I wasn't doing music, I'd probably still be folding jeans.'

Soon, she would join a rather more prestigious establishment. Her education had rather gone off the rails while she was at the Chestnut Grove school in Balham, a place that might have been expected to have suited her better. It specialises in the visual arts and media, but she was not happy there and often bunked off classes. 'I was really mouthy and ended up playing truant,' she said. Part of her frustration was normal adolescent stuff. She did, though, feel that not enough support was being offered to her and her fellow pupils. 'They didn't really encourage me,' she told *The Times*. 'I knew I wanted to do music but even when I was in Year 7 and wanted to be a heart surgeon they didn't encourage that … It was just, "Try and finish school and don't get pregnant," ha, ha, ha.'

Speaking of music classes, she said, 'They gave me a really hard time, trying to bribe me, saying that if I wanted to sing I had to play clarinet to sing in the choir. So I left.' Summing up her mood immediately before she left, she shows how lacking in optimism she had been at that point in her life. 'Things were looking quite bleak,' she said. The only thing that kept her pecker up was music and her increasing interest in becoming a singer herself. 'As soon as I got a microphone in my hand, when I was about 14, I realised I wanted to do this,' she remembered. She was blissfully free of the problem that holds some people back: self-consciousness in hearing their own voice. 'Most people don't like the way their voice sounds when it's recorded. I was just so excited by the whole thing that I wasn't bothered what it sounded like.'

Then she managed to get accepted at a new school. Here, she was in the sort of environment that would expertly nurture her burgeoning creative talent on a daily basis. It was an absolutely pivotal moment for her when she joined the BRIT School. 'Everything changed when I went there,' she said.

As she first walked into the BRIT School, Adele took one huge step closer to international fame, huge success and a multi-million-pound fortune.

CHAPTER TWO

BRIT POP

When Adele was on tour in America in 2011, she was taken to one side and told she had made chart history. Her album *21* had topped the charts for a record-breaking 10 weeks. In celebrating this achievement, she immediately knew who she wanted to pay tribute to. 'Thanks to the BRIT School,' whispered Adele. 'A wonderful place that I still miss a lot.'

The BRIT Performing Arts and Technology school has sometimes been compared to the New York High School for the Performing Arts. Its US counterpart was the inspiration for the 1980s film and hit television series *Fame*, although the BRIT School is in Croydon, slightly less glamorous than the Manhattan location of the home of *Fame*. BRIT is funded by the government, but operates independently of the local education authority's control. It was established in 1991 after Conservative minister Kenneth Baker had approached entrepreneur Richard Branson with a proposal. From its second year, it received sponsorship from the BRIT Trust, which is the body behind the music industry's annual Brit awards ceremony.

It is estimated that graduates of the school have sold more than 10 million albums in the UK and amassed 16 Brit award nominations and 14 Grammy nominations between them. Yet, even away from the performing focus, the school's academic record is admirable: over 90 per cent of its pupils gain five or more GCSE passes. And, naturally, it has a glittering alumni. The list of those who have studied at the BRIT includes Leona Lewis, Amy Winehouse, Imogen Heap, Katie Melua, Katy B and members of the Kooks, the Feeling and the Noisettes. As we shall see, some of these coincided with Adele's time at the school.

The prevailing atmosphere and unofficial mission statement of the BRIT School, which mark it out from other arts establishments, very much suit Adele's personality and approach. As one teacher put it, the BRIT School is designed for 'the non-type. The school fits round their personality, rather than asking them to form their personality round the school.' Few true talents would have it any other way but Adele more than any suited such an ethos. A promotional video the school put together speaks of the importance of dreaming. 'The musician realises that they have more influence on the mindset of the world than politicians, parents or popes,' it declares. Certainly, Adele's influence has become immense as her accomplishments have mounted. One teacher, Dec Cunningham, is keen to emphasise that, though it is an arts school, BRIT still has the same responsibilities and issues to face as any other state school. 'It's important to remember that the BRIT School is basically a local comprehensive,' he said.

Adele said she stumbled into the school's arms due to a crisis in her mind. 'The only reason I ended up studying music at the BRIT School was because I knew I was going to fail all my GCSEs, so I panicked,' she said. As her account has it, she was not joining the BRIT School to pursue a career as a music artist. Rather, she says, at this stage she expected to be involved in the music business in a behind-the-scenes capacity. This frame of mind proved helpful, as it meant she took the trouble to learn production skills, including how to soundcheck microphones, amplifiers and speaker systems. 'It's handy,' she said later, ''cause you don't have to pay people to do it for you.'

But first she had to find her way to the school. To do so, it has been said, one should take the train from London Bridge, alight at Selhurst station and then 'follow the teen wearing bright-yellow drainpipe jeans, a leather motorcycle jacket and bird's nest hairstyle'. Adele followed such a trail – which still has some truth today, although fashions and trends change – and reached the school's two main buildings. One is an oblong pavilion, the other a redbrick structure which was built over a hundred years ago. The structures sit, somewhat awkwardly, among typical Croydon terraced housing. This is the area that no less a critic than David Bowie (who spent his formative years in south London) had previously described as 'concrete hell'. But Adele quickly grew to love life at BRIT. The discomfort and lack of motivation that she had felt in Balham seemed a long way away.

Getting *into* the BRIT School as an enrolled pupil, though, was not as easy as finding the buildings themselves. As a state-funded, creative powerhouse of an institution, it attracts a lot of applicants, two-thirds of whom will be unsuccessful. The school has some 850 pupils at any given time, accepting youngsters from the age of 14 to 19. The success of its most famous students have further elevated its appeal. 'The likes of the Kooks and Amy Winehouse have put Croydon on the map,' said Adele. 'Even though they're not originally from Croydon, they've been nurtured here, which should make everyone proud – I certainly am.'

Later, Adele herself would help to keep Croydon on the map with her debut album *19*. BRIT's location made it always seem to be a slightly more down-to-earth version of the Sylvia Young Theatre School, which has been housed in Drury Lane, Marylebone and now Westminster. Indeed, Adele had originally wanted to go to the fee-paying Sylvia Young, mostly because Spice Girl Emma Bunton had gone there – 'but my mum couldn't afford it,' she said.

It was fortunate then that BRIT was so suited to what she needed. 'I could just listen to music every day for four years,' she said. 'A lot of people feel trapped by youth, but at BRIT I felt fucking alive. They taught us to be open-minded and we were really encouraged to write our own music – and some of us took that seriously and some of us didn't. I took it very seriously.' Having felt unsupported at her previous school, she now felt that she was in good hands.

Indeed, the school's prospectus makes it a point of pride to describe the assistance it gives pupils. 'The school has a unique atmosphere of support and respect which helps cultivate the ability and talent of our young people,' it reads. Many of its alumni are in agreement with this boast, including Adele. She also confirms that there is some truth in the comparison that is often made to the legendary American home of performing dreams. 'It was a bit like *Fame* sometimes – you get people doing their ballet stretches and singers having sing-offs... I'd rather that than someone pulling out a knife!' She actually credits the establishment with saving her from a less exciting childhood. She believes that her fellow pupils helped lift her away from a mundane road. 'I hate to think where I'd have ended up if I hadn't gone,' she said. 'It's quite inspiring to be around 700 kids who want to be something – rather than 700 kids who just wanna get pregnant so they get their own flat.' She expanded on how she became confronted by this contrast. 'Nothing against it, but all of my friends from [her previous] school have kids,' she said. 'Not because they didn't have things to do but that's just what you did. It's rubbish. Things were looking quite bleak. Then I got to go to school with other kids who wanted to be something.'

She felt she took a major step up in the world when she

moved her schooling from Balham to Croydon. Not that the new environment made her a 'goody two shoes' character, nor anything like it. The land of slumber often delayed her arrival. 'I'd turn up to school four hours late,' she said. 'I was sleeping. I wasn't doing anything... I just couldn't wake up.'

Once up and about, though, she was a popular, gregarious student, one of those teenagers who seemed to know and be known by everyone. However, she does not recall Leona Lewis from her time there, even though their paths will have coincided. 'That Leona Lewis must've been a quiet horse as I can't remember her at all,' said Adele, 'and I knew everyone there.'

As for Lewis now, though she has spoken of a desire to duet with Adele, she has never spoken of any memories of her at the BRIT School. But Lewis too has spoken in glowing terms of her own experience at the school, despite what was a lengthy commute for her as a young student: 'It took nearly two hours door-to-door, but was so worth it 'cos it's such a great education there. There's no other place like it and it gave me so much.'

Adele continues to be little short of gushing in her praise: 'I loved it there, it's such a great place and the support you get is amazing. Some of the shows they put on are amazing – better than any of the shows on in town at the moment.' When she was selected to take part in one such production, she was late. 'My heart exploded in my chest. It was pretty horrible. I almost did get kicked out of school for that. Now I'm always on time.' Indeed, she traces her boisterous nature back to her schooldays. 'Sometimes I'm so loud that afterwards I cringe, but I can't help it,' she said. 'I like being the life of the party. At school I was the class clown, trying to bust jokes all the time.'

There were challenges, too, at BRIT. All of those creative, sometimes sensitive, souls created an interesting vibe. Many of the pupils felt moments of frustration as their temperamental natures came to the fore. Adele was one of these. 'Sometimes I wanted to leave because when you are creative you can be quite frustrated,' she recalled. 'I never really paid attention in my studio lessons. Whenever I go in the studio, I'm always nervous. I have never conquered that fear.' That fear plagued her time at school, too. Her concern was compounded by the fact that she still wondered if she was ever going to make a career in the industry. 'I don't think I was frustrated because of the school,' she said. 'I never thought my being a professional singer was going to happen, so I sometimes thought it was a waste of time pursuing something that most likely was not going to happen.'

She did not exactly excel in the more conventional parts of the curriculum. Her mind was even then becoming increasingly focused on purely creative matters. 'My academic side went downhill and I played the class clown too often,' she said, 'but I loved the music lessons.' The mere experience of being at the school changed so much about her, not only her talents but her tastes, too. 'I am much more open-minded about music having been there,' she said. 'When I went there, I made friends who were into music I was unaware of or dismissive of, like atmospheric dub step or heavy hip hop. It was an eye-opener as a teenager.' The laidback element of the curriculum and its delivery also suited her just fine. 'Of course you do actual lessons but they don't force anything on to you,' she said. 'They just aim to help you develop. They nurture you, you know.'

That said, she had criticisms of the place. Sometimes, she has said, she felt that the musical parts of the BRIT curriculum were too focused on the smaller details of songs. She prefers not to overanalyse music, for much the same reason she had until recently eschewed singing lessons. Indeed, for Adele, one of the best ways to learn more about vocal prowess is simply by listening to the greats, analysing what makes them great and attempting to replicate it yourself. 'They kind of try to teach you to dissect music but I don't want to do that,' she said. 'I've had one singing lesson in my life. It made me think about my voice too much. You can teach yourself. I listened to Etta to get a bit of soul, Ella for my chromatic scales, Roberta Flack for control.' With Adele supplementing professional guidance from the BRIT with her own, straightforward self-tuition, she had begun to develop her already strong singing voice into the breathtaking affair it is today.

While her classes and home-lessons developed her song, it was sometimes her fellow pupils who helped spur on her ambition and focus. In her second year, she met someone who would inspire her to seek ever greater things. A singer called Shingai Shoniwa moved in next door to Adele – who was very impressed with her. Indeed, she liked not just what she saw, but what she heard. 'She's an amazing singer,' said Adele.

Shingai Elizabeth Maria Shoniwa had a tough start in life, one that Adele will have related to as they talked. Shoniwa grew up in south London, raised mostly by her mother after her father died when she was young. 'Wanting to escape from reality can inspire the greatest and most trivial creative natures in people,' she has commented. Shoniwa's voice is exceptional and unforgettable. *Rolling Stone* magazine would later describe it as 'a living, breathing manifestation of the rock'n'roll spirit, with a voice that is equal parts Iggy Pop and Billie Holiday'. She also has considerable and natural charisma about her. In her early days as a musician, when she was playing a gig at a squat, she played her guitar with a loaf of bread instead of a plectrum. She would later dislocate her shoulder due to excessive leaping around during live performances. She speaks with visceral emotion about music: 'When you look at someone like Grace Jones, David Bowie or Jimi Hendrix, you see part-human transcending that part-beast who can't really control their own surroundings.'

Hers was a voice that captured the imagination of Adele back in the school days before either of them was famous. 'I remember when Shingai Shoniwa was rehearsing I used to press my ear to the wall and listen to her, entranced,' said Adele of her unofficial audience. 'I used to hear her through the walls. I'd go round and we'd jam and stuff like that. Just hearing her and her music really made me want to be a writer and not just sing Destiny's Child songs.' Shoniwa went on to enjoy success with a band called the Noisettes – however, most important for our story is the ambition that she fired up inside Adele. (Later, Adele would share a producer with Shoniwa's band.)

So, what did Adele's fellow pupils make of her? Pop singer Jessie J was at the BRIT School at the same time and she recalls Adele as the belle of the BRIT ball. 'At school she was very kind of loud and everyone knew her, and she was the girl everyone loved and up for a laugh and you could hear her laugh from a mile down the corridor,' said Jessie. Creatively, their paths also crossed. 'She was in music and I was in musical theatre. We used to jam at lunchtime and someone would play guitar and we both would just sing.' Something of a tradition was set back then which the two young women continue to this day. 'We're so common when we're together, it's hilarious,' said Jessie, who has become another hugely successful BRIT graduate. She came top in the BBC's Sound of 2011 poll, was named the critics' choice winner at the Brit awards in the same year and had a UK No 1 with her catchy song 'Price Tag', a dominant part of Britain's 2011 pop soundtrack.

Katy B also attended the same time as Adele. 'Jessie and Adele were both in the year above me and they were singers I really looked up to,' said Katy, who went on to study at Goldsmiths College, University of London. These years really were particularly ripe ones for BRIT. Katy paints a portrait of a building that was fit to burst with musical creativity: 'You walk into the foyer and somebody is always playing an acoustic guitar or singing,' she said. For her, the presence of Adele was a joy and an important part of the appeal of school life. 'Having people like Adele pass around knowledge and information and being so passionate about what you are learning is amazing,' she said. 'One of my favourite singers is Jill Scott and the person who introduced me to Jill was Adele. I was doing a project with her and she got me into soul. She'd always say you have to listen to this or that.'

Kate Nash was another of Adele's fellow pupils who went on to make it big. Adele said that Nash was an absolute scream at times. Nash was 'so funny. She was always doing impressions during lessons,' said Adele. One can just imagine her cheeky, booming laugh ringing out in response to Nash's wit and mimicry. Katie Melua was yet another pupil and, said Adele, 'lovely, too. She was straighter, but she had a wicked voice.' Since leaving BRIT, Nash has stayed loyal to her fellow students by employing many of them as dancers.

The director of music at the BRIT School is Liz Penney. She had interviewed Adele for her place and by chance this was the first time Penney had interviewed a prospective student. Not a bad first effort for her to have made. She remembers Adele only too well. 'She was great fun,' said Penney. 'She was here for four years and sometimes she worked really hard and sometimes she didn't work quite so hard. She was quite chatty... but she always made me laugh. From the time she came here – when some of the other students weren't so into songwriting – she was from the moment she arrived.' Addressing her former star pupil, she proudly added, 'Adele, well done, love. The girl done good. I'm really proud of you, as are all the music staff here.' Hearing these words brought tears to the eyes of Adele.

The fact Adele went to BRIT School is a key part of her story, one that is frequently recounted as a central point in most articles that are written about her. From the school's point of view, this is a positive. Indeed, for the entire educational genre of the performing arts, it is a plus. In the eyes of some, Adele has made the concept of the stage school a cool one. While some commentators find it all too easy to dismiss graduates, people like Adele and Amy Winehouse have made it credible in the music industry. Rock singer James Allan, who is the frontman of Oasis-esque indie outfit Glasvegas, changed his thinking after meeting Adele. 'Growing up, something like the BRIT School was the least cool thing you could admit to,' he told the *Daily Star*. 'But you meet some people and it makes you more open-minded and helps you understand where they come from. I can say that I met Adele one night, I didn't know who she was. We were in this bar and when I spoke to her I thought she'd got this amazing soul, a really soulful person. You know all that karma crap, well I got a great vibe off her, whether she's been to stage school or not. I'm really glad that she's doing so well.'

The *Guardian*'s Tim Jonze also believes that Adele runs contrary to the normal perception of the stage-school graduate. 'She is as far from the dead-eyed, all-singing, all-dancing stage-school desperado as imaginable,' he wrote. The *Sun* newspaper listed the BRIT as one of its ONE HUNDRED PLACES THAT MAKE BRITAIN BRILLIANT in June 2011. It included Adele's connection with it as the key piece of evidence for its brilliance. Adele herself defined the place as its most popular graduate. Previously, Amy Winehouse had held that honour but her dismissive comments about the place – it 'was shit' – had rather sullied the connection for both parties.

Another old boy, Luke from the indie band the Kooks, is also somewhat dismissive of the place but with a more measured tone. 'I have mixed feelings about the BRIT,' said the man who attended some years before Adele. 'Some people get really wrapped up in fame – there are kids from the middle of nowhere and their parents treat them like they're already celebrities 'cause they're at this famous school.'

Adele remains a glowing ambassador for the place. She has even spoken of an ambition to form a female supergroup featuring female singers who have passed through the BRIT School's doors. In the line-up alongside Adele would have been Kate Nash, Katie Melua and – until her tragic death in the summer of 2011 – Amy Winehouse. Adele said the band would 'represent most women in the world. If we were in a band I think it would be the best band ever.' She would not necessarily limit the line-up of her fantasy supergroup just to BRIT alumni, saying that she also hoped Lily Allen would join.

While the BRIT School has unquestionably nurtured a

respectable slice of the female vocal talent that has entered the industry in recent years, the charts have also been home to lots of female singers who took different routes to the top. Among these are Lily Allen, Joss Stone, Duffy and Dido. The soul singers among them have all attempted to conquer America. Adele could watch the experiences of Stone, Duffy and Winehouse in particular for evidence of how to succeed in the US. Meanwhile, in the UK, she could consider herself a key part of a new trend, as the British pop public went bonkers for female solo artists. Indeed, Adele spoke glowingly of Amy Winehouse and how she led a new charge of talented female singers from the Croydon institution and beyond. This, the childhood Spice Girls fan might have paused to reflect, was true 'girl power' in action. 'I think Amy has paved the way for me and Duffy,' she said. 'There used to be only one girl a year in the industry but now six or seven of us have come through in the last few years: Amy, Duffy, Lily and Kate.'

In 2007, as the BRIT School kept hitting the news because of the rush of its graduates in the charts, particularly female vocalists, Adele put the trend in what she saw as its correct context. 'Before this year the BRIT School didn't actually produce anyone. All this money was being pumped into it and nobody was coming out of it and doing well, so I think they were getting a bit worried. I think the BRIT School's produced loads of great people that nobody knows yet but, off the back of Amy, it's been getting more support. Suddenly all these great girls came forward in this great outburst of talent – I think it's just luck and timing, to be honest.'

Yet with her trademark frankness, she has admitted that BRIT has also had some real duds through its doors. 'Some of the people there are atrocious, really bad,' she said. 'They all wanna be fucking soul singers! I'm all up for people who are in development, but not people who are in there for four years and start when they're shit and leave when they're even worse.'

Alongside this trend of stage-school graduates, it has also been noted that there is a growing number of pop stars who have been privately educated. Artists such as Laura Marling, Florence Welch, Jack Penate, Jamie T and Coldplay's Chris Martin join members of folk bands Noah & the Whale and Mumford & Sons in this category. Even Lily Allen, despite her 'mockney' image, was privately educated at a leading British boarding school. Adele's *Pop Idol* hero Will Young was also privately educated. In the past, so-called posh pop formed a part of the industry. Indeed, the contrast between well-spoken, art-school types like Blur formed a dynamic contrast with working-class bands like Oasis. However, Adele stood aside from these trends: as we have seen, as the daughter of a single mother, she spent the earliest years of her life in Tottenham. After moving between a few state schools, she did move to an arts college, but, of course, BRIT is a state-funded institution.

Her interviews became legendary. Few could believe that this young woman with such a soulful and rich singing voice could have such an everyday, down-to-earth speaking voice. While she remains a working-class girl, the fact is that she is – rightly – not ashamed of her background and she has no intention of singing about her humble upbringing and the challenges it offered her. Indeed, she loathes musicians who sing about class issues from such a stance. 'It's all, "Oh, I come from nothing." Shut up, man! It doesn't matter. If you're good, you get places, full stop. But I do get pissed off when people say my friends are apparently posh. Jack Penate went to a public school on a scholarship, you know. You should see Jamie T's house – it's rank. And Kate Nash has never even spoken about her background. Just 'cos she sings with an accent doesn't mean she's trying to say that she's working class. Nobody likes a posh voice, do they?'

Adele's graduation was a big step, just as it is for so many school leavers as they step nervously into the exciting and scary realities of proper adult life. Looking back on it, Adele offered a perspective on what it felt like to leave the BRIT School and enter the big world outside. 'You're a huge fish in a small pond, whereas, when you leave and go out from your comfort, you're a goldfish in an ocean,' she said. To continue with the aquatic metaphor, Adele would quickly become a large fish in that very ocean. As such, she is by most standards one of the most successful and impressive graduates of BRIT. When they accepted her into their fold, they had made a wise decision. The budding Adeles of Britain now only want to go to one place. There can be no greater kudos for a place such as the BRIT School than watching one of its alumni set the world alight with their music.

CHAPTER THREE

THE HOMETOWN HERO

Adele and her mother moved from Brixton to West Norwood while Adele was at BRIT. They lived on the high street in a modest flat above a discount shop next to a garage. These could hardly have been less romantic surroundings. However, the area would reach a whole new level of glamour and become almost iconic after Adele wrote some of her biggest hits while there. The first Norwood song was actually about Tottenham, the place where Adele had grown up with Penny. By the time she started writing it, her musical ambitions were already on the way to becoming realised.

Adele was no longer merely flirting with the idea of becoming a singer. By the time she was 16, the notion was a fully fledged ambition. It had been a class project that led Adele to stardom. 'Part of my course at the BRIT School was recording lessons,' she said. 'I used to record demos in order to pass my course. I didn't know what to do with them.' But soon she would share them with a record label and quickly her life would change forever.

XL Recordings is a fascinating record label. In some ways, it is reminiscent of Creation Records in the heyday of Oasis. One of the similarities comes in the shape of its chairman and part-owner, Richard Russell. Like Alan McGee, the man at the helm of Creation, he is part-entrepreneur, part-creative music lover. Both of them have been as adept at closing deals and masterminding other aspects of the business as with the creative side. This is particularly true with Russell, who has produced music for such acts as Gil Scott-Heron and Major Lazer, as well as mixing tunes for leading British rapper Roots Manuva.

Certainly, his infectious enthusiasm is reminiscent of McGee at the peak of his Creation powers in the mid-1990s. Russell has even appeared on the promotional video for a song – with long hair, he looked more like a raver himself rather than a staid company boss. Russell stumbled into the industry, having found that music was a great escape from the boredom he felt in the north London suburbs he grew up in. He recorded mixtapes as a young man and sold them in Camden market. He also DJed and worked in a record shop. Then he worked for Island Records. 'It was an incredibly exciting, vibrant place,' he said. 'You could smoke dope in the warehouse.' He became involved in XL Recordings, and took over the reins when its founder, Tim Palmer, retired in 1995. The label signed the likes of the Prodigy and was soon making millions of pounds each year. Once the likes of Radiohead and the White Stripes joined the roster, XL was a major player, one with artists who drew both respect and sales from the record-buying public.

The philosophy of the label that signed Adele is simple. 'I look for originality,' said Russell. 'Quality and originality and the hunch that someone might have longevity.' He claims that, unlike much of the music industry which has a notoriously short-term view, he is very much focused on the long run. 'You're never really signing anyone on the strength of what they're doing at that moment; you're trying to recognise the potential of what someone does,' he said. Adding that he feels his policy has been vindicated, he said, 'Now we've got a roster of artists delivering records, we're working with people who've obviously got great work to come.'

Many XL acts have reciprocated this admiration and praised the label and its staff, including Liam Howlett of the Prodigy. 'It's always about the artist with those guys,' he said of Russell and his colleagues in January 2009. 'That's why they've survived.'

So much of his philosophy sounds like common sense. However, he feels that his simple and sensible method of operation is something that has got lost in 21st-century showbusiness. 'Record companies work well as small units closely connected to the music, closely connected to the artists,' he says. 'People have got distracted from the idea that you've got to have great artists, you've got to have great music.' Here, he positions himself as a proponent of back to basics for the music industry. He does not believe that the music industry is involved in some sort of battle with new digital technology. Fear of such innovations and what they might mean for record labels is commonplace in music business circles. Some are terrified of it, while others point out that, several decades ago, when people began to record records on to blank cassettes that was also meant to be the death knell for record labels.

Russell is not one to dwell on fear of new technology. 'That's a funny phrase, "Fight the internet",' he said. 'You're gonna fight the internet?' He even, in a sense of adventure and experimentalism, undertook a dummy run of promoting some music of his own on MySpace. He recorded a song using his computer, knocked up some artwork for it and then published the package on MySpace. He noted the statistics of how many people had come to listen to his song. 'And I was like, all right, this is fucking exciting,' he said. So he decided to search for new acts he could potentially sign up. The first discovery he made online was Jack Penate, who he found on MySpace. No wonder Russell is excited by the potential of the internet. 'It's so frenetic and there is so much going on. It is the wild west out there,' he said. 'The whole thing is on its fucking head.'

All these developments were taking place at the same time as the quality of the British music scene was becoming ever better. As we have seen, a lot of new female acts were emerging. This was just part of what some music commentators were identifying as a quality renaissance. Russell felt that, while all time periods have their fair share of good-quality acts, these were good times indeed. 'It's incredible,' he said in 2007. 'Absolutely incredible.' By this stage, he had discovered and signed up Adele.

Adele's first batch of material was almost ready for release. She was actually signed in September 2006 and the story of how they found her is interesting in itself. There is an element of symbolism in the fact that, while she was at the BRIT School, one of the few times that Adele clashed with teachers was over the power of the internet. She felt that the staff were behind the times when it came to the marketing power of the worldwide web. 'The BRIT teachers were a bit out of touch,' she said. 'I tried to teach them a bit about the internet, but they seemed to think everyone bought records and stuff.' If there were any doubts in their minds about what she had told them, these would have been dispelled by the way in which she launched her own career after graduating. Here, more than ever, was compelling, unarguable proof that the web is a fertile ground for music promotion.

She recorded two demos and sent them to an online publication called Platforms Magazine. The first song was called 'Daydreamer', the second 'My Same'. It was the fourth issue of Platforms Magazine, not the biggest online venture, which took the honour of being the first public space to host Adele's music, which is a fair old boast to be able to make. 'I used to record my demos and give them to my friends and they set me up in music MySpace,' she said, showing how normal the process seemed at this time. One friend in particular took ownership of this process. Adele trusted him, because he was very well versed in the ways of the internet, especially social-networking websites. She nicknamed him Mr MySpace UK. What happened next was about to launch her to a proper record deal. 'It literally kicked off from there,' she said. She recognises that, though her talent is undeniable, there is an element of good luck in the fact she was discovered and so easily. 'I didn't have to face the real world – everything fell into my lap,' she said. 'I've been very fortunate.'

Suddenly, she began to be in demand. 'I was still at school, I wasn't doing any gigs, I wasn't on the circuit, I didn't know anyone and I was getting emails from record companies,' she remembered. 'My mate was like, "I've got all of these people from record companies emailing. What should I say?"'

However, far from jumping for joy as these messages appeared in her inbox, she remained grounded out of a sense of scepticism as much as caution. 'I thought, yeah, whatever. I didn't believe you could get signed through MySpace.'

So, when she first set up her MySpace page, in December 2004, it was not with a sense that this move would change her life forever. In fact, MySpace and other online social-networking sites have proved a popular forum for the launching of mainstream music careers. The most spectacular example of this comes with Sheffield indie band Arctic Monkeys, who sped from being a MySpace band to making the fastest-selling debut album of all time. The band, formed in 2002, began by playing small gigs in tiny, cramped venues. Taking that route, they could easily have imploded before being discovered properly. Then, their music began to be shared on the MySpace website. The band have said that they didn't take an active involvement in what happened next, preferring to say that the flames of the online wildfire that built their name were all fanned by ordinary fans.

The detail is hardly important. What matters is that the Monkeys were quickly building a following online. Naturally, the music industry soon got to hear about all the fuss and began to circle in the hope of grabbing the band's signature. And their first single, 'I Bet You Look Good on the Dancefloor', was a UK No 1 hit in 2005 and their debut album, the following year's *Whatever People Say I Am, That's What I'm Not*, sold more copies on its first day alone – 118,501 – than the rest of the Top 20 albums combined. They have never looked back, continuing to be a hugely popular and successful band. 'The internet is the root of it all,' said a publicist for the band. 'They're part of that generation.'

Another British act to use the internet rather than more traditional routes to promote music is Lily Allen. She had been rejected by several record labels and was on the brink of giving up on her pop dream when she decided to try posting demos of her music on MySpace. She swiftly amassed a substantial online following, as tens of thousands of people lapped up her tunes. As the media took notice of her, she secured a mainstream record deal. Millions of albums, an Ivor Novello and a Mercury prize later, Allen was a true star.

Other acts from around the world to have used the internet to launch their careers include American singer Savannah Outen, Portuguese star Mia Rose, Dutch vocalist Esmee Denters and many more. Perhaps the most spectacular beneficiary of new media in recent years is Canadian pop sensation Justin Bieber. His rise to fame began when his mother filmed him singing in a local talent show and posted the footage on YouTube to share with family and friends. More and more people watched the videos which eventually came to the attention of a small online promotions group. They helped him to build his YouTube following before a young American entrepreneur called Scooter Braun saw the videos and secured young Bieber a record deal with Island Records. Even once signed, Bieber continued to use the internet as his primary promotional tool. His Twitter following is now into its millions and it is there that he communicates and connects with his fanatical, global teenage fanbase. An online presence can be potent: by keeping his original YouTube channel and Twitter account running, Bieber builds in his fans a sense that it is they who have made him and taken him to the top. That sense of ownership builds fierce loyalty, the results of which can be seen in the gargantuan size of his hysterical following.

Bieber had yet to appear on the scene when Adele was signed via MySpace. She hadn't seen evidence that the effect of the online world could be translated into solid success. However, that was exactly what was about to happen. 'I didn't know that MySpace was that influential at the time,' she said. 'Then Lily Allen and Arctic Monkeys were on there and it blew up.'

XL Recordings were watching and listening and they loved what they had heard of her. The song that stood out for them was 'Hometown Glory', the song she had written when she was 16. The song's political slant appealed to the staff of a label which appreciated acts who wrote songs with messages – though, if they expected such social commentary to be a regular feature of her songs in the future, they were to be disappointed.

Adele says that it took her just ten minutes to write 'Hometown Glory'. Impressive stuff: that's less than three times the time it takes to *hear* the finished product. And it was composed when she was just 16. The song has a haunting and melancholy tune, the powerful emotions of which remain long after the track has finished. As love songs to cities go, it is a far from sunny one. As mentioned, she launches into politics in the song, about how the government and the people take different sides. The people are united, she sings, not going to take anything lying down. Given the political slant of the song, it sounded like it could have been written in the 1980s. Her admiration for Billy Bragg, the politico folk singer of that decade, was easy to spot in this song. Indeed, the Style Council – Paul Weller's soulful, at times eccentric, 1980s combo – would have loved a song such as this. The section about people protesting was influenced by her experiences of the huge protest marches against the Iraq war. 'It was just such a moment, to see all these people come together to stand against something,' she says. 'There were these mohawk punks next to rude-boy kids in hoodies. It was great to be a part of.

'I wrote "Hometown..." on the guitar ... and it was actually the first song I ever wrote from start to finish. It was kind of about me and my mum not agreeing on where I should go to university. Because, though at first I'd wanted to go to Liverpool, later I changed my mind and wanted to go to university in London. But, because I love being at home and I'm really dependent on my mum, she still wanted me to go to Liverpool so that I'd have to learn how to do things on my own, rather than still be coming home for dinner, having her do my washing and stuff like that. So in that way it was a kind of protest song about cherishing the memories – whether good or bad – of your hometown. Whereas – having only been to Liverpool about twice – there's nothing there that comforts me, here in London, even if I'm having a really shit day there's still something I love about the place. So really, yeah, in general it is an ode to the place where I've always lived.' In short, the song, she said, contained 'all my fondest memories of London'.

The song might have been written in response to pressure from her mother for Adele to leave London and go to university elsewhere but Penny has since agreed that Adele made the right decision in staying in the capital and pursuing her musical dream. 'She's over the moon!' said Adele. 'She was like, "Get a job, get a job" for so long and I was like, "No… I can't be bothered!" Then I went and got a record deal and all this happened and now I'm definitely allowed to stay in London.'

Indeed, it was this very first song that captured the imagination of XL Recordings. So impressed were they with her demos that they emailed her and asked her to come to their offices for a meeting. For a while, she ignored their message. She had not heard of the label and was unaware of their impressive and artistically brilliant track record. Back at XL, they must have wondered why she was proving unresponsive. Perhaps, they might have wondered, she had already been signed by another label.

'I didn't realise they did all these amazing names,' said Adele of this period of silence. The only label she really recognised at this stage was Richard Branson's Virgin Records. 'When I was getting enquiries, I didn't know what to do,' she said. 'I didn't know who to believe. I didn't know if they were genuine.' She assumed that the best thing that could have come from a meeting would be an offer of an internship. So she took a friend along when she went to meet XL. You can't be too careful, she later said she had reasoned, when meeting somebody you have only known over the internet. 'I made my guitarist, Ben, come along to my first meeting with XL Recordings,' she said. 'He's puny, Ben, looks like a dwarf, but I'd never heard of XL so I thought I might be on my way to meet an internet perv or something.'

XL convinced her they were the real deal and it was then time to find Adele a manager. 'The first person who told me about Adele was actually the guy that eventually ended up signing her, Nick Huggett, who was at XL at that time,' said Jonathan Dickins, the man who would end up managing Adele. 'He said I should check this girl out. I just got a MySpace URL.'

Jonathan Dickins comes from a family steeped in music history. The black-haired, east Londoner's grandfather, Percy Dickins, was the co-founder of the music weekly *New Musical Express*, and in 1952 he came up with the idea of a pop music chart based on record sales. Before Dickins, popularity had been worked out on the basis of sales of sheet music. Meanwhile, Jonathan's uncle was the chairman of Warner Brothers in the UK for many years and his father is a booking agent who has worked with a galaxy of stars including Bob Dylan, Diana Ross and Neil Young.

As the younger Dickins himself said, the music industry was his family trade: 'It's all I knew.' He wanted to follow in their footsteps but bided his time as he looked for his own niche. 'I was very conscious of trying to make my own career in music and not follow in their footsteps – not doing the same things as they did, but hopefully being successful in my own sphere of the music industry,' he told the Hit Quarters website. After working in A&R, he eventually opted for artist management and in 2006 started his own company, September Management. He retains his enthusiasm for his job partly through having a policy of only working with artists whose music he himself loves. 'I still do it the old-fashioned way,' he said. 'I always go with a gut feeling: would I buy it; would I listen to it?' His own manager heroes include David Geffen and Elliot Roberts, and as part of his philosophy of music management he believes that the best way to break a new act is via live concerts. He thinks that radio and other routes are less dependable, though he is forever open-minded, analysing changes in the industry.

When he met Adele, he decided he wanted to work with her. As much as anything else, this decision was based on a simple incident: he made her laugh. 'Literally stomach cramps the day after,' she said.

For him, this decision was clear-cut. 'It was the most simple, straightforward thing I've ever done in my life, really.' What a promising start to what has become a strong and important relationship for both. 'We had one meeting and just got on great,' he said. They discussed music and which artists they enjoyed. Adele was swung in part due to the presence in his roster of one of her favourite acts. 'She was a massive fan of Jamie T. She was 18, just out of college, and wanted to make a career in music. We started working together in early June 2006 and eventually we signed her to XL in the end of September 2006.'

A criteria that he uses to help him decide whether or not to work with an act includes how focused they are on what they want from their own career. 'One thing that every great artist has is a clear sense of what they are and what they want to achieve,' he said. 'That's absolutely essential for me.' This is something that Adele impressed him with. 'This business is completely and utterly driven by great artists, not by managers, lawyers, record companies, or radio.' In Adele, he had indeed found a great artist, as well as one whose personality would always want to be in the driving seat. She is no shrinking violet, content to stand on the sidelines. 'Adele is incredible,' he said in the early days of her success. 'For a girl who's just turned 20 years old, it's unbelievable how focused she is in terms of what she thinks is right for her career,' he said. 'So, I listened and threw in some ideas, and generally it just clicked. It wasn't about me going, "This is what I can do, blah, blah, blah..." I try to let the artist take the lead with matters now.'

However, her future management needed to be sure that the voice in the demo songs was really something as special as it seemed. So a concert was arranged in Brixton for them to hear her voice in full flow in person. Once they had heard her, they were ready to sign. 'The key to great singers is believing every single word they sing,' said Dickins of the wider authenticity of his new artist. 'And I think you believe every word that comes out of Adele's mouth.'

The label were impressed by Adele's personality as well as by her talent. 'She had an extremely strong idea of what she wanted to do,' Russell said. 'I don't think you get that from BRIT School. You get that when you have great instincts.' Discussing the early material they worked on with Adele, Russell found one theme that was common to many singers of her generation. 'It's very hard to find anything that is not influenced by black American music, in one way or another,' he said. 'Everything is rooted back to the blues. What we've seen in the UK is an amazing wealth of talent shared by young female solo artists and there's maybe an unspoken competition there. There's something about her voice. It connects to you very directly. Her subject matter – being hurt – she talks about it in a way that's so easy to relate to. It's very honest. She's incredibly focused... That focus is only as useful as it has been to her in combination with the talent she was born with.'

It was, said Adele – who was worth around £6 million by 2011 – a modest initial record deal. Off the back of it, she only made one notable lifestyle change. 'I used to smoke rollies but then I got the record deal and switched to Marlboro Lights.' Great riches were just around the corner. As she came to terms with the fact she was now a musician proper, with a recording contract and high hopes for the future, she took time to look back into her past, and credit those she saw as having given her the most assistance: the staff and facilities of the BRIT School. 'While at first I was very like "I ain't going here! It's a stage school! I can do it on my own!", I think I do owe it *completely* to the BRIT School for making me who I am today, as cheesy and embarrassing at it may sound. Because, while my mum is the most supportive mum on *earth*, she wouldn't have known how to *channel* me. With her I'd probably have gone down the classical music route or maybe Disney or musical theatre... But at the BRIT School I found my direction, because the music course was really wicked.'

She was still keen to draw a contrast between BRIT and the image of theatrical schools that is more prevalent in popular imagination. 'It's not your typical stage school full of kids that are pushed into it by their parents. It's a school full of kids that will dance at a freezing-cold town hall, barefoot, for eight hours solid. And, whereas before I was going to a school with bums and kids that were rude and *wanted* to grow up and mug people, it was really inspiring to wake up every day to go to school with kids that actually wanted to be *productive* at something and wanted to *be* somebody.' She felt that her early days in the industry proper were comparable in some senses to the atmosphere of the BRIT School. She stepped, she said, directly 'from the bubble of the BRIT School straight into another bubble'. There was no intermediary period. When lots of people her age would be looking ahead to university, or starting work in offices, shops and factories, or simply immersing themselves in a period of laziness, she was moving straight from education into the music industry. She could be forgiven for feeling overwhelmed, which she did. Later in life, she might go on to take a step aside from music to enjoy a belated gap year. But, back then, having written just three songs, she had the attention of major record labels, one of which had signed her. Yet as exciting as these developments were, there was a feeling of low confidence for Adele as she found her feet in her new world. For nearly a year, she did not write another song. During those months, she said, 'the future wasn't looking bright for me'.

Things began to look far brighter in June 2007 when Adele made her first television appearance on *Later... with Jools Holland*. This brought back memories for her of being allowed to stay up late as a child, watching the live music show with her mother Penny. She went on to say she could hardly believe she was there. For her to appear on *Later...* at such a tender age was remarkable enough in itself, but the true wonder is that she was invited to do so before she had any release to her name. She sang 'Daydreamer' with just her acoustic guitar as accompaniment. The quirky Holland announced her with a simple sentence: 'Making her TV debut, will you welcome from Brixton... Adele.'

It was a catchy, if slightly nervous performance. Her nerves were understandable. Not only was she thrown into the deep end of television, having never so much as dipped her toes in previously, but she was also surrounded by music royalty. 'They usually put you in the middle of the room, but for some reason they put me at the end, right in front of the audience, with Björk on my left, Paul McCartney on my right and my mum crying in front of me,' she said. 'I met them afterwards and couldn't stop crying.'

As far as the *Later...* team was concerned, Adele had passed the test with flying colours. 'We sandwiched her between Sir Paul McCartney and Björk before she'd even released a record,' confirmed a producer. 'But like any confident, self-assured, sassy 19-year-old, south London girl, it didn't faze her one bit.' So how had they decided to book Adele at such an early point in her career? 'When we fall for somebody, we have to have them,' said *Later...* producer Alison Howe. 'She's a classic. She doesn't fit anywhere; she just has a great voice. I would hope that, by this time next year, she will have sold as many records as Amy [Winehouse], and I don't see why she shouldn't.'

Her performance was not flawless. The BBC website would in due course say it had been 'brim with nervous caterwauling'. But it had been good enough to win her a new army of fans from among the 600,000-odd musical devotees who regularly tune in to *Later...* The media championing of Adele began in earnest. Other early journalistic admirers included the *Guardian*, BBC Radio 1 DJ Zane Lowe and *Q* magazine. Soon, the *NME* would describe her as 'London's new heartbroken soul laureate'.

She was already in a strong position before the release of her first single on 22 October 2007. Even some successful acts had to release several records before they attained the profile she already had. 'Hometown Glory' was initially a vinyl-only release on Jamie T's Pacemaker label. It was first released this way in keeping with a vow Adele had made to him. 'He was like, "But you promised I could put out 'Hometown' back in the day…"' she said. Weeks before its release, it was being played to radio listeners. It had been playlisted at Radio 1 on the B list and Radio 2 on the C list, meaning it got regular on-air spins.

Dickins was pleasantly surprised by these significant developments. 'The expectations around this single from our point of view were not huge, although we obviously think it's a great bit of music,' he said at the time. 'It's amazing how well it's done in terms of being picked up by press and radio. It's really just a brief introduction, before her first single is released on XL next January.'

The sleeve for the release featured Adele sitting reflectively in a cafe. Two members of the waiting staff, decked in white uniform, are chatting in the background but Adele is sitting thinking, with a tea cup sitting on the table in front of her. As the *Observer* newspaper later put it: 'A certain tone had been established.'

The public response was promising from the start. For the B-side, she chose to record a cover of 'Fool That I Am' by favourite singer Etta James. She had originally become interested in the song because she wanted to add something to her live performances. 'I felt I needed to beef up my live set by introducing covers, I decided to include "Fool That I Am" in my show,' she said. 'You know, it was a song that just changed everything for me. It inspired me to want to write my own songs, to be honest and to try and touch people. Basically, I think it's a beautiful song, I love singing it… And so I thought it would be nice for my fans if I included it on this single.'

On the Rock Feedback website, writer Chris O'Toole heaped praise on Adele. He said that she 'sings with accomplishment and passion and could bring a tear to the eye of the most hardened cynic'. Turning specifically to 'Hometown Glory', he attempted to put the song in what he saw as its correct context. 'The fire has burned down to the final embers. You have hit the bottom of the final bottle of corner-shop wine. The lady you are failing to seduce is reaching for her coat and asking you to call a cab. You reach for "Hometown Glory" and perhaps, just maybe, everything will work out.'

Sarah Walters, on City Life website, described the song as: 'Soulful – if a little lacking in direction.' She added, 'There's still enough room for Adele to shine as a unique star.'

The song failed to chart on its first release, but due to the fact such a limited edition of vinyl had been pressed this was inevitable. It is a song that was to subsequently benefit from inclusion on the soundtracks of several high-profile television series. In April 2008, it was featured on the popular Channel 4 teenage drama series *Skins*. It captured the mood of the programme and the imaginations of those who watched it. It soon entered the charts. Within weeks, it was included on the American teenage drama *One Tree Hill*. As well as earning Adele royalties in its own right, this development also introduced her music to millions of hip young Americans. However, an even more significant television exposure for the song was just around the corner.

The American medical television series *Grey's Anatomy* regularly pulls in audience figures of around 20 million in America. It has also won numerous awards and is watched by millions more around the world. To have a song included in the soundtrack of an episode is a huge deal for any artist. So, when 'Hometown Glory' was played during the finale of season four, it was a major boost for Adele's fledgling career. The song had been chosen after Alexandra Patsavas, who has worked as a music selector for countless big television series in America, went to see Adele sing at the Hotel Cafe near Sunset Boulevard in Los Angeles. She loved the song and knew it could fit in well. She spoke to her friend Jonathan Palmer from Columbia and soon the song was slotted into the series.

The television suitability of 'Hometown Glory' became all the more clear when it showed up on a raft of other television series back in Britain during 2008. In the second half of the year, it was included three times in the long-running Channel 4 soap opera *Hollyoaks*. It seemed a song that was perfect for the soundtrack of fictional young lives and the heartache and challenges of life. For instance, it was used on *Hollyoaks* during an episode in which one of the show's most popular characters died. Other shows it appeared on during 2008 included *The Secret Diary of a Call Girl*, and the American reality show *So You Think You Can Dance*. As we shall see, this would not be the end of its cultural influence on television and beyond.

By the summer of 2008, the song had been re-released properly – and Adele's life was changing fast. 'I went overnight from being a support act to every newspaper writing stories about me,' she said. Her introduction to fame was abrupt and she explained how it felt being thrown into the proverbial deep end. 'I did one interview and it went everywhere. The first time you get quoted out of context is the scariest thing. You can't remember what you said but you think, I would never say that... *Did* I say that?'

It had been 'Hometown Glory' that had grabbed the attention and her manager analysed how quickly she became popular and successful. He believed it was a simple case of quality being rewarded. He eschewed any explanations that go far beyond that. 'She's just brilliant; I don't think there's any science to it,' he said. 'She is possibly the best singer, or one of the best singers, I've ever heard in my life. That voice is incredible. A combination of that voice with a song like "Hometown Glory", which was the song that really started her, was incredible – it completely and utterly stood out.'

Standing out was exactly what Adele was starting to do, as awareness of her talent swept Britain like an unstoppable, and increasingly fierce, fire.

To help her with the transition, she not only had her management and record company but also a growing army of creative friends. In 2006, she had met singer and label-mate Jack Penate at the 333 club in London's Hoxton, at a night called Troubled Mind, and they became good buddies. She went on to work with him, and for his part he could not have been more appreciative of her natural, raw talent. She has twice contributed backing vocals on Penate tracks. The first was on 'My Yvonne' on his 2007 debut

Matinee. The second occasion was in 2009 and came about very casually. 'Adele was in Notting Hill and I just phoned her and said, "Can you do this song?"' he said. 'As always, she came in and killed it. Her voice always makes such an impact on anything because it's the most beautiful thing.'

She also hit it off with respected music producer and industry royalty Mark Ronson. She had been a fan of the musical genius since 2003, when he released the *Here Comes the Fuzz* album. He invited her to New York where he showed her round his favourite haunts.

'Mark is so funny,' she said. 'I always think he's about 24, but he's 32. He's old!'

Adele assembled a group of people around her which has since become known as Team Adele and been lauded for the brilliance of its operation. There is a family feel to the group, both metaphorically in the sense of its closeness, and literally, given that Dickins' sister Lucy joined its ranks. 'I met her separately from Jonathan and loved her and didn't put two and two together,' said Adele. 'I went to him and said, "I've found this agent. Her name's Lucy Dickins." He said, "Oh, yeah, that's my sister."'

Kirk Sommer of William Morris, the giant entertainment agency, also joined the ranks. 'I heard her name in a few key places and tracked down some music online,' Sommer told a trade music magazine. 'It was love at first listen. I got in touch with Jonathan and pursued it for several months. I stayed on it, and the more I listened, the more eager I was to work with her.'

Brad Hunner is another key part of Team Adele. He is a

hardworking radio plugger who works for an organisation called Radar Plugging. Given the enormous on-air presence that Adele swiftly established, his contribution cannot be doubted. Radio play is key in breaking a pop artist, even in these days of online marketing and digital downloads. Hunner did Adele proud, breaking her name to national radio stations long before she had released a record. Hunner had previously worked for Anglo Plugging, but in 2006 he launched his new independent radio promotion agency. It was based at the XL Recordings office in Notting Hill, taking him into the heart of the operation that was about to launch Adele to the world. On his arrival there, the XL managing director Ben Beardsworth said Hunner's presence would 'step things up'.

When these fine minds and safe pairs of hands came together to mastermind Adele's career, it wasn't just the singer herself who benefited. While the massive record sales that she has generated have naturally been to the advantage of Adele, her management and record label, the entire music industry has been delivered a much-needed shot in the arm by the triumph. A hit machine such as Adele is exactly what it had been hoping for. The confidence that music business people such as Russell have in modern technology is to a large extent vindicated by her achievements. Two of the biggest-selling artists of recent times were both discovered via the internet: Adele and Justin Bieber. The many millions of records these two very different artists have sold worldwide are stark proof that the internet can be the best friend, rather than the enemy, of the mainstream music business.

As 2007 drew to a close, Adele could not have doubted that she had an amazing year ahead of her. In October, she had been the subject of the *Guardian*'s Flash Forward feature. In the text, Sarah Boden noted Adele's talent and the fact that she made for an unlikely soul singer. 'With her milky-soft complexion, feline sooty eyes and sixties girl-group hairdo, the 19-year-old doesn't look much like a soul crooner,' wrote Boden.

Two months later, Adele received some sensational news. She was in the running for the first ever critics' choice award at the next Brit awards ceremony. Over a thousand music industry insiders and critics had selected her for the award, specifically created to highlight those acts expected to break through in the year of the ceremony. She had been up against some tough competition. The other acts in the frame included Oxford sensations Foals and the Welsh soul and jazz singer Duffy.

As a result of this honour, the media was beginning to really take notice of Adele. In the eyes of those who already admired her, she was getting the attention she so richly deserved. There were some detractors who thought she had been overhyped. The coverage was inescapable, and even Adele herself reacted, with typical humour, when she learned that she had been featured in the *Daily Mail*, that bastion of middle-market, middle-England media. 'The *Daily Mail*? I'm in the posh papers! I read the *Sun*.'

Inevitably, reports sometimes focused on her appearance. In the image-conscious 21st century, in which many pop stars are far more beautiful to look at than to listen to, Adele was a reminder of times gone by. She reminded us of the days when we cared more about the music rather than the image of artists. Speaking to the *Guardian*, she laid out her manifesto in regard to her weight. 'I read a comment on YouTube that I thought would upset me,' she says, '"Test pilot for pies" – but I've always been a size 14–16 and been fine with it. I would only lose weight if it affected my health or sex life, which it doesn't.' She did, though, add a qualifier to this fine statement: 'I might lose a lot of weight if I'm pressurised.'

As the issue kept being raised in the media, Adele came to accept that she would need to live with the fact that this was an angle that would forever be used. While some of the comments made were in no way nasty or critical, her appearance was something that was often cited. The fact she is not a super-skinny woman and that her appearance was not that of a conventional supermodel did indeed fascinate the media and provoke strong feelings. For some, it was seen as an advantage and a positive. They installed her as the poster girl for non-poster girls: a famous woman who defied the rules that normally govern female celebrities. Some other commentators and journalists were just bitchy. As for Adele, she preferred to not make a big deal of how she looked either way. 'The press are always trying to bring it up,' she told the *Daily Telegraph*, 'but I really don't give a toss. If I wanted to be on the cover of *FHM*, then of course I'd be, like, "Fuck, I need to lose weight" or "I need some fake tan" or "I need to get my teeth fixed". But I'd rather be on the cover of *Q* for my music.' Fortunately, she said, she had no inherent desire to take up extreme physical exercise, nor to 'run up a hill' or anything like that. 'I'd rather weigh five tons and make an incredible album than look like Nicole Richie and make a shit one,' she said, cigarette in hand. As a final benchmark, she added, 'If you ever see me rail-thin, then you'll know there's something really wrong with me.'

Therefore, she did her best to make light of the issue, even offering one journalist a soundbite description of how she felt she came over. 'Being told how to look is about being a product and I don't want to be a product,' she said. 'I'd say my look is shabby-chic. I just wear big jumpers over tight jeans and carry a huge bag and that's it. I don't want people to notice how I look. Although that's probably not working because I'm bigger than most people doing this job, but I want people to just listen to me.' She explained that she had always been one to keep the issue of her appearance in perspective. Adele came over as a fun-loving lady and one who would only pay attention to how she looked insofar as such thought and effort did not get in the way of her having a good time. 'I don't care about clothes – I'd rather spend my money on cigarettes and booze,' she said. 'I've never felt that pressure. Me and my friends will eat a bucket load of pasta if we're hungry – we don't care. It's my gay friends who are more concerned with their weight. They'll be like, "I can't eat carbs!" It's never been an issue for me – I don't want to go on a diet, I don't want to eat a Caesar salad with no dressing. Why would I do that? I ain't got time for this, just be happy and don't be stupid.' It's good, common-sense advice delivered with charismatic conviction and the public paid attention to what she said.

Her style was something that many women were interested in – not despite her attitude, but because of it. She kept continuity in the products she used on her face and in her scents. 'Because I wear a lot of make-up when I'm working I like to use skin food by Weleda because I feel really replenished when I do,' she said. 'My skin feels back to life and not caked in foundation. I'm also obsessed with lip balms and I use loads of different makes. I've got about ten on the go at one time. I love Chanel make-up, perfume-wise I wear Christian Dior's Hypnotic Poison.' Her false eyelashes were a striking part of her image. And, characteristically, Adele was jokey as she discussed her favourite sources for eyelashes. 'Oh yes, I love Shu Uemura and MAC eyelashes,' she said. 'I like to look like a drag queen. I've never had those eyelash extensions you can get though. My mum has them and she wakes up in the morning looking like she's hungover because they're all bent! I can't maintain my eyelashes myself so I need someone to do them for me and false ones work on me.' Her icon when it comes to pulling off a great eyelash look was the singer Shakira. '[She] looks amazing with her big eyelashes and no other make-up, but I don't think I could get away with that look. I like false lashes and plenty of eye make-up.'

Adele could be very generous to other women when it came to icons of beauty. Despite being in the public eye, she wasn't one to be gratuitously bitchy. Those included in this hall of fame formed a varied group, and it's notable that Adele most looked up to women whose charm was mostly natural. 'I think Fearne Cotton always looks really beautiful and really fresh and like she hasn't made much of an effort,' she said. 'She looks like she's just rolled out of bed looking that amazing. I can't do that – I need a lot of prep – but she's naturally lovely. Halle Berry always looks pretty nice too and Queen Latifa has got the most amazing skin ever. She actually looks better without make-up than with it.'

Adele herself talked of how she had developed an obsession with designer handbags. She has said that she has bought enough to turn her bankrupt. And it was true that she was rarely seen without a flash bag over her shoulder or wrist, some of them costing her thousands of pounds. One of her most expensive models was made by Chanel. A quilted, purple handbag, it set her back more than £2,000. For Adele, it was worth every penny. The same was true of the Burberry Knight handbag. The large, studded accessory cost around £1,300. Other designer handbags she has splashed out on include the Jimmy Choo Rosabel, the Louis Vuitton Monogram Canvas Galliera bag and the extravagantly named and priced Caviar Monochrome number from Chanel.

But it wasn't all high spending for Adele. For instance, one day she followed a visit to a Louis Vuitton store – during which she had spent a small fortune – by visiting the knockdown clothes store favourite Primark. She was a big fan. 'Love the one-pound knickers with all the designs and the funny jokes on them,' she said. 'And bows. You can only wear them once 'cos they just fall apart.' She wore acrylic nails, too. She called them her 'ghetto nails' and said they make her 'feel like a woman'.

When it came to relaxing at the end of the day, she was a

well-known fan of red wine and unpretentious about which variety she drank. 'Not really fussed, Cabernet would do,' she said. Meanwhile, among her favourite food was the traditional Sunday roast with onions and as a snack she loved egg sandwiches and ready-salted crisps with Worcester sauce. 'Fuckin' amazing,' she said. These good down-to-earth tastes counterbalanced her more expensive tastes elsewhere.

Looking ahead to 2008, she talked about how she had to take a deep breath and steel herself for what she could already sense would be a dramatic 12 months. It was clear her level of fame and recognition would rocket. Inevitably, this would bring pressures and challenges as well as new freedoms and joys. She had a straightforward attitude to the future. 'If I don't like [success], I'll walk away,' she said. 'You don't have to lose your privacy. If you're in control of your career, you won't get followed. Just don't go to celeb hangouts.'

One of the first challenges to come would be managing her own reaction to the public response to her Brit award. 'I'm really chuffed and flattered to have won the new category,' she said. 'It's fantastic to have lots of people supporting me. I've always wanted a Brit award and I'm made up to be getting one so early on!' The chairman of the Brits committee, Ged Doherty, described her as a 'worthy winner', adding, 'Huge congratulations to Adele, I know the competition was tough.'

But Adele soon realised that the news of her success wasn't greeted with universal approval. As she spoke to the media, she was already aware there was some cynicism about both the award itself and the fact she had won it. She admitted from the start that there was something slightly strange about the story. 'I found out in December, after I did the Jonathan Ross show,' she said. 'But someone had told me about the award a month before, that the Brit awards were setting it up. I didn't believe them, I was like, "Yeah, whatever". And then my manager told me, so I went around to all my family, saying, "I've been nominated for this Brit award," but my manager said, "No, you've won." So it's a bit weird. It's a bit weird getting an award before you've done anything, isn't it? Haha! But all good.' She responded directly to the suggestion that the award had been dreamed up purely as an excuse to give her a publicity boost. 'I don't think it was invented for me. That would be really, really funny if it was, wouldn't it? I mean... oh, my gosh!' she said. 'But, yeah, you know, I think it's a really good award. The impression I got from the award and why they announced it in December was to bring the spotlight on the person that won it. I'm getting a lot of coverage at the moment so it's very successful in what it set out to do. So I think they should have it every year.'

One interviewer wondered aloud whether she had considered rejecting it out of fear that it would bring so much pressure and hype that she might not be able to cope. 'No, I'm an opportunist! Haha! Course I'm not going to turn it down! I've always wanted one, as well. You know, the hype and all that, there's not a lot I can do about it. I'm getting a bit sick of seeing myself in stuff but I haven't actually done many interviews. It's just people writing about it. It happens, you know!

As she arrived at the Brits, she gave a series of interviews on the literal and metaphorical red carpet. She seemed excited about the night to come but was keeping matters in perspective. 'I like watching it. It's not as glamorous as it looks, you know. But it's really fun and you get to meet lots of people and I've just seen some friends, which is fun.' The Brits weren't the only thing on her mind, as Adele had received her finished record as well. 'I'm really excited, I got the finished thing today, with all the packaging and so on, which was really exciting.'

She was asked what she had been up to of late and how she felt. 'Been all right, thank you, I've been busy. Promoting my record and releasing my album and doing the tour.' Pointing to the line of press at the event, she added, 'And doing this for about five days.' With a part in a Mark Ronson medley on the cards for her as well that evening, she seemed full of trademark Adele excitement about the prospect. 'It's not really a song you'd think I'd do. It's quite mellow, quite sultry.' Speaking of the other acts involved in the Ronson medley, she added, 'I think, even if we're all rubbish, it's going to be amazing.'

Asked who she was looking forward to seeing perform, her list went on and on until it had encapsulated nearly every act due to perform. Such an excitable woman, you had to love her. Asked if she thought the presenters, the wildcard Osbourne family, would swear on live television, she said, 'Oh, I hope so, I hope so. That would be great.' Then it was time for her to reveal how she built her confidence for such a daunting night. 'Have some Dutch courage, a bit of tipple – yeah.' She added that she was a bit nervous for her part in the Ronson medley.

For Adele, still so new to the celebrity game, it was a strange experience to be around so many other famous faces on the night. For them, such evenings were more commonplace. Adele was still fresh to it all and, as she spoke about how she felt, her words connected with the audience at home. Like her, they could never play it cool in such surroundings. For the average viewer, following the Brits from home, there was no mystery in the nerves of a new attendee like Adele. 'It's been amazing but it's been daunting,' admitted Adele.' I act like such an idiot around other stars. It's really weird being in an arena. It takes like half an hour to get out of an arena. A big difference from Barfly in Camden – but it's good!' Asked if she got star-struck, she made a distinction between the acts who did faze her and those who did not. Pointing at the Klaxons and Kaiser Chiefs, she said, 'Not by them lot,' adding that she already knew them. 'But if I see, like, Leona Lewis or Kylie I'll probably be a bit nervous.'

In fact, Kylie herself spoke of Adele and the impact she had on her. 'Adele, with that breakthrough song, it's just divine. In fact, that's what I've been singing to myself all day.'

One of Adele's most entertaining pre-show interviews was with BBC radio star Chris Moyles and his sidekick Comedy Dave. Adele began by saying that the knowledge she was definitely the winner helped her compose herself ahead of the event proper. 'It's quite handy knowing already,' she said. With the element of surprise taken away from her category, she explained that she was going to arrive from backstage to collect the gong, as opposed to do the more traditional walk to the stage from a table. This lessened the chance of the comic disaster she had been worrying about. 'Yeah, at 8.21 I go and get it,' she told them with notable precision. 'But I don't walk up, I go backstage and then I walk on. I was quite looking forward to the walk up, but I suppose this saves me falling flat on my face.' She added that she had nothing polished and prepared to say in accepting her award. 'I don't know... I had a speech but I scrapped it.' She joked about the fickle nature of awards ceremonies and the tendency of the unlucky nominees to try to conceal their disappointment. Already keenly aware of how fleeting the music game is, she said, 'Next year, if I'm nominated and then I don't win, I'll have to do that fake smile, like, "Oh, I'm so pleased she won it," which I'm not very good at.'

She then took the conversation down ever more giggly territory. Moyles asked her if she was attracted to him, but she replied with a stinging: 'You look like my dad's brother.' Not quite the response he might have hoped for. 'This is sounding almost seedy,' said Moyles, 'I didn't want it to sound seedy.' To up the entertaining tension, she reminded him, 'You are a lot older than me, Chris.' Moyles, loving the banter, was back as quick as a flash, telling her, 'Yeah, but I'm loaded.' But in Adele he had met his match, and he had hardly finished his sentence when she retorted: 'So am I.'

This particular strand of repartee did not come completely out of the blue, for Adele had indeed once revealed, to a somewhat aghast nation, that she found Moyles attractive. It was during an interview with Jo

Whiley on BBC Radio 1's Live Lounge. Adele said later that she did not realise the interview was live. Needless to say, Moyles made merry when he learned of the news. 'He spent the whole week going on about how I liked him, but my type always changes,' she said. 'I like Chris Moyles, Colin Firth, Ryan Phillippe and Jamie Oliver.' That is indeed a broad collection of men, from the roguish Moyles, with his fulsome physique, to the more gentlemanly Firth and foppish, pretty Phillippe. But then Adele has always had varied tastes, as we saw with her teenage crushes on Will Young and Mike Skinner. 'I like a good back,' she continued. 'I like Jake Gyllenhaal's back. In that film with Jennifer Aniston, *The Good Girl*, when he's banging her, his back was so fit, even my mum was like, "Wow!" So a good back and a sense of humour. I don't like fit boys who aren't funny. I'd prefer an ugly boy who was really funny.' Got it?

She later said that, as she waited backstage to collect her Brit, she'd been thinking back to previous ceremonies she had seen. Most notably, in 2006, she had been among the audience right in front of the stage. Pupils at the BRIT School are given tickets to be in the pit right in front of the stage. Adele was there, watching, as the likes of Kaiser Chiefs, Coldplay and James Blunt won awards. She watched Paul Weller, Kelly Clarkson and Prince perform. Just 24 months later here she was, backstage, waiting to collect an award herself. What an amazing turn her life had taken. She heard Sharon Osbourne introduce her category. The famous host explained the connection between the presenter and recipient. 'To present her with this award is a man who holds a very special place in her heart,' said Osbourne. 'You see, she got suspended from school for fighting over him. Shame, if only she knew what we all know about him. Anyway, please welcome, the gorgeous Master Will Young.'

Master Young then arrived on the stage and launched into his announcement. 'Good evening, everybody. Now, this is a new Brit award, and it's given to an act that our most eminent critics believe will break through in 2008. This year's winner has already proven the critics right, because her debut album *19* went straight to No 1 in the album charts. It looks like it will stay at the top of the charts for a good long time. It's appropriate that the winner should have graduated from the BRIT School because... they're all standing in front of me. Because, this event, through its trust, helps fund the BRIT School.

'The BRIT School roll of honour is getting longer each year, with Amy Winehouse, Katie Melua, Kate Nash along with the members of the Kooks and the Feeling all being former pupils. And now, another hugely talented artist joins their ranks. It gives me enormous pleasure and please give a big cheer for the gorgeous Adele.'

The audience cheered wildly as she arrived. The BRIT School pupils in particular were loud and proud with their admiration. Adele was and is an inspiration to them. She is a living embodiment of the possibility that their own dreams could come true.

'Hello,' she said nervously as she arrived at centre stage. 'Hello, woo! It's really nice to be here, at last, it's been going on for, like, three months. I'm not going to talk for too long, 'cos I think speeches are really boring but I'd really like to thank some people. Erm... I've got my heart beating so fast. Everyone who voted for the critics' choice award, thank you very much. My manager, Jonathan, who's been there since day one, I love you very much. And my beautiful mum. Alison Howell, everyone at XL and Beggars, Nick Huggett who's moved on but I still love ya. Jamie T, Jack Penate, BRIT School... and everyone for buying my album – thank you so much!' She was already walking off-stage as she completed her speech, saying, 'Have a good night!'

In her reference to how long the build-up to the presentation had gone on for, Adele had hinted how tired she had grown of talking about the award. But, having finally got her hands on it, she was mistaken if she thought she was about to get any immediate respite from such discussion. Her first post-presentation chat was with television presenter Fearne Cotton. Trying to up the energy and excitement levels backstage, Cotton said to Adele, 'This is the first year for this award, and here it is!'

Adele looked at the award and said, 'Cool, thanks,' before giggling. The awkward atmosphere continued when Cotton asked Adele if it had yet sunk in that she had won it. 'Nearly,' said Adele, reminding Cotton that she had found out three months ago that she had won it. It was an awkward but amusing moment, typical of these sorts of interviews. The media is bursting with enthusiasm to discuss topics at length that are not half as significant as the attention suggests. Adele continued to have mixed feelings about the award. She later admitted, during an interview with the website Clash Music, that it had come at a price. 'It was a bit overwhelming, I felt quite uncomfortable by it all,' she said. 'Everyone assuming... you know what I mean? It wasn't actually like, "Oh, she's won a Brit award 'cos she's done well." It was everyone assuming I was gonna do well.'

As her public profile continued to rise, Adele was mindful of the dangers ahead. She was a shrewd and switched-on lady as her reflections on the potential pitfalls of fame showed. 'It's a death trap, this industry,' she told the *Daily Telegraph*. 'I mean, you play to two thousand people who adore you, then you go back to your hotel room alone. That's quite a comedown.' How to deal with the high after the show has long been a puzzle which has caused pain for entertainers of all hues. 'People don't tend to make it through intact, do they?' However, she has cause to be confident that she will survive the rigours of fame. Although she has often been compared to tragic Amy Winehouse, she says she had a major advantage over her fellow former BRIT pupil. Despite freely confessing to 'a serious cigarette and red wine habit', Adele insists she has never taken anything stronger. 'I've never taken an illegal drug in my life,' she said. 'I want to be known for my music. I don't want to be in the press for having coke up my nose, because my nan will see it.'

That said, she has empathy for Winehouse and the way her life and career had been challenged by her hedonistic ways. Her tribute to Winehouse following her death in July 2011 was, as we shall see, particularly eloquent and touching. As Adele herself has said, she was not a drug user but she enjoyed a drink. Consequently, she was mindful that, while her following in Winehouse's staggering footsteps seemed unlikely, she could not rule out such a fate. 'I do worry about it,' she has said. 'I'm sure if you'd asked Amy Winehouse three years ago whether she was worried about ending up like that she'd have said, "No". But it's easy to fall into. I don't do drugs, I've never done a drug in my life, but I'm a big drinker. And when I do a show and I've got six hours to kill, I just get drunk because I'm bored. So I can see how it could happen.'

Indeed, she felt that not just boredom but something in her very make-up would make drug use a particularly dangerous road for her to go down. 'Coke is everywhere,' she said when asked what she most dislikes about the music industry. 'It would be so easy to fall into it. I am an addictive personality: if I start something I don't stop. I smoke 30 cigarettes a day, I drank a lot in the past. I know I would go on to other things and I don't want that.' Instead, her wildest social plans involved the desire to go to a novelty party at a nightclub. 'I wanna go to a foam party in a wetsuit – no one will notice me,' she laughed. 'Apparently people get naughty.'

It is understandable that Adele felt that the Brits critics' choice was a mixed blessing for her. 'I was the critics' choice all the time – not the public's,' she said, 'and people naturally back the underdog, not the person who's shoved in their face the whole time. So, I guess, to me, the success is sweeter because of that... I don't feel pressurised but all the journalists who tipped me are going to look like right fucking idiots if I just disappear, aren't they?' She was busy adjusting to the sudden new demands of fame. 'I don't like photo sessions that much. That side of things is a lot harder than I thought it would be, in a good way, though. I mean, I never really thought about being a pop star and I never thought about all the behind-the-scenes stuff that would come with it. I just thought I'd release a single and that would be that.'

Having been launched through a record label discovering her on the internet, Adele intended to keep that arm of her marketing strategy going. Just as the likes of Lily Allen and Justin Bieber had maintained and built the online networks that launched them, so Adele kept on communicating with fans in that same way. 'It's a great way of getting stuff out there,' she says. 'I'd much rather five million people heard my music than I earned £5 million. I write bulletins and blogs and I listen to what people say, maybe too much sometimes. If someone emails and they're like, "You've been out of the UK too long, it's not fair," I'll be like, "Right, I'm coming straight back." It's also easier to tackle gossip on your blog as it gets so out of control – "Actually I'm not going out with Johnny Borrell" or "I'm not a lesbian", you know.'

It was not just Adele who felt the pressure of gossip but those around her, too. 'I started seeing this boy a couple of months ago,' she said, in the spring of 2008. 'It was really amazing and I started trying to write songs again and then he turned around and told me he couldn't go on with it – he couldn't handle the paparazzi, plus he was paranoid that I was going to write about him.'

As she watched the media attention intensify, Adele too became concerned that it would just as easily knock her down. Though she was delighted when the BBC voted her the most promising new artist for 2008, this development also added to her concern that the public might turn against her. Her continued fears were not groundless. People in some places did begin to question just who she thought she was. Others declared that she was not half the talent that Amy Winehouse was. Both of these whispers were unfair. Adele had never done anything to suggest she harboured the sort of arrogance that would merit anyone asking, 'Who do you think you are?' Also, she had never compared herself with anyone else or encouraged others to do so. In time, Adele would eclipse even Amy Winehouse and emerge from her shadow. For some time still, though, she would continue to be referenced only in connection to the troubled 'Rehab' songstress.

Things had been more intense for her than many might have suspected. A year later, looking back on this turbulent period of her career, Adele told the *Daily Mail* that she even considered suicide after she had won her Brit award. That is how desperate she felt. She turned to a more experienced pop star for advice. Given his own sometimes emotionally unstable ways, Robbie Williams' advice on this occasion proved to be of enormous help and support to Adele. 'I met Robbie Williams shortly after the awards show and told him how uncomfortable I felt about the prize,' she told the *Daily Mail*. 'I was getting criticised for the first time, with people saying I only won because I'd been to the BRIT School. They thought I'd been manufactured.' This, she felt, was unfair, as she had 'paid my dues with some tough gigs'. She continued

Above: Adele in full flow in 2011.

Below: Barnstorming the Brits in 2011.

Above: The BRITS school helped to make Adele a star.   © *Rex Features*

Below: The young Adele with her name in lights.   © *Getty Images*

Left: Adele with collaborator Eg White.

© *Getty Images*

Right: Another associate is Mark Ronson.

© *Rex Features*

Inset: Legendary producer Rick Rubin helped Adele's sound.

© *Rex Features*

So proud – the two Grammys Adele won in 2009. © Rex Features

Above: In the BBC's Maida Vale studios in early 2011.   © *Getty Images*

Below: A (mostly) new generation of divas in 2009 – Adele (second from right) on stage in New York with, from left, Miley Cyrus, Kelly Clarkson, Jordin Sparks, Paula Abdul, Jennifer Hudson and Leona Lewis. © *Getty Images*

Right: Designer Barbara Tfank, an invaluable fashion resource for Adele. © *Getty Images*

Left: Will Young with his early admirer Adele.

© *Rex Features*

Above: Jonas Brothers – Kevin, Joe and Nick – and Adele backstage together.

Below: The theme to 2012 hit Bond movie *Skyfall* won Adele a double whammy of awards with a Golden Globe in January 2013 (*below left*) and, close to tears, an Oscar the following month (*below right*).

Adele performing at the Grammys in February 2012 and going home from the ceremony with two armfuls of awards. © *Rex Features*

to unload her feelings on to Williams. 'Robbie, who has had his fair share of criticism, was brilliant,' she said. 'He told me the prize was just a leg-up: it had put me in a position where people would listen. That helped.' Her newfound perspective on the issue came when she told one interviewer that she planned to keep the award in her toilet.

To help her shake off the blues, she could focus on the release of her second single, 'Chasing Pavements'. It is an intriguing title for a song, no? A strange one, even, as Adele admitted. 'It doesn't really make sense, does it? "Chasing Pavements" is about chasing a boy – even if you know something's gonna go wrong, you really want it to go right, so you just don't give up. I can't write other people's drama, and I can't glamorise a microwave or anything like that so I end up writing songs about things I've experienced.' She had co-written the song with songwriter and producer Eg White. The actual story behind its inspiration was the stuff of typical Adele drama. She had a fight with her boyfriend in a nightclub and found herself running down the street in the early hours of the morning. 'There was no one chasing me and I wasn't chasing anyone,' she said. 'I was just running away. I remember saying to myself, What you're chasing is an empty pavement. It's a metaphor. It's impossible to chase a pavement but I was chasing that pavement.' As an attention-grabbing title, it had a lot going for it, even if some listeners thought she was singing 'Chasing *payment*'.

There was a striking meteorological and geographical contrast for Adele between the circumstances of the song's recording and those of its release. It had been recorded in the summer in the Bahamas in 2007 and was released in Britain in the middle of winter, in early 2008. The B-side she chose for the song was an acoustic cover of the Sam Cooke song 'That's It, I Quit, I'm Movin' On'. She had first introduced the main track to the nation at the end of 2007 on the BBC's popular chat show *Friday Night With Jonathan Ross*. With viewing figures of up to five million, Ross's show was a superb place for any artist to appear. Acts that were far more established and known than Adele was in 2007 could only watch with jealousy as she showed up there. The sleeve for the release featured Adele on a sofa, with her right arm draped over the side.

Meanwhile, the promotional video was broadcast regularly on the airwaves. It centres around a car crash in which a man and woman have been hurt. As the drama plays out, Adele approaches the scene on foot, singing the lyrics. She then stands overlooking the scene as the medical team treats the victims, singing with palpable detachment. There are split narratives, one of which sees the victims taken away. The other features them coming to life and dancing. It was directed by Matthew Cullen, whose company described the video as 'surreal'. 'When I listened to the song, I was inspired by the idea of following after someone you love even though it will never work out,' said Cullen. 'The unconscious couple coming to life to retell the story of their relationship was a perfect storytelling device for the themes.' He explained that capturing on film the shadows that the dancing couple cast against the pavement presented the biggest challenge because there was only a 30-minute window of suitable daylight each day. 'Light is your best friend and your enemy but in the end it worked,' he said.

It did indeed: his video won an MTV award for Best Choreography. In due course, as we shall see, the song itself would net Adele some prestigious prizes.

Meanwhile, as she promoted the song, she was again interviewed widely, bringing her to the attention of ever more people. During her chat with the Digital Spy website, she was asked by the interviewer to define her sound. As she began to receive worldwide attention, plenty of critics, fans and other people would offer their own definitions. For now, Adele said of her music. 'I'd call it heartbroken soul – pathetic love songs about being pathetic! I was listening back to my album the other day, and I just thought, Oh, my God, I'm so pathetic when it comes to boys!'

She got more used to the demands of the media and always understood the importance of media promotions, particularly so earlier in her career. She found television appearances 'boring' backstage. She complained that, because 'everyone's an arsehole' there, she found the experience ruined her own enjoyment of television as a viewer.

A bizarre turn of events occurred when a misunderstanding in America led to the song being banned. A school of thought developed in the US that 'pavements' in the song meant gay men. The theory sprang up after an entry was added to the popular website Urban Dictionary, which lists definitions of youth slang terms. It is an open website, meaning entries can be added easily by readers. 'Because of that some radio stations in the States wouldn't play it,' said Adele. 'The guy wrote it on Urban Dictionary, which I've used for years and "chasing pavements" was never on there before.'

However, that was a mere blip for her progress in the long run. Just like 'Hometown Glory', 'Chasing Pavements' proved a popular song for television dramas to use as a soundtrack. It featured on several episodes of *Hollyoaks*, and on American show *90210*. It was also included in the film *Wild Child*. All of the various promotional routes paid off. 'Chasing Pavements' reached UK No 2 and remained in the top 40 for many weeks. In fact, by the time 'Chasing Pavements' slipped out of the top 40, Adele was already promoting a new, weightier release. Just a fortnight after her second single had been released, she unleashed her first album. She was nervous ahead of its release, and wondered how well it would fare. There is obviously much more emotional investment in a full body of work, particularly in the debut album. It is this release that gives the most solid sign yet of where an artist's fortunes might be.

Adele need not have worried: it went straight to UK No 1.

CHAPTER FOUR

19

Few talented pop artists ever went poor by writing catchy songs about heartbreak – it is one of the most fertile genres in showbusiness. But Adele insists she had never made a deliberate decision to write so many sad love songs, the like of which formed the majority of her debut album. 'In the past I've tried to sit down and think, Right, this is what I'm going to write about – but I can't because you can't force it. All my songs are a bit sad and full of drama because when I'm happy I haven't got time to write songs, y'know? When I've had my heart broken, I end up feeling sorry for myself and writing songs.' Such music dominated her debut album, *19*. Though there were occasional diversions from the theme of heartbreak, it was that which unified the majority of the tracks. The collection was one of the most eloquent and moving – as well as musically impressive – expressions of romantic pain that the album charts had known for some time.

So much has been written and said about *19*. Yet the coverage, though overwhelmingly positive, has largely ignored the eclectic use of styles and genres. Adele insisted that there was no contrived plot for the album, that it was just produced quite naturally. 'I had no specific plans for my album,' she told Blues And Soul website. 'In fact, I *still* don't know exactly what kind of artist I want to be! You know, for me the album was just about making a record of songs to get a boy off my chest and include all the different kinds of music that I love.' While she knew that she would be painted as a 'white soul girl', she had not aimed for that or any other kind of label for her debut. 'You know, the album genuinely did just come together very naturally and very organically,' she said. The independent streak that Adele and her mother had developed after their family became a single-parent one had an influence on the songwriting process. Attempts to pair her with co-writers were largely met with a thundering rejection from Adele. 'People kept trying to put me with writers,' she said, demonstrating her annoyance. 'I was like, "I'm better than that!" so I thought, I'm writing on my own.'

Asked why she chose to name the album *19*, she initially quipped that she simply had been unable to think of any other title. This, despite the fact that she considers album titles important, particularly titles for debut albums. Her two favourite such titles are *Debut*, for Björk's first album, and *The Miseducation of Lauryn Hill*. 'They're ones that everyone just knows, that don't make you think too much and are just quite obvious,' she said. In the end, she went for *19* because she felt that the album 'very much' represented her age. She felt that she 'became a bit of a woman' when she was 19, so she named the album in homage to that important time in her life. When she was signed to XL Recordings, she was 18 with just three songs under her belt. Soon after she turned 19, though, 'a load more just suddenly came out of me'. She has never responded to the suggestion that her choice of name was a sly dig at the management company of Simon Fuller, 19, which launched the Spice Girls and the *Pop Idol* genre. Given her love of that band and the genre of talent show, it seems unlikely – all the more so given that she followed the age-related theme when it came to titling her follow-up album.

Adele's emotions are raw throughout the album. 'I was very sad when I wrote it,' she said. 'And I think that genuinely does come through in the music.' The opening track is 'Daydreamer', an acoustic folk song of much prettiness. It is a gentle start. Adele's soft vocal delivery is accompanied only by a gentle, acoustic guitar. The song is so sweet it prompts a daydream in the mind of the listener as they listen to Adele's touching lyrics about an ideal man. Not that this is an entirely tender, romantic song. The line about the man who feels up his girl ensures that it retains a more rugged element, in keeping with Adele's image and personality. It was influenced by the time she fell for a man without realising he was bisexual. 'I had no problem with that,' she said, 'but I get so jealous anyway and I can't fight off girls and boys. When I told him that, he said not to worry. Two hours later, he was kissing my gay best friend next door.'

The wistful theme continues in the first verse of track two, 'Best for Last'. She starts by hoping that her man will be a perfect lover, with a way with words. These wishes are interrupted in the second verse, as she reveals that the man has played her and that she now no longer thinks he'll be around for long. She moves between the yearning for ideal romance and angry realisation that she will not find it with this man throughout this raw, jazz- and gospel-tinged song with its minimalist backtrack. It works well, many women – and indeed some men – will relate to the dual narratives of romance. The raised hopes which are dashed, only to somehow resurrect themselves afresh.

After the aforementioned 'Chasing Pavements' comes 'Cold Shoulder'. It is here that the album takes a musical step up, as is fitting given that the man at the production desk was the legendary Mark Ronson. Lyrically and thematically, the album springs into life. Having started wistfully, introduced elements of heartache and then mild frustration, Adele here is angry and defiant. Backed by a full band in fine funk fettle, she berates her man for gracing her with a cold shoulder, and showering her with cutting words. She also sings that, when her man looks at her, she wishes that she could be the other woman in his life. In the process of which she dismisses his suggestion that she is imagining the problem. While she acknowledges that he may not have felt satisfied by their relationship, she adds that she is starting to share that feeling.

This is the sound of a woman who has seen her man for what he is. She has also seen her own faults and realises that she has repeatedly acted dumb, even in the face of clear evidence of his misgivings and errant behaviour. Just four tracks into the album and the gentle, sweet Adele of the opener has turned into a furious, determined woman. What happened to the Adele of 'Daydreamer'? She returns, in part at least, in 'Melt My Heart to Stone'. Musically, this is a gentle, softly sung effort. The tune is not remarkable in itself, but Adele's vocals carry it home. The sense of a woman wising up to the realities of a flawed relationship remains. She mournfully admits that she is forgiving her partner's behaviour, as well as pretending he is different. This is her favourite song on the album. 'I just love singing it. When I wrote it, I was crying,' she said. 'The song is about breaking up a relationship.'

In a curious turn of phrase, she feels this denial on her part melts, then burns, her heart to stone. She concludes that of the two she is the only one in love. At the end of 'Melt My Heart to Stone', she confronts the object of her song with the fact that, as she stands her ground, he takes her hand – thus depriving her of the self-confidence she is trying to establish. She closes with the accusation that he builds her up, only to leave her dead. Having shown the power of her ability to make recriminations, Adele is in a different mode in 'First Love'. She sings sweetly and admiringly of her first love and asks him to forgive her as she needs to end their relationship. Accompanied by just a keyboard and triangle, she announces that she needs to experience a kiss from someone new.

The defiance of 'Cold Shoulder' is reprised in 'Right as Rain'. This is a happy tune, detailing the upside of heartbreak. If there is an 'I Will Survive' on *19*, it is here. In this up-tempo song, Adele and her backing singers ask the listener, who wants to be firing on all cylinders? There is an excitement about the drama of heartache. Anyway, at least she can tell herself that she chooses to be alone. Having cried her heart out, she is in no mood to make up with her ex. She is tired, she announces in the song's percussion-less middle eight, of playing games. She has decided that life is harder when you're on top. The defeatist sentiment is contrasted by the happy and funky soundtrack.

The ninth track is her cover of Bob Dylan's 'Make You Feel My Love'. This was a song Dylan released in the late 1990s. It has since been covered by artists including Billy Joel, Neil Diamond, Garth Brooks and Bryan Ferry. Adele's cover came about at the suggestion of her manager, Jonathan Dickins. He explained that he 'played [it] to her, and she loved it and that got on the record'. This, he added, was not a rare intervention on his part: 'I like to be hands on and be creative and have a musical opinion, even if the artists disagree with it sometimes.' On *19*, Adele takes Dylan's track to new, gospel-infused heights. It is the album's most tender, warming track. As we shall see, it is also a song that – through Adele's cover of it – has had a significant impact. 'The song is so convincing,' she said.

'But when I first heard it, I couldn't understand the lyrics. When I finally read them, I thought they were amazing. The song just kind of sums up that sour point in my life I've been trying to get out of my system and write into my songs. It completes the shape of the album which is not sad, but bitter.'

It is back to original material for the remainder of the album. Track ten is 'My Same' – a song she wrote about a friend when she was 16. If there was a mission statement behind the song, it would be an acknowledgement that opposites attract. It is a jolly song about a friendship that should not work – but does. For years Adele did not sing the song live, as she had fallen out with her friend and did not want to give her the satisfaction of knowing she was singing about her. As of 2011, Adele added the song to the set list for some shows at least, after making up with her friend. 'It was probably over something stupid, I can't even remember why I stopped talking to her, that's how pathetic I was,' said Adele. She added that the irony of her initial refusal to play the song live was that it showed her stubborn streak – a major theme of the song.

'Tired' is a song that expresses how Adele feels after trying to make a relationship work, only to find that she gets nothing in response. Why bother? she wonders. During an anomalous, almost psychedelic middle-eight, Adele reproaches herself by whispering that she should have known. Then it's back to the simple but catchy main melody. The music has a strong beat and is one of the more energetic tracks on *19*, though the electro-pop beeps are a strange inclusion on this otherwise impressive tune. Yet, while she might indeed sound a little tired in 'Tired', she certainly does not seem exhausted. Indeed, she sounds more tired on the album's closing song, the aforementioned single 'Hometown Glory'. The theme of this song is different to those of the album's other songs, but the mournful air and haunting melody make it very much at home on *19*. It is a short song, but one that lingers in the memory and the heart long after it has finished. So does *19* as a complete piece of work.

Many listeners responded to the end of the album by simply clicking 'Play' on whatever equipment they used so they could hear it afresh once more. But would the critics be as impressed as Adele and her team hoped they would be? In the main part, yes. The *Observer*'s brilliant Caspar Llewellyn Smith noted that, for a lady her age, Adele had produced a surprisingly mature record. 'Of course, "mature" might be a synonym for "boring", but this is also a perfectly paced record – not one to dissect for the MP3 player – and there are enough contemporary notes struck in the production to make it feel anything but retro,' he said. Perhaps the highest praise in his review came in the shape of his comment that Bob Dylan would 'envy' her for her cover of 'Make You Feel My Love'. The reviewer also compared her to Dusty Springfield and Aretha Franklin, 'albeit of [London] SW2'. The BBC website said: '*19* is a great start, a solid base to build a career on and a wonderful reminder of just how great our home grown talent can be.' On Amazon UK, the staff review said Adele was 'in possession of something special'. Looking ahead, he wondered, 'Who dares to dream what bigger numbers could bring.' Within days of the album's release the Amazon page would be bombarded with glowing customer reviews as the punters had their say. Elsewhere in the online publishing world, Digital Spy's Nick Levine wrote that the biggest strength of *19* was Adele herself: 'She's an engaging presence – alternately sassy, vulnerable, needy, apathetic and even, on "Hometown Glory", a little bit political,' he wrote.

The main negative review came in *Uncut* magazine. It was written by Barney Hoskyns and, though it made some valid and fair criticisms, it started from a peculiar place. He pointed out that the early 1980s saw a raft of new white soul singers, including Mick Hucknall, Marti Pellow and Alison Moyet. 'Nobody gives a toss about 'em today,' he said. Not entirely true, but also an irrelevant point. It is an *extremely* rare chart artist who is still followed and popular three decades after their heyday. Though he humorously described himself as a 'gnarled rock-scribe veteran', this seemed to be very sceptical. He said 'Make Me Feel Your Love' was 'emotionally vapid' and 'Crazy For You' 'wants to be Patsy Cline via Etta James but isn't'. Given the middle-aged male demographic of *Uncut*, perhaps this publication was never destined to be a cheerleader for a young woman like Adele. *NME*, too, was lukewarm, giving *19* just five out of ten. 'It's clear that, for all the hype, Adele is not yet ready to produce an album of sufficient depth to match her voice. Popular wisdom holds that Winehouse didn't hit her stride until after her debut: perhaps that's the case with Adele,' wrote Priya Elan.

This was one of several reviews that concluded with a comparison to Amy Winehouse. *The Times*' review was peppered with similar points, speaking of 'a post-Winehouse thing' and Adele's 'nu-Amy status', though also conceding that there might be laziness in applying that label to her. Leaving, appropriately enough, the best of his review until last, Peter Paphides wrote that, as he listened to *19*, he wanted to give Adele some warm milk and biscuits and tell her that no man is worth all the heartache she was expressing in the songs. He speculated that she may well agree with such a thought. 'But would she believe it if you told her that no album is worth this sort of heartache?' he continued. 'Probably not. And, when you hear *19*, neither will you.' He gave the album four out of five stars.

Refreshingly, Dorian Lynskey, of the *Guardian*, wrote that the Winehouse comparisons 'are as misleading as they are predictable'. Welcome words, but the rest of his two-star review was damning. 'There is scant emotional heft behind Adele's prodigiously rich voice, little bite to her songwriting,' he said. Having dismissed the Winehouse comparisons, he nonetheless made a gin-flavoured one himself, saying that, if *Back to Black* was 'Tanqueray-strength heartache, *19* is more of an alcopop.' For the red-wine-favouring Adele, this might have been a hard analogy to swallow. However, his review was almost positive compared to that on the Sputnik Music website, which concluded that *19* was 'music for fat, pubescent girls to get dumped to'. Thank goodness for *Q* magazine, which cheered that 'Adele's songs possess an ageless classification'. However, *Q* also reached the same conclusion that many other critics of *19* had: that the best for Adele was yet to come. There was a definite feeling that she had only scratched the surface of her talent. It was as if many listeners felt more impressed with Adele herself than they did with *19*. The critical response would be so much more positive for her next album, as critics took note of her undoubted improvement and also scrambled to add their names to the bandwagon that Adele was now majestically travelling in. She could then have afforded a smile as she noted the urgency with which the critics chased her, suddenly keen to glorify her. In part, this reflected a tangible improvement in her work, but it also reflected the fact that, despite doubts expressed by many of their number about *19*, the record-buying public had given the album a far less ambiguous response. It came in straight at the top of the charts in its first week on sale. Adele was delighted.

Although she was a fan and lover of music, she was also possessed of a shrewd, commercial mind, and the fact that *19* was a UK No 1 was of huge significance. Adele is the people's pop singer and therefore it is the people whose verdict means most to her. Though in general she has drawn much praise from reviewers, it is the verdict of the girl browsing the shelves of HMV – as she did as a teenager – that means more to her than that of the jaded, middle-aged critic.

As for the music industry itself, it had been waiting some time for an artist that would create 'events' in terms of sales. Though it would be her follow-up album that saw her break records and shift units in terrifying numbers, the word had already got round the industry in 2008 that Adele was a major prospect. But it wasn't just about product – she was mindful that in writing about her own heartbreaks she could assist others in coming to terms with theirs. She hoped she would. Nobody was more aware than Adele, as she has said, of the healing potential of music. While she was frank enough to admit that this was not her primary motive, it was a side effect that she was aware of and delighted by. 'To help me get over something and be able to help other people is the best thing ever,' she said. *19* earned a Mercury prize nomination, announced in July 2008. Up against her was a fine mixture of talent, including Elbow, British Sea Power, Radiohead and Rachel Unthank & the Winterset. The winner was Elbow, with *The Seldom Seen Kid*. However, to have even been nominated for such an award was an exciting honour for Adele. In just a few years, she would be nominated for even more – and would win many of them.

Meanwhile, she was also dealing with a process familiar to many who have become suddenly famous and successful. As soon as any person becomes known publicly, people often want to join in. This can either take the form of hangers-on, eager for a place in the spotlight or simply people keen to make a bit of money. Adele has said that the latter trend afflicted her after *19* became a hit. During a chat with the *Sun*, she claimed that the ex-boyfriend that influenced *19* had been in touch with an audacious request – he wanted a cut from the royalties. 'For about a week he was calling and was deadly serious about it,' she told the newspaper. 'Finally, I said, "Well, you made my life hell, so I lived it and now I deserve it." He really thought he'd had some input into the creative process by being a prick. I'll give him this credit – he made me an adult and put me on the road that I'm travelling.' Again, the Winehouse comparison was striking: her debut album *Frank* was influenced by an ex-boyfriend she had met while working as a trainee reporter.

Given her feisty nature, the media sometimes tries to drag Adele into spats with other female artists. Such conflict always makes for entertaining stories. She rarely bit, as was seen on one of her early television appearances. By the summer of 2011, the consensus was that BBC light-hearted music panel show *Never Mind the Buzzcocks* had probably seen better days. It had peaks during the successive reigns of presenters Mark Lamarr and Simon Amstell. Since the latter host departed, the show has rotated hosts and guests regularly have to contend with outrageous mickey-taking as part of the game. Back in its heyday, things were quite different. For instance, Amy Winehouse made two appearances on the show, one of which became legendary. She joked, spat and traded wisecracks with Amstell, providing the sort of entertainment and irreverent wit that many a stand-up comedian would have been proud of, let alone a musician. Since then, no musician had approached the level of fun that she had created.

However, when Adele first appeared on *Buzzcocks*, in 2008, she was entertaining enough. Amstell, introducing her, said, 'She normally spends her time chasing pavements. Well, pavements can take a night off because tonight she's chasing points!' Joining her on guest captain Mark Ronson's team was Australian comedian and singer Tim Minchin.

In the opening round, her team was asked to name what had once caused a delay to a Kylie concert in Brighton. She took the opportunity to comment, 'I love Kylie.' Amstell continued his chat with Adele saying, 'Do you want to know why I like you? Because you're down to earth, you're likeable, you're like the perfect human being. You're real, you tell it like it is, and you're honest.'

Sensing she was being set up by Amstell, Adele said, 'Yes?'

He added, 'So tell us who you hate most out of Lily Allen, Kate Nash and Duffy.' As she giggled, Amstell added, 'Tell us why you hate Duffy so much.'

Adele said, 'No, I don't hate Duffy. But I'm Welsh as well and I wish people would know that, because my nanna gets quite upset. No one recognises that I'm Welsh. But she is full Welsh, but then she's north Welsh.'

At this point Phill Jupitus chipped in to quip, 'Yes, because I can tell from your accent that you're more south Welsh.'

Amstell pursued his quest to encourage Adele to be controversial, saying, 'Also, in interviews you feel that Duffy comes across as a bit fake, right?'

With a sheepish, uncomfortable smile, Adele replied, 'Why are you doing this?'

Amstell continued to press, asking Adele if she thought Duffy was older than she claimed to be. To her credit, Adele laughed along with the banter, rather than taking it at all seriously. She certainly was never going to let fly about her so-called rivals in the same way Amy Winehouse did on *Buzzcocks* when she said she would 'rather have cat Aids' than work with Katie Melua.

In the introductions round, in which two contestants do their best to give a vocalised rendition of the start of a song so the third team member can guess what it is, Adele and Ronson were to sing Nerd's 'Lapdance' to Minchin. 'I can't pretend I'm an instrument,' Adele protested when Amstell teased her about her vocal performance during her intro. Finally, when they came to the mystery line-ups – in which contestants try to identify a forgotten musical personality from a line-up including four lookalikes – Adele at last delivered a little of the controversy that Amstell had been hoping for. The panel began to discuss Lindsay Lohan, then the partner of Ronson's sister Samantha. When Ronson said he thought Lohan was 'a really talented actress,' Adele looked shocked. 'What?' she asked with humorous indignation. 'I think she's lovely, but she's not an actress,' she added with one of her roaring laughs.

In truth, it has normally been a hard task to get Adele to be rude about other female singers. The rivalry that the media hopes to stir up between female singers is largely non-existent. True, there are occasional spats and criticisms, but in the main – from Adele at least – there has been more promotion of a sisterhood in mutual support. 'I don't really need to stand out, there's room for everyone,' she said in 2008. 'Although I haven't built a niche yet, I'm just writing love songs.' Love songs that were proving popular across the world. As well as reaching UK No 1, *19* was a Top 10 hit in many countries including Australia, Belgium, Canada, Germany, the Netherlands, Ireland and Norway. It was also selling well in that golden market where so many other massive British acts have spectacularly failed.

Adele was proving a hit in America.

CHAPTER FIVE

AN AMERICAN DREAM

The list of hit machines who have failed to translate their enormous worldwide popularity into the States is not only long but also contains some prestigious names. From the UK the likes of Sir Cliff Richard, Marc Bolan, Take That, Robbie Williams, Busted, Oasis and Ms Dynamite failed there, as did Irish neighbours Westlife. Most recently, Cheryl Cole has had to take an early flight home, after her plan to launch herself there as an *X Factor* judge, solo star and all-round celebrity fell at the first hurdle. Even the pop queen that is Kylie Minogue has found America a tricky proposition. There are so many hurdles to jump, including the soul-destroying, lengthy promotional tours of radio stations and endless meet-and-greets that involve weeks on the road with little guarantee of a positive outcome. Indeed, it is fair to say that there is a good chance that such acts will not break America, but rather America will break them.

No wonder that British acts who have found fame in America are therefore a rarity. The most obvious examples remain the Beatles and the Rolling Stones. These acts have one crucial and simple thing in common in this regard: their material is, essentially, American music. It was why Amy Winehouse did so well there. The US market has long enjoyed having its sounds sung back to it by outside artists. Given the nature of her sound, Adele was in a stronger position than most to crack America. Still, there were no guarantees and, given that Adele was a wise, cautious and realistic artist, she took nothing for granted about any market, least of all the American one.

Her first north American tour began in March 2008. It would include promotional commitments such as those inevitable radio interviews and also live performances. Among the latter were slots at Joe's Pub in New York, and the Hotel Cafe in Los Angeles. Then came a fusion of promotional commitment with live performance at the SXSW music conference and festival in Austin, Texas. It was Joe's Pub, though, that constituted her first significant live outing in America. The venue brought with it a certain symbolism, for it was there that Amy Winehouse made her first ever live performance in America. It has quite a reputation, rated widely as one of the best small music venues in the world. Publications and outlets from the *Village Voice* to *Newsweek* and BBC radio have all given it sufficient praise for it to attain legendary status. It is the sort of place where the barrier between artist and audience is so slight as to be almost non-existent. As Alicia Keys, who has played there, said, 'You get all the sweat and heat from the performances'. A fitting place for Adele.

She looked relaxed and composed as she took to the stage, though the nerves became clear in time. She even apologised between songs, saying that she was suffering from a heavy cold. She started her Joe's Pub gig with 'Daydreamer' and the ten-song set continued with 'Crazy For You' and other tracks, before concluding with an emotional rendition of 'Hometown Glory'. She had her eyes closed during much of the performance and her anxiety was hard to deny. Yet she needn't have worried. One online music reviewer wrote that the short set was so entrancing that it flew past. He added that the performance 'pretty much showed why she's the real deal and no trendy, flash in the pan. By far, she is the best new voice in music on both sides of the Atlantic.' He also noted, with approval, her personality, observing of her patter between the songs, 'She's just a big goof-ball with a thick British accent.'

She played a second show at Joe's Pub and then just 24 hours later she was on the west coast of America, playing at the Hotel Cafe. Dressed in a characteristically dramatic black outfit, she sang beautifully and put in a stellar performance in front of a packed house. Many of those present rated the show as the best they had seen in their lives. Recordings of her songs that night have become popular among fans. She then played two shows in Canada, at the Cabaret in Montreal and the Rivoli in Toronto.

Then there was more promotional business to be undertaken back in the US. It would involve lots of travelling and work, but Adele left in a determined mood. 'She wants to work it properly and put in time there,' XL's Richard Russell told *Billboard*. 'People are really excited about her over there.' They were excited about British acts in general, particularly female soul singers. Among the other popular names in the US at the time were the likes of Corrine Bailey Rae and Duffy, and Joss Stone was also going down something of a storm. Lily Allen, too, had received some recognition. Adele noted the achievement of other Brits in America and was only too happy to follow the trend. 'I'm very proud to be a part of it,' she said. 'I'm very pleased to be riding the wave.'

The appeal of UK acts had not always been entirely about the music. Given the growth in political correctness in America, the UK's often more outspoken and rough-around-the-edges artists bring something new and exciting to the market. The likes of Amy Winehouse and Adele in particular were unpredictable, opinionated and have – to differing extents – openly hedonistic lifestyles. In the land of *American Idol* and other reality shows and *Disney*-friendly pop, this is a breath of fresh air. This is not true of everyone. It is to the eternal credit of Leona Lewis that she has succeeded in America even though her image and personality are far from fiery. In her case, her immense talent simply outweighs all else.

Adele was aware that launching herself in the US brought with it new challenges but she was also of the opinion that there were advantages to how things worked there. 'Well, obviously the US is a lot bigger and there is a little more work involved,' she said. 'There's politics: if you do one thing, you can't do another thing. You don't do this and you won't get that. That stuff doesn't exist in the UK. I guess because there are so many different kinds of markets in the US, you need to define your niche. I think that's probably it.' She was completely correct. It's been said that a British star is more likely to win the lottery than to successfully break the American market. Yet Adele, far from being overwhelmed by the scale of the task ahead, actually felt that in America there was more focus on talent rather than more superficial things. 'You can't go to America and be shit. You could have an amazing figure and they won't buy it,' she said. It is talent alone that matters there. 'I could wear a bin liner and they'd still like me.'

The prospects were indeed soon looking very promising. As her bookings and commitments continued, on-stage she was in fine form. She sometimes changed the lyrics to 'Chasing Pavements', altering the key word to 'sidewalks'. The fans were loving her and one night they presented her with a bouquet of flowers and a card that thanked her for 'staying true' and wished her well for the future. During one concert she interrupted her song mid-verse to ask if she could have a margarita. One night, she had more than a few drinks and ended up beyond tipsy on the tour bus. She slurred her words and sat with a woolly hat, lopsided, on her head. 'Amy Winehouse: eat your heart out.' Captured on camera for release on a bonus disc, it made for a cute filmed document of a fun and exciting adventure for our heroine.

That said, she still needed to work hard in order to fully bring such a vital audience on her side. She also missed home a lot. '[The experience was] amazing – but also really difficult because I'd never been away from home that long ever in my life,' she said. Asked how she found the relentless promotional work involved with cracking America, she replied honestly, 'Horrible – hate it.' She then laughingly said that she had tried to kill herself twice, such was the pressure. With a smile, she added, 'Only joking. It all helps... all helps.' Chief among the challenges of the tour, she explained, was the fact she was sharing a tour bus with 'six stinky guys'. One of the motels they stayed in had cockroaches and then there was the day that the tour-bus toilet got blocked with tissue paper. Then, after playing the *David Letterman Show* in Manhattan, she was approached and then chased by the paparazzi. She hid in a secluded Russian vodka bar. 'Four hours later I emerged... Oh my, I was flying down Broadway, very drunk,' she said. A creative, and fun, solution to the pressures of fame, typical of Adele.

As she told Digital Spy, the television commitments over in the US confused her a bit. Firstly, she did not appreciate right away the high calibre of the shows she had been booked on. Then, she got mixed up over whether she was recording live or part of a pre-record. 'Yeah, I did *Letterman* and the *Today Show*,' she told Digital Spy. 'I had no idea what they were the equivalent to because obviously we don't have them here. I was like, "What's the *Today Show*?" and they were like, "Imagine *GMTV* but on a much bigger scale." It was live and there were like 50 million people watching so I literally just shat myself! *Letterman* was pre-recorded so I wasn't quite as nervous, but I forgot that during my performance. I got halfway through the song and couldn't remember whether it was live or not. Look it up on YouTube – you'll see my face just drop!'

There were perks to make up for the stress along the way, including her finding and buying a pair of Manolo Blahnik shoes of the kind featured in an episode of *Sex and the City*. The fashion fan was absolutely chuffed: 'I've been looking for these for three years.' Sometimes, she said, she needed humouring to keep her energy up. Other times, though, she was providing the humour herself. She saw the funny side when a hotel booked her and her tour manager into a room with just one kingsize bed. When they stopped off in Portland, she said it was 'just like Croydon'. When she saw someone scrambling for deserted cigarette butts on the pavement outside a venue, she recalled a similar experience herself. Her mother had refused to give her a cigarette, and she was craving some nicotine so much that she ended up looking for butts. At first in her story, she painted her mother as the villain of the piece, then admitted, 'But then I was 13 or 14.'

As well as bringing her own music to the performances, she also tried some cover versions. Among these was an imaginative cover of 'Last Night', by Manhattan indie giants the Strokes. Her cover started in a slow, blues style that scarcely resembled the lively, rocking song. However, one verse in, the full band kicked in replicating the sound of the original. It was an unexpected choice of cover, yet she did it justice, managing to combine both originality and familiarity in a very well-known song.

Despite her belief that she could wear a bin liner for all anyone in America cared, she could not escape questions about her appearance. With many of her promotional engagements and live performances taking place in big, hip cities on the east and west coasts of America, it was perhaps inevitable that talk would once more turn to Adele's weight. After all, in cities such as Los Angeles and New York, many people are extremely conscious of their appearance. One does not have to stroll far down Manhattan's Fifth Avenue or LA's Sunset Strip to see plenty of women who are stick thin as a fashion statement rather than looking natural. So Adele was expecting questions about her own appearance. 'I knew people would ask me – especially here with the whole Hollywood thing – if I felt pressure to lose weight,' she said. 'I don't think it is important. I think it used to be more important, and I think there are aspects of it now where people will talk about what you look like, not what you're doing. I made a record. I don't want to be on the front cover of *Playboy*. I want to be on the front cover of *Rolling Stone* with my clothes on.' She soon would be.

On her return, she spoke enthusiastically about her time abroad. Here again, she said, the internet had played an important role in spreading word of her. 'Amazing – and it's all so unexpected,' she said when asked to sum up how the tour had gone. 'I was a bit scared when my American agent said he was going to put me on a 15-date tour over there but, thanks to the power of the internet, people showed up at my gigs and knew all the words and it all went amazingly.' To celebrate her return to Britain and to officially shrug off the extra responsibilities and pressures she had been under there, she went out partying in London with her oldest mates. With them, in her home city, Adele could be herself again. It was a great way to return to normality and, as ever, to concentrate on keeping her feet on the ground. She had missed her friends, she admitted. 'I love my friends so much that I do get quite moody when I'm away from them,' she told Digital Spy. 'It was five weeks this time which is quite a long time, but the shows were so good that it made up for missing them.'

On 10 June, she would be able to gauge how much of an impact her American tour had made when her album *19* was officially released over there. But it would only be later in the year that it truly captured the US public's imagination. As it was, in 2008, she cancelled a series of commitments in America after problems and tensions in her private life made her feel unable to travel abroad. She had really missed home during her first travels in America, saying she was on her knees with homesickness. But it would be another year before she felt able to discuss what happened. 'We refer to that period as my ELC, my Early Life Crisis,' she explained. Her use of the third person to describe herself was no coincidence. Using the plural, she said, allowed her to feel less vulnerable and exposed. Even with the passage of a year, she still felt uncomfortable and embarrassed by the cancellation. 'Now I'm sober, I'm like, "I can't believe I did that." It seems so ungrateful.' What she said really haunted her was not that she had possibly blown her chance of making *her* dreams come true. Instead, she felt the burden of having thrown away '*everyone*'s dream'.

Expanding on the 'crisis' that led to her cancellation, she added, 'I was drinking far too much and that was kind of the basis of my relationship with this boy. I couldn't bear to be without him, so I was like, "Well, OK, I'll just cancel my stuff then."' She knew that this caused enormous problems and discomfort, but insisted there was no other option. 'I got in trouble for wasting people's time but I was desperately unhappy,' she said. It was not just American dates that were cancelled as part of Adele's 'ELC' and nor was it her relationship that was the sole cause of it. She just felt she was starting to miss out on real life. The bubble of success brought with it a lot of fun, plenty of fame and no shortage of fortune but she missed something more important: friendship. 'It had got to the stage where friends would call, and I'd be working in Norway or somewhere and they'd ask me to come round and I'd get annoyed that they didn't know I was abroad,' she said. 'So for three months I went to the pub, barbecues, saw my cousins.'

At the same time, Adele found it hard to step off the promotional and professional treadmill. Suddenly, she had space and time again. Having demanded it, she then found she was not sure what to do with it. 'I told everyone not to call me for six months as I was turning my phone off,' she said. 'I wasn't even going to have a Blackberry. I was going to have a Nokia pay-as-you-go. But within a few days I was like, What am I meant to be doing? It was really weird going from being so busy and having a schedule to having to rely on yourself again to organise things.'

Whatever the different motivations behind the cancellation, the message that Adele was sending out was clear. Here, she was drawing a line in the sand and declaring that she was a free person and not to be used by her management or record company. 'I can't be a product; no one can do that to me,' she said. 'I have all the say. I have power over everything I do.' We were back to the Adele of her childhood: the strong-willed girl who demanded to be in control and this was the attitude that would serve her well. She already had cause to feel cautious optimism about the early sales of *19* in the US. She said she viewed its performance as 'an underground thing'.

In November 2008, Adele had been booked to appear on the hit American television show *Saturday Night Live* after a producer from the show saw her perform live in Manhattan. Although an appearance on *SNL* is a big deal for any artist, she could not have predicted what would happen. 'It was just meant to be like a normal show,' she said. 'Then we walked in on Saturday and Sarah Palin was there!'

The vice-presidential candidate chosen by Republican John McCain, Palin was a contentious figure from the off. Her image as a hockey mom – a tough, family woman – her stringent right-wing opinions and attitudes, together with a questionable grasp of geopolitics, made her a divisive, much-discussed and oft-mocked public figure. While many conservatively minded Americans admired her, more metropolitan and Democrat-supporting people thought she was at worst dangerous, at best ridiculous.

Palin's presence had turned this episode of *Saturday Night Live* into a juggernaut of a media event in America. For weeks, one of the show's witty presenters, Tina Fey, had delighted the nation with her cutting impersonations of Palin. So, when Palin herself agreed to appear on the show, it guaranteed massive attention. What had already been a big slot for Adele became massive. At its peak, the episode was being watched by 17 million Americans, the long-running show's highest figures for over a decade. So, when Adele sang 'Cold Shoulder' and 'Chasing Pavements', she could scarcely have got a more high-profile slot. Immediately after the show, *19* began to be downloaded by tens of thousands of viewers. Soon, she was at No 1 in the American download charts. Her album also rose to No 5 at Amazon.com. Meanwhile, 'Chasing Pavements' also reached the Top 25. Adele had been fortunate in the way her own campaign collided with Palin's – but she richly deserved such a stroke of luck.

She had an embarrassing moment backstage, when she mistook Palin herself for Fey. 'I fucking love Tina Fey and I was, "Tina, Tina". She didn't even acknowledge me, she was just completely oblivious,' recalled a mortified Adele. Once they did speak, it was all civil enough. 'She was really nice backstage, but I'm a hundred per cent chuffed to pieces that Obama won,' said Adele later. 'I'm not a fan of her – at all.'

Indeed, when Palin had approached Adele, she had been wearing what she described as a 'massive' Obama badge.

She had wanted to wear the badge as she sang live to the nation. Her manager Dickins was horrified at the prospect of such a divisive gesture at such a delicate point in her American promotional campaign. It was reported that he told her he would cut her hands off if she tried such a controversial move and in the end she didn't wear it. Generally, Adele herself was against musical artists making statements on events in the wider world. Despite the political lyrics in 'Hometown Glory' and the fact that a politician had inadvertently boosted her career in America, Adele was largely content to stay out of contentious current affairs issues. 'Obviously, I've made a few comments here and there in the past, but I don't think musicians should be talking much about politics,' she said.

She returned to America several months later, to solidify and build on the popularity she had gained through *Saturday Night Live*. Tickets for her shows were in major demand – so much so that some changed hands for up to $200. She was in triumphant form as she played shows that were, in every way, bigger than anything she had done in the US before. This time, she was at bigger venues, all of which were jam-packed. She had more musicians with her on-stage, she played longer sets and the audiences sang her words back to her throughout. She kicked off a typical set with a storming rendition of 'Cold Shoulder' and finished with 'Chasing Pavements'. Sandwiched between those songs, those she had performed on *Saturday Night Live*, were a combination of her own numbers and a few cover versions. The icing on the cake was her chatter and banter.

For American fans, her chirpy, cockney voice was irresistible. In a land where many musicians feign indifference on-stage, in the hope of achieving coolness, Adele's patter was a breath of fresh air. The fans, which one Boston newspaper described as 'a newly formed American cult', lapped it all up.

At the end of 2008, Adele could reflect on a remarkable year. So much had changed in her career and in her life in general. So many random, strange things had happened to her along the way. She was asked what the most random moment would be and it turned out to be one of the events on the other side of the Atlantic that most stuck out in that regard. 'It must have been on *Saturday Night Live* when Sarah Palin turned up and Alec Baldwin and then Marky Mark – who isn't really my era, but my mum loves Marky Mark, so I sent her a text, and my aunts love him too,' she said. 'The whole year's been a bit random, the fact that [*19* has] done so well, all the time I'm like, What's going on? It's a bit bizarre, but I wouldn't change anything for the world.' She admitted that the reality of what had happened to her over the year had yet to sink in. 'I don't think it ever will. It's all gone so fast that it's impossible to notice everything that's happened, let alone take it all in. I tried to develop a tough skin for a while and kept ignoring everything that was going on, which made me come across a bit confrontational and cocky, I think. But in fact I'm the complete opposite: I couldn't be happier with what's happening, but I'm trying not to think about it in case I shit myself.'

The following month, her popularity in the US was

confirmed with the breathtaking development that she had won two Grammy awards. Artists often feign surprise or disinterest when they learn they have been nominated for awards. It is a protection mechanism to stop themselves from getting their hopes too high and to play it cool in front of their fans, whatever the outcome. For her part, Adele said she was aware there was a possibility she might be nominated for a Grammy in 2009, but added that she was of the impression that this was a long shot. So she did not even tell her mother ahead of the nomination announcements that she could be in the mix. The evening the nominations were announced, Adele went online to see whose names had been announced. She said she was only looking in order to discover how many categories Leona Lewis had been nominated in.

While she was searching, she received a text message from American celebrity blogger Perez Hilton. He informed her that she had been nominated in three categories. She was still reeling with excitement from that news when her publicist rang. At first Adele assumed the call was to celebrate the news of three nominations, but her caller then informed her she had been nominated in a *fourth*. 'I was screaming,' said Adele. 'I had to put the phone down. It was the proper death of me. I didn't think anyone would ever really care until my third or fourth record so I wasn't bothered that [my label] thought it was a long shot. My manager came over to my house at, like, 4.30 in the morning with a bottle of champagne that I'd bought him in September for his birthday because he's... cheap.' It was a jolly and unexpected toasting of some exciting news that had shaken both of them.

The unexpected nominations were for Best New Artist, Record of the Year, Song of the Year and Best Female Pop Vocal. Coldplay and Radiohead were the only UK acts to receive more nominations. 'It was Adele, Adele, Adele, Adele,' she recalled. 'I never thought in my wildest dreams with my first record that I'd be included.' When she admitted publicly that she did not believe that artists should win a Grammy when they have released only one album, the story was twisted. Soon, headlines were appearing that suggested Adele said she didn't want a Grammy at all. She clarified her position and added, 'It's like [actors who win] an Oscar too soon, it puts a dampener on the rest of their career.' Duffy, another British nominee, also caused offence when she said that she had only very recently even heard of the Grammys. As for Adele, her shock at her nominations continued for some days. 'I'm waiting for someone to say, "You mug, we're only joking!"' she said the following week.

In February 2009, the shock of the nomination was dwarfed when she went on to win in two of the categories at the ceremony in Los Angeles.

It was the 51st ceremony. Adele looked sensational on the night, as had been expected after it was revealed that *Vogue* editor-in-chief Anna Wintour had given her style advice for the night. Wintour is a notorious figure, nicknamed 'Nuclear Wintour' by some, due to her stern and demanding personality. The film *The Devil Wears Prada*, starring Meryl Streep, is said to be largely based on her.

Adele had paid a visit to the *Vogue* office as she was the subject of a photo shoot. While she was there, the legendary Wintour summoned her. 'It was just like *The Devil Wears Prada*,' Adele said, of the conversation in which Wintour offered to style her for the Grammys. 'I got a really nice dress ... I [usually] wear dresses with tights and flat shoes and a cardigan. But I am going to get my boobs out and everything. It's going to be quite a big deal.'

In fact, Wintour had commissioned designer Barbara Tfank to put together the outfit for the singer. 'Adele came to my office,' Tfank remembered. 'We sat down at a table and I said, "Tell me about when you're on-stage and how you like to feel and how you like to look." She had this very cool beehive hair from the night before and that inspired me, too.' Tfank had enjoyed and appreciated the chance to work with Adele and hoped that Wintour's interest in the singer's style heralded an increased acceptance of fuller-figured ladies in the world of fashion and style. 'I think we're finally coming to a better place of realising that not all people are alike,' she said.

Meanwhile, the black ensemble was enough to raise appreciative eyebrows when Adele arrived at the Grammys. She wore a black, reserved 1950s-style dress with the waist nipped in. She looked every bit the winner she was to be that night. Like many of the ladies present that night, Adele worked for her look. 'Am I having fun? Yeah. But my feet hurt,' she admitted as she collected one of her awards.

Other Brits to score on the night were Welsh singer Duffy, Estelle, Coldplay, Radiohead and veteran singer Robert

Plant. Coldplay had been among the biggest winners of the night, collecting awards in three categories. They were dressed in *Sgt Pepper*-style Beatles outfits, for which they apologised to Paul McCartney, who was present. The biggest disappointment among British acts was felt by Leona Lewis, who left empty-handed despite having been nominated in three categories. When Adele collected her Best New Artist award, Adele addressed the acts who had been up against her for the gong. She said, 'Thank you so much. I'm gonna cry... Duffy, I love you, I think you are amazing. Jonas Brothers, I love you as well'.

Given that the Grammys had been criticised for some years for favouring commercial acts over critical successes, Adele's triumph over the teen pop Jonas Brothers earned the award fresh brownie points among the more discerning viewers. She had earlier also won Best Female Pop Vocal for 'Chasing Pavements'. Little could anyone watching have known that several tracks on her second album would vocally eclipse her performance on 'Chasing Pavements'. Better was yet to come for Adele, yet, given how early in her career she had won two Grammys, she could afford to be ecstatic in the moment.

'Amazing,' she said. 'It's starting to sink in, now I'm talking to people.' She added that she still felt shocked and that she just wanted to see her mother. Adele had chosen not to take Penny with her in case she did not win anything. Instead, Penny had stayed behind in London, following the proceedings in Adele's flat. Adele said she had chosen to be there 'so she can smell me' and in that sense be closer. 'I called her afterwards and she was just crying her eyes out.' Emotional times for mother and daughter. Both might have looked back at the journey that had taken Adele to such prominence and respect in the music industry. But it wasn't just congratulations – in case Adele got too carried away, her mother was going to help keep her feet on the ground. Penny told her she was not impressed to see her daughter chewing gum as she picked up the Best New Artist gong.

Adele was asked what came next for her. 'I'm going to go and put my jeans on... and go and have some cigarettes and hang out with my manager and my friends,' she said. It was a very Adele way to celebrate: she wanted to come back down to earth quickly.

After she had won her two awards, there was still time for one memorable encounter when she bumped into pop star Justin Timberlake. He approached and congratulated her on her success when he saw her backstage. At first, she did not realise who it was. 'In the hallway after I'd won two Grammys, he grabbed me and he's like, "Congratulations,"' she said. 'I was so totally overwhelmed about the Grammys that I didn't even realise it was Justin. Then, ten yards down the huge hallway in the Staples Center, I just heard this huge scream and realised I was screaming my head off.' It had been another unexpected and overwhelming experience for Adele. Her fame and fortune had engulfed her so quickly that she was ill at ease with the A-list circles she could now move in. The fan inside her found it hard to accept that not only were global superstars in her midst, but also that they recognised and respected her. Speaking to *People* magazine soon after, she directly addressed Timberlake. She apologised for their awkward Grammys encounter and then offered a slightly sycophantic reason for it. 'Justin, I love you and I'm really sorry ... for making it seem like I didn't want to meet you,' she said. 'I really did – and I don't think we can ever be friends because you're just too much. You're too good!' Naturally, such cute and self-deprecating sentiments only made her more adorable to her fans, old and new.

Adele also kept in touch with Anna Wintour after the Grammys, and was styled again by Tfank for future appearances and promotional commitments. Adele had enjoyed meeting Wintour, who she found far less scary in reality. 'Anna Wintour was lovely,' she told *Grazia*. 'Nothing like I'd feared before I met her. I was expecting Meryl Streep in *The Devil Wears Prada*. Anna was wonderfully articulate and really friendly. She turned me into a lady, and she introduced me to Barbara Tfank who made my Grammys dress and who has continued to make me pieces for videos and shows, and more recently my outfit for the Royal Variety Performance. I felt a bit awkward at first, when I had an Anna Wintour makeover. I couldn't walk in the shoes so I ended up wandering around the Grammys barefoot. But after a while, the more Barbara and I kept working together, I started to enjoy fashion. Once I'd discovered what I like and what suits me, I've kept that look up to an extent.' The lasting influence of this brush with high fashion is clear: Adele's style has become more sophisticated and focused since her earlier days.

Her double win at the Grammys increased media

attention for her in America. CNN ran a special report about her, introducing her as having a 'retro soul sound, voluptuous curves and unfiltered opinions that burst out of her mouth in cockney soundbites'.

Adele told them less what she is, and more what she is not. 'I'm not like, some, like, blonde, skinny, fake-boobed, white teeth, really stupid,' she said with a giggle. 'I'm nothing like that, and I think that appeals to people. I hope that I never start looking like a model.' Proving the report's assessment of her outspoken nature, Adele said that she 'hates the paparazzi', adding 'I think they're disgusting,' before miming a spit on the floor. It was a defiant way of expressing the fury that pushy photographers provoked inside her. Her hatred for them is indeed intense – one day, she popped to the local shop for some bread, milk and cigarettes. This normal, everyday errand took on a surreal dimension when she returned home and found a photographer on her doorstep. She was furious, and told later how she 'nearly beat the shit out of him'. The threat of a beating from Adele seemed to do the trick. 'Since then I haven't had the paparazzi at my house.' These media intrusions have also come between Adele and people that she had previously considered friends. When Adele found out that some people she knew had colluded with the paparazzi, her reaction was unequivocal and uncompromising. 'I don't talk to those people no more,' she said.

In the wake of the Grammys haul, Adele's label announced a new set of dates in America. In March she would play in San Diego at the House of Blues and conclude a brief tour later that month in Cleveland. She was also booked to appear at the Roseland Ballroom in New York on 5 May in celebration of her 21st birthday and she announced another date on the west coast of America, at the Hollywood Bowl in Los Angeles in June. What a domino effect her success was having. A combination of hard work, talent, suitability for the market and the entirely unexpected Palin effect were all taking Adele deep into the heart of many Americans. However, she has not ignored other territories. 'I want as many people as possible to hear my music,' she said. 'I want to do well in Europe, Asia and Australia. It's so weird to come all this way to do shows and have them sell out. It's ridiculous and amazing how many people want to talk to me.'

It was amazing for her how many people wanted to talk *about* her, too. One of these was the singer Estelle, who said that Adele's tracks could not be considered soul music. 'I'm not mad at [Adele and Duffy], but I'm wondering – how the hell is there not a single black person in the press singing soul?' Estelle said to the *Guardian*. 'Adele ain't soul. She sounds like she heard some Aretha records once and she's got a deeper voice – that doesn't mean she's soul. That don't mean nothing to me in the grand scheme of my life as a black person. As a songwriter, I get what they do. As a black person, I'm like: "You're telling me this is my music? Fuck that!"' Ironically, this outburst was published just days after Estelle had said she did not want to be involved in commenting on other artists. 'When people ask me about other singers, I just don't really – what's the word – care,' she said. 'I've been working on my own record for such a long time that I don't want to take away from it by talking about or dissing other artists.'

Her subsequent comments touched on a theme we shall return to. For now, Adele did her best to ignore Estelle's reported statement. 'I don't really care,' Adele told Digital Spy in response. 'I don't read my press, so I only heard about it, I didn't read it. It's an opinion and I like people with an opinion, so if that's what she thinks then fine. She doesn't listen to me like Aretha, but you know I didn't ask her to, so whatever. I'm sure it was a bit misquoted – people always misquote people and I know that, but whatever, I don't care. I'm doing my thing and she's doing hers.'

Back at home, Adele's new single was 'Make You Feel My Love' and it reached UK No 4. The cover featured a simple close-up shot of her, looking at the camera through heavily eye-lined eyes from over her shoulder as if to underline how she was becoming an unlikely icon. The video for the song featured a gaffe which was to create a nightmare for its director. Somehow his phone number was included and it duly became an internet sensation. Soon he was receiving thousands of unsolicited calls from pranksters who had spotted the crucial digits. 'I've had more than five thousand calls,' he said. 'Some people sing the song down the phone, others shout abuse. It's making my life a misery.' It was also a single that once again proved popular on television soundtracks. It featured on British school drama *Waterloo Road*, as well as American shows *One Tree Hill*, *Ghost*

Whisperer and *Parenthood*. It was also used in other dramas including *EastEnders* and *Hollyoaks*.

In November 2008, Adele won in the Best Jazz category of the Urban Music Awards. She was nominated in the *Q* magazine awards in the Best Breakthrough category, though she missed out to Duffy. Another nomination came from the MOBO (Music of Black Origin) awards, in the Best Female category.

Meanwhile, she was living in a new home after a July 2008 move. Taking advantage of her new riches, Adele would attempt to go it alone and live in independent splendour. However, the sweet family girl inside won the day and she was soon back with Penny. The initial move had been to an apartment in west London. Adele tried to play it down. 'It's just a one-bedroom flat in Notting Hill above a shop,' she said. 'My [step]dad works for Wickes, so I should be able to get cheap DIY stuff. I get lonely sometimes but I love it.' However, the quality of the property and the love she brought to it made it a nicer project than her self-deprecating description made out. 'It looks like it is straight out of the film, in a row of white houses,' she said.

With her newfound independence, Adele took driving lessons. 'I learned to drive, but that didn't really work,' she said. 'Apparently I'm a very spatially aware, considerate driver, according to my driving instructor. I didn't keep up my lessons. I was recovering from a severe breakup, so I was drinking a lot. I imagine I was over the limit for most of my lessons!'

Adele also started to cook for herself. Early meals she whipped up in her new kitchen included chilli con carne, stir fries and lasagne. For Christmas, she invited Penny over for dinner. 'I'm going to attempt to do a proper Christmas dinner with loads of roasties and those little sausages with bacon wrapped round them – I love them,' she said. As for festive decorations, Adele was straight to the point in describing what she had gone for. 'I've got a fake Christmas tree 'cos after a while I think the real ones smell like piss.' Indeed, when asked what epitomised the festive spirit, Adele's answer was that it was the Christmas specials of the soap operas. 'You know it's Christmas when someone dies in a soap,' she said. 'Do you remember when Tiffany hit her head on the kerb on Christmas Day trying to escape from Grant? I was about ten and I was so distraught because I didn't know anyone who'd died until my grampy. I felt like I knew Tiffany. I remember going to the bathroom upstairs and being really shocked and shaking and crying.' For Adele, the Christmas of 2008 was a calmer affair.

The following July, she made some changes to her home for the arrival of a dog. 'I'm getting a new floor put in my flat in a couple of weeks 'cos I'm getting ready for my little doglet,' she told the *Daily Star*. 'He's so cute!' Her dog, a dachshund called Louis, nearly ended up with a weirder name. For a while, she considered naming him Britney because he was born the same night as she was watching Britney Spears in concert. 'I almost called him Britney even though he was a boy. [But] it only lasted a few hours until my hangover stopped,' she said. Then she toyed with calling him Aaron Lennon after her favourite Tottenham Hotspur player. Once she settled on Louis he became a fixture of Adele's life. He was attacked by a Jack Russell in the park, but in the main he was a hassle-free friend for Adele. She said that if she ever got another dog she would call it Ella, after the jazz singer Ella Fitzgerald.

The more immediate future contained another move – this time she was going to live in a new place with Penny after missing the warmth of their proximity. It was in November 2009 that she decided enough was enough. 'After my first record I moved out of my mum's and moved to Notting Hill on my own. My life fell apart. My phone got cut off, my credit card got cut off, the house was a mess. It was awful. I couldn't function without my mum so I moved back in with her.' She was aware that this move in a sense represented an admission that she had failed in her quest to live alone – but she didn't care. 'I'd rather be defeated than one day come in and the rats would be eating me,' she said. 'My mum and I don't live in a tiny place. It's a big apartment, she can be at one end and me at the other.'

Penny could not have been prouder of her daughter – wherever she chose to live. Her girl's career was building fast, but Penny was as impressed by Adele's character and loving nature. The bonds they had formed as Penny raised Adele single-handed remained strong, even as the little girl became a young woman, revered across the world for her music. How quickly Adele had become known and loved – the popularity of *19* was immense, but that success would be dwarfed by her follow-up.

Following her Grammy glory, Adele continued to receive nominations in other award ceremonies. She received three for the 2009 Brits – for Best British Female, Best British Breakthrough and Best British Single in 'Chasing Pavements', although, this time, none translated into awards. Later in the year, she received a different, and slightly unconventional, honour. Prime Minister Gordon Brown wrote to her to thank her for the part her music was playing in keeping the British public's mood buoyant in difficult financial times. Adele was surprised to receive it, but also strangely touched. 'It was really nice. It went, "With the troubles that the country's in financially, you're a light at the end of the tunnel." It was amazing. I'm fighting the credit crunch on my own!'

In 2009, Adele continued to receive offers for side projects. One of these was a request from Israel to use 'Hometown Glory' in an advertisement to endorse a new egg timer. It would have earned her a nice, simple payday, but Adele turned it down. She did not want her music associated with the product. 'They were paying really good money but I was like, "No",' she said. 'Even though nobody in England or America would probably ever see it, I definitely had to turn that down.'

She did take up an offer to make a cameo performance on the long-running American television show *Ugly Betty*. A Golden Globe-winning series, it had become a hit around the world. Other famous celebs who have made cameo appearances include Naomi Campbell, Lindsay Lohan, Lucy Liu and Victoria Beckham. Adele appeared as herself, singing 'Right As Rain' at a photo shoot which three leading characters are working on for an assignment. She said it made her feel like a 'superstar' for a moment. 'It was like seconds on camera but, you know, I felt like Julia Roberts for the day!' she added. 'It was the best really.'

Adele was following in Lindsay Lohan's footsteps on *Ugly Betty* and Lohan remained a fan of Adele. In the same week as a *Q* interview, Lohan praised her online. 'I love Adele's "Rumour Has It" off her new record,' she wrote on Twitter. 'Such a good vibe to it. Makes me happy.'

In the same week, Lily Allen also used Twitter to big up Adele. 'So happy for Adele,' she wrote. 'So good when good things happen to nice people. CONGRATULATIONS ADELE on being No1EVERYFUCKINGWHERE!.'

Adele did indeed seem to be everywhere after her album *19* was released. People the world over had taken the songs to their hearts and most had done the same with the woman who had sung them. It was not just the richness of the songs and the power of her voice; Adele's sincere and vulnerable personality had also struck a chord. However, if she seemed to be 'everywhere' after *19*, then the reaction to her follow-up album would make her truly ubiquitous. It was to be nothing short of sensationally popular.

CHAPTER SIX

THE GOLDEN KEY

Adele spent her 21st birthday in the US. She had kicked off her mini tour at San Diego on 9 March 2009. She then played in Arizona, Austin, Houston and Cleveland before arriving in New York. She performed at the Roseland Ballroom on her birthday on 5 May. Then she flew to the west coast, where she co-headlined a show at the Hollywood Bowl with her idol Etta James. There were exciting times, a great way to be celebrating this milestone birthday in her life. And she went on to mark the occasion in style by naming her second album *21*.

Musically, Adele's second album was influenced by a host of artists including country star Garth Brooks, early Dolly Parton, the Steeldrivers, Loretta Lynn and the Carter Family. 'I hadn't even heard of Garth Brooks until around 15 months ago,' she said at the time of *21*'s release. New folk stars Mumford & Sons, too, were a factor in the developing flavour of her music. She said their music 'literally goes into my chest and beats me up, and makes me completely fearless.'

The other inspiration for the album was her latest ex-boyfriend. He was a man she never named, but who she described as 'the most amazing person who has ever been in my life'. She had enjoyed an intense relationship with him. So the breakup naturally hit her hard. 'It's going to take me ten years to recover,' she said in the painful aftermath of that relationship. This pessimistic self-diagnosis was understandable in part, given that at the time she had considered it her first genuine relationship. Part of the recovery process was the composition of her second album. It was a recording which would send her fame soaring to unimaginably high levels. 'It broke my heart when I wrote this record, so the fact that people are taking it to their hearts is like the best way to recover,' she said. She insisted on keeping his identity secret, saying, 'It's not interesting. If he were a celebrity, people would want to know.'

What was known was that her partner had been an older, accomplished man. This was the first time she had dated such a character. As a result, the relationship had given her a new, mature perspective and interest. 'It was the biggest deal in my entire life to date... He made me totally hungry... He was older, he was successful in his own right, whereas my boyfriends before were my age and not really doing much,' Adele said. His influence on her had been cultural, too. She added, 'He got me interested in film and literature and food and wine and travelling and politics and history and those were things I was never, ever interested in. I was interested in going clubbing and getting drunk.' It was fitting that Adele grew in this sense during the relationship – for the one thing that most critics agreed on when her second album was unleashed was that she had matured.

Musician and producer Ryan Tedder worked in the studio with her on many of the ideas and tracks that took shape on *21*. He was abiding by the crucial principle of letting her keep in overall control. 'I'm letting Adele be Adele,' he told the BBC while they were still in the middle of recording sessions. '*19*, that album was so absolutely mind-blowing to me, so simple and beautiful that I don't want myself as a fan to interfere with her sound. Yesterday the song we did was very much Adele – it was 10 per cent Ryan, 90 per cent Adele. [I told her,] "I don't want to put you through the Ryan Tedder machine where you end up with a song that sounds as much like Ryan Tedder as it does Adele."'

At much the same time, Adele was saying that she was not going to hurry work on the album. 'I'm writing it slowly but surely,' she said. 'You're only as good as your next record so if you rush it you end up losing that little niche you've created for yourself and you'll end up with a shit record.' A few weeks earlier, she had also admitted she was worried about how her new work would be greeted by her existing fanbase. 'I'm a bit scared. Obviously there are new avenues that I want to go down with the sound and I don't want to leave behind the fans who might not like the new sound I am going for. So I'm a bit wary of that.'

Adele claimed that, though it was the big dramas of life that were influencing and inspiring her writing, she could actually write a song about almost any event, however trivial. 'The littlest things I can write about, it doesn't have to be some drama. The littlest things – about not putting a cup in the dishwasher. I can write a song about that as well,' she said. In the end, the album would deal with the bigger trials of existence.

Though the title of the album followed the format of her debut, she had considered naming the album after one of its tracks – 'Rolling in the Deep'. As she told *Rolling Stone* magazine, the song reflected one of the most significant things she felt she had lost with the breakup of her relationship, the reassurance that she had someone looking out for her in life. 'The phrase "rolling in the deep" is sort of my adaptation of a kind of slang, slur phrase in the UK called "roll deep", which means to have someone, always have someone that has your back and you're never on your own. If you're ever in trouble you've always got someone who's going to come and help you fight it or whatever like that. And that's how I felt in the relationship that the record's about, especially "Rolling in the Deep". That's how I felt, you know, I thought that's what I was always going to have and it ended up not being the case.'

She not only had a change of mind about the album title but also about the emotional feel of its songs. She had originally wanted her second release to be a more upbeat piece of work. On reflection, she had found *19* to be too serious. She felt it did not reflect her personality, which is 'fun, cheeky, loud and sarcastic'. Certainly, the Adele of the songs on *19* was an entirely different character to the one she showed in her interviews and was in her private life. She wanted to show that she has a lighter and spirited side. To that end, she was partially successful. That lighter side does show its face at several points on the album. More broadly, though, there is no doubt this is a successful, wonderful piece of work. In both its sadder, slower, happier and more lively moments, it consistently impresses. Each song has its own strengths and charms: together they unite to form one of the most enjoyable, emotional and impressive albums to be released by a UK artist for many, many years.

21 opens with 'Rolling in the Deep'. This makes for a defiant, almost rallying, start to the record. Adele has said this song is the musical equivalent of saying something in the heat of the moment and 'word vomiting'. Thematically and musically, she is serving notice from the off that *21* is a different, fuller, more brassy piece of work than her debut had been. The song also has a bigger production than anything on *19*. Lyrically, she is berating her ex-partner throughout, telling him that they could have had it all but that he has thrown it away. Not only that, she vows to unleash revenge on him. He will, she warns him, reap just what he had sown after the way he had played her heart. Given her reputation as one who only sings the gently sad, heartbroken tunes of a broken woman, 'Rolling in the Deep' is clear proof that there is more to her than that. She has commented that this song was a 'fuck you' to the suggestion that, as a single woman, she would not amount to anything.

'Rolling in the Deep' was produced by Paul Epworth. It is, in Adele's words, a 'dark, bluesy gospel disco tune'. The fact it was produced by a stalwart of the indie music scene is clear to the listener: it has more attitude to it than anything on *19*. This was a musical collaboration that Adele was at first anxious about. Epworth, who has worked with Primal Scream, Maximo Park and the Rapture, is very much grounded in the indie sound and, as Adele says, she is 'known for being very pop'. This was a meeting of opposite styles and minds. As such, she could not help but wonder to herself how it would turn out and was delighted to find it was 'a match made in heaven'. She found he was full of ideas and that he brought the best out in her voice. 'There are notes in that song that I never even knew I could hit.' Vocally, it is indeed her most powerful moment to date. She belts out the defiant lyrics, remaining totally dominating in the song's rich musical soundtrack. In every sense, then, the album's opener is a declaration of strength. As the listener first luxuriates in its warmth, they quickly are filled with excitement at what more there is to come on *21*.

Far from toning down the music or rhetoric in the second track, Adele essentially carries the spirit of 'Rolling in the Deep' into 'Rumour Has It'. She taunts the object of her previous song now, mocking the disastrous turn that his relationship with the woman he left her for has taken. She turns a line around to give the story of the song a twist. From saying that the rumour is that her ex-partner is leaving his new girl for Adele, at the close of the song she suggests that it's her leaving him for the new girl. Musically, this is another up-tempo song and it is also heavy on percussion. She described it as a 'bluesey, pop, stomping song'. On this form, her fans will hope that long will she stomp. She said the lyrics were inspired by nights out with her friends in which they would bombard her with the latest gossip about her ex-partner. She knows some people took the 'rumour' of the title to refer to the relentless cycle of media rumours. She insisted it refers to the way her own friends often believe rumours about her, a fact that she said leaves her 'pretty mortified'. The song, which in some ways is reminiscent of Duffy, was produced by Ryan Tedder.

Having turned the tables with her lyrics in track two, she put a song called 'Turning Tables' in third position. This was a song that would be more familiar to fans of *19*. She co-wrote it with Tedder and it was produced by Jim Abbiss, who has worked with Arctic Monkeys among others. It is gentle, sparse, mournful and slow. Looking back on the relationship she is leaving, she sings that she can no longer bear being under his thumb and being the focus of his games that see him turning tables. She feels she could not even breathe while under his spell. Though leaving him is a challenge, she will brave the storms that the task brings with it and will walk away. This is a beautiful song, with the piano, strings and Adele's voice combining to create an experience that is cleansing. However, it was born out of anger. Adele arrived at the studio one day ranting about a man. 'Who the fuck does he think he is, always turning tables on me?' she asked. Ryan Tedder seized on the term, and together they built it into the song.

In 'Don't You Remember', Adele returned to the more vulnerable soul of *19*. It was, fittingly enough, a song that was difficult to forget, such was its power. Here, she is shaken and stunned to have lost her lover. She had no idea, she sings, of the state they were in. She has had to endure the abrupt ending of their relationship, but she hopes that, if he remembers what had first made him love her, he will come back. This is a traditional ballad, one whose mellow verses build into a big chorus. It was one of the last songs she wrote for the album. She did so after realising that, as she looked over the songs about her ex, she had 'made him out to be a complete twat'. She chastised herself for this she said in an interview, suddenly feeling she had been 'childish'. So she wrote a song that recalled the glorious times they had together, when she was completely besotted and electrified by him.

The next song on the album, 'Set Fire to the Rain', saw Adele again sway between competing emotions. It is, she said, a song about the contradictions of romance. She recalled the strength and warmth that her partner had given her. However, she then became wise to other sides of his personality that were unexpectedly less pleasant. She then flits between acknowledging that she cannot help but wish he would return, and hoping the fire will 'burn'. She said she was 'really heartbroken when I met who the song is about and he really brought me back to life and put me back together – and he was a dickhead as well'. Musically, it has a busy, heavy production, and is one of the more commercial tracks on *21*. Yet, despite its mainstream sound, it was not picked for one of the early single releases. Most casual fans of Adele would not list it as one of her songs of which they are aware. This says something about the quality of her music.

In the Rick Rubin-produced 'He Won't Go', Adele repeats the trick of turning a lyric round so it is seen from each side of the relationship. It was about two real-life friends that she met, one battling heroin addiction. She became inspired by their lives. The song's characters have created space between each other and, even though the girl is assured by her friends that she is better off without the man, she keeps stumbling over reminders of him and it prevents her closing the door completely. In the early choruses, she chants that she won't go, insisting that she is not prepared to give up on the relationship. By the end, this is turned round. It's the partner who won't go, who has had the space to think about things and decided that he will take another stab at their relationship. After all, they conclude, if what they have is not love, then what is? Musically and thematically, this is something of an oddity in Adele's canon of work: lively, imaginative and upbeat.

Then came 'Take It All', one of the first songs written for *21*. It had been a spontaneous creation: one day, writer Eg White played a single chord in the studio and Adele just began to sing lyrics to it. In the final product, she can be heard in full-on martyr mode, the phase that many people go through after a hard breakup. She has given everything she could to her lover and asks plaintively whether it was not enough. 'It's about devotion,' said Adele, and how that devotion can be responded to by its focus 'taking the piss out of me' in return. She promises to change, pleads that she will change and thinks that, if only he knew that everything she does is for him, he might see it differently. In the end, in full drama-queen mode, she tells him not to look back at her but instead to take it all, with her love.

'I was still with my boyfriend then,' she said of the writing process, 'which was obviously a sign that things were going downhill.' That was the only track to emerge from the sessions prior to her split from her partner. It was once that split happened that the rest of the album came pouring out of her. Heartbreak, it once more proved, was a major creative spark for Adele. 'It's all tied together by my voice … I don't have a definitive sound,' she said. 'I have no idea what I sound like yet, so, until I do, all my records will have a kind of mixtape vibe going on.' Showing how comfortable she is with the gospel sound, Adele's slightly husky delivery takes that genre to new, earthy places. That said, her most earthy vocal performance of *21* would come later in the album.

Having thus waved her man off, did Adele leave the door ajar for him, for a possible future reconciliation? She did, in the next track, 'I'll Be Waiting'. Here we have a more contrite, apologetic Adele, singing that she was a child before and that in the future she will be different, if only he will give them another chance. The time had been wrong before, and they had a long-distance relationship but in the future things could be different. She has faith in what they have together. After dark times, she says the sky is blue and she sees her future with him again. This song was, Adele said, 'almost like the soundtrack to my life'. While writing and working on it, Adele was very happy. When she spoke about the song, she reconnected with that happiness and it came across in her words. In terms of the sequencing of *21*, 'I'll Be Waiting' takes the album back up a gear. The energy was welcome and judiciously positioned.

In 'One and Only', she moved from presenting her wishes for a reconciliation from a hope to expressing them as a dare. She was asking for one more chance from the subject of the song, but she was now daring him to drop his own objections and defences, presenting it as a challenge, perhaps to appeal to his sense of male competitiveness. Produced by Rick Rubin, this was, she said, 'another happy song', reflective perhaps of the fact that it was not about the figure who had inspired the majority of the songs on the album. Instead, it is about a man she had known for many years. Even though they had never been an item, despite their close bond, she predicted she might well marry him one day.

The middle eight of 'One and Only' was, Adele said, 'cheesy'. It was inspired by a scene in the Drew Barrymore movie *Never Been Kissed*, in which the world slows down in the moment of a kiss. 'It's like a fairytale,' Adele said of such a moment, adding that 'One and Only' was 'like a daydream song'. It was one of the finest vocal performances on the album and of her career to date.

Moving away from her own material, she went on to cover 'Lovesong' by the Cure. In doing so, she returned in spirit to the first live concert she ever saw, when her mother took her along to the Cure in Finsbury Park, London. It was suggested that Rubin had originally rearranged the track with the intention of recording it with Barbra Streisand, who decided not to pursue it. And so the idea was passed to Adele. The lyrics declare the sense of completion, freedom and cleanliness that the protagonist gets from being with their partner. It closes with a declaration of eternal love. 'It's a really touching song,' Adele said. She was missing home when she recorded it in Malibu. She felt overwhelmed by the experience of being so far from everything she knew. Those emotions come across in the raw take on the song that made its way on to *21*. 'I felt quite heavy,' she said, 'and that song really set me free.' She described the recording as 'stunning' and 'amazing'. This was due in part to the fact that she had lost her voice a bit on the day she recorded 'Lovesong'. She felt that really suited her version.

The album's closer was the iconic 'Someone Like You'. Here, Adele was at her most gut-wrenching and empathy-inducing. As she said herself, the emotions and sentiments of this song did, in a way, contradict those expressed in 'Rolling in the Deep', *21*'s opener. It meant the album had gone full circle. For some listeners, 'Someone Like You' provided a sense of emotional closure to the album as well. The listener followed Adele on a poignant journey from defiance, to heartbreak, to pleading. In 'Someone Like You', she wishes her ex-partner well. Though she begs him to not forget her, she seems as serene and resigned to the facts of the album's story as she could be. However, Adele insisted that this was the sound of a woman on her knees. In being so raw, it was not just the standout song of the album, but of her career to that point. It was reminiscent of the closing track of *19*, 'Hometown Glory'. And those fans who came to the studio version of 'Someone Like You' having heard her live performance at the Brits might have found the recording to be a surprise in some senses. The studio version is less sad than the performance she gave at the Brits. The chorus seems even more sincere. She said she had aimed to balance the perception of her ex-partner. She felt he deserved to be shown in a positive light as well. 'If I don't write a song like this, I'm just going to end up becoming a bitter old woman forever. It was about putting us at peace, and coming to terms with the fact that, though I'd met the love of my life, it was just bad timing.'

Even long after the release, the standout song continued to be 'Someone Like You'. Could any of the team behind it have known quite the extent to which it would capture the public's imagination? Indeed, they insisted that they had consciously avoided trying to go down the everyman route too heavily with the song. 'We didn't try to make it open-ended so it could apply to "anybody",' said co-writer and producer Dan Wilson. 'We tried to make it as personal as possible.' It certainly came across as deeply personal to its listeners.

For Adele, it was therapeutic. 'After I wrote it,' said Adele, 'I felt more at peace. It set me free. I'm wiser in my songs. My words are always what I can never say [in real life]. But I didn't think it would resonate … with the world! I'm never gonna write a song like that again. I think that's the song I'll be known for.'

The relationship that much of the album is about brought positivity as well as hurt. 'It changed me in a really good way,' she said. 'It's really made me who I am at the moment,' she added. 'I can imagine being about 40 and looking for him again and turning up and he's settled, he's got a beautiful wife and beautiful kids, and he's completely happy and I'm still on my own.' It was a thought that haunted and scared her.

Looking over the album as a whole in an interview, she compared the Adele of *21* with that of *19*. In the debut, she said, she sounded 'really naive and childish', despite the fact that people have long described her as wise beyond her years. However, by *21* she felt she was 'more grown-up and mature and sincere'. Among the lessons that have informed that maturity was the one at the centre of 'Someone Like You', the concept that you have to move on and wish people the best. It was something she learned in recovering from heartache. She said she felt 'better and lighter' for the realisation. 'I wanted the songs not to have anything glittery or glamorous about them, like an organic tapestry rather than like a Gaga album,' she told *Rolling Stone*. 'I mean, I love Gaga, but I didn't want to get wrapped up in all that European dance music.' Instead, she looked more to country for her inspiration. Having spent so long on the road in the US, she had become fascinated with several country artists. Lady Antebellum and rockabilly pioneer Wanda Jackson were particularly strong influences. 'I've really gotten into that kind of stuff over the last couple of years,' she said. 'One of my

American tour-bus drivers was from Nashville and he would make up compilations of all his favourite country, blues, bluegrass and rockabilly songs.'

Thinking logically, her newfound affiliation with country acts made a lot of sense. So many of these acts wrote music that reflected the heartache and other obstacles that they had to face in their lives. This was, literally and metaphorically, music to Adele's ears.

'She'd definitely been exposed to things that opened her eyes musically,' said Paul Epworth. 'So much of the music from the US over the last century was formed from various trials and tribulations and I think that's reflected on Adele's record – that she identified with these artists singing about their lives.'

Epworth was just one of a world-class team of producers and songwriters to have worked with Adele, a group which also included Rick Rubin, Ryan Tedder and Francis 'Eg' White. There was a definite sense that *21* was a project about which she very much meant business. Of Rubin, she said, 'I like how he thinks about music and how he bases all his decisions about music on how it makes him feel.'

However, Rubin wasn't the only one in the production frame. The album had almost been helmed by former White Stripes frontman Jack White. 'We were doing a lot of collaborations, but we never got around to it,' said Adele. She recorded a version of 'Many Shades of Black', originally by another of White's bands, the Raconteurs. Jack White himself was involved in the session – 'I met him and it was lovely' – and after the 2009 Grammys they were due to reunite. 'We were going to finish some tracks in Detroit and then it never happened. It'll happen at some point, though. I definitely want to follow it up.'

A future musical collaboration between these two musical talents is a tantalising prospect. White's songs with the much-missed White Stripes had been indie tunes fused with blues and country. Working with Adele, he could potentially produce some material which straddles many of the sounds that influenced her as a child.

Meanwhile, on the brink of *21*'s release, she declared she was less tense than she had been prior to the release of *19*. 'I was nervous and uptight because it was all brand new,' she said, remembering how she felt when her debut hit the shops. 'The reception was so unexpected that everyone just sort of went along with it. Not that I'm saying I'm a professional now. But I've learned to sit down and enjoy it all. I feel more free than I ever have.'

Industry experts were already purring with appreciation having heard the album, even before any reviews were published. 'She's got a little more swagger now,' said executive vice president of music and talent relations at VH1, Rick Krim.

When the reviews came in, it was apparent that critics were almost unanimous in their admiration for the progress in her work. Will Dean wrote in the *Guardian* that Adele 'comes of age sounding as wise beyond her years as she did in 2008'. Noting the two-year gap between *19* and *21*, Dean concluded, 'A progressive, grown-up second collection, it ought to ensure Adele is around for *23*, *25*, *27* and beyond.'

The *Daily Telegraph* gave *21* five stars and heaped corresponding amounts of praise on it. 'Where previously her slight, observational songs seemed barely able to carry her powerful voice, the emotional and musical heft of styles enables her to really spread her vocal wings,' wrote Bernadette McNulty. 'And her voice is a thing of wonder.'

Elsewhere, there were further accolades. Holy Moly said, 'We can't imagine we'll hear a better album this year.' Remember – this was said in January. The BBC website's review said, '*21* is simply stunning. After only a handful of plays, it feels like you've always known it... Genuinely brilliant.'

In the *NME*, Chris Parkin said that *21* 'flattened all memory' of *19*. He added that the opening two tracks, 'Rolling in the Deep' and 'Rumour Has It', were superior to the music on her debut album. For him, this raised an issue. 'They're light years ahead of the supermarket-brand hurt Adele bled all over *19*, which begs the question: why allow that pastel-pink mush to reanimate in the opener's wake?' The website Consequence of Sound also questioned the sequence, saying, 'The album suffers from a somewhat uneven feel overall – the track order just seems off.'

One of the more critical reviews was in the *Observer*, which had been very glowing in its review of *19* and had featured and promoted her work in other ways. Writer Kitty Empire complained that 'the shivers don't come as often as they should' on *21*. She imagined that the producers had been 'working with a sign saying: "More than two million albums sold; don't screw this up" taped on the mixing desk. Too many songs start promisingly, then swell to a predictable, overdramatic billow (that's you, "He Won't Go").'

In the US, the album went down well, perhaps in part due to the apparent American influence. Jon Caramanica, in the *New York Times*, compared *21* with its predecessor and liked what he saw. The new songs were, he wrote, 'as sturdy as before, helped along by a small cavalcade of classicist producers and writers with an ear for careful tweaks. Where *19* could feel like a period piece at times, *21*, the rare breakup album as scornful of the singer as her subject, aims to show just what sort of odd details those frames can support.'

Greg Kot of the *Chicago Tribune* was less impressed. While he agreed *21* was an improvement, he felt it was not improvement enough. He noted that she had some fine producers working with her, but said, 'Too bad the songs themselves aren't better. It's only the sheer conviction of Adele's voice that prevents "Don't You Remember" from drowning in its own sap or the tortured turns of phrase in "Set Fire to the Rain" from collapsing.'

Rolling Stone summed up how Adele had changed since *19*, by saying, '[She] has toughened her tone, trimmed the jazz frippery and sounds ready for a pub fight.' Although the reviewer had criticisms, he gave *21* four-and-a-half stars and concluded, 'When the grooves are fierce, Adele gives as good as she gets.'

Barry Walters of *Spin* magazine was more favourable and more eloquent. He wrote that the weakness of *19* had been too many 'folksy guitar ballads' and cheered, 'Those have vanished; ditto Adkins' Tottenham accent. Instead, she wails harder and writes bolder, piling on the dramatic production flourishes to suggest a lover's apocalypse. If you're looking for a record that'll make you wanna trash your beloved's belongings and have make-up sex amid the ruins, *21*'s your jam.'

Margaret Wappler of the *LA Times* looked further ahead and hoped Adele would stay faithful to one of the production team. 'Who knows what damage she'll exact for *30*, but let's hope Epworth is along for the ride,' she wrote.

The *New York Daily News*, a popular Manhattan tabloid, was the most positive of all. Indeed, in describing *21* as 'perfect', it could scarcely have been more admiring. One can only imagine Adele's delight when she read this review in which Jim Farber said her album 'floats beyond countries and time'. His review was full of glorious, laudatory phrases about Adele, casting her as someone with 'handsome tone' and 'ample lung power'. He showered *21* with admiration, writing, 'From start to finish, it shows Adele in alpha mode, ready to outshout any bigmouth singer of the last two decades, from Celine to Christina to (sigh) Whitney.' Praise indeed. In conclusion, he aimed to lay down a gauntlet to other stars. *21*, he wrote, 'draws an unequivocal line in the sand that announces to every other diva around: "Beat this".'

More generally, comparisons with Amy Winehouse continued – often in the most tenuous of ways. For instance, one reviewer wrote that, by releasing a second album that was better than her debut, Adele had followed in the tradition of Winehouse, whose second album *Back to Black* was, in the opinion of the reviewer, superior to her debut *Frank*. The fact that countless musical acts have improved between their debut and follow-up album was not enough to get in the way of another comparison between Adele and Winehouse.

The commercial and critical rewards Adele took from *21* were obvious and mighty. However, such an emotional, wrought album had also taken a lot out of her, as had the experience that influenced the writing of the album. 'It broke my heart when I wrote this record, so the fact that people are taking it to their hearts is like the best way to recover. 'Cause I'm still not fully recovered. It's going to take me ten years to recover, I think, from the way I feel about my last relationship,' she explained. If nothing else, he had influenced an almightily great album. Even if Adele never recorded another song, *21* would guarantee her place in the hearts of millions of music lovers for good.

But, as far as Jonathan Dickins was concerned, this was just the start for Adele. 'She's made a great record that we're immensely proud of,' he said. 'And it's just another step in a long, fruitful career. Everything we try to do – every decision – is absolutely focused on the long term.'

Given that Adele's classic sound and style of music is one that definitely improves with age – unlike the modish pop sounds of some artists her age – it is to be hoped that Adele will continue and enjoy the sort of development that Dickins hoped for. The Winehouse comparisons have frustrated both Adele and her fans and nobody would want her to go off the rails as the 'Rehab' singer did. Fortunately, there was little sign of that in the wake of *21*.

Dickins was far from being alone in predicting that the album would lead to even bigger things for its young star. Her potential to be a worldwide sensation was only just beginning to be realised. 'Really, we are just on our first single and we think there are probably five, so I think it's just the beginning,' Rick Rubin told *Billboard* of the star's US campaign. 'And she's barely toured at all so really it's in the baby stages. I think it's a beautiful album that we're all really proud of and it's amazing that it's connecting with people in the way that it is and we just hope it continues to do so. She is an incredible singer. She bares her soul in her songwriting, and it's the real thing... She uses her vocal instrument in a way that we don't get to hear a lot. What she is doing, it's a very pure expression of herself and it resonates with people. There is no trickery involved. It's a really honest album.'

Meanwhile, we keep returning to the relationship that prompted and influenced *21*. Despite the astounding fortunes and fame that album brought her, Adele still wished she had given up music and stuck with the relationship. 'I don't think I'll ever forgive myself for not making my relationship with my ex on *21* work, because he's the love of my life,' she told *Out*. 'I would still be singing in the shower, of course, but yeah – my career, my friendships, my hobbies. I would have given up trying to be the best.' The relationship left her with lots of hurt and tears, yet it also left a positive legacy. It would be the one that she measured all future boyfriends against. She described the rapport she and her ex-partner had with palpable and surprising emotional power. 'He was my soul mate,' she said. 'We had everything, on every level we were totally right. We'd finish each other's sentences and he could just pick up how I was feeling by the look in my eye, down to a T. We loved the same things, and hated the same things and we were brave when the other was brave and weak when the other one was weak - almost like twins, you know. And I think that's rare when you find the full circle in one person and I think that's what I'll always be looking for in other men.'

She had taken steps to move on, even signing up to an online dating website in the hope of finding a new man. 'I just signed up for eHarmony,' she said. 'I can't put a photo of myself, so I don't get any emails!' Instead, she tried to find other ways of reaching closure. That process proved challenging. 'I must have written him about five or six letters at different stages of the recovery. I've written, put in an envelope, stamped and everything, but never sent. I've got a little box of stuff that reminds me of us and they're still in there.'

What an astonishing impact this man had on her life, and what a significant impact and influence he continued to play on her emotions and imagination. During her next major television appearance of 2011, Adele would be singing about him and thinking about him as she did. She could not help but wonder if he was among the audience as the nation was watching. Soon afterwards, the video of the performance would be watched by millions across the world. It was Adele at her very finest.

CHAPTER SEVEN

SOMEONE LIKE US

It was an emotionally charged performance that would change Adele's life forever.

The Brits 2011 were held at London's vast 02 arena. With its 20,000 capacity and high ceilings, it has a grand and somewhat intimidating feeling. The ceremony was due a positive focus, as for so many years the most notable moments had been controversial rather than musical. Among these incidents had been the time Liam Gallagher tossed his award into the audience in 2010, the spat between Sharon Osbourne and Vic Reeves in 2008 and other such headline-grabbing moments of petulance as Jarvis Cocker interrupting Michael Jackson's performance in 1996. How long had it been since an artist had dominated the evening for what really mattered: their performance?

On Tuesday, 15 February 2011, Adele might simply have been recovering from the pain of Valentine's Day as a single woman. Instead, she was putting in a magnificent, spine-tingling appearance at the Brits. In front of some 16,000 at the venue and nearly six million watching from home, she would reach new heights as a live performer. In little more than three minutes, she would distil the most painful emotions all people experience at some point in life into song. Both the fans in the seating around the edge of the venue and many of the notoriously cynical music business bigwigs sitting around tables on the floor were to be stunned by her gut-wrenching performance.

Host James Corden had promised that his style on the night would be 'warm and sensitive'. He was as good as his word. 'There's nothing quite like the feeling when you're listening to a song written by someone you don't know, who you've never met, who somehow manages to describe how you felt at a particular moment in your life,' he said. 'This next artist is able to do that time after time. It's for that reason that she's currently number one in an astonishing 17 countries. If you've ever had a broken heart, you're about to remember it now. Here, performing "Someone Like You", it's the beautiful Adele.'

As she prepared to sing, Adele might have reflected on her various Brit experiences. The times she had watched the ceremony at home with her mother. The shows she attended in person as a fan, squeezed into the pit in front of the stage alongside fellow BRIT School pupils. Then came her appearance in 2009, when she was the winner of the first ever critics' choice award. Since then, she had heard occasional whispers that she had not won that award through merit and that she had benefited from some sort of fix. This scepticism plagued modern Britain, stretching far and wide across the psyche of people who struggle to be pleased for those chasing and fulfilling their dreams.

Well, on this night she was going to answer all the cynics and critics in style. Wearing a vintage dress and fine diamond earrings, she certainly looked the part. The other live performers on the night had favoured huge productions. Take That had come on-stage surrounded by dancers in riot gear. Rihanna had sung with her usual full-on pomp and ceremony, while Plan B had reprised Take That's lawless theme with a breathtaking production that included a dancer dressed as a policeman who ran on to the stage in flames, leaving many of those watching at home unable to decide at first whether it had been a stunt or a disaster. Adele's performance could not have been more different. It was just her, a pianist and a light shower of glitter towards the end. This was not to be about gimmicks or attempts at controversy – it was to be about the music.

She looked particularly stunning as the camera swept to her. That would continue to be the case throughout the song, but one other aspect of her appearance would change radically. She stood with enormous poise at the beginning of the song. It seemed to those watching that her body language was successfully camouflaging her real feelings. She waved and pointed her arms a lot. As the song continued, particularly towards the end, her nerves came bubbling to the surface. Throughout, she was picked out by a single spotlight, standing next to the pianist. This was a truly, brilliantly old-fashioned performance. During the first chorus, where the vocals naturally take a step up in power, she seemed to give them a slightly bigger kick. The extent to which the audience was with her became clear as applause, cheers and screams of appreciation greeted the chorus. As the song drew to a close, that golden glitter rained over the stage. By this point, the emotion of the audience had reached its peak. Everything about the conclusion of the performance was raw and genuine. Pieces of glitter even got caught in the front of her hair and on her neck. During the final line, she pumped her fist to underscore the emotion of the song. As she sang the final words, it was as if she had come back to reality. She scrunched up one eye slightly bashfully. It was an amazing moment, this woman who was singing so brilliantly to thousands in person and millions at home was suddenly struck by girlish nerves, the sort that might strike a schoolgirl speaking in front of a class or at a school play. It was a look that said: 'Was that OK?' The answer would soon become obvious. Then her vocals were over and, as the piano part drew towards its conclusion, the tears that had been threatening to spill out for a while did just that.

'Thanks,' she mouthed to the audience as it roared with both delight and empathy. She had moved everyone, including herself, and the applause was as much to support her emotionally as it was to appreciate her professionally. The love and compassion that people felt for her was tangible. She then nervously bit her thumb, in one final act of vulnerable theatre. Immediately, the audience rose to its feet. At home, television viewers were similarly impressed, and flooded Twitter with statements of appreciation and awe.

The focus then returned to Corden. The sincerity of his introduction just a few minutes earlier had been clear. He had expected big things of her and she had more than delivered. 'Wow,' he said with a tone of disbelief, as the standing ovation continued around him. 'Wasn't that amazing? You can have all the dancers, the pyrotechnics, laser shows you want but, if you sound like that, all you need is a piano. Incredible.' He spoke for the nation.

Adele's verdict on the night was more concise: 'Shat myself,' she said.

Given the curious blend of scepticism and expectations which surround the Brits, there are few moments during it that create anything approaching a consensus among viewers. Adele impressed and moved just about everyone else with her visceral and vulnerable delivery. Talk about washing your emotional linen in public. Clearly, a large part of the emotion she had displayed was connected with the subject of her song – her ex-boyfriend. Later, speaking to ITV2, she offered more specific insight into what had gone into her performance. 'I was really emotional by the end because I'm quite overwhelmed by everything anyway, and then I had a vision of my ex, of him watching me at home and he's going to be laughing at me because he knows I'm crying because of him, with him thinking, Yep, she's still wrapped around my finger,' she said. The response from the audience had proved the tipping point, she said. 'Then everyone stood up, so I was overwhelmed.'

It was not only a momentous time for her emotionally. Physically, too, she had been in a strange place before she even took to the stage. She had been on a health kick prior to the ceremony and a post-show party was not the first thing on her mind. 'I've been on a detox, man!' she said. 'Five days without fags, I'm five days clean! I ain't drinking, I ain't smoking, no fizzy drinks, no sugar, no dairy, no spicy food, no citruses... no bloody nothing!' She later revealed that even her beloved post-show glass or two of red wine was off the agenda. 'I haven't been well so I've been very boring tonight. I've had laryngitis so I'm not even supposed to be talking, never mind singing. It's rubbish – no drinking, no talking and no partying.'

Vocal problems would continue to be a problem for her in the first half of 2011 and she would go on to talk about how she became quite concerned as the year went on. Even in February her frustration was clear in her interviews. The effect that live performances had on her was telling even without the extra burden of illness. She might make her talent seem effortless, but make no mistake about it – Adele always paid for her brilliance. Behind the scenes, she had to dig deep to build the confidence to sing. Indeed, Adele has admitted that she often gets extremely nervous prior to live performances. 'I'm scared of audiences,' she admitted soon after her Brits triumph. 'One show in Amsterdam, I was so nervous I escaped out the fire exit,' she recalled. 'I've thrown up a couple of times. Once in Brussels, I projectile vomited on someone. I just gotta bear it. But I don't like touring. I have anxiety attacks a lot.'

For a short time, Adele made many focus on what the Brits should always be about: the sheer brilliance that can be achieved in the UK's music industry. In those three minutes, she more than repaid and vindicated the faith that had been shown in her when she won her critics' choice award just a few years previously. The reaction took her fame and popularity to new heights. As soon as the performance was uploaded to YouTube, the video spread around the world like wildfire. People who had previously not heard of Adele were suddenly watching footage of her at her peak. As of the summer of 2011, this video had been watched nearly six million times. It had become a TV to YouTube crossover to rival the first audition of *Britain's Got Talent* runner-up Susan Boyle.

The mainstream media heaped praise on Adele. Her *Telegraph* cheerleader Neil McCormick was one of the first to commend her for 'delivering a heart-rending ballad armed with nothing but a big voice, a monster melody, a piano and a shower of glitter'. Word spread around the world, with, for instance, the *Seattle Post* observing that Adele 'looked genuinely moved at the end and you could feel the emotion that she put into that performance. It was stunning'. In many other newspapers and magazines, Adele was highlighted as the star not just of the night but of the moment in general. What an amazing response there was.

However, perhaps the true marker of the influence of her

Brits performance came in the pop charts. The song had been outside of the Top 40 before her appearance but, as the nation wiped its collective eyes after watching her sing at the 02, many of them hit the download button, sending it back up the charts. It is quite usual for those who appear at the Brits to enjoy a boost in sales as a result, with 70 per cent increases being quite common, but nobody had ever got quite the response Adele had. 'Someone Like You' soared straight back to the top of the singles chart, where it dislodged Jessie J's 'Price Tag'. This meant Adele had two songs in the Top 5 simultaneously – 'Rolling in the Deep' was at UK No 4. She held the same positions in the album charts. *21* stayed at UK No 1, while *19* crept back to UK No 4. This was the first time since 1964 that one act had two positions in the Top 5 of both the single and albums chart at the same time. Adele was in good company – the act who previously achieved the same feat was the Beatles. 'I Want to Hold Your Hand' and 'She Loves You' were their singles and the albums were *With The Beatles* and *Please Please Me*. Then the live version of 'Someone Like You' that Adele had sung was released on iTunes and quickly topped the chart there. Indeed, all of the live performances from that year's awards were made available to download with proceeds going to the BRIT Trust.

The fact Adele held off a challenge in the singles chart from Lady Gaga, with 'Born This Way', only made it more impressive. Gaga was gracious in the face of this, revealing during an interview on BBC radio what a fan she is of the girl of the hour. 'I love Adele,' she said. 'I think Adele is wonderful and I'm so excited at the success she has had over the past couple of weeks with the Brits and everything. It's so wonderful.'

Adele was similarly unstinting in her praise of fellow artists. Her simple performance had been praised and contrasted to the raunchier, louder performances by the likes of Rihanna, but Adele had herself been turned on by Rihanna's appearance. 'You look at someone like Rihanna and, my God, her thighs make me love her,' she told the *Daily Mirror*'s Celebs on Sunday after the Brits. She had been out partying just a few months earlier, she said, when dancing along to Rihanna's hit 'What's My Name?' brought her an enormous sense of connection with the US star. 'Over New Year's and Christmas, I had time off and I went to all my friends' parties singing it,' she said. 'Doing the dance moves, I was convinced I was Rihanna. She was possessing me with that song, I swear.' Returning to the Brits, she also said she had been 'inspired' by Mumford & Sons, who shared the billing. The act's appearance on the night had led to some commentators claiming that there was a 'folk revival' in the offing in the British music industry. Some of these noted folk influences in Adele's music and included her in the trend.

Looking back later, Adele was still puzzled and overwhelmed by the entire Brits experience. 'It's really bizarre – at the Brit awards I was so frightened,' she said. 'I've never actually been so scared in my life but it ended up being the most life-changing night of my life. Everyone stood up. I've never been given a standing ovation by my peers and by the industry. It was amazing. I was really embarrassed when I was singing that song because I hate getting emotional about my ex-boyfriend. I'm fine about it now but I realised in that four minutes that actually I'm not fine about it. That's why I broke down. I saw my manager and he looked proud and I love making him proud.'

Certainly, she had set a high bar for performers at future ceremonies. The Adele effect is one that all will want to repeat each year, but it will be a tall order to make that one happen. Even Adele herself would need to work hard and have a bit of luck to define a Brits ceremony so strongly again. But at least she can say she has already done it.

The next high-profile live performance of 'Someone Like You' from Adele came at the iTunes Festival at London's Roundhouse in July. Adele was back to performing after at last having been told by doctors that she was over her bout of laryngitis. She'd announced the good news a couple of days before the show during an interview with her beloved BBC Radio 1 friend Chris Moyles. Adele gave a brief description of the problem. 'It's basically a hole in your vocal cord but I sang through it so that's why it popped. I'm better now. It's fine, I got the all clear,' she said. She had been scared when she first realised she had lost her voice. 'It's never happened before. My voice went off, like a tap,' she said. She had to sit in silence for nine days. Caffeine, alcohol and cigarettes were all banned during this period. Adele said that in order to make her wishes understood she had to have 'a chalkboard around my neck. Like an old school mime. Like a kid in the naughty corner. Like a Victorian mute.' On one particular occasion, her desire to communicate had become almost overwhelming. Typically for Adele, it was a particularly exciting episode of the BBC soap opera *EastEnders* that so excited her. However, the issue was not one she felt she could laugh about at its peak, when she had begun to wonder whether she would ever sing again. What a relief it was for her not to lose the gift that she had only just begun to use professionally and which had given her astounding levels of fame and fortune so quickly. Losing one's voice for good is a fear that haunts many singers. Few have come as close as Adele to genuinely believing that the nightmare will come true. But, if her performance at the iTunes gig was anything to go by, she was entirely restored.

'This song changed my life, it's my most amazing achievement,' she said, introducing 'Someone Like You' as the closing song of the set. 'I'm singing for you guys so thank you very, very much for coming. I really do appreciate it, it means the world to me – so thank you very, very much. This is "Someone Like You". Have a wonderful night and get home safe, yeah?' She seemed to be curiously calm and collected during the first verse, even pulling a cheeky smile between lines. During the bridge to the first chorus, she seemed more moved and involved. After the middle eight, she smiled to the audience and, removing the microphone from its stand, asked the audience, 'Sing it to me?' They did so with enthusiasm, and she joined in with them mid-chorus. 'One more time,' she said, setting up a new choral sing-along. 'Roundhouse, thank you so much,' she said, as the audience applauded the end of the song. With her emotion bubbling, she added, 'Thank you, I'll see you soon. I'll be back in September.' To keep them going, an EP featuring a selection of tracks from her performance was released on iTunes. One critic wrote of the EP with admiration, concluding, 'She keeps right on thrilling.'

That night had been a barnstorming performance from Adele, with the usual banter including an observation that her ex-boyfriend would probably be watching the show on television. She crowned that thought by raising a middle finger to the cameras. Between songs she sipped on a warm honey drink to help her vocal cords. 'I'd rather be drinking red wine,' she told her fans. She also covered the Bonnie Raitt single 'I Can't Make You Love Me' and the Cure's 'Lovesong', as well as performing plenty of hits of her own. It was a triumphant return to the stage after her illness. 'I'm really relieved,' she later said. 'And it went great and my voice ain't hurting, so I'm really pleased.'

Any doubts that she would return impaired were taken away when she launched into 'Hometown Glory' from the wings. At the end of the first verse, the song paused as she walked on-stage to delighted cheers and screams from her fans. ''Ello!' she said cheekily, before launching back into the song. In doing so, she swiftly encapsulated the contrast between her singing voice and persona and her speaking voice. That was why the audience loved *her*, as well as her ability.

She had been on witty form throughout the set. Having chastised herself for swearing too much between songs, she sure enough managed to swear again soon after taking herself to task. 'I bet I fuck this up,' she said. 'Oh, shit! I swore again, said I wouldn't do it!' When she introduced 'If It Hadn't Been Love', she said, 'It's about shooting your wife – something I've felt like doing to some of my ex-boyfriends.' She also cracked a joke about Beyonce's hair when the superstar had played the previous month at Glastonbury. The audience loved it all. Adele was well aware of how entertaining her between-song chatter was for the audience. She said it was pure nerves that drove her onwards. This loquacious side of her character was one she felt she inherited from her grandmother. 'I get so nervous on stage I can't help but talk,' she said. 'I try. I try telling my brain, Stop sending words to the mouth. But I get nervous and turn into my grandma. Behind the eyes it's pure fear. I find it difficult to believe I'm going to be able to deliver.'

Adele's outspoken chattiness had begun to carry more weight as she moved from star into superstar territory. Her words would garner so much attention and discussion that they would sometimes place her at the centre of a media storm. This was just one of the costs of fame. Luckily for Adele, she felt fairly comfortable at her newfound level of celebrity.

CHAPTER EIGHT

FAME'S MANY FACES

Some pop stars can go years without dipping their toes into controversy or without saying anything remotely amusing or insightful. On a good day, Adele can scarcely go a paragraph without entertaining and provoking. It is as if all the personality and opinion lacking in bland pop stars was handed in full to Adele. Witness her robust remarks about taxation in 2011: 'I'm mortified to have to pay 50 per cent,' she said. 'While I use the NHS, I can't use public transport any more. Trains are always late, most state schools are shit and I've gotta give you, like, four million quid – are you having a laugh?'

This was truly headline-grabbing talk. To say the world was not bursting with sympathy would be an understatement. That de facto 21st-century barometer of the public mood, Twitter, featured outbursts against Adele from angry users. 'That quote from Adele moaning about her tax bill and slagging off public schools has really pissed me off,' read one. Another user wrote: 'Got my paycheque today. Looking at the amount I take home after tax and national insurance is just depressing.' Other users were more succinct, describing Adele as 'silly'. Music fans rarely fall over with sympathy when they hear popular artists complain about the trappings of fame. But Adele was hardly alone. When U2 moved their business interests out of Ireland and in doing so reduced their tax bills, many were disgusted. Some protestors even disrupted live performances by the Irish rock giants. The Rolling Stones spent time in the south of France to avoid British tax. Non-musical stars to complain about tax have included actor Michael Caine and Formula 1 driver Lewis Hamilton.

It's not something that appeals to fans. As far back as the Beatles in the 1960s with their track 'Taxman', and the Kinks who also complained in song about high tax rates, audiences have rarely taken well to bands complaining about money. This highlights a wider issue facing wealthy musicians – how to stay in touch with the masses of fans who dipped into their pockets to hand them that haul. One of the challenges for musicians is to continue speaking, and singing, sentiments that do not alienate them from their fans. In Adele's case, the press, naturally, went to town on the comments. The media is so frustrated by the tendency of many celebrities to dodge controversy that, when one does speak out on an issue, journalists leap all over the story. A *Guardian* writer tackled each section of Adele's outburst. On the NHS, he reminded Adele that unless taxes were paid it would disappear. As for public transport, he argued that, as she had said she does not use it, the complaint about late trains was hollow. He argued that recent statistics showed most state schools are not 'shit' and that it was tax revenue that prevented them from becoming so.

The traditionally right-wing *Daily Telegraph* was more sympathetic. James Delingpole noted, 'Adele, your openness, fearlessness and integrity puts the rest of your industry to shame.' Such support was rare, though. Many pointed out that Adele's musical career had been helped by the fact she attended the state-funded BRIT School. The *Daily Mirror*'s iconic columnist Tony Parsons wrote, 'Everybody loves Adele – until she starts talking about tax.' But he wasn't exactly in the opposing camp. Like many of the more reasoned observers at the time, he understood how someone paying 50 per cent tax could be frustrated by such a burden. He also dismissed those who were suggesting that Adele could leave the country if she did not like it. After all, he said, she would then be making no tax contribution at all.

Perhaps the most supportive voice, and almost certainly the most surprising one, came from the thinktank the Adam Smith Institute (ASI). The fact that such an august organisation was even discussing Adele showed how widely the ripples from her comments had spread. The ASI said that there was nothing strange in Adele's feelings and that they were shared by many Brits across the social spectrum. 'There are lots of people out there who wonder why they have to cough up so much of the money they earn just to pay for late trains and bad schools,' it said. 'Welcome to the club, Adele.'

The storm that had been created was not entirely fair. Adele had built her career the hard way and from humble roots. Her nature was in no way greedy at all, as those closest to her have attested. She has shared her success, in all senses of the word, with her loved ones. As well as supporting her mother, she has helped out other family members and has taken time out from her fame, turning down lucrative offers, to spend afternoons with her old friends. Her long-term aspirations, too, seemed to show a genuine character less interested in money than she was in happiness and sincerity. 'I feel like I'm here to be a mum,' she has said. 'I wanna look after someone and be looked after, give my all to someone in marriage and have a big family, have a proper purpose.'

The British music scene needs characters and controversy. It would be a sad day if one of our most entertaining and forthright personalities felt intimidated into avoiding sensitive subjects. Journalists who bemoan anodyne celebrities should not jump on those who do put their heads above the parapet or they will find that there will be nobody left to inject a bit of charisma into the music business.

It is worth pausing at this stage to consider the pace at

which the progression in Adele's career and level of recognition was travelling. Unknown at 19, Adele was known in British music circles by the time she turned 20. In the 12 months that followed that anniversary, she became, among music fans, an international star. She managed – through a combination of effort and inherent tendency – to remain as normal as possible amid the changes. For instance, she was not won over by the celebrity restaurants that she had the opportunity to visit. 'I went to the Ivy, I hate it, I think it's shit,' she told interviewer Liz Jones. 'And Nobu. They are all rubbish.' Instead, as we have seen, she said she preferred an afternoon in the park with her longstanding friends. They drank cider, reminisced about old times and generally had a good giggle. In as far as it was possible, it was as if Adele had never become famous. She stuck with her old friends because she did not know any different. To her it was not a question of choosing between her showbusiness friends and her existing ones. There was room for both in her life. She could move in famous circles and also step back into more familiar company.

It wasn't so obvious what room her life had for love in 2011. She had admitted to dating some well-known – but unnamed – people. 'I've been on a few dates with celebrities but I don't like it,' she said. 'You go out and everyone looks at you both. I'm not going to say who. We go to really established places that know how to keep their fucking mouths shut. But then, everyone wants to fuck a celebrity so I wouldn't trust them.'

She was asked what her 'type' of man is, but replied that she prefers to not limit herself in that sense. 'I don't have a type,' she told *Glamour*. 'Never have. Older, but not as in 50. Not younger than me. I'm pretty young so it would be like fucking Justin Bieber! Any colour. Any shape. But they've got to be funny.' Asked to name a famous man she currently fancied, she joined in the royal-wedding spirit that dominated 2011 after Prince William married Kate Middleton. For Adele, it was William's younger brother who carries the most allure. 'I'm after Prince Harry,' she said. 'I know I said I wouldn't go out with a ginger, but it's Prince Harry! I'd be a real duchess then. I'd love a night out with him, he seems like a right laugh.'

Certainly, Harry's more wild and unpredictable ways would have been a good fit for Adele. The thought of cockney, outspoken Adele joining the British monarchy was irresistible. It's a shame it's so unlikely to happen. She also said, in February 2011, that she was beginning to date a funnyman. 'It's early days,' she said of the relationship. 'He wants to be a comedian. He makes me laugh.' Given how hearty and memorable her laugh is, it brought a smile to the lips of many to think of her dating someone who could have her cackling regularly. She added, 'We're still getting on, so, yeah, it's nice.'

What of the rumours linking her in 2011 to rapper Kanye West? Adele and West had first met at the Grammys in 2009. That night, as he presented Adele with an award, he told her that he had cried while listening to her first album. 'I think his honesty threw her because he explained that her lyrics describe the heartache he felt over his mum's death in 2007 perfectly, as well as how he often feels at the end of a relationship.' The stories were sourced to unnamed 'insiders' and so could not be verified one way or the other. 'It's no secret that Adele is happier than she's been in a long time,' said one quoted in *Look*. In fact, the pair had traded public expressions of professional admiration as far back as 2008. Writing on his blog, West had mentioned her song 'Chasing Pavements'. He wrote, 'This shit is dope!'

Adele was touched by this vote of confidence from such a respected musical talent. 'I'm amazed,' she said. 'He's like a megastar. I'd like to collaborate with him too.'

This was far from the only time that she had mentioned a desire to collaborate with another well-known artist. A longstanding feature of her career has been to publicly float the idea of such creative hook-ups. 'I wanna make a bluegrass record so I would like to do that with Jack White,' she said of the White Stripes man she did 'Many Shades of Black' with.

Other acts have independently spoken of wanting to duet with Adele. Hardly surprising, given the scale of critical respect for her and the commercial potential she carries. Alicia Keys was among the interested parties, saying of Adele, 'She is a great lady, I definitely see that there is a strong possibility we will do something together,' she said. However, the rumours that Keys and Adele were having a romantic relationship were dispelled.

'I think my own husband started that rumour,' she joked. She is married to rapper and artist Swizz Beatz. 'He is so excited, we love Adele!'

Beatz confirmed that he was hot on this idea, adding that he did not care whether he or someone else produced such a collaboration – he simply wanted it to happen so he could enjoy the result. 'I just thought that, man, this would be a great moment for both of them because they have amazing styles and they both respect each other,' he said. 'They're fans of each other. So let's make this good for music.' Asked how likely it was that such a duet would really happen, he said, 'We're looking good, we're looking good, we're looking good.'

London-based rapper Wretch 32, who covered 'Someone Like You', also dreamed of collaborating with Adele. 'That would be magnificent, but I think it would be impossible so I don't even want to say it. She is one of the best this country has ever seen,' he said.

Then there was the duo LMFAO, too. 'We'd love to work with Adele,' said Redfu, one half of the Los Angeles team.

Back home in the UK rapper Tinie Tempah said in May 2011, 'We're working on something together. It's going to be something amazing. You'll all hear about it very soon.'

But despite the constant speculation about a host of different duets – some of it prompted by Adele herself – she has herself dampened the excitement by suggesting that any sort of studio-based duet was not on the immediate cards for her. 'I think most duets always go unnoticed and I don't think anyone's ever gonna do one as good as Marvin Gaye and Tammi Terrell,' she said. 'But, saying that, I think Estelle and Kanye on "American Boy" was great and I loved "No Air" by Chris Brown and Jordin Sparks.'

Estelle later spoke with awe of how Adele's music was proving such a hit, describing her as 'winning across the world'. Yet in terms of collaborations in the recording studio, Adele pretty much ruled them out for good. 'I'm not doing any collaborations,' she said. 'I think I ruin collaborations. I love to sing with people live, rather than on record.' However, she added, 'If I could do one with anyone – Robbie? Any day, I love a bit of Robbie.'

She also talked widely about her likes and dislikes, revealing as she did what was at the heart of her musical vision. 'I am in love with Gaga and Rihanna and Drake and all that, but I wouldn't be like, "Let's do a song like [Drake's] 'Find Your Love',"' she told *RWD*. 'I love that Chipmunk and Tinchy [Stryder] and all these lot are doing so well but I hate that they're having to rap over Swedish dance music. I find it really discouraging. I want to make organic music, just me and a band in a room, sticking to my roots. Whether it succeeds or not, at least I can hold my head high.' It was an approach shared by another new young artist, Laura Marling, on her 2010 album *I Speak Because I Can*. 'I'm such a fan of Laura Marling and always was before she even released her first album,' Adele told the BBC. 'She just gets better. She leaves me wanting more and I'm always really curious about her songs. Sometimes I can relate to them but sometimes I don't understand. She constantly leaves me curious. That's what I like in an artist. She really sticks to her guns.' She had been speaking about Marling's music for a few years. Indeed, in 2008, Adele had plugged her during an interview with Digital Spy, quipping that she was doing so for musical credibility. 'She's on my MySpace,' she said. 'She's a brand-new artist – I'm trying to be really cool by mentioning her!' It was a cute, self-deprecating endorsement from a woman who knew her words carried weight, but was not so arrogant as to believe she was some sort of musical prophet.

The rumours of duets persisted, with the most frequently named partner being Beyonce. The American soulstress had vigorously praised Adele, something that she finds hard to come to terms with. 'It's weird,' she said. 'I was meant to meet her at *Saturday Night Live* when I played. She asked for a ticket but then couldn't come – she had to go fly somewhere else. I'm the biggest Beyonce fan! Destiny's Child are my life. They kind of made me not just wanna be plain pop, like [with an] auto-tuned, "effect"ed voice. Hours on end I used to try and copy Beyonce, I love her, I think she's amazing. I love all three of them.'

In 2011, Beyonce had been the surprise headliner at the Glastonbury Festival at the end of June. She might have been thought too mainstream to play such an alternative event, but once there she absolutely commanded the stage, capturing the imagination of the audience on the night and the millions following it from home.

Were it not for laryngitis, claimed the *Sun*, Adele would have joined Beyonce on-stage for a duet. Adele had talked about the throat condition after the Brits earlier in the year and now it meant she had to turn down Beyonce's offer. 'Adele was absolutely gutted, Beyonce is one of her big heroes. It would have been the stuff of dreams to perform with her – the gig of her life. But docs have told her she's got to rest her voice or risk damaging her prized asset. She hopes one day they can do something together.' Adele's illness had already affected her latest US tour, which she cancelled earlier in the month with great regret. Yet she was already making plans to reschedule later in the summer when she hoped to be fully restored.

The day after the Glastonbury show, Adele got to hear Beyonce sing at an intimate concert in London's Shepherds Bush Empire. Other famous faces in the crowd alongside Adele included Jessie J, Tinie Tempah, Gwyneth Paltrow, Jay-Z and cast members from the television show *Glee*. The star-studded guest list also included Ewan McGregor, Alexandra Burke, Stella McCartney, Sugababes star Jade Ewen, JLS singer JB and Paloma Faith. Adele looked fantastic in a low-key way, as was appropriate for a gig in a small former theatre. She wore a long black blazer, matching leggings and an understated multi-coloured top. Jessie J was more striking: her multi-coloured top was louder than Adele's and she was also on crutches due to a broken foot. All the same, the arrival of Adele, Jessie and Tempah provoked a storm in the venue. 'It's safe to say that the crowd practically threw up on themselves with excitement,' wrote the *Mirror*'s showbiz correspondents of that moment.

It wasn't the first time that Adele had seen Jay-Z on his trip to the UK. 'Jay has been making the most of his trip over here,' ran one report. A key part of that fun was meeting with our heroine. 'It's not often he is overwhelmed by people when he meets them, but Adele was on top form as usual. She talked him under the table. He was chuckling all the way through their chat. He told her he was going to Glastonbury and she gave him a guide of what to see. She said he must catch Paolo Nutini. She said he was the must-see act of the festival.'

On-stage at Shepherds Bush, Beyonce was on fine form. She opened her set with 'Run the World (Girls)' and at the end of it she included hits such as 'Listen', 'Single Ladies (Put a Ring on It)' and 'Halo'. 'You'll have to forgive me because I'm still high from yesterday,' she told Adele and the rest of the crowd. Then she did her cover of the Queen hit 'Bohemian Rhapsody'. 'You know what? There was a song I was supposed to do, but didn't have time. It's called "Bohemian Rhapsody".'

It had been a wonderful night for all in attendance. Just as Adele was said to be excited to see and meet some of the celebrities in the audience, so some of them were overawed to meet her. Gwyneth Paltrow announced on Twitter that she had 'swooned' when she met the singer.

The following morning, as Adele reflected on a great evening out, news came of her part in another record-breaking achievement. The number of digital albums sold in the UK in 2011 reached the 10 million mark in record time, new data from the official charts company showed. Adele was the key player in this statistic, selling more than 600,000 digital albums, with *21* becoming the first album to pass the 500,000 downloads mark. On the same day, further good news came for her from the other side of the world. Despite the fact that she had never so much as set foot in Australia, let alone performed there, she reached No 1 in both the singles and album charts Down Under when 'Someone Like You' knocked LMFAO's 'Party Rock Anthem' off the top.

The news came hot on the heels of another stunning milestone in the US. The return of *21* to the top of the Billboard Top 200 in June 2011 made it the first UK album this century to clock up ten weeks at No 1, while 'Rolling in the Deep' also became the second-longest Hot 100 chart topper by a British female in history.

As more and more stories broke around Adele, the rock band Linkin Park recorded a live acoustic cover of 'Rolling in the Deep' in Germany. They had performed it first on television and then reprised it at the iTunes Festival in London in July 2011. The performance came as part of a five-song encore that was greeted with wild cheers. Former Pussycat Dolls singer Nicole Sherzinger has also covered the song during a private concert in Monaco.

On and on came the good news for Adele. In July, 'Someone Like You' became the first single of the decade to sell more than a million copies.

For her part, Adele revealed that her own playlist in 2011

included the eponymous album by Bon Iver: 'I'm pretty convinced it's my record of the year already,' she wrote on her blog. 'You know when someone's life flashes before their eyes in a film, and every memory flashes before their eyes. It happens when you listen to him sing, but you survive it!' She closed the post with a plea to her fans. 'Please listen if you haven't already. So, so special! The soundtrack to my heart.'

There was no doubt that praise by Adele for the American indie-folk singer's work boosted his sales. Given the scale of her fanbase, an endorsement from Adele was a valuable thing.

In mid-July, *21* became the biggest-selling digital album of all time in the US. Just one week after Eminem's *Recovery* had become the first album to sell one million digital copies, *21* overtook it to claim a significant milestone. There was a pleasing sense of a full-circle here. Having launched her career via online formats such as MySpace, Adele was now the queen of online sales in America. As a US music industry figure commented, her appeal straddled several demographics, from the kids who digitally downloaded individual tracks to older, more considered customers who bought a full album. However, the commentator described her as being first and foremost a 'full-package artist', meaning that many of those who enjoyed her singles felt compelled to explore and purchase her entire body of work. This explained the sustained commercial performance of both her albums. As she became the biggest-selling digital artist in US history, *21* returned to the top of the conventional charts in Britain.

Putting Adele's fortunes into a wider context, it is worth noting that, alongside Beyonce and Lady Gaga, she was standing at the centre of a female revolution in pop. For many years, it was boy bands that seemed to rule the roost in the charts. Then came young Justin Bieber, whose terrifying level of popularity only underscored the fact that a pretty male face was a sure-fire winner in the pop charts. However, it has since been female acts – and particularly the terrific trio of Adele, Beyonce and Gaga – that increasingly called the shots in the charts. After considering their combined influence, popularity and commercial clout, one can then look at the talent of those who are just behind them in the race: the likes of Rihanna, Leona Lewis, Katy Perry and Nicole Scherzinger. This was *true* girl power.

Among all these records, milestones and other developments, Adele was still doing what mattered most to her fans: performing. In May, she played in New York, at the Beacon Theatre in the Upper West Side. One reviewer described Adele, who kicked off with a particularly lively rendition of 'Hometown Glory', as 'dynamic and graceful, delivering casual augmentations to her songs that suggest her musical ease'. Commenting on the ever-entertaining between-song chatter, the reviewer noted her 'cheeky, unpretentious presence between songs, dancing self-consciously and glibly dissing that idiot ex-lover who inspired *21*'s sad couplets'. It had been a mixed audience and among the comments overheard by the reviewer was: 'I'm gonna buy this album and send it to that asshole... and also my boyfriend.' As the crowd left at the end of the night, some were crying, some were whistling, some were smiling. Everyone, it seemed, was moved profoundly in one way or another.

Significantly, she also appeared at the GAY nightclub in London after the gay pride festival. It was particularly important because Adele had said how she adored her gay friends and gay fans alike and seemed at ease in front of the crowd. By the time she sang 'Someone Like You', the atmosphere was one of enormous emotion and mutual admiration. The audience sang along with every word, through both the choruses and the verses. When she sang about finding 'someone like you', she pointed at the audience as she sang 'you'. She had, with exaggeration for comic effect, said that all her friends are gay and added that she played the role of something of a mentor to them. 'My sex life's pretty lonely but I've got a lot of drama in my life,' she told gay magazine *Attitude*. 'I'm like the agony aunt, they're always coming over my house at four in the morning in tears.'

Meanwhile, the good news just kept coming as it was revealed her name had been mentioned in the context of some prestigious events. There was even talk that she would have a special role at the 2012 Olympics in London. And it was Adele who was installed as the bookmakers' favourite to sing the theme for the next James Bond film. She was the 3/1 favourite, with Beyonce and Leona Lewis behind her. Her track 'Someone Like You' had been coveted by filmmakers of all genres and it seemed perfect for a big-screen outing. Adele was in no hurry to close such a deal and said she would be particular about where it might go. 'I'm holding out for an amazing indie movie,' she said. 'It's a bit too personal, that song, I'm not giving it to fucking Hollywood.' More specifically, when asked if she would like a song of hers to appear in a certain, popular vampire series, she said, 'I don't wanna be on *Twilight*.'

With the popularity of big stage productions with their flash and sometimes gaudy costumes and other promotional gimmicks, Adele was a refreshing reminder that there is no need for anything else when the song is superb and the voice delivering it is also special. We are reminded of her performance at the Brits in 2011, when it was just her and a piano on the stage. The following day, it was Adele that people remembered over the huge productions of Take That and others. 'My music's not stylised – it's not sold by image or by my sexuality or aloofness or anything like that,' she said. 'I think it would be really bizarre if I started doing gimmicks and stunts – it wouldn't suit my music.' It was entirely in keeping with her principled stand that she was uncomfortable with any idea of her music being snapped up by corporations or brands. And yet this was something that many artists did as a matter of course. Selling a song to a company to be used for an advertisement was a massively profitable venture. Indeed, with much music being downloaded illegally, it was one of the few ways remaining to make serious money. While such deals are undoubtedly big payers, these associations damage credibility in the eyes of some purists.

Speaking of artists who she thinks have 'sold out' by going down the endorsement route, Adele said, 'I think it's shameful, when you sell out I think it's *really* shameful. I have become a brand myself and I ain't doing shit that people will be, like, "Why's she done that?" It depends what kind of artist you wanna be but I don't want my name anywhere near another brand ... I found it really unnecessary, there was no need.'

She was equally opposed to the other money-spinning sidelines that some artists are tempted by, including having their music released in deluxe formats. This can often take the form of the original album with a few B-sides and perhaps a demo or live track thrown in. For a record company, this was a great way of increasing revenue from an album. Adele herself expressed her strong disapproval with her own label when they released such a version of her breakthough *19*. She said any act who exploited the deluxe album route would be a 'fucking desperado'. Indeed, she feared that releases ultimately alienate a performer from their following. 'B-sides don't make a record because they're shit, do you know what I mean?' she told *Q* magazine. 'Just muggin' off your fans! I've bought deluxe ones and I'm "These songs are shit!" And it makes you not love 'em as much, "You're muggin' me off!"'

Adele had never forgotten the feelings she had way back

when she was just a fan herself, even as she acquired millions of fans of her own. Her policies on what she would and would not do as an artist were clearly defined. For instance, Adele vowed that she would not perform at any major outdoor festivals again. 'The thought of an audience that big frightens the life out of me,' she said. 'I don't think the music would work either.' She felt her material was too slow and mellow to work for a festival audience. As someone who attended festivals as a fan, she made the call about ballads at festivals by following her own tastes and instincts. Unless it was Coldplay on the bill, she did not want to hear any ballads or slow music. Indeed, when she was in the crowd, it was sometimes in a dance music tent. Similarly, just as she wouldn't play to large festival crowds, she also preferred not to play at London's massive O2. Her tour promoters had attempted to sell the idea to her by pointing out that playing at smaller venues entailed more dates and more travelling. She told them, 'I'd rather do 12 years at the Bar Fly [a tiny north London venue] than one night at the O2!' She added that, having made so many strict decisions about what she will or will not do, she was at peace. For her, these were the choices that she has had to make to remain happy in her own career and life. She accepted that 'some people think I'm mad', but for her that was fine.

There were a few offbeat exceptions to her firm rule. As a big fan of the long-running Australian soap opera *Neighbours*, she harboured a dream of one day appearing on the soap and performing a cameo song alongside the stuffy Harold Bishop, played by Ian Smith. 'I love *Neighbours* and especially Harold,' the singer said. 'He plays the tuba so I'd love to ask him to play on some of the tracks. In return I could do a cameo on *Neighbours* like Lily Allen did. But I have to overcome my fear of flying all that way first.' Having been in *Ugly Betty*, a part in *Neighbours* would be perfectly suited to Adele. After all, this was the woman who defined her Christmas by what happened on the festive soaps.

Meanwhile, the nominations and awards just kept on coming. In July 2011, it was announced that Adele's songs were up for no less than seven categories in the MTV video music awards, including Video of the Year award. In that slot she was up against Katy Perry, for the 'Firework' promo. The two ladies were also to go head-to-head in six other categories – Best Female Video, Best Pop, Art Direction, Cinematography, Directing and Editing. Other key nominees included Kanye West, Beyonce, Eminem, Thirty Seconds to Mars and Nicki Minaj. Adele described herself as 'flabbergasted' by the news of her nominations and offered 'huge props to Sam Brown the director of "Rolling in the Deep"'. She was quickly booked to perform during the awards ceremony, joining the likes of Chris Brown and Lil Wayne on the bill.

The same week, she learned she had been nominated for a yet more prestigious honour: a Mercury Prize for *21*. She faced competition from PJ Harvey and Elbow and nine other acts. 'I'm unbelievably chuffed to be nominated for the Mercury. Thank you so, so much, totally unexpected,' she wrote on her blog. 'I found out yesterday on my way home from Paris.' She added her best wishes to the other nominees and her 'own nod' to indie band Wild Beasts.

Reaction to Adele's nomination was not without controversy. This was not surprising in itself, as dissenting voices are part of the tradition of the annual announcement of Mercury nominees. This time, it was suggested that it was wrong to include Adele in the nominees because, they argued, she had already received enough critical and commercial support and the awards that often follow both. Why include such a celebrated and decorated album?

These doubters misunderstood the essence of the Mercury Prize. Since its inception in 1992, when it was won by indie band Primal Scream, it has existed solely to champion UK music and nominations are made on the basis of the quality of music alone. Both unknown and successful acts are therefore absolute equals as far as the panel is concerned. This is why, in recent years, obscure and accomplished acts alike have won. For every unknown, such as Antony and the Johnsons and Speech Debelle, there were recipients at the height of their powers, such as Franz Ferdinand and Arctic Monkeys.

The cultural debate on the merit of Adele's inclusion took place as bookmakers drew up their own lists of who they thought most likely to win. Adele was the favourite, her odds just shorter than those for PJ Harvey with *Let England Shake*. As discussion over Adele's inclusion continued, perhaps people were losing sight of the scale of Adele's achievements and their impact on the music industry.

Whatever she does, whatever musical genres she considers or tries, Adele will always be able to fall back on some basic facts which set her ahead of the pack. One of the key producers of *21*, Rick Rubin, probably put it best. He said, 'She doesn't carry any of the baggage of many of today's pop stars and it truly is about the music first and her voice and her lyrics and baring her soul with what she's saying. I would say what she makes is her art, and at no time does it feel like product.'

This sense of sincerity in her work was indeed a powerful asset for Adele. The 21st century so far has been dominated by cultural scepticism. People no longer believe that pop stars are truly singing live on stage, others doubt the authenticity of the reality-television contests that launch new acts ever year. In an era where trust is at such a premium, Adele has been one act that people feel they can believe in.

It would be hard not to feel love for a person who could be so entertaining in interviews. Her chirpy voice, raucous laughter and ability to constantly go into random streams of consciousness positioned her a million miles from those pop stars whose undoubted good looks are not matched by their personality. For instance, an Australian interviewer once asked Adele how difficult it was to get up and out of bed early in the morning to fulfil a promotional slot on breakfast television. Before long, Adele was off on one of her conversational riffs and turning in all sorts of directions as she did so. 'I love a card. You know, cards? At birthdays? I collect them. There's this place in London, in Soho, does the best cards. Upstairs. My friend took me, she knows I love a card. Downstairs. A sex dungeon. Oh my *gawd*, the toys. All my best mates are gay, they love it. I've seen things... nothing like *this*. My eyes were watering.' Let us hope she never changes.

Adele herself has said one of the most important benefits of her career was that it allowed her the freedom to include her friends in her journey. On BBC Radio 1, she told Chris Moyles and his listeners, 'I flew my friends out to New York and I made them come to all the shows. I think they were a bit bored by the end. I get to share it with my friends, which is really nice and I never got to do that before. I don't like talking about it when I come home, because all I ever do is talk about what I do. So I like to just be normal with my mates.'

She will also hopefully remain entirely star-struck by artists she admires. Adele regularly provoked excitement aplenty in fans and admirers who have encountered her in person. She understood these reactions – because she still has them herself. On just one evening out in America, she saw a galaxy of stars she either admired, fancied or both. Her excitement and nerves were palpable in these words. 'I was sitting about five rows from [Etta James] at the Fashion Rocks [concert] in New York – nearly died, nearly fainted,' she said. 'Justin [Timberlake] was about two rows in front of me and I could smell him and he smelled amazing. Rihanna was really nice about me in a British interview she did, so I was going to walk over and say, "Hi, Rihanna, I'm Adele," but I got too nervous. I've got the biggest crush on Chris Brown and he was all oiled and all moisturised, he looked so perfect. I didn't say "hello" to anyone.'

A vocal minority have suggested that the reason white soul singers do so well in the British pop charts is because of an inherent racism in the industry and society at large. People point at Adele, Amy Winehouse and Duffy as proof – white girls singing black music. 'I think it is a very valid point and, if it is the case, I think it's disgusting,' said Adele. 'But, having said that, I don't think it is the case. I think, if you're good, you get heard. Whether you're black, white, Indian or whatever, I think, if you make a good enough record that people believe in, they will push it.' She accepted that the fact that 'a Jewish girl, a ginger girl and a Welsh girl' were all dominating a black genre was 'weird', but argued it was not for sinister reasons.

Adele has showed no signs of letting negativity slow her down, but not all her plans have been musical. 'In five years' time I'd like to be a mum,' she said in 2008. 'I want to settle down and have a family, definitely sooner rather than later.' She has also spoken of moving to Nashville, Tennessee, to learn about country music. There she would get a chance to truly immerse herself in the genre. She was in the US when she conceived her second album and the effect of America was plain for all to hear. It could be similarly interesting for her to work in Nashville. 'I might take a few years out and see what it's like, for my third album or something,' she said.

Yet she missed the UK when she was overseas, even when she was only away for a few weeks. It wasn't uncommon for her professional commitments to last longer than that – they frequently ran into months on end. Adele would get particularly homesick for very specific brands such as Lenor fabric conditioner, Flora sandwich spread and, more generally, gherkins. She may have become big in America and beyond but she remained a Brit at heart.

So, she said, perhaps she would end up staying at home to record the record – quite literally, for she is planning to have a studio built in her house. As before, this was as much to do with keeping control as anything. 'I want to write it all, record it all, produce it all and master it on my own,' she said. 'I think it'll take a lot longer because I want to do it this way. When I move house in the summer, my sound engineer is going to come and help me install a studio and teach me how to use it.'

Given the slight, smooth transition in genre between *19* and *21*, lots of people wonder what new influences and styles will be heard on her third album. During a chat with *Rolling Stone*, she joined in the speculation with a typically humorous, stream of consciousness response. 'I think I might make a hip-hop record, because all I'm listening to is Nicki Minaj and Kanye West and Drake and stuff like that,' she said. 'No, I doubt I'll make a hip-hop record. I don't think I'd have the swagger to get away with it, not with this accent anyway. It would be annoying. It would be like a kind of sketch show if I did it.' So we can rest assured that Adele won't be rapping about her homies or wearing neck-straining gold chains any time soon.

She has also said that she would never make a full-on country album. Pop was a genre she was a little more tempted towards. However, the huge stage productions which seem to be more or less compulsory in modern pop, particularly for female stars, put her off. 'I don't like productions,' she said. 'I feel [more] comfortable just standing on a stage with a piano than with a band and dancers and routines and sparkly lights... I'd love to do it, but the thought of it just makes me want to jump off a building.'

She issued teasing comments about the third album 'I have five tracks ready to go,' Adele revealed in May 2011. 'One of them is quite upbeat – a real "girl power" type of song.' She added that she might cover the INXS track 'Never Tear Us Apart', saying it 'is probably my fave song of all time'. Her final remark about the work in progress was: 'The whole album will have quite a live feel to it.' The public awaited it with feverish expectation.

She managed her own expectations carefully when it came to how well the next album would perform on the market. 'I'm not expecting my next record to be as big as this record,' she said, referring to *21*'s gigantic sales. 'That's impossible.' She said that it would be extremely helpful to her writing process to meet another man and have similar dramas to those which inspired her first two albums. 'I fucking hope I meet someone in that time so I'll have something to write about,' she said. 'But if I'm happy, I don't think I'll be writing another album at all!'

These statements proved challenging for Adele's fans: on the one hand they crave more musical material from their heroine, yet which true fan would want her to endure unhappiness?

Perhaps the answer would be for Adele to make a break with tradition and write material from a happy place. The lady herself was unconvinced such a scheme could work. 'It would be fucking awful if my third album was about being happily settled down and maybe on my way to being a mum,' she said. But neither does she want to become the cliched successful music artist who, after becoming rich and famous, writes about the supposed 'challenges' of celebrity. Such songs inevitably fail to strike a chord with their fans who cannot relate to the lifestyle of the international superstar. 'I get annoyed when all singers write about is cars, limos, hotels, boring stuff like missing home, complaining,' she said. 'I have a real life to write about.' At the same time, she would obviously not destroy a fruitful relationship in order to create new material about a broken love. 'Not yet, maybe about ten records in,' she quipped. 'If something is only all right, I make it into a bad thing. I won't if it's really good.'

Although she had become a symbol for many heartbroken women, it might be inaccurate to describe Adele as any sort of martyr figure. While she was open about how much men have hurt her, she did not paint herself as an entirely blameless figure in her failed relationships. Indeed, nobody was quicker to list Adele's failings than the lady herself. 'I used to think I was such a great girlfriend but I'm not at all, I have my flaws as well,' she said. 'I expect too much. At the time I don't realise that. I expect too much but never tell them. I'd never say, "Look, I'd really like it if you did this for me." I always moan about it but never tell them to their face. And if someone goes, "Why don't you just tell him what you want?" I'll be, like, "Well he should be able to pick it up, to sense it." I can be stubborn, very, very stubborn, but only in my relationships. I think everything I do is golden, I think I'm Princess Diana.'

Similarly, it would be wrong to describe Adele the person as a musical purist or snob. Some chin-stroking musos have expressed admiration for her classic sound and low-key stage performance but, as we have seen, Adele – as a fan – always loved the sort of music such commentators contrast her with. 'I adore get-your-tits-out music,' she said memorably. 'Katy Perry, Rihanna, Britney Spears and Kylie are all great girls and delivering top music. It's just that I'm not the right fit to perform like that so I'm going down my own path. I'm a huge fan of pop music. I love it. I don't listen to music like my own. I just seem to click with acoustic, honest and moving music.'

There is something admirable about an artist eschewing a golden opportunity to take the cultural high ground and instead speaking with such believable admiration of acts such as Perry and Rihanna. Were she to turn on them, she would have plenty of admiring ears. That was not Adele's style, though. Neither does one have the sense she was merely being polite. Her happy-go-lucky personality was indeed more fitting of someone in the pop world.

Adele's music could go on to define the second decade of the 21st century. Musically, the first ten years were dominated by reality-television acts and indie bands. Some of those artists, in both categories, were admirable. Leona Lewis, Girls Aloud and Alexandra Burke all gave reality television a good name, while the Strokes, the Libertines and Arctic Monkeys were fine examples of indie rock. However, for each of these admirable six acts, there were countless poor imitations. As the two movements became bandwagons, the public grew tired of each. Who better to refresh our enthusiasm than Adele? Tired of bland, playing-it-safe mediocre reality acts? Adele was enormously talented, bursting with personality and entirely unafraid of ruffling a few feathers with her opinions. Meanwhile, Adele was in all senses a contrast to the bandwagon of skinny young men desperately trying to recapture the excitement of the early years of the Strokes. Though she began by being compared to Amy Winehouse, Adele has simply eclipsed all. She remains, as one influential music magazine put it, simply too magical to be compared to anyone.

The scale of her influence can be seen in how popular her songs have become among the hopefuls who audition for the *X Factor* and other reality-television contests including

American Idol. On the latter show, contestant Haley Reinhart performed 'Rolling in the Deep'. A long line of wannabes throughout the 2010 season also announced that the song they wanted to sing to showcase their talent was '"Make You Feel My Love", by Adele'. Putting aside the fact that it was a cover version of a song originally written and sung by Bob Dylan, the sheer number of times the request was heard made it harder for producers to create a balanced show.

Adele continued to prove to be a popular choice when auditions began for the 2011 series – and the standard of performance didn't always do her material any favours. 'This year the contestants have been mostly murdering Adele,' revealed host Dermot O'Leary during filming.

Indeed, so tired of poor attempts at Adele's music did everyone become that new host Gary Barlow took to directly questioning whether contestants had another option. 'Are you sure that's wise?' he asked yet another singer who announced an intention to cover Adele.

Long-serving host Louis Walsh was of the same mind. 'So far it's been Adele overkill,' he said during a break in filming. 'I love her, she's fabulous – but you have to be really good if you are going to take on an Adele song. Most people just aren't up to the task.'

Soon, the judges and producers considered imposing a moratorium on Adele covers.

However, when a reality-show contestant does justice to an Adele song, it makes for captivating television. Two acts who had successfully covered Adele on UK reality shows were Rebecca Ferguson and Ronan Parke. In the 2010 series of the *X Factor*, Ferguson sang 'Make You Feel My Love' during the live finals. Her rich, soulful voice delivered the song well. It was one of the less vulnerable performances that runner-up Ferguson gave. Walsh was impressed: 'I can definitely see you getting a recording contract.'

Even Simon Cowell was full of admiration. 'That was absolutely fantastic,' he said, adding that she could become an 'ambassador for Britain'.

The following year, in *Britain's Got Talent*, 12-year-old singer Ronan Parke also covered 'Make You Feel My Love'. It was surprising that such a young contestant could so brilliantly sing such a song. 'It was effortless,' said judge Amanda Holden.

Simon Cowell added, 'I have to say that you totally and utterly nailed that. I tell you what, if Adele's watching now I think she'd be really happy.'

Adele herself is aiming for more happiness in all aspects of her life after enduring the contrasting twin narratives of huge success and terrible heartache. Among other plans on the horizon for her in the summer of 2011 included a crack at giving up meat. 'I'm trying to be veggie,' she said in July. 'Whenever I'm about to eat meat I always see my little dog's eyes.' She also revealed that she had tried to give up smoking. Despite the fact that her time away from tobacco improved her voice, she had eventually decided that life without cigarettes was not a price worth paying. 'I gave up smoking for two months,' she said in June. 'It was fucking grim. I had laryngitis about a week before the album came out and it was so frightening. I stopped smoking, drinking, eating or drinking citrus, spicy foods or caffeine. It was so fucking boring. When my album went to [UK] No 1 and in America, I just sat in my room and watched telly because I couldn't go out and talk to anyone! My voice was better when I wasn't smoking. Within a week I noticed it had changed, but I'd rather my voice be a bit shit so I can have a fucking laugh!'

She was aware that she is a role model to many. Mothers often approach her in the street to tell her that they are so happy that their daughters are fans of her. For Adele, this brought with it a weight of responsibility that she was not entirely at ease with. 'It's a bit worrying,' she admitted. This goes a long way to explaining her down-to-earth personality, and refusal to take herself at all seriously during her media appearances. 'Sometimes I get letters from people asking me to sign wedding photos because their first dance was to "Make You Feel My Love" and I start crying and then I'll sign them,' she said.

Adele remains a reluctant hero and one who is keen to knock over any pedestals her fans might have in mind for her. She continues to be uncomfortable with some parts of being famous – particularly the stranger elements of those who follow her. 'The other day I was up north and there were these – well, I don't think they were fans actually, they were like eBayers,' she told the *Sun*. 'I'd be at the venue, they'd be there. I'd leave the venue and they'd be there. Then they started taking pictures of my dog doing a shit and stuff like that. It was really weird. I was on my own taking Louis out for a walk. One of them just got in the lift with me and I got really panicky. Luckily there was a cleaner on the floor I was on. I was just thinking – imagine being someone like Cheryl Cole or Katy Perry or Gaga, where you've got to be conniving to have a normal day. That scares the life out of me. I don't think I'd be able to carry on doing music if it got to that point. I don't think it ever will – I don't think I'm the kind of artist where that will happen.'

Away from her career, the urge to continue to be a genuine person was high on her priority list. She has spoken of loathing the idea of fame changing her as it has so many other stars. She has insisted that she has never been more normal than she has been since becoming a worldwide celebrity. She is a sharp woman, though, and so is more than familiar with the traps that lie ahead. Occasionally, she has said, she would find herself momentarily acting up. One day, during a long and draining photo shoot, she found herself sitting up a ladder, smoking a cigarette. When she accidentally dropped it, she asked one of her team to pick it up and return it to her. Her request was given short shrift and denied.

She still tries to ignore both the praise and the criticism that her music has been met with. At this stage in her career, it is praise that almost exclusively comes her way, although there has been some criticism and she is fully aware that in times there might be more. For any artist, the healthiest response is to shrug off both praise and criticism as far as possible. 'That stuff goes right over my head,' she said. 'I'm 22. So those things don't really interest me! I just love singing, innit?' she said. 'I mean, I'm really proud of making some people really proud in England. I've never seen my mum so happy. She's like, "Oh, well, this is just ridiculous now, surely not, fuck off Adele." It makes me... really emotional actually. It's pretty overwhelming. It's very extreme. I wasn't ever expecting any success like this,' she said.

Those who hope Adele will never change the basic parts of her character that make her such an admirable and attractive soul will be relieved to learn that she is determined to not let fame alter her. During her years as a celebrity, she has observed other famous people who have become fake or arrogant as a result of their popularity and riches. She has said she hopes never to become like that and even has a plan if she felt she was starting to. 'I've met people I admire and people I don't admire who are completely affected by their success, and I fucking hate them,' she said. 'There's so many people who believe their own hype and treat people like shit and if I was ever like that I would absolutely stop doing what I'm doing for a while and go and find myself again. I find it grotesque when people change because of it, but maybe it's because they're not as good at keeping in contact with the people who love them for a reason.'

CHAPTER NINE

GRAMMY GRABBING

In October 2011, Adele faced the biggest challenge of her career to date when a dogged medical condition forced her to cancel her US tour. The problem was the vocal cord haemorrhage that had been troubling her for some time. It was something that no doubt would have infuriated her. Some UK dates also had to be cancelled as she reluctantly wiped clean her schedule for the remainder of the year. The fans were disappointed and so was Adele. She announced that she was, in fact, 'devastated' by the cancellation. 'I have absolutely no choice but to recuperate properly and fully or I risk damaging my voice forever,' she explained.

It is easy to imagine the frustration Adele probably felt at this time. Here, the sincerity of her character made the pain all the worse. If she were a less authentic personality, she could have spun the predicament to her advantage by granting a string of rare interviews to the celebrity weeklies over the crisis. In between these crisis chats she could have carefully choreographed paparazzi shots of her. None of this was in her nature, though – she just wanted to be able to sing again.

Ironically, just as her professional future was in limbo, her present could scarcely have been brighter: her albums and concert DVD *Live at the Royal Albert Hall* continued to fly off the shelves. But, in her darker moments, she would have been forgiven for wondering if she would ever record or perform again. Putting aside the financial dimension of the issue, the effect such an outcome would have had on her emotionally is incalculable. 'Singing is my life,' she said. Despite the success and multi-million pound fortune she had gathered, she was hungry for more.

All concerned held their collective breath as, a month later, she underwent laser microsurgery in America. Dark rumours began to circulate online, all unfounded. One was that she was suffering from throat cancer. Soon, it was being suggested that her life itself was under threat. Then Adele revealed that, in fact, the surgery had been a success. She would have to slowly rebuild her vocal confidence – she earmarked February 2012 for a return to live performance – but everything was suddenly peachy. 'I'm doing really well, on the mend, super happy, relaxed and very positive with it all,' she said. 'It's been the most erratic year,' said Adele, looking back over 2011. 'It's been fucking brilliant and exciting and emotional.' Just a bit.

The successful surgery gave Adele a dose of perspective. She went into the treatment thinking and speaking like a woman terrified of losing the momentum of her career and therefore determined to return as soon as possible. However, with the surgery completed and her recuperation underway, she began to express a wish to take some time out, 'and just "be" for a bit'. Although she has thought a lot about her third album – she talked of having a bluegrass vibe on it – she was, in the wake of the surgery, in no hurry to actually start work. 'I'm really looking forward to some time to do nothing,' she said. 'I imagine I'll be 25 or 26 by the time my next record comes out, as I haven't even thought about my third record yet. There will be no new music until it's good enough and until I'm ready.' This statement shocked some of her fans – and Adele had to leap into action to scotch the perception that she intended to disappear for years.

Meanwhile, an unexpected reminder of her appeal was inadvertently gifted to the world by Karl Lagerfield, the elderly fashion designer. He was asked during an interview what he thought of the current crop of female pop stars. 'The thing at the moment is Adele,' he said. 'She is a little too fat, but she has a beautiful face and a divine voice.' There was immediate outrage over his comment about her weight. Lagerfield had horrified much of the public but Adele seemed to be the least upset by it.

'I've never wanted to look like models on the cover of magazines,' she told *People*. 'I represent the majority of women and I'm very proud of that.'

Although Lagerfield subsequently apologised for his remark, his criticism of her weight had served a useful purpose for Adele. She had been out of the public eye for a while. The controversy galvanised the fans afresh behind their heroine. It also reminded the world that, for many of us, Adele was not admired *in spite* of her figure but *because* of it.

Her place in the hearts of the public was confirmed – but everyone still wanted her to return to the frontline as soon as possible. Before undergoing surgery, Adele had issued a defiant rallying cry for the future as far as live performances are concerned. 'I will be back and I'm gonna smash the ball out of the park once I'm touring again,' she vowed.

Her first opportunity to get her plan underway came at the Grammys in February. She was nominated in six categories at the prestigious ceremony, including Record of the Year, Album of the Year, Song of the Year, Best Pop Solo Performer and Best Pop Vocal Album. An amazing, almost imperious list of nominations – and she was widely tipped to make a clean sweep. As Elton John had joked in 2011: 'Next year a large woman will win everything – and it won't be me.'

Expectation buzzed round the industry that she would win all six categories. This prediction would prove correct, but nobody would have expected the tragedy that would occur on the eve of the ceremony and cast a shadow over the evening. Whitney Houston's sudden death, at the age of 48, shook the music industry. At the start of the ceremony, LL Cool J said, 'There is no way around this – we've had a death in our family. So at least, for me, the only thing that feels right is to start with a prayer for the woman that we love, for our fallen sister Whitney Houston.'

However, the show had to go on and the evening was ultimately dominated by Adele, who looked magnificent with a new blonde hairstyle and a sophisticated black dress. She was her usual witty self when she collected her awards. As she accepted the trophy for best pop solo performance for 'Someone Like You', she said: 'Seeing as it's a vocal performance, I need to thank my doctors, I suppose, who brought my voice back.' When she got the Album of the Year award she was in tears, and, in a moment only a Tottenham girl could bring to such a glitzy ceremony, said, 'Oh, I've got a bit of snot!' As her success mounted throughout the evening, she said that she was sad her mother was not present at the ceremony. 'Mum – girl did good,' she said.

The girl had indeed done good. There was an electric atmosphere as the award-laden singer prepared to perform. Many held their breath as she took to the stage to sing 'Rolling in the Deep'. The performance did not begin with its familiar guitar – instead, she sang the chorus a capella first. In that opening 18 seconds her face portrayed a range of emotions from a dreamy distance to raucous ecstasy, cheeky nonchalance and side-gazing suspicion. Talk about charisma. Her voice, to widespread relief, was as strong as ever. She had already laid down a statement and the song proper was only just starting. Adele could scarcely have been more assured and iconic – she looked and sounded sensational. Rihanna and Paul McCartney were among those saluting her from the enraptured, star-studded audience.

Within weeks she was at another leading awards ceremony – the Brits. Following her breathtaking rendition of 'Someone Like You' in 2011, she sang 'Rolling in the Deep' this time. Given that the performance was part of her comeback from surgery, it still held considerable significance, albeit not as emotionally as the previous year. Back then, she had announced her presence to anyone in the nation yet to hear of her. This time, she was the nation's princess, reaffirming her place in our hearts. It was not, though, to be her singing that the nation was discussing the following morning.

Adele won two awards on the night: Best Female Artist and Album of the Year. When she accepted the latter gong, at the climax of the evening, she embarked on an emotional acceptance speech during which she spoke of her pride at being British. 'Nothing beats coming home with six Grammys and then coming to the Brits and winning album of the year,' she said. 'I'm so proud to be flying the British flag for all of you.' It was at that point that host James Corden was forced to interrupt her speech and introduce Blur, who were to see the evening out with a medley of songs. Given the live broadcast of the ceremony, the evening had to run to a tight schedule for ITV.

As a clearly embarrassed Corden sheepishly interrupted Adele's speech, she said, 'Are you about to cut me off? Can I just say then, goodbye and I'll see you next time round.' She then turned away and flipped her middle finger at a section of the audience. She explained later that her gesture had been to the corporate elements of the audience. 'I was about to thank the British public for their support,' she said. 'They cut me off, sorry if I offended anyone but the suits offended me ... that finger was to the suits at the Brit Awards, not to my fans.' The reaction on Twitter suggested that few viewers were offended by Adele's gesture. Many felt that cutting short an artist in her prime was the truly offensive part of the episode.

As the year wore on, more astonishing facts kept emerging. For instance, in the wake of her Grammys triumph, her album *21* spent an appropriate 21st week at the top of the US chart. Meanwhile, three of her singles occupied the Billboard singles chart – making her the first woman in the single chart's history to do so. Then, in Australia, *21* became the longest-running No 1 album in the chart in the 21st century and the second longest-running No 1 of all time. The *Sydney Morning Herald* described her as 'seemingly unstoppable British songstress'.

She was an increasingly wealthy British songstress, too. In April she topped the list of richest young British musicians as her estimated fortune was reported to have soared from £6m to £20m over the previous 12 months. Her nearest rivals on the *Sunday Times* Rich List of young British musicians were Cheryl Cole, Leona Lewis and Katie Melua – each reported to have a comparatively meagre £12m. Times were tough, girls.

Over in the US, Adele made the Top 10 of the Billboard's sixth annual Money Makers ranking. Hot on the heels of this came the news from home that *21* had outsold Michael Jackson's *Thriller*, to become the fifth biggest-selling UK album of all time.

There was a certain swagger in the fact that, when she won 12 awards at the 2012 Billboard Awards in Los Angeles, Adele was not even present to collect them. She had been nominated in a staggering 18 categories including Top Artist, Top Female Artist and Top Pop Artist, all three of which were among the dozen she won.

Adele turned 24 in May 2012. As she celebrated with her boyfriend Simon and other friends, she received a birthday cake in the shape of a bosom sent by the pop star Rihanna. It came adorned with a message that the Barbadian beauty also tweeted to her own followers: 'Happy birthday to my lover, Adele'. At 24 years of age Adele had achieved so much and had so many things to celebrate. Yet by the time of her next birthday she would have something much more significant to smile about.

CHAPTER TEN

SKYFALLER

For an increasing number of modern celebrities, fame is akin to running on a treadmill set to a sharp incline and high speed. Only by relentless, breathless activity, they have come to believe, can they remain in the place the love most: the fickle spotlight of showbusiness. Albums, films, clothing ranges and other projects are released at a prolific rate. In between such spikes, the celebrities continue to grasp for any opportunity to remind the public they exist, however desperate or ungainly those opportunities.

This is a very 21st century phenomenon. Once upon a time, most artists were more confident than that. They essentially disappeared from public life between projects, confident in the knowledge that the quality of their craftsmanship would ensure popularity. Only a small minority of contemporary artists conform to this old-fashioned approach. Chief among them is Adele and the fact that her fame has not been diminished since she went to ground is vindication of her approach. If a theme runs through the events of this chapter – including motherhood, award ceremonies and the prospect of a third album – it is the sense of quiet dignity, privacy and restraint of our heroine.

Not that she has been on an all-out sabbatical. In October 2012, she was back in the charts when 'Skyfall', her title song for the James Bond film, was released. Sony approached her for the project because they hoped she could evoke the sort of power that Shirley Bassey had. Sony Pictures president of music, Lia Vollack, said she admired the 'soulful, haunting, evocative quality' of Adele's voice. Bond actor Daniel Craig also felt she was the right girl for the job, telling a US show: 'When Adele's name came up I just jumped at it, I just said, "We have to get her." I just thought that she has the voice and she's got the tone that we wanted.'

Despite some initial misgivings, she accepted the offer and composed 'Skyfall' with producer Paul Epworth after she read the film's script. The movie has a more sombre undertone than previous Bond outings and Adele felt it was imperative to reflect this in the theme song. It needed, in fact, to be a paradoxical affair and Epworth said he found it 'interesting' to aim to produce a song that was 'simultaneously dark and final, like a funeral, and to try and turn it into something that was not final'. He said the song would have: 'A sense of death and rebirth.'

He has long seen Adele as having an 'an open mind musically'. Yet when she joined him in the studio, he was taken aback by her professionalism, poise and pace. 'Within

10 minutes, she put down most of the vocals,' he told hollywood.com. 'She had the lyrics ready in her head when she drove over. It was the most absurd thing. She's fast, but it was really quite phenomenal.' He was amazed when Adele sang what he called 'the Bassey-esque slurs' of the opening'. He added: 'She has a lot of finesse and skill. She's not just a powerhouse – it's a lot of careful technique. That's why she's an amazing vocalist. It's all control.' The lavish production was enhanced with classic Bond orchestration.

Anticipation of new material from Adele is always huge. Her involvement in the film's soundtrack created excitement as soon as it was rumoured. Those whispers started long before the deal was officially confirmed. The lady herself had hinted at the project during an interview with Jonathan Ross. 'I'm going back in the studio in November, fingers crossed,' she said in 2011. 'Well, this is actually a theme, what I've got to do for, um, wow... That's really giving something away isn't it?'

Once the news was made official, she spoke of the 'instant spotlight and pressure' that comes with agreeing to perform a Bond song. 'But I fell in love with the script and Paul had some great ideas for the track and it ended up being a bit of a no brainer to do it in the end,' she told *The Sun*. 'It was also a lot of fun writing to a brief, something I've never done, which made it exciting.' As the song built from the basics to the rich extravaganza of its final form, it struck Adele just how exciting this project was. She said: 'When we recorded the strings it was one of the proudest moments of my life. I'll be back combing my hair when I'm 60 telling people I was a Bond girl back in the day I'm sure!'

The melody of the opening lines of the verse echoes the classic, central Bond theme, and then Adele's voice, more sultry than ever, joins the arrangement. The song builds into a lively chorus and it continues to grow throughout the track. Backing vocalists join Adele for the second chorus and the strings become stronger and richer throughout. Upon its release in October – her first release proper for nearly two years – it was lavished with praise by the critics. The *Los Angeles Times* said it was 'big' and 'bold', the *Wall Street Journal* felt it had 'sweep' and 'drama', while the Huffington Post concluded that it fitted 'perfectly alongside the work of Shirley Bassey in the oeuvre of James Bond title tracks'. Neil McCormick's review in the *Daily Telegraph* was more nuanced; he described it as 'classy' but 'overly predictable'.

As a promotional gimmick, the single was released for download at 0.07am – as in 007 – on 5 October 2012. The release formed a part of a global James Bond day which marked the 50th anniversary of *Dr No*, the first Bond movie. Adele's song reached the top of the iTunes chart within hours, knocking Rihanna's 'Diamonds' off the perch. It reached UK No 2 in the singles chart, tying with Duran Duran's 'A View to a Kill' as the highest charting Bond theme song. In the US it became her first song to debut in the Top 10 and the first Bond theme to chart in the Top 10 in a decade. As this book first went to the press, the single had sold over five million copies worldwide.

The sales of the song helped Adele to top the next young musicians rich list as her estimated personal fortune soared to £30m. Yet more records sold, and broken, by Adele – but the most significant milestone of her life was just weeks away as *Skyfall* was released. On 19 October, she gave birth to a baby boy. She and Konecki were reported to be 'ecstatic' at the arrival of their son. The couple were keen from the start to avoid making the event into a media circus. Their spokesperson issued a curt message explaining they were 'not releasing a statement at this time'.

Adele's preference not to turn her precious son into a publicity-boosting commodity continued throughout the first year of his life. On the odd occasions that photographers glimpsed her out with her baby she would use a blanket to protect the boy from prying camera lenses as best she could. She kept her son's name officially secret. Asked at a press conference how motherhood had changed her, she merely said: 'I am exhausted, that's how it's changed me. That, and eczema from boiling bottles.' It was only some eight months into the baby's life that the media caught a clear photograph of him, when a paparazzo grabbed the prized snap at New York's Central Park Zoo.

Adele's low-profile approach to fame was done to evade rather than seek cheap recognition, but she got just that when she topped a poll to find the 'celebrity mum of the year'. She was the winner of a celebrity stork award run by Bounty. 'Real mums identify with Adele,' said a spokeswoman. 'They respect the fact that she hasn't fallen for the "fame game" and has done everything she can to keep her son away from the media circus. Mums really seem to appreciate those celebrities who try to raise their families out of the limelight.'

Her true recognition came from awards for her music. As of

the spring of 2012, she had already won over 70 significant awards, including Ivor Novellos and honours at the BRITS and *Billboard* ceremonies. That was a remarkable haul for an artist who was then just 24 years of age and whose career had not yet completed a sixth year. The remainder of 2012 and the first half of 2013, were relatively quiet times for Adele, yet the awards kept coming and her collection swelled both in volume and stature.

At the beginning of 2013, as Britain shivered through a prolonged and hellish winter, Adele was in the sunshine of California, picking up three major awards between the middle of January and the end of February. It was astonishing that after so long out of the limelight, she was still being handed so many top awards.

In January she won a Golden Globe for the *Skyfall* theme. It was her first official public appearance since becoming a mother. When Jennifer Lopez announced the winner, Adele turned to Daniel Craig, who was sitting at her table, and high-fived him. Not for her the tearful theatrics or faux modesty beloved of thespians at such moments. Her acceptance speech, too, was gloriously Adele-esque. It was at once irreverent and respectful; it combined vulnerable human emotion and profanity. 'Oh my God, oh my God,' she said, giggling like a naughty schoolgirl who had just got away with a prank. 'Honestly, I've come out for a night out with my friend. We're new mums. We've literally come for a night out, I was not expecting this. It's very strange to be here – and thank you so much for letting me be part of your world for a night. It's amazing, we've been pissing ourselves laughing at you.'

She then dedicated her award to Konecki, and, her voice almost breaking with genuine emotion, 'my lovely son'. Backstage, she told a press conference that she had always felt she had taken a risk in accepting the challenge of a Bond song. 'I had my child two weeks before the film came out so it was bad timing,' she told them. 'It was such an honour to be involved. Normally I write about my misery and this time I wrote according to someone's script.' It had been an exciting night out for Adele. Her fans were as delighted to see her back in the spotlight as they were over her award itself.

The following month she won an Oscar. She arrived at the ceremony dressed in a stunning, embellished black Jenny Packham gown. Her lightened hair looked magnificent. Her overall look was arguably the most glamorous and radiant she has looked since becoming famous. She sang 'Skyfall' as part of a special tribute to the Bond franchise. It was her first public singing performance for some time, yet there was little sign of nerves as she sang. As she sang the line of dreaming of a particular moment, she pointed meaningfully at the floor, perhaps hinting at how keenly she had anticipated *this* very moment. She owned the stage from the beginning, yet that custodianship seemed to swell more the longer the song went on.

Then it was back to cheeky Adele for a while: as she left the stage, she kicked off her sparkly Louboutin platform shoes. 'I'd pick them up but I can't bend over,' she said, indicating her tight dress. Later, as she accepted the Oscar she was more emotional than she had been at the Globes ceremony. A four-strong panel announced her as winner: Richard Gere, Renée Zellweger, Queen Latifah and Catherine Zeta-Jones. She thanked co-writer and producer Epworth for 'believing in me all the time', and paid tribute to Konecki, who she called 'my man'. Choking back tears, she added: 'Thank you so much, this is amazing'. Epworth then thanked Adele for being 'the best person I've ever worked with'.

Asked backstage how she would be celebrating, she said: 'I think I'm going to the *Vanity Fair* party, so that'll be quite nice. But I've got to get up at 6am so one glass of champagne and I'm gone these days.' Back in the UK, considerable pride was felt that a British singer had won an award at two big awards ceremonies. A fellow British star paid tribute to her, in the form of Elton John. 'She's authentic, she doesn't lip synch, she comes on and she sings, she's the real deal,' he said. 'She's not slick, she's human, she's imperfect, she's what every entertainer should be.' Again, we see how it is her authenticity, that increasingly elusive commodity in show-business circles, which connects with her admirers.

A hat trick was completed at the Oscars as she had also won a Grammy earlier in February. She had been handed the first award of the night – taking the best pop solo performance for 'Set Fire to the Rain'. Jennifer Lopez had, as at the Golden Globes, handed Adele the trophy, both ladies acknowledging the Latino singer was becoming Adele's good luck charm. Adele, who was wearing a red floral number rather than her customary black, later turned from recipient to dispenser when she handed Mumford & Sons the album of the year gong for their record *Babel*.

So it seemed that her step away from the spotlight had done nothing to diminish the affection and esteem she was held in.

Indeed, if anything, respect for her grew. She has become an icon for many people to draw strength from. During 2013, misogyny had become a central issue again, with a growing sense that society has either regressed slightly or had never moved on to the extent people hoped. Television presenter Jameela Jamil cited Adele as a role model as she spoke out against media sexism. 'I use humour to get my point across because you have to fight fire with fire and banter back with men,' said Jamil. 'That's why Adele is a champion. Yes, she's beautiful, but she doesn't sexualise herself to sell records – she lets her talent speak for itself. So many women think if they don't look a certain way they won't do as well. We're apologetic about ourselves before we even begin.' Adele was recognised in a similar way by BBC Radio 4's *Woman's Hour* programme, which included her on its power list of 2013.

Then came the royal seal of approval. In June, it was announced that she was to receive her most prestigious honour to date. She was named an MBE in the Queen's birthday list alongside fellow singer-songwriter PJ Harvey and comedians Rob Brydon and Tony Robinson. Some commentators felt that, at the age of 25 and with only two albums to her name, Adele was too young. However, plenty of others were simply delighted for her. *The Sun*'s headline captured this mood: ONE LIKES YOU, ADELE. *Heat*'s headline was less succinct, but summed up the moment well in its own way: YAY! ADELE ADDS 'MBE FOR SERVICES TO MUSIC' TO HER MASSIVE SHELF FULL OF AWARDS!

Amid the huge affection felt for Adele was the unanswered question of when she would release a new album. Her fans had been patient in their wait for new material and concerts. What with surgery and motherhood, she's had plenty of reason to take a break and step outside the spotlight. Rumours of a new album rubbed shoulders in the media with contrasting reports claiming she was years away from even starting work on her next recording.

When told her fans were keen for a new release, she said: 'Tell me about it, so am I.' Speaking about writing new tracks, meanwhile, she added: 'They'll come when they're ready and when I've got something to sing about.' As she was since she wrote the tracks for *19*, Adele was keen to only write about real things, all the better for producing memorable tracks which make listeners shiver in recognition. Sources close to her say that all she really wants is to be a mother for a while. She is besotted by her boy and he remains her priority. As the saying goes, class is worth waiting for. If this saying is true, then there is no artist on the current scene more worth waiting for than Adele.

CHAPTER ELEVEN

25

What a haunting moment it was when she resurfaced. In October 2015, in the midst of a commercial during the X Factor, a voice emerged softly out of a black screen. 'Hello, it's me...' it sang. Only one singer has pipes like that – so everyone knew right away it was Adele. The long, long wait was over. She was coming back.

She had warned us we were in for a wait. Back in 2011, Adele told *Vogue*'s Jonathan Van Meter she needed a long break from the spotlight. Or, to quote her in full, direct splendour, she told him: 'I am fucking off for four or five years.' And as we have seen that is, more or less, what she did.

Aside from her release of the *Skyfall* title song in the autumn of 2012, and appearances at a clutch of awards ceremonies, she disappeared from public view. As her popularity and success reached stratospheric levels, Adele took one last gaze at the frenzy she had sparked, shrugged her shoulders and sauntered away, leaving a vacuum where she once stood. For her fans, it was a painful departure.

Celebrities have the potential to play so many parts in the lives of their fans that a complete withdrawal is felt deeply. In terms of album releases, Adele's prolonged absence can be measured against the output of other female artists. Between the release of *21* and the autumn of 2015, her fellow female acts were busy: Taylor Swift released two albums (*Red* and *1989*) and became something of a spokeswoman for a generation; Rihanna also tossed out a brace (*Talk That Talk* and *Unapologetic*) and got snapped on the beach a lot; Lady Gaga offered two (*Born This Way* and *Artpop*), while Katy Perry released just the one (*Prism*).

But it is not merely the absence of new music that caused Adele's break to cut so deep. No, what was so special about her hiatus was that she did not bother with the ancillary aspects of her career, either. No interviews, public appearances or cynically engineered publicity stunts were fixed to keep her profile up. Although Adele had once sung: 'Don't forget me, I beg' to a former lover, she was not going to make a similar plea to the public. She rarely even tweeted.

But most of all, she cleaved to a very clear rule: that she would only release new material that she thought improved on the tracks that were on her previous two works. Ever the endeavouring perfectionist, she was only interested in moving forward creatively, not lazily treading water or simply trading on her past popularity. Even if such a stance meant less commercial success, she was not willing to budge at all.

'I won't come out with new music until it's better than *21*,' she said to a mixed reception at her record label. 'I'm not expecting to sell as many records, but I don't want to release shit.' Only having drawn that clear line in the sand could she set about the colossal, bewildering task of bettering *21*, of coming out with an album which improved on one that included such classics as 'Someone Like You' and 'Rolling in the Deep'. The first track to be released from her new album was 'Hello'. Co-written by Greg Kurstin and the lady herself, its whimsical, smoky verses build into a power ballad chorus that smothers you in goose bumps. She described the song as a 'massive breakthrough for me with my writing because it'd been pretty slow up to this point, and I felt after I worked with Greg Kurstin on this, it all poured right out of me.'

Its release was met with frenzy. The video for new single 'Hello' broke Taylor's Swift's records for the most views on Vevo in 24 hours. 'Hello' accumulated 27.7 million views in its first day online, trouncing the 20.1 million views that Swift's 'Bad Blood' attracted in its first 24 hours.

It is a fine lead track for the album. The music industry generally considers an artist's second work to be the standout challenge of their career – the much-discussed 'difficult second album'. While *21* had been a challenge for Adele – a collection that she had put enormous work and attention into – for her, it would be the third album that proved the true challenge. As to the material itself, several of those who worked with her during the creation of it claimed that a pair of moods dominated her approach: a sense of paranoia over it becoming public too soon, and a general crisis of confidence. Though, as we shall see, there is a very different side to that story.

Album three was a project for which Adele drew on an army of potential creative support. It has been reported that the album could feature songs recorded with a galaxy of musical stars: OneRepublic's Ryan Tedder, producer Danger Mouse, Canadian singer-songwriter Tobias Jesso Jr and writer-producer Max Martin (of Britney Spears and Backstreet Boys fame). Other acts rumoured to have teamed up with Adele are Pharrell Williams, Beyoncé, Sia and Kelly Clarkson. In truth, a full list of those who either have, or are rumoured to have, teamed up with her could fill a chapter in itself, albeit a rather un-engaging one.

Pharrell Williams's experiences with Adele, which he discussed in 2015, offer an insight into how strongly willed and single minded she was for this project. 'I've seen her recently,' he told US broadcaster Ryan Seacrest. 'She's kinda like, "OK guys, I'm gonna open my diary for 20 minutes". So it's like, OK, you have 20 minutes, or 32 minutes really.' The 'Happy' singer, who purringly describes Adele as a 'masterful writer', adds: 'Then she gives it to you and closes it up and disappears, and she's off with her beautiful boy – and that's what it's all about.'

Speaking of masterful writers, in early 2014, the revered tunesmith Diane Warren revealed that she had worked on a few songs with Adele. Born in the 1950s, Warren has worked with dozens of top acts, including Beyoncé, Celine Dion, Whitney Houston, Mariah Carey, Cher, and Kelly Clarkson. Perhaps her most famous song of all was written for Aerosmith: 'I Don't

Want to Miss a Thing'. To put the esteem in which she is held in some sort of context, the hugely influential Peter Reichardt, a former chair of EMI Music Publishing UK, said of Warren: 'She's the most important songwriter in the world.'

So this regal figure in songwriting circles was quite the character for Adele to work with – and she enjoyed the experience. Warren prefers to work alone generally, but her collaboration with Adele and their sessions at RAK Studios in north-west London was something she relished. 'It was just great,' said Warren. 'I don't really write with people and we spent a lot of time together and really clicked and really connected and I really like her as a person... I'm really excited about the stuff we did.' However, Warren conjured a more cautious note over the fate of the songs she wrote with Adele, saying: 'We did some great songs but I don't know if they've made the record. I don't think anybody does.'

A similarly ambiguous tone was heard from the Blur and Gorillaz frontman Damon Albarn on the fate of his spoils. The mockney muso touched heads with Adele on five tunes but he did not walk away from their collaboration hopeful that any of the quintet would make the final cut for the album. In fact, his tail seemed somewhere between his legs. In a rather downbeat chat with *The Sun*, he said that Adele approached him and he 'took the time out for her'. If that sounds somewhat spurned in tone, when asked what came of the sessions he went further. 'I don't know what is happening really,' he said. 'Will she use any of the stuff? I don't think so.' He also hinted that Adele herself was feeling uncertain about the project, when he added: 'The thing is, she's very insecure.

And she doesn't need to be, she's still so young.' Commenting on the material Adele had put down with Danger Mouse, Albarn sniffed: 'It's very middle of the road.'

He was not the only musician to emerge from the project with their feelings seemingly bruised. The soul-pop veteran Phil Collins also spoke rather disparagingly. The 'Against All Odds' singer told *Q* magazine: 'She's a slippery little fish is Adele.' He added: 'She got hold of me and asked if I would write with her. She gave me a piece of music to finish and at first I didn't know if I'd failed the audition as I didn't hear back from her. Then she said, "No, no, I'm moving house and the baby's taking up a lot of my time, I'm not actually doing anything at the moment." And now I've heard there's [an album] coming out. I'm not on it, I know that.'

The hurt feelings of Collins are palpable, and concern for the egos of the creatives Adele hooked up with do not seem to have been uppermost in her mind as she drew a wide net. She also held a tentative meeting with producer Emile Haynie, collaborator with Eminem, Kanye West and Lana Del Rey, amongst others. 'We got along well as friends when we met in February,' he said in April 2015, 'and I hope we can cut some songs, but Adele is taking her time. I'd push for it to happen, but we'll have to wait and see.'

Thank goodness, then, for Ed Sheeran, who spoke more positively and gallantly of the Queen of Pop. The gregarious, guitaring gargantuan beamed that he had heard only good things about the album. 'I haven't heard [the record], but everyone I know who've worked on it is just like, "Dude... that record!" Apparently it's really good.' (Sheeran and Adele, by most measures the biggest UK artists of the past six years, have been friendly for a while. In 2013, the guitarist revealed that Adele cheekily pinched a toy parrot he had as part of a pirate costume he was wearing at an event. 'Adele nicked my parrot,' he revealed, memorably. 'I was dressed up as a pirate and I had a parrot on me and she nicked it for her kid.')

The Australian singer-songwriter Sia managed a more productive outcome from the experience of working with Adele. The pair wrote two songs in three days for the album, but as far as the Aussie understood, none would make the album. One of them, 'Alive', will certainly not feature. When she was told of this, Sia asked Adele if she could pitch the track around other artists, starting with Rihanna. Adele, ever protective of her material, and keen to avoid any leaks ahead of the album's release, told Sia: 'Yeah, but can you take my vocal off it because I don't want my vocal floating around out there on a demo.'

However, there was a twist in the tale. Once Sia re-cut the vocals for 'Alive', she played it to friends and family and they urged her to not give it away to another artist, but to keep it for herself. So she did just that, and released it as a single in September 2015. This track, about survival against the odds, is sultry in the verses, then defiant and powerful in the choruses, and one can perhaps grasp Sia's thought that Rihanna would be a suitable performer. It would be fascinating to hear the version Adele recorded, if she ever felt like sharing it further down the line. It's a cracker of a tune, which in itself says great things about Adele's album. After all, provided her selection is wise, if she rejected 'Alive' it suggests the songs that made the cut will be exceptional.

Just what Adele's third album will actually sound like has become something of an obsession for many music fans over the last three years. All sorts of styles have been rumoured. As far back as 2011, she had begun to speak of the album, offering hints of its tone and style. 'It won't be a big production,' she told *Q*. 'I want it to be quite acoustic and piano-led. I want to write it all, record it all, produce it all and master it on my own. I think it'll take a lot longer because I want to do it this way.'

Adele has, elsewhere, spoken of a country or bluegrass direction for the new album, a possibility that was echoed by the US singer Kelly Clarkson. The *American Idol* winner told *The Wall Street Journal* in 2015 that she had 'heard' that Adele was 'doing something more country influenced with this next record'.

Perhaps the most enthusiastic trail for the album came from Ryan Tedder. The OneRepublic singer, who was involved with some of the tracks on *21*, having heard 'most of' the tracks for its successor, said: 'This album's gonna be crazy.' With all these tantalising glimpses and hints of what the album may sound like, music fans became ever more excited to hear it. Thus began a period of false starts, unconfirmed rumours and unfulfilled hopes. Adele's fans – many of whom call themselves 'Daydreamers' – found they had to wait for the dream of a third album to come true. Not only that, as they waited they were subjected to several delays and disappointments.

For example, in May 2014, she prompted a flurry of excitement on Twitter when she posted a photo on the social network, captioned: 'Bye bye 25... See you again later in the year x'. Her messages on the micro-blogging site tend to carry enhanced gravitas, as she is a very rare tweeter. As of October 2015 she had sent just 273 tweets, compared with Lady Gaga, who had posted 6,967 messages. Her 'Bye bye 25' tweet made for an ambiguous message. Sent on the eve of her twenty-sixth birthday, it was widely interpreted to signify both a farewell to being twenty-five years of age, and a hint that her next album would be called '25' and would be released by the end of 2014.

Two months later this particular theory intensified after the official Twitter account of the World Music Awards sent out a tweet stating that Adele had 'confirmed' a 2015 tour 'after the release of her new album 25!' However, the tweet has since been deleted, and the chairman Martin Mills of Beggars Group, the parent company of XL Recordings, shot down the rumour, telling *Billboard* there was 'no truth' in the claims made in the online posting.

Producer William Orbit was also caught up in a premature rumour. No sooner had he confirmed that he would be working with Adele on the album than reports began to claim that his work was done and that, as he was the final person to be involved with the material, Adele was now readying the album for release.

In February 2015, something far meatier emerged – only to then disappear. The producer and sound engineer Matt Chamberlain tweeted a photograph of Adele at work in a recording studio. He also confirmed that he had worked with her on her album. However, the tweet – along with his entire Twitter account – was deleted shortly afterwards. On and on came the teases. In September, the celebrated photographer Matthew Castle tweeted that he had done a photo shoot with

Adele for a magazine cover. He tweeted: 'New mag cover of @OfficialAdele coming very soon! I would imagine there will be official news attached to that.'

Adele may seem nervous and controlling about the album, but she has misgivings, too, about the touring that will be expected to follow it. 'When I am busy and on tour, I feel like I'm stuck in this bubble, and all my friends are going forward with things. But if I get emotional about it and Skype them, they say, "There's nothing going on here. Absolutely nothing." So that's what wears me out. Constantly feeling paranoid about my life, that it's going to disappear and they are all going to forget me.'

Although she suffers from normal pre-show nerves, it is not so much live performance itself that Adele has her main issue with. Instead it is the relentless grind of touring – weeks, sometimes months, at a time away from home, moving from hotel to hotel, sitting in the same vehicle. Many musicians hate touring, and often none more so than solo artists. Without the comradeship of proper band-mates around them, it is easy for solo singers to feel a lack of empathy for the ups and downs of the experience. Since becoming a mother, Adele has a whole new, beautiful reason to feel misgivings about setting off on the road again – and he is called Angelo. According to reports in the summer of 2015, she had turned down an £80m offer to tour the forthcoming album. The reports claimed that she preferred to enjoy her 'quiet family life' with partner Konecki and their two-year-old son. 'In fact, people at the label admit they are clueless about whether Adele will tour at all,' said a source.

However, she will do well not to buckle under the pressure for her to tour the new album – and she may have done so behind the scenes some time ago. She has stated in interviews that she 'absolutely' will tour the US when the album is out, adding: 'I can't wait.' She has also indicated that she will tour Brazil, stating in a note to a fan there: 'I will be coming to Brazil with my next record and I look forward to seeing you there'. So it seems like she has long been committed to the idea of a world tour.

The break from the public eye has suited her, and she will return to the spotlight refreshed, more mature and poised than ever. She had spoken of a 'need to lay some concrete' before she signed off. 'And I think that will really cure my paranoia of feeling like I am missing home, missing out.' With the concrete laid, and her nest with Konecki and Angelo made, she will hope she can set off on tour without any fears, albeit with a heavy heart as she kisses goodbye to her loved ones.

The central question of how much confidence she has can be seen in quite a different way to Albarn's aforementioned angle. Her refusal to play the twenty-first-century publicity game, her insistence that she will wait however long it takes to get her music right before releasing it, and her mixed feelings on touring, suggest a deep-seated artistic confidence rather than doubt. She has always been more interested in the artistry of her craft rather than cheap attention, a stance that seems a bit quaint in the twenty-first century, but which is very welcome. Would that more acts followed her dignified example, and put aside their tendency to shriek for the spotlight on a tiresomely regular basis.

Diane Warren notes the result of this. 'She has a mind of her own,' said the songwriter. 'Nobody rushes Adele or makes decisions for her, which is probably why she's a great artist. She wants to get it right.' Paul Epworth, Adele's long-time studio ally, has been asked many times when the album will hit the shelves. 'That will come when it's ready,' he said. These words do not speak of insecurity – quite the opposite. Adele was this confident even before *21* jettisoned her to global superstardom. 'I can't be a product; no one can do that to me,' she said as far back as 2009. 'I have all the say; I have power over everything I do.'

She will, ultimately, release the new album from a significantly different position than she did when she released *21*. For many months, and in some cases years, after that album was released, people were still discovering her music for the first time. Therefore the album, which has become the fourth best-selling album in the UK of all time behind Queen, The Beatles and ABBA, was released relatively quietly, certainly so for a recording that was set to become such a commercial juggernaut. Its sales simply grew and grew. Unlike many hit albums, where the sales peak in the early weeks of release, *21* was selling double the number of units a year after its US release as it was over the first few weeks.

(And as *BuzzFeed* humorously noted, the world itself was a different place when *21* came out. It listed a series of lost trends that existed in 2011: 'People were addicted to playing Angry Birds'; 'Charlie Sheen was #winning'; and 'Rebecca Black's "Friday" made nearly everybody go crazy'. Ah, such heady days.)

Adele looks back at the comparative calm with which she put out *21* with wistful affection. Compared with the almost asphyxiating anticipation ahead of her third album, those were days of borderline anonymity.

She says the new collection will be thematically different to its heartbroken predecessor. 'My last record was a break-up record, and if I had to label this one, I would call it a make-up record,' she wrote. 'Making up for lost time. Making up for everything I ever did and never did. 25 is about getting to know who I've become without realising. And I'm sorry it took so long but, you know, life happened.'

For the retail industry itself, the new album could prove a milestone. With sales of CDs dropping off in the face of the growth of downloads, some industry analysts have predicted that Adele's third album could be the final big smash from any artist in which CD sales are significant. No wonder retail chains were clearing spaces for the album even before the release date was definitively, officially announced. The fourth quarter of 2015 was set to be a huge one for the music retail industry, with albums from One Direction and Justin Bieber set to join Adele's comeback release.

The new album could yet bag her further awards, and in January 2014 she was back among the gongs when 'Skyfall' won a Grammy. The new honour stood alongside the song's previous awards: an Academy Award, Golden Globe, and Critics Choice nods. It took a Grammy for Best Song Written for Visual Media. Celebrating her tenth Grammy, Adele, who was not present at the ceremony, sent a tweet saying: 'Wish I was there! Thank you for the grammy! (My 10th one! Whhaaa?) Have a wonderful night. I'm in bed, now feeling very restless x.'

That restlessness will jettison back into our lives, and the public, who so *love* as well as respect her, will welcome the songbird back with open arms. She will be the familiar, warm, candid Adele who is so adored, but with a somewhat different air. On a personal level at least, she has less to prove than she did when, heartbroken, she offered us the divine 'Someone Like You'. One of the aspects of her romance with Konecki that Adele celebrates most is his healthy disinterest in her professional fortunes. 'He's wonderful,' she said. 'And he's proud of me, but he don't care about what I do or what other people think.'

So prepare for an altered Adele. For the first time, she will bask in the public's attention as a contented private figure. 'I'm done with being a bitter witch' she says. A harsh assessment of her own previous persona, but, having 'fucked off for four years', she will return the least fucked off we have ever known her. The Queen of Pop has let other pretenders enjoy the stage for too long, it is time for her to come and resume her reign. And yet, despite her undoubted majesty, her charm will as always centre on the fact that she is, when all is sung and done, someone like you.

Her new family had been a factor in the lengthy pause between albums two and three. 'I didn't do anything [musically] until my kid was like eighteen months old or nearly two years old,' she said. 'It was pretty obvious pretty quickly that I wasn't ready in my head space to concentrate on accessing my creativity, so I didn't want to waste anyone else's time. So I decided not to do it until I felt ready.' Once she was ready, she went to work.

CHAPTER TWELVE

THE BEST OF ADELE IN HER OWN WORDS

On whether fame has changed her: 'I've never been more normal than I am now.'

On her grandfather's influence: 'I painted him as this Jesus figure in my life.'

On vocal influences: 'I taught myself how to sing by listening to Ella Fitzgerald for acrobatics and scales, Etta James for passion and Roberta Flack for control.'

On her favoured outfits: 'I'm like Johnny Cash. I only wear black.'

On smoking: 'I used to smoke rollies but then I got a record deal and switched to Marlboro Lights.'

On the upside of heartbreak: 'It can definitely give you a deeper sensibility for writing songs. I drew on a lot of heartbreak when I was writing my first album, I didn't mean to but I just did.'

On nerves: 'I get so nervous on stage I can't help but talk. I try. I try telling my brain: stop sending words to the mouth. But I get nervous and turn into my grandma. Behind the eyes it's pure fear. I find it difficult to believe I'm going to be able to deliver.'

On meeting Justin Timberlake: 'I wanted to say to him, "I love you, let's get married and have children," but instead I just barked at him, woof.'

On not posing naked: 'I don't like going to the gym. I like eating fine foods and drinking nice wine. Even if I had a really good figure, I don't think I'd get my tits and ass out for no one.'

On weight loss: 'It's never been an issue for me – I don't want to go on a diet, I don't want to eat a Caesar salad with no dressing, why would I do that? I ain't got time for this, just be happy and don't be stupid. If I've got a boyfriend and he loves my body then I'm not worried.'

On her appearance: 'The focus on my appearance has really surprised me. I've always been a size 14 to 16, I don't care about clothes, I'd rather spend my money on cigarettes and booze.'

On intimate live shows: 'I love hearing my audience breathe.'

On taxes: 'When I got my tax bill in from the album *19*, I was ready to go and buy a gun and randomly open fire.'

On her mum: 'Mum loves me being famous! She is so excited and proud as she had me so young and couldn't support me, so I am living her dream, it's sweeter for both of us. It's her fortieth birthday soon and I'm going to buy her forty presents.'

On celebrity restaurants: 'I went to the Ivy, I hate it, I think it's shit. And Nobu. They are all rubbish.'

On losing her voice in early 2011: 'I had to sit in silence for nine days, chalkboard around my neck. Like an old-school mime. Like a kid in the naughty corner. Like a Victorian mute.'

On dancing – or not: 'I have the passion to dance, I just don't have the rhythm.'

On 'Someone Like You': 'I was like "This guy actually deserves to be shown in a good light as well. If I don't write a song like this I'm going to end up becoming a bitter old woman. It was about meeting the love of my life and it just being bad timing."'

On the same relationship: 'I expected too much, I was needy, I was jealous even though I'm not a jealous person. We both said a lot of things in the heat of the moment.'

On recording that hit: 'On "Someone Like You" I am really crying. You can hear it towards the end.'

On men: 'I don't have a type. Never have.'

On her fellow female artists: 'I love seeing Lady Gaga's boobs and bum. I love seeing Katy Perry's boobs and bum. Love it. But that's not what my music is about. I don't make music for eyes, I make music for ears.'

The essence of Adele: 'I'm really happy to be me, and I'd like to think people like me more because I'm happy with myself and not because I refuse to conform to anything.'

Final word: 'I don't make music for eyes. I make music for ears.'

APPENDIX

AWARDS

By the summer of 2015, Adele had won over 90 significant awards, having been nominated for more than 170. Here is a selection of those she won.

AMERICAN MUSIC AWARDS
2011
Favourite Adult Contemporary Artist
Favourite Pop/Rock Female Artist
Favourite Pop/Rock Album

☆

BILLBOARD AWARDS
2012
Top Artist
Top Female Artist

Top Billboard 200 Artist
Top Digital Songs Artist
Top Radio Songs Artist
Top Hot 100 Artist
Top Digital Media Artist
Top Pop Artist
Top Streaming Song
Top Alternative Song
Top Billboard 200 Album
Top Pop Album

BT DIGITAL MUSIC AWARDS
2011
Best Independent Artist or Group

THE BRITS
2008
Critics' Choice
2009
Best British Female
2012
Best British Female
Mastercard British Album of the Year

GOLDEN GLOBES
2013
Best Original Song

☆

THE GRAMMYS
2009
Best New Artist
Best Female Pop Vocal Performance
2012
Album of the Year
Best Pop Vocal Album
Record of the Year
Song of the Year
Best Short Form Music Video
Best Pop Solo Performance (twice)
2014
Best Song Written for Visual Media

☆

IVOR NOVELLO AWARDS
2011
Songwriter of the Year
PRS for Music Most Performed Work

☆

MOBO AWARDS
2011
Best UK R&B/Soul Act

MTV
2011
Best UK/Ireland Act
Song of the Year

NICKELODEON UK KIDS CHOICE AWARDS
2012
Best UK Female

☆

OSCARS
2013
Best Original Song

☆

Q AWARDS
2011
Best Female Artist
Best Track

☆

URBAN MUSIC AWARDS
2008
Best Jazz Act

☆

DISCOGRAPHY

ALBUMS
19 (XL, 2008)
21 (XL, 2011)
25 (XL, 2015)

☆

SINGLES
'Hometown Glory' (XL, 2007)
'Chasing Pavements' (XL, 2008)
'Cold Shoulder' (XL, 2008)
'Make You Feel My Love' (XL, 2008)
'Rolling In The Deep' (XL, 2010)
'Someone Like You' (XL, 2011)
'Set Fire To The Rain' (XL, 2011)
'Rumour Has It' (XL, 2011)
'Turning Tables' (XL, 2011)
'Skyfall' (XL, 2012)
'Hello' (XL, 2015)

ABOUT THE AUTHOR

Chas Newkey-Burden is a leading celebrity biographer whose subjects include Amy Winehouse, Simon Cowell, Brangelina, Tom Daley and Stephenie Meyer. His books have been translated into 14 languages. He has also co-written books with Kelvin MacKenzie and Julie Burchill. He is a regular guest on BBC Radio London and a columnist for the *Jewish Chronicle*.

Follow him on Twitter: @AllThatChas

THE
CRYSTAL BIBLE

THE
CRYSTAL BIBLE

A DEFINITIVE GUIDE TO CRYSTALS

Judy Hall

 A GODSFIELD BOOK

First published in Great Britain in 2003
by Godsfield Press, a division of
Octopus Publishing Group Ltd
2–4 Heron Quays, London E14 4JP

20

Copyright © 2003 Godsfield Press
Text copyright © 2003 Judy Hall

Designed and produced for Godsfield Press by The Bridgewater Book Company

Additional photography by Mike Hemsley at
Walter Gardiner Photography

Printed and bound in China

ISBN-13: 978-1-84181-175-8
ISBN-10: 1-84181-175-0

NOTE: An asterisk* placed after a word indicates that the word or
term may be looked up in the Glossary section (see pages 378–383)
for a full explanation.

CAUTION: The information given in this book is not intended to act
as a substitute for medical treatment, nor can it be used for diagnosis.
Crystals are powerful and are open to misunderstanding or abuse.
If you are in any doubt about their use, a qualified practitioner should
be consulted, especially in the crystal healing field.

CONTENTS

CRYSTAL REFERENCE

CRYSTAL DELIGHTS

Everyone is attracted to gemstones. Diamonds, Rubies, Emeralds, and Sapphires are prized the world over. These are indeed precious stones; they uplift the heart. Their brightness is what most people think of when they hear the word "crystal." Equally prized are the semiprecious stones such as Carnelian, Garnet, Rock Crystal, and Lapis Lazuli. They have been used for ornamentation and as a symbol of power for thousands of years. But such crystals were valued for more than their beauty—they each had a sacred meaning. In ancient cultures their healing properties were as important as their ability to adorn.

Crystals still have the same properties today but not all are as flamboyant as gemstones. There are quieter, less outwardly attractive crystals that are nonetheless extremely powerful. Gemstones themselves can easily be overlooked when in their natural, uncut state but their attributes remain the same, and an uncut Sapphire, for instance, which costs a fraction of the price of a faceted stone, is as effective as the most scintillating cut gem.

Most people are familiar with the crystals that have been around for years such as Amethyst, Malachite, and Obsidian but nowadays new crystals such as Larimar, Petalite, and Phenacite are finding their way into

stores. These are "stones for the New Age." They have made themselves known to facilitate the evolution of the earth and all those upon it. These crystals have an extremely high vibration that raises consciousness and opens the higher chakras* to communicate with other dimensions. Knowing how to use these crystals is vital if you are to make use of the gifts they offer.

This book has been divided into sections that will help you to find your way around the crystal kingdom. Containing everything you could ever need to know, these sections tell you about the delights of crystals, their healing use and decorative features, how they were formed, and how to take care of them. There is a Crystal Reference at the front so that you can look up a particular crystal by the name by which you know it, and then find its properties in an extensive Directory section, which also enables you to identify crystals. The comprehensive Index at the back is cross-referenced to symptoms and attributes; you can use this to find a crystal for a specific task, or for your particular purpose. The Glossary on pages 378–383 defines terms that you may not be familiar with.

Crystals come in numerous shapes and many of these have now been given names that signify their function, such as channeling or abundance crystals. If you want to identify a particular facet shape or to know what a certain type of crystal looks like, browse through Crystal Shapes. This section is followed by Quick Reference pages that give you useful information such as the Body and Zodiac Crystal Correspondences, Gem Remedies, Healing Layouts, and a Love Ritual.

CRYSTAL BACKGROUND

The more you understand about crystals, the more effective they are. In this section you will find background information on how crystals are formed, advice on how to choose and care for your crystals; how to use them for healing and decoration, and the way to dedicate them.

Dedicating and programming your crystals helps them to work more efficiently. It is part of the ritual of working with crystals. As crystals are powerful beings in their own right, they need to be approached with respect. If you do this, they will be only too pleased to cooperate with you. Many people like to have a "crystal day" when they cleanse their crystals and then meditate with them to attune more strongly to their energy. Doing this regularly enables your crystals to talk to you and to show you how you can use them to enhance your life and well-being.

Taking the time to cleanse your crystals is extremely important. Crystals are efficient absorbers and transmitters of energy. One of their functions is to cleanse and transmute negative energies. If you leave your crystals to do this without regular cleansing, most become saturated and unable to do their work, though a few are self-cleaning.

CRYSTAL FORMATION

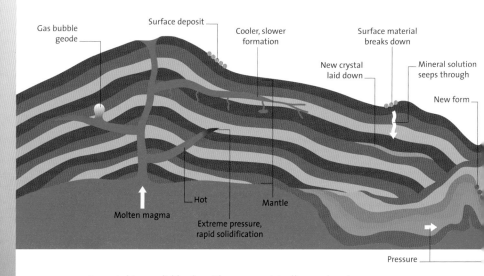

Gas bubble geode

Surface deposit

Cooler, slower formation

Surface material breaks down

New crystal laid down

Mineral solution seeps through

New form

Hot

Mantle

Molten magma

Extreme pressure, rapid solidification

Pressure

A crystal is a solid body with a geometrically regular shape. Crystals were created as the earth formed and they have continued to metamorphose as the planet itself has changed. Crystals are the earth's DNA, a chemical imprint for evolution. They are miniature storehouses, containing the records of the development of the earth over millions of years, and bearing the indelible memory of the powerful forces that shaped it. Some have been subjected to enormous pressure, others grew in chambers deep underground, some were laid down in layers, others dripped into being—all of which affects their properties and the way they function. Whatever form they take, their crystalline structure can absorb, conserve, focus, and emit energy, especially on the electromagnetic waveband.

14

THE CRYSTAL LATTICE

Because of chemical impurities, radiation, earth and solar emissions, and the exact means of their formation, each type of crystal has its own specific "note." Formed out of an array of minerals, a crystal is defined by its internal structure—an orderly, repeating atomic lattice that is unique to its species. A large or small specimen of the same type of crystal will have exactly the same internal structure, which can be recognized under a microscope.

This unique geometric crystal lattice is how crystals are identified and means that some crystals, such as Aragonite, have several very different external forms and colors, which at first glance could not possibly be the same crystal. However, because the internal structure is identical, they are classified as the same crystal. It is this structure, rather than the mineral or minerals out of which it is formed, that is crucial to crystal classification. In some cases the mineral content differs slightly, creating the various colors in which a particular crystal can be found.

While a number of crystals may be formed out of the same mineral or combination of minerals, each type will crystallize out differently. A crystal is symmetrical along an axis. Its regular external planes are an outward expression of its internal order. Each matching pair of faces has exactly the same angles. The internal structure of any crystalline formation is constant and unchanging.

Crystals are built from one of seven possible geometric forms: triangles, squares, rectangles, hexagons, rhomboids, parallelograms, or trapeziums. These forms lock together into a number of potential crystal shapes, which have generic names based on their internal geometry. As the name suggests, a hexagonal crystal is formed from hexagons built into a three-dimensional shape. A collection of squares forms a cubic crystal, triangles a trigonal, and rectangles a tetragonal

Triangle   Square   Trapezium

Rectangle   Rhomboid   Parallelogram   Hexagon

crystal, while rhomboids form an orthorhombic crystal, trapeziums a triclinic, and parallelograms a monoclinic crystal. The outer form of the crystal will not necessarily reflect its inner structure.

At the heart of a crystal is the atom and its component parts. An atom is dynamic, consisting of particles rotating around a center in constant motion. So, although a crystal may look outwardly serene, it is actually a seething molecular mass vibrating at a certain frequency. This is what gives a crystal its energy.

THE EARTH'S CRUST

The earth began as a whirling cloud of gas, out of which was created a dense dust bowl. This contracted into a white-hot, molten ball. Gradually, over eons, a thin layer of this molten material, magma, cooled into a crust—the earth's mantle. The crust is relatively about as thick as the skin on an apple. Inside that crust, the hot, mineral rich, molten magma continues to boil and bubble and new crystals form.

Some crystals, such as Quartz, arise from the fiery gases and molten minerals in the earth's center. Superheated, they rise toward the surface, propelled by stresses caused by movement of huge plates on the earth's surface. As gases penetrate the crust and meet solid rock, they cool and solidify—a process that may take eons or may be fast and furious.

If the process has been relatively slow, or if the crystal grows in a gas bubble, then large crystals can grow. If the process is fast, then the crystals are small. If the process stops and starts, effects such as phantom or self-healed crystals are possible. If the process is exceptionally fast, a glass-like substance, such as Obsidian, is formed rather than crystals. Crystals such as Aventurine or Peridot are created at high temperatures from liquid magma. Others, such as Topaz and Tourmaline, are formed when gases penetrate adjoining rocks.

Yet other forms arise when magma cools sufficiently for water vapor to condense into a liquid. The resulting mineral-rich solution lays down crystals such as Aragonite and Kunzite. When it penetrates fissures in surrounding rock, the solution is able to cool very slowly and lay down large crystals and geodes such as Chalcedony and Amethyst.

Aragonite ("sputnik" form)

Crystals like Garnet are formed deep in the earth when minerals melt and recrystallize under intense pressure and enormous heat. These crystals are known as metamorphic because they have undergone a chemical change that has reorganized the original lattice.

Calcite and other sedimentary crystals form from an erosion process. Rocks at the surface break down and mineralized water dripping through rock or traveling as a river lays down weathered material as new crystals, or the minerals become cemented together. Such crystals are often laid down in layers on a "bedrock" and tend to be softer in texture.

Crystals are often found still attached to the bedrock on which they formed or cemented together as a conglomerate. This bedrock is known as the matrix.

CRYSTAL DECORATION

Crystals are highly decorative, especially when shaped and polished, although some stones are stunning in their natural form. You can now buy decorative objects wrought from an enormous variety of precious stones, all of which greatly enhance their surroundings, especially if you choose them for their esoteric properties too.

Gemstones such as Emeralds and Sapphires are vibrant stones. They make excellent jewelry, for men as well as women, but all crystals can enhance your environment and look superb as well. A carefully placed crystal can magically transform its surroundings.

Wearing gems used to be a royal or priestly prerogative. The high priest of Judaism wore a breastplate set with precious stones. It was much more than a badge of office; it conveyed power to the wearer. As far back as the Stone Age, men and women wore crystal jewelry and talismans. They had a protective as well as a decorative function, guarding their wearer against harm.

Crystals today carry the same power and jewelry can be selected not just on the basis of its outward attraction. Wearing crystals, or simply having one in close proximity, can boost your energy (Orange Carnelian), clean your space (Amber), and attract wealth (Citrine). Carefully positioned, crystals can change your life. You can choose stones to enhance your intuition (Apophyllite), increase mental abilities (Green Tourmaline), and boost confidence (Hematite). You can select

Amber jewelry

abundance (Tiger's Eye) and healing (Smithsonite), or attract love (Rhodonite).

CRYSTAL PROTECTION

Certain crystals, such as Smoky Quartz and Black Tourmaline, have the ability to absorb negativity and electromagnetic smog*. They put out pure, clean energy. Wearing a Black Tourmaline around your neck protects you against electromagnetic emanations, including cell phones and computers, and turns back psychic attack*. Amber and Jet jewelry will also protect your energies.

Smoky Quartz Celestial

A large Smoky Quartz cluster or shaped point can look stunning as a decorative object, belying its practical cleansing purpose. Place one between you and a source of electromagnetic smog or geopathic stress* or position it on your desk. An Amethyst geode has the same effect. If you find that computers have a debilitating effect on you, place a Fluorite cluster or a piece of lustrous Lepidolite beside it, and you will be amazed at the difference in how you feel—and your computer will work more in harmony with you.

CRYSTAL ATTRACTION

A large Citrine geode is highly decorative. A beautiful object in its own right, it will not only attract wealth but will also help you to keep it. Place it in the Wealth Corner of your home (farthest left rear corner from the front door).

Citrine geode

Selenite is one of the newer stones. Its pure white, finely ribbed form looks angelic and, not surprisingly, it attracts angelic energy into your life. It can link you to your soul's purpose. You can pop it under your pillow, but it is at its most beautiful as a pillar with the sun behind it or set on a light box.

Many transparent crystals have their effect heightened by being placed on a light box or catching the sun. Care should be taken as clear Quartz, for instance, focuses the sun's rays and may start a fire, and colored crystals can fade in sunlight.

Selenite

SEMIPRECIOUS STONES

Semiprecious stones have as much power as gemstones. Some are found in several colors, which can affect their attributes. Topaz, which sheds golden light on your life's purpose, is often used for rings. In its blue form, it can be worn at the throat because it stimulates the ability to put your thoughts into words.

Herkimer Diamonds have a clarity and sparkle every bit as attractive as Diamonds themselves, and they come in bigger and more affordable sizes. Many Herkimers display wonderful rainbows in their depths. Used for earrings, they heighten your intuition and increase your creativity. But their power is such that it is better to wear them in your ears for a few hours only. Wearing them for too long can set your head buzzing and may cause insomnia. Peridots are known as "poor

Herkimer Diamond

man's Emeralds," but this visionary stone has the power to ameliorate jealousy and anger, reduce stress, and release negative patterns. As with many stones, in its unpolished form it could easily be overlooked. But faceted and polished, it is a jewel fit for a queen.

BRINGING LOVE INTO YOUR LIFE

If you are seeking love, crystals will help. Place a large piece of Rose Quartz in the Relationship Corner of your house (farthest right rear corner from the front door), or put a piece beside your bed. Its effect is so powerful it might be wise to add an Amethyst to regulate the attraction. You can also wear Rhodochrosite jewelry—its softly banded pink is pretty as well as potent. Love will soon come your way.

Amethyst geode with Snow Quartz crystal

21

CRYSTAL HEALING

Malachite

Crystals have been used for millennia to heal and bring balance. They work through resonance and vibration. To gain maximum benefit from crystal healing, you need to be properly trained or to be treated by someone who is well qualified and experienced. But you can find benefit in crystals for common ailments and they are effective first-aid remedies, especially when made into gem essences (see page 371).

Some crystals contain minerals that are known for their therapeutic properties. Copper, for instance, reduces swelling and inflammation. Malachite has a high concentration of copper, which aids aching joints and muscles. Wearing a Malachite bracelet allows the body to absorb minute amounts of copper in exactly the same way as a copper bracelet does. In ancient Egypt, Malachite was powdered and applied to wounds to prevent infection. Today it is a powerful detoxifier but, as it is toxic, it should only be applied externally. This property of toxic crystals to detoxify is rather like the homeopathic principle of "like cures like." Crystals safely deliver infinitesimal, vibrational doses of something that, taken in large quantities, would be poisonous.

Crystals are used in modern medical practices. They are piezoelectric, which means that electricity, and sometimes light, is produced by compression. This property is harnessed in ultrasound machines, which use a piezoelectric crystal to produce a sound wave. Sound is now being applied at the leading edge of surgery. A tightly focused beam of ultrasound can cauterize wounds deep within the body and blast tumors apart without the need for invasive procedures. Shamans and crystal healers of old were familiar with this ability of crystals to focus sound and light vibrations into a concentrated ray, which was then applied for healing. Rotating a crystal wand on the skin causes compression, which releases a focused beam to the organ beneath.

Carnelian

Ancient healers also knew that, whereas some crystals are either energizing or calming, there are crystals that will both sedate an overactive organ and stimulate a sluggish one. Magnetite, with its positive and negative charge, does exactly this. It sedates an overactive organ and stimulates an underactive one. There are crystals that will heal quickly, but may provoke a healing challenge, while others work much more slowly. If you want to deal with pain—a signal that something is wrong in your body—you can do this with crystals. Pain could result from an excess of energy, a blockage, or a debility. A cool and calming crystal such as Lapis Lazuli or Rose Quartz will sedate energy, whereas Carnelian will stimulate it, and Cathedral Quartz is excellent for pain relief no matter what the cause.

Lapis Lazuli

Crystals are excellent for dealing with headaches. Lapis Lazuli will quickly draw off a migraine headache. But you need to know from where the headache stems. If it is caused by stress, Amethyst, Amber, or Turquoise placed on the brow will relieve it. If it is food-related, however, a stone that calms the stomach, such as Moonstone or Citrine, will be appropriate.

23

HOLISTIC HEALING

Crystals heal holistically. That is to say, they work on the physical, emotional, mental, and spiritual levels of being. They realign subtle energies and dissolve dis-ease*, getting to the root cause. Crystals work through vibration, rebalancing the biomagnetic sheath* that surrounds and interpenetrates the physical body and activating linkage points to the chakras* that regulate the body's vibrational stasis (see page 364). By bringing the chakras back into balance, many states of physical and psychological dis-ease can be ameliorated.

Most illnesses result from a combination of factors. There will be dis-ease at subtle levels. This dis-ease may be emotional or mental, or a sign of spiritual unease or disconnection. There may be misaligned connections between the physical body and the biomagnetic sheath. Other energetic disturbances may be caused by environmental factors such as electromagnetic smog* or geopathic stress*. Simply placing a Black Tourmaline or Smoky Quartz crystal between you and the source of geopathic or electromagnetic stress can magically transform your life. But you may need to go deeper into the cause of dis-ease. Crystals gently deal with the cause rather than merely ameliorating the symptoms.

Larimar

You can lay crystals on or around your body for ten to thirty minutes (for sample layouts see pages 365 and 374), or use them like a reflexology tool to stimulate points on your feet—Larimar is particularly useful for this as it locates the source of dis-ease. Crystal eggs (see page 331) can also be used on the feet. Crystal wands are helpful if you need to stimulate a point on the body. Rotated gently, they lift pain and dis-ease. Throughout the Directory you will find crystals to treat illnesses and imbalances on all levels.

Crystals have been connected with particular parts of the body and its organs for thousands of years (see page 368). Many of the connections come from traditional astrology, both Western and Eastern. Traditional Chinese Medicine and Indian Ayurveda, both over 5,000 years old, still use in modern medical prescriptions crystals that appear in formulas in ancient texts. Hematite, for instance, is said to calm the spirit and so combats insomnia. But it is also used for blood disorders as it is believed to cool the blood, arresting bleeding. Hematite is used by modern crystal healers to relieve those same conditions.

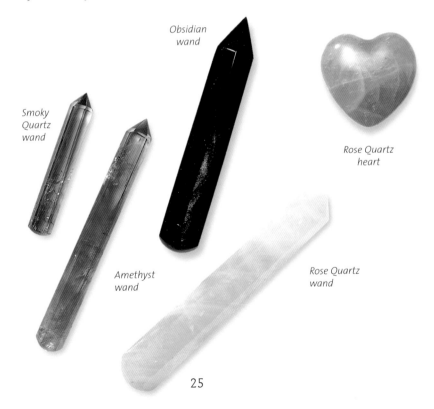

Obsidian wand

Smoky Quartz wand

Rose Quartz heart

Amethyst wand

Rose Quartz wand

25

CHOOSING A CRYSTAL FOR HEALING

To choose a crystal, or crystals, for healing, you can work from symptoms to deeper cause (preferably with advice from a qualified crystal healer). Each entry in the Crystal Directory lists the conditions it heals at the physical, emotional, psychological, mental, and spiritual level. The Index has a comprehensive cross-reference to help you link symptoms with relevant crystals.

So, for instance, if your symptom is a digestive problem, you could choose a Citrine point to aid healing. Laying it on your abdomen, or wearing it on your little finger, which connects to the small intestine meridian*, could calm your digestion. The crystal works directly on the physical body. However, at a deeper level, digestive problems could well relate to a lack of abundance. Money worries often translate themselves into dis-ease*. Citrine is the stone of prosperity. It attracts wealth and abundance into your life (especially when placed in the left corner of you home that is farthest from your front door). Wearing a Citrine reenergizes you and stimulates motivation and creativity—which brings abundance.

Angelite

At a deeper level still, fears around money often stem from a feeling of being unsupported by the universe. This fear is not merely emotional dis-ease, it is spiritual disconnection. Citrine's ability to activate the crown chakra*, which is where the spiritual connection is made, could enable you to strengthen your trust in the universe.

Citrine

Having identified spiritual disconnection as a probable root cause of your dis-ease, you might then want to look to other crystals that will support that level of your being. Stones such as Petalite and Phenacite link you to a spiritual reality with a very high vibration. Phenacite aids in grounding the spiritual into everyday life but, if this is your first experience of working with crystals to stimulate spiritual contact, it may be too powerful for you. A better choice might be Angelite or Celestite, which gently attune you to the celestial realm*. Angelic presence induces a powerful sense of being supported by the universe.

Brown Celestite

As some crystals support each other and others cancel each other out, care should be taken when using crystals for healing. If in doubt, consult a qualified crystal healer.

SOURCING YOUR CRYSTAL

The best source for your crystal is a local store where you can browse at your leisure. Such stores are usually listed in Yellow Pages under Crystals, Gemstones, or Minerals. The Internet can also point you in the right direction—although there are hundreds of thousands of entries and it can take time and persistence to narrow a search down. There are also Mind-Body-Spirit, Healing, and Crystal and Mineral fairs where you will find crystals for sale. These are listed in Lepidiary Journal, Mind-Body-Spirit journals, or advertised locally.

CRYSTAL SELECTION

Within these pages, you will find crystals that are familiar and others that you have never seen before. With so many crystals to choose from, it can be difficult to know which is the right one for you. If one is gifted to you, it makes it easy. But if you wish to buy one for yourself, browsing through this book first will be invaluable.

If you want to choose a crystal for a specific purpose, the Directory and the Index will help you to find exactly the right one. Look up possibilities in the Index and then check out the crystals themselves in the Directory. If you have no idea what you want your crystal for, but are attracted to the idea of wearing one, then your date of birth is a good starting point and you will find your birthstones on pages 362–363. You can select one that resonates to your zodiac sign, earthing celestial energies.

You can also pick out a crystal at random. Trust your intuition. Browse through the Directory until one attracts your attention and go out and buy that type. There will no doubt be several in the store to choose from. The crystal that speaks to you will be right (never buy from a source that does not let you handle the stones first and, if buying through the Internet, ensure that crystals can be returned if inappropriate—see page 27). Handle several, allow yourself to be drawn to one, or put your hands into a tub of crystals until one sticks to your fingers. If that crystal makes you tingle, it is the one for you. Remember that big or outwardly beautiful is not necessarily most powerful. Small, rough crystals can be extremely effective.

Before you use your crystal, remember to cleanse it first (see page 31).

PROGRAMMING YOUR CRYSTAL

Crystals need to be dedicated to the purpose for which you use them. Dedicate a new crystal as soon as you have cleansed it (see pages 30–1). This focuses the energy.

Hold the crystal in your hands. Picture light surrounding it. (If you find this difficult, hold your hands in front of a light source.) Say out loud: "I dedicate this crystal to the highest good of all. May it be used in light and love."

To program your crystal, hold it. Let yourself be open to higher guidance. Consider the purpose for which you wish to use it. Be specific. If you want it to attract love, describe exactly what kind of love you are looking for. If you are seeking healing, say precisely for which condition and what you want to happen. When you have formulated your program, attune to the crystal. Ensure that this is exactly the right crystal for the purpose. When you are totally in tune, say out loud: "I program this crystal for [your purpose]."

Then put the crystal in a place where you will see it frequently or keep it in your pocket. It can be helpful to hold it two or three times a day, or more. You may need to repeat the programming several times.

Crystals are highly responsive. Hold in the palm of your hand for dedication, programming, or to select the right crystal for you

CRYSTAL CARE

Many crystals are fragile or friable. Crystals that are layered or clustered can separate. Crystals such as Selenite are water soluble. Polished surfaces or natural points are easily scratched or damaged. Tumbled stones are more durable. Endless hours turning in fine grit gives them a tough surface. You can keep tumbled stones together in a bag but other crystals should be kept apart.

When not in use, wrap your crystals in a silk or velvet scarf. This prevents scratching and protects the crystal against absorbing foreign emanations. Crystals need to be cleansed when you buy them and after wearing or using for healing. Always cleanse jewelry that comes to you from someone else, as it can hold their negative vibrations and pass them on to you.

A few crystals never need cleansing. Citrine, Kyanite, and Azeztulite are self-cleaning. Clear Quartz and Carnelian cleanse other crystals, and are especially useful for delicate and friable stones, but may need cleaning themselves afterward.

Tumbled stones can be kept in a small bag

CRYSTAL CLEANSING

Crystals that are not friable or jointed can be held under running water or immersed in the sea or in salt water. As you do so, hold the intention that all negativity will be washed away and the crystal reenergized. Placing the crystal in the light of the sun or moon for a few hours can also recharge its batteries provided it is not a stone that fades in sunlight and care is taken not to focus the rays where they could start a fire—remember that the light from the sun moves around in an arc as the day progresses.

Friable crystals or clusters can be left in sea or rock salt overnight. Gently brush every speck of salt off afterward as they could damage the crystal, especially in a damp atmosphere.

Certain crystals have the ability to cleanse other crystals. Keep a Carnelian in a bag of tumbled stones and you will never need to cleanse them using any other method. A small crystal can be placed on a Clear Quartz cluster and left overnight.

You can smudge* crystals or pass them through the light from a candle. You can also visualize them surrounded by light, which purifies and reenergizes them.

Cleanse crystals in water or salt

One of the easiest ways to purify a crystal is to use a purpose-made cleanser available over the Internet. You only need to put a drop or two on the crystal, or spray it with an atomizer of water to which a few drops of cleanser have been added—this does not damage friable crystals if sprayed lightly.

31

CRYSTAL MEDITATION

Meditating with a crystal is one of the easiest ways to attune to its energy. Cleanse your crystal before beginning so that its energies will be pure. Meditation is a way of shutting off mind chatter. It has many benefits—alleviating stress, lowering blood pressure, etc.—but it also allows you to get to know your crystals. In the stillness of meditation, the crystals talk to you.

Meditation is like opening a door to another world, especially if you choose a crystal that has fault lines* and occlusions* within it. You lose yourself within the crystal. In the peace that follows, solutions and insights rise up into awareness. It is beneficial to meditate with each of your crystals in turn, taking a few days to tune into each one and come to know it fully.

Some people like to have a "crystal day" when they tune into each of their crystals. Start with the red crystals to energize and awaken, moving through the rainbow spectrum into orange, yellow, green, blue, purple, violet, and clear. This brings you to the highest crystal vibration and you could well feel blissed out*. You may need to earth your energies again with one of the black crystals. Earthing, or grounding, your energies after meditation is important as you may otherwise feel floaty and not quite here. Boji Stones are excellent for this as they settle you into your body instantly but gently, and immediately bring you fully present.

Agate   *Amber*   *Sulphur*   *Peridot*   *Agate*   *Amethyst*   *Fluorite*

CRYSTAL MEDITATION EXERCISE

Making sure that you will not be disturbed, especially by a phone, settle yourself comfortably with your crystal. Hold it in both hands or place it on a low table in front of you.

Breathe gently, letting each out-breath be a little longer than the in-breath. As you breathe out, let go of any stress or tension you may be feeling. As you breathe in, let peace flow with your in-breath passing right through your body. Allow your breathing to settle into an easy rhythm.

With softly focused eyes, look at your crystal. Notice its color, its shape, its weight if you are holding it. Feel its vibrations passing into your hands. Allow yourself to wander within the crystal, exploring its inner planes. When you are ready, close your eyes. Quietly contemplate the energies of the crystal and let it teach you about itself.

When you have completed the meditation, open your eyes and put the crystal aside. Place your feet firmly on the floor. To ground yourself, hold a Smoky Quartz or Boji Stone.

CRYSTAL DIRECTORY

Crystals come in all shapes and sizes, and the same crystal may occur in several forms or colors, or be known by several names. The appearance of many crystals is enhanced by cutting or polishing, but they are as effective in the raw state. A crystal in the raw may be difficult to identify as many of its characteristics are less easy to spot.

Throughout this Directory you will find crystals illustrated in various forms and colors to make identification easy. You will be able to see what a rough crystal looks like when it has been cut and faceted or tumbled. You will see large clusters and small points, polished palm stones, and geodes.

Crystals can be used for healing or environmental enhancement as well as personal adornment. Their subtle vibrations affect the physical, emotional, mental, psychological, and spiritual levels of being. They bring out particular qualities, and open the gateway to spiritual understanding. This Directory contains all the knowledge—practical and esoteric—you need to access their miraculous properties and to position stones for the greatest benefit.

CRYSTAL ATTRIBUTES

Within this section you will find all the information you need on the general attributes of each crystal, together with its psychological, mental, emotional, and spiritual effect and its use in healing—all of which are cross-referenced in the Index. You will also learn how to place your crystal for maximum effect.

Each crystal is listed with all the colors it takes on and the names by which it is known. Where there is more than one color or a form of the crystal that has additional properties, these are listed after the main entry. Thus, the general properties of each crystal are shown under the generic heading, followed by the crystal's unique attributes.

You can also use the Directory to select a crystal for healing, protection or some other purpose. The Index will help you here. Look up the condition for which you need the crystal. You will probably find several page references. Look at each crystal in turn and note which one has the strongest attraction for you. This will be the most appropriate.

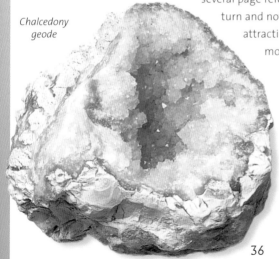

Chalcedony geode

IDENTIFYING A CRYSTAL

The sources for each crystal are shown in the box beneath the heading, together with a description of its color, appearance, and size. This means that if you happen to pick up or are given a crystal, you can identify it.

36

If you need to identify a crystal, look at it closely. Note its color and its form. Does it have clear crystals with faceted points? Is it rough or has it been tumbled smooth? Is it dense and grainy or translucent? Look through the illustrations until you spot the one most like your stone. The photographs in the Directory show many but not all of the colors in which each crystal is available. If your crystal is similar in appearance and is one of the colors listed but not shown in a photograph, then this is most probably a correct identification. (If you are in any doubt, most crystal stores will be pleased to help you further.)

CRYSTAL BEINGS

Many crystals contain beings or guardian spirits who actively want to work with you to use your crystal to its fullest potential. Meditating with your crystal (see page 32) puts you in touch. You may find that the being is in another dimension with which the crystal forms a bridge. Some crystals have their own angel or connect with higher beings.

Blue Chalcedony being

AGATE

*Natural
Agate (sliced)*

COLOR	Clear or milky white, gray, blue, green, pink, brown, often artificially colored
APPEARANCE	Waxy and soft, usually banded, sometimes translucent with small crystals, various sizes. Often sold as artificially colored slices that have no additional therapeutic properties
RARITY	Common
SOURCE	United States, India, Morocco, Czech Republic, Brazil, Africa

ATTRIBUTES Formed from microscopic crystals of quartz laid down in bands, this is a very stable crystal. Agates are grounding stones, bringing about an emotional, physical, and intellectual balance. They aid in centering and stabilizing physical energy.

Agate has the power to harmonize yin and yang, the positive and negative forces that hold the universe in place. A soothing and calming stone, Agate works slowly but brings great strength. Its multiple layers can bring hidden information to light.

Psychologically, Agate gently facilitates acceptance of one's self. This builds self-confidence. It aids self-analysis and perception of hidden circumstances, bringing to your attention any dis-ease* that is interfering with your well-being.

Agates enhance mental function as they improve concentration, perception, and analytical abilities, leading to practical solutions. Agate's love of truthfulness encourages speaking one's own truth. Agates with clear crystals can stimulate memories.

Emotionally, this crystal overcomes negativity and bitterness of the heart. It heals inner anger, fostering love and the courage to start again. It is useful for any kind of emotional trauma. It creates a sense of safety and security by dissolving internal tension.

Spiritually, Agate raises consciousness and links into collective consciousness and awareness of the oneness of life. It encourages quiet contemplation and assimilation of life experiences, leading to spiritual growth and inner stability.

HEALING Agate stabilizes the aura*, eliminating and transforming negative energies. Its cleansing effect is powerful at the physical and emotional levels. Placed on the heart, it will heal the emotional dis-ease that prevents acceptance of love. Placed on the abdomen or taken as an elixir, Agate stimulates the digestive process and relieves gastritis. It heals the eyes, stomach, and uterus; it cleanses the lymphatic system and the pancreas; it strengthens blood vessels and heals skin disorders.

POSITION Hold or place on appropriate body location.

Blue Agate (natural)

SPECIFIC COLORS AND TYPES In addition to the generic properties, specific colors have additional properties:

Blue-Green Agate is usually artificially made glass and has no therapeutic properties.

Green Agate

Green Agate enhances mental and emotional flexibility and improves decision-making. It is useful in resolving disputes.

Pink Agate promotes love between parent and child. Position over the heart for optimum effect.

Pink Agate

Botswana Agate Found only in Botswana, this Agate is excellent for anyone connected with fire or smoke. It is beneficial for smokers and those who want to quit smoking. Botswana Agate looks to solutions rather than dwelling on problems. It helps you to explore unknown territory and your own creativity. At a mental level, it helps you to see the bigger picture. At an emotional level, it gently releases repression. This agate often has nodules or ovoids and, being gray and usually found as a nodule, it looks like the brain, with which it resonates. It is particularly useful in helping the body to assimilate oxygen, benefiting the circulatory system and the skin. It also aids depression. At a nonphysical level, it stimulates the crown chakra*, bringing energy into the auric field.

AGATE: **BLUE LACE AGATE**

Polished and tumbled

Raw

COLOR	Pale blue with white or darker lines
APPEARANCE	Banded, often small and tumbled
RARITY	Readily available
SOURCE	As Agate

ADDITIONAL PROPERTIES Blue Lace Agate is a wonderful healing stone. Its soft energy is cooling and calming, bringing peace of mind. It is particularly effective for activating and healing the throat chakra*, allowing free expression of thoughts and feelings. It opens the way

41

to experience of the higher energies. This is one of the great nurturing and supportive stones. It will neutralize anger, infection, inflammation, and fever.

Psychologically, Blue Lace Agate counteracts the repression and suppression of feelings that stem from fear of being judged and rejected. Judgment is often present in the parent–child relationship, both in childhood and adulthood. As a result, feelings are held back and the lack of self-expression blocks the throat chakra and may affect the chest—the feeling being of suffocation. Blue Lace Agate gently dissolves the old pattern of repression and encourages a new mode of expression. It is useful for helping men to release and accept their sensitivity and feeling natures.

Mentally, Blue Lace Agate assists with verbal expression of thoughts and feelings and counteracts mental stress. Emotionally, the peaceful energies exuded from this stone neutralize feelings of anger.

Spiritually, Blue Lace Agate clears the throat chakra so that the highest spiritual truths can be expressed. It is a stone that links thought to the spiritual vibration and brings in deep peace.

HEALING Blue Lace Agate is a powerful throat healer. Its property of counteracting blocked self-expression releases shoulder and neck problems, thyroid deficiencies, and throat and lymph infections. It lowers fevers and removes blockages of the nervous system, and treats arthritic and bone deformity, strengthening the skeletal system and healing fractures. It also aids capillaries and the pancreas. As an elixir, it treats brain fluid imbalances and hydrocephalus. Blue Lace Agate can also be used to enhance sound healing—it focuses and directs sound to the appropriate place.

POSITION As appropriate, particularly at the throat.

AGATE: **DENDRITIC AGATE**

Shaped and polished

COLOR	Clear, brown, green
APPEARANCE	Transparent with fern-like markings, often small and tumbled
RARITY	Readily available
SOURCE	United States, Czech Republic, India, Iceland, Morocco, Brazil

ADDITIONAL PROPERTIES Dendritic Agate is known as the stone of plenitude. It brings abundance and fullness to all areas of life, including business and agriculture. It can be used to enhance the yield of crops or to maintain the health of house plants.

43

Dendritic Agate creates a peaceful environment, both inner and outer, and encourages the enjoyment of each moment. This crystal has a particularly strong connection with the plant kingdom and can enhance communication with that realm. It deepens your own connection to the earth.

However it is used, Dendritic Agate works slowly and takes time to be fully effective.

Psychologically, Dendritic Agate encourages you to remain centered in times of strife or confusion, bringing stability. It lends you perseverance and the ability to see difficulties as a challenge.

Spiritually, Dendritic Agate urges you to remain connected with your roots as you grow. Dendritic Agate opens and aligns the chakras*, enabling them to integrate higher consciousness.

HEALING At a subtle level, Dendritic Agate heals dis-ease caused by chakra imbalances. Within the body, Dendritic Agate resonates with anything that branches, such as blood vessels and nerves. It heals the nervous system and conditions such as neuralgia. This stone treats skeletal disorders and aligns the skeleton to one's physical reality. Dendritic Agate reverses capillary degeneration and stimulates the circulatory system. Placed on the site of injury or pain, it provides pain relief. It is a useful stone for healing plants and the earth itself. It stabilizes the vortices within the earth's energy field and can overcome geopathic stress* or "black ley lines*."

POSITION Hold or place on the appropriate point. Wear for long periods to gain maximum benefit. Tuck into plant pots.

AGATE: **FIRE AGATE**

*Natural
formation*

COLOR	Brownish red, orange, blue, green
APPEARANCE	Swirling, luminescent, small stone
RARITY	Obtainable from specialist stores
SOURCE	United States, Czech Republic, India, Iceland, Morocco, Brazil

ADDITIONAL PROPERTIES Fire Agate has a deep connection to the earth and its energy is calming, bringing security and safety. With strong grounding powers, it supports during difficult times.

Fire Agate has a strong protective function, especially against ill-wishing. Building a protective shield around the body, it returns harm back to its source so that the source understands the harm it is doing.

Physically, Fire Agate, as its name suggests, links to the fire element and aids sexual endeavors, fires up the base chakra* and stimulates vitality on all levels. Psychologically, Fire Agate dispels fear and instills deep security.

Holding a Fire Agate encourages introspection, effortlessly bringing up inner problems for resolution. It helps to eliminate cravings and destructive desires and can be useful in treating addictions.

Spiritually, this protective stone aids relaxation so that the body "mellows out," enhancing meditation. Said to represent absolute perfection, it instills spiritual fortitude and aids the evolution of consciousness.

HEALING This stone heals the stomach, the nervous and endocrine systems, and circulatory disorders. It aids eyes, strengthening night vision and clearing vision at the inner, intuitive levels and outer, physical levels. It resonates with the triple-burner meridian* and can be applied to bring it back into balance, reducing hot flashes and removing heat from the body. Fire Agate brings vitality into the body, preventing energy burn-out. Placed on a blown chakra*, it gently brings it back online. At a subtle level, Fire Agate clears etheric blockages and energizes the aura*.

POSITION Fire Agate can be worn for long periods, or placed on the head or body as appropriate.

AGATE: **MOSS AGATE**

Polished

Tumbled

COLOR	Green, blue, red, yellow, brown
APPEARANCE	Transparent or translucent with branching markings like foliage or moss, often small and tumbled
RARITY	Common
SOURCE	United States, Australia, India

ADDITIONAL PROPERTIES A stabilizing stone strongly connected with nature, Moss Agate is said to refresh the soul and enable you to see the beauty in all you behold. It is helpful in reducing sensitivity to weather and to environmental pollutants. This stone is extremely beneficial for anyone employed in agriculture or associated with botany.

A birthing crystal, Moss Agate assists midwives in their work, lessening pain and ensuring a good delivery. It is a stone of new beginnings and release from blockages or spiritual fetters.

47

A stone of wealth, Moss Agate attracts abundance.

Moss Agate can act with a dual purpose. It helps intellectual people access their intuitive feelings and, conversely, assists intuitive people in channeling their energy in practical ways.

Psychologically, Moss Agate improves self-esteem and strengthens positive personality traits. It releases fear and deep-seated stress. It helps to develop strength and the ability to get along with others, and encourages expanding one's personal space and growth. It strengthens the ability to try one more time, inspiring with new ideals after a period of stagnation.

Mentally, Moss Agate promotes self-expression and communication. It balances the emotions, reducing stress and lessening fear. It encourages trust and hope, being a highly optimistic stone. It is helpful for anyone suffering from depression through life circumstances or brain imbalances. No matter how difficult those circumstances may be, Moss Agate gives insight into the reason behind them.

HEALING Moss Agate speeds up recovery. It can be used to counteract long-term illness. It is anti-inflammatory, cleanses the circulatory and elimination systems, encouraging the flow of lymph, and boosts the immune system. Moss Agate eliminates depression caused by left–right brain imbalance. It helps prevent hypoglycemia and dehydration, treats infections, colds and flu, and lowers fevers. It is anti-inflammatory and reduces swelling in lymph nodes. As an elixir applied to the skin, Moss Agate treats fungal and skin infections.

POSITION Place or hold on the appropriate point in contact with the skin.

AMAZONITE

Polished and tumbled

Raw

COLOR	Blue, green
APPEARANCE	Opalescent with veins, various sizes, sometimes tumbled
RARITY	Common
SOURCE	United States, Russia, Canada, Brazil, India, Mozambique, Namibia, Austria

ATTRIBUTES Amazonite has a powerful filtering action. At a physical level, it blocks geopathic stress*, absorbs microwaves and cell phone emanations, and protects against electromagnetic pollution. It should be placed between you and the source of any pollution or taped to a cell phone. At a mental level, it filters the information passing through the brain and combines it with intuition.

This is an extremely soothing stone. It calms the brain and nervous system and aligns the physical body with the etheric*, maintaining optimum health. It balances the masculine and feminine energies and many aspects of the personality. It is a stone that helps you to see both sides of a problem or different points of view. At an emotional level, Amazonite soothes emotional trauma, alleviating worry and fear. It dispels negative energy and aggravation.

Spiritually, an elixir of Amazonite is extremely beneficial to all levels of consciousness. The stone itself assists in manifesting universal love.

HEALING Amazonite heals and opens both the heart and throat chakras* to enhance loving communication. It also opens the third eye* and intuition. The stone dissipates negative energy and blockages within the nervous system. It is beneficial in osteoporosis, tooth decay, calcium deficiency, and calcium deposits, balancing the metabolic deficiencies that create these conditions. The elixir rectifies calcium problems. Amazonite also relieves muscle spasms. A major property is the protection it affords from the health hazards of microwaves and other sources of electromagnetic smog*.

POSITION Hold or place over the affected point, or wear to protect against microwaves. Place near computers or tape to your cell phone.

AMBER

Shaped

Yellow, clear

COLOR	Golden brown or yellow—green is artificially colored
APPEARANCE	Opaque or transparent resin, insects or vegetation trapped inside, various sizes
RARITY	Easily obtained
SOURCE	Britain, Poland, Italy, Romania, Russia, Germany, Myanmar, Dominica

ATTRIBUTES Strictly speaking, Amber is not a crystal at all. It is tree resin that solidified and became fossilized. It has strong connections with the earth and is a grounding stone for higher energies. Amber is a powerful healer and cleanser that draws dis-ease* from the body and

51

promotes tissue revitalization. It also cleans the environment and the chakras*. It absorbs negative energies and transmutes them into positive forces that stimulate the body to heal itself. A powerful protector, it links the everyday self to the higher spiritual reality.

Psychologically, Amber brings stability to life but also motivates by linking what is wished for to the drive to achieve it. Its warm, bright energies translate into a sunny, spontaneous disposition that nevertheless respects tradition. It can help counteract suicidal or depressive tendencies.

Mentally, Amber stimulates the intellect, clears depression, and promotes a positive mental state and creative self-expression. It brings balance and patience and encourages decision-making, being a useful memory aid. Its flexibility dissolves opposition. Emotionally, Amber encourages peacefulness and develops trust. Spiritually, Amber promotes altruism and brings wisdom.

HEALING Amber is a powerful chakra cleanser and healer. At a physical level, it imbues the body with vitality and has the power to draw dis-ease out of the body. By absorbing pain and negative energy, Amber allows the body to rebalance and heal itself. Amber alleviates stress. It resonates with the throat, treating goiters and other throat problems. It treats the stomach, spleen, kidneys, bladder, liver, and gallbladder, alleviates joint problems, and strengthens the mucus membranes. As an elixir and for wound healing, it is an excellent natural antibiotic. It can stimulate the navel chakra and help in grounding energies into the body.

POSITION Wear for prolonged periods, especially on the wrist or throat, or place as appropriate. If treating babies or children, it is beneficial for the mother to wear the stone first.

AMETHYST

Purple Amethyst

COLOR	Purple to lavender
APPEARANCE	Transparent, pointed crystals. May be geode, cluster, or single point. All sizes
RARITY	One of the most common crystals
SOURCE	United States, Britain, Canada, Brazil, Mexico, Russia, Sri Lanka, Uruguay, East Africa, Siberia, India

ATTRIBUTES Amethyst is an extremely powerful and protective stone with a high spiritual vibration. It guards against psychic attack*, transmuting the energy into love. A natural tranquilizer, Amethyst blocks geopathic stress* and negative environment energies. Its serenity enhances higher states of consciousness and meditation. Amethyst has strong healing and cleansing powers, and enhances spiritual awareness. Traditionally, it was worn to prevent drunkenness and has a sobering effect on overindulgence and physical passions, supporting sobriety. It overcomes addictions and blockages of all kinds. Used at a higher level, Amethyst opens to another reality.

Amethyst is extremely beneficial to the mind, calming or stimulating as appropriate. When you meditate, it turns thoughts away from the mundane into tranquility and deeper understanding. Mentally, it helps you feel less scattered, more focused and in control of your faculties. It enhances the assimilation of new ideas and connects cause with effect.

This stone facilitates the decision-making process, bringing in common sense and spiritual insights, and putting decisions and insights into practice. Mentally, it calms and synthesizes, and aids the transmission of neural signals through the brain. It is helpful where insomnia is caused by an overactive mind and protects against recurrent nightmares. Amethyst enhances memory and improves motivation, making you more able to set realistic goals. It can help you to remember and understand dreams and facilitates the visualization process.

Amethyst balances out highs and lows, promoting emotional centering. It dispels anger, rage, fear, and anxiety. Alleviating sadness and grief, it supports coming to terms with loss.

Amethyst is one of the most spiritual stones, promoting love of the divine, giving insights into its true nature, and encouraging selflessness and spiritual wisdom. It opens intuition and enhances psychic gifts. This is an excellent stone for meditation and scrying* and can be placed on the third eye to stimulate it. Sleeping with Amethyst facilitates out-of-body experiences* and brings intuitive dreams. It transmutes "lower" energies to the higher frequencies of the spiritual and etheric* realms.

HEALING Amethyst boosts production of hormones, and tunes the endocrine system and metabolism. It strengthens the cleansing and eliminating organs and the immune system. An excellent cleanser for the blood, Amethyst relieves physical, emotional, and psychological pain or stress, and blocks geopathic stress. It eases headaches and releases tension. This stone reduces bruising, injuries, and swellings, and treats hearing disorders. It heals dis-eases of the lungs and respiratory tract, skin conditions, cellular disorders, and dis-eases of the digestive tract. It is beneficial for the intestines, regulating flora, removing parasites, and encouraging reabsorption of water. Amethyst treats insomnia and brings restful sleep.

At a subtle level, Amethyst balances and connects the physical, mental, and emotional bodies*, linking them to the spiritual. It cleanses the aura* and transmutes negative energy, and stimulates the throat and crown chakras*. It is helpful for people about to make the transition through death. Amethyst can stabilize psychiatric conditions but should not be used in cases of paranoia or schizophrenia.

POSITION Wear or place as appropriate, especially as jewelry. Clusters and geodes can be placed in the environment and single points are used in healing. Place the point in toward you to draw in energy, and away from you to draw off energy. Amethyst is especially beneficial worn over the throat or heart. For insomnia or nightmares, place under the pillow. Amethyst fades in sunlight.

Amethyst point

SPECIFIC COLORS

In addition to the generic properties, the following colors and forms have additional properties:

Violet-Lavender Amethyst has a particularly high vibration. Double-terminated lilac crystals take you into beta brain waves. They also stimulate and then calm the throat and heart chakras. Violet "flowers" bring light and love into the environment.

Lavender Amethyst flower

Chevron Amethyst is one of the best third-eye* stimulators. It enhances inner, intuitive vision and outer, physical vision, and out-of-body journeys. It has powerfully focused energy that dissipates and repels negativity. This stone cleanses the aura and aids in auric diagnosis. It has a strong healing field, bringing harmony to the organs of the body and stimulating the immune system. It helps you to find and implement a positive answer to any problem.

Pineapple Amethyst has small nodules covering the sides above which emerge the termination points. Looking like the turrets of a castle in a fairytale, it facilitates contact with the mythic and fairytale realms and stimulates the imagination. It is a powerful archetypal healer for family and collective myths.

Amethyst wand

Pineapple Amethyst cluster

AMETRINE

Polished

Raw

COLOR	Purple and yellow
APPEARANCE	Transparent crystal, combination of Amethyst and Citrine, often small and tumbled
RARITY	Readily available though obtained from only one mine
SOURCE	Bolivia

ATTRIBUTES Ametrine powerfully combines Amethyst and Citrine. It is fast and effective in its action, and is particularly useful in long-standing illness as it brings insight into causes of dis-ease*. Ametrine connects the physical realm with higher consciousness. This stone facilitates and protects during astral travel* and relieves psychic attack*. It clears stress and tension from the head, calming the mind and bringing greater focus to meditation. Ametrine opens the third eye, promoting healing and divination. It unites masculine and feminine energies.

Psychologically, Ametrine enhances compatibility and acceptance of others. It shows where everyone is linked, overcoming prejudice. An extremely energetic stone, it stimulates creativity and supports taking control of one's own life. It is a stone that can overcome apparent contradictions.

Mentally, Ametrine brings clarity, harmonizing perception and action. It strengthens concentration and aids thinking things through, encouraging exploration of all possibilities, bringing creative solutions. It takes the intellect beyond everyday reality to link into higher awareness.

Emotionally, Ametrine releases blockages, including negative emotional programming* and expectations, facilitating transformation, bringing insight into underlying causes of emotional distress. Ametrine promotes optimism and a well-being that is not disturbed by stressful external influences.

HEALING Ametrine gets to the bottom of things. Its powerful cleansing properties disperse negativity from the aura*, and toxins from the body. An exceptional blood cleanser and energizer, it regenerates the physical body and strengthens the immune system, aids the autonomic nervous system and physical maturation, stabilizes DNA/RNA, and oxygenates the body. Ametrine heals chronic fatigue syndrome (CFS)*, burning sensations, depression, gastric disturbances and ulcers, fatigue and lethargy, tension headaches, and stress-related dis-ease. It releases blockages in the physical, emotional, and mental subtle bodies*.

POSITION Wear directly on the body for prolonged periods, placing on solar plexus. Holding Ametrine brings deep-seated issues to the surface so that they can be communicated and healed.

ANGELITE

*Sliced and
lightly polished*

COLOR	Blue and white, sometimes flecked with red
APPEARANCE	Opaque and often veined like wings, largish stone
RARITY	Easily obtained
SOURCE	Britain, Egypt, Germany, Mexico, Peru, Poland, Libya

ATTRIBUTES Angelite is one of the "stones of awareness" for the New
Age. It represents peace and brotherhood. As its name suggests,
Angelite facilitates conscious contact with the angelic realm*. It
enhances telepathic communication and enables out-of-body journeys*

to take place while still maintaining contact with everyday reality.

Angelite is a powerful stone for healers because it deepens attunement and heightens perception. It also provides protection for the environment or the body, especially when taken as an elixir.

Angelite is formed from Celestite (see page 96) that has been compressed over millions of years, and it shares many properties with that stone.

Psychologically, Angelite helps you to speak your truth, whatever it may be. It also helps you to be more compassionate and accepting, especially of that which cannot be changed. It alleviates psychological pain and counteracts cruelty. Mentally, Angelite has been used to enhance astrological understanding and to bring deeper understanding of mathematics. It also facilitates telepathic contact between minds.

Spiritually, Angelite is filled with compassion. It transmutes pain and disorder into wholeness and healing, opening the way for spiritual inspiration. It creates a deep feeling of peace and tranquility. It helps connect to universal knowledge and raises awareness. Angelite facilitates the rebirthing process, stimulates healing, and opens psychic channeling*.

HEALING Applied to the feet, Angelite unblocks meridians* and energetic pathways. It resonates with the throat, alleviating inflammation and balancing the thyroid and the parathyroids. This soothing stone repairs tissue and blood vessels, balancing the fluids within the physical body, and can act as a diuretic. It is useful in weight control, and relates particularly to the lungs and arms. Angelite can cool the pain of sunburn. At a subtle level, Angelite balances the physical body with the etheric realms.

POSITION Hold or place on the body as appropriate.

ANHYDRITE

*Natural
formation*

COLOR	Clear, blue, gray
APPEARANCE	Long bladed or short crystals, usually on matrix
RARITY	Obtained from specialist stores
SOURCE	Italy

ATTRIBUTES Anhydrite gives support and strength on the physical plane. It promotes acceptance of the physical body as a transient vessel for the soul. It helps you face with equanimity what tomorrow may bring. It is useful for people who have difficulty in coming to terms with incarnation and who long for the "post-death" state. Teaching acceptance of all that life has brought, releasing a hankering for the past, it assists past-life healing, showing the gift in all that has been.

HEALING Anhydrite treats disorders of the throat, especially those caused by a difficulty in expressing oneself through a physical body. It removes retained or excess fluid and disperses swelling.

POSITION Place on the throat or over the thymus gland.

61

APATITE

Blue

COLOR	Yellow, green, gray, blue, white, purple, brown, red-brown, violet
APPEARANCE	Opaque, sometimes transparent, glassy, hexagonal crystal, various sizes, often tumbled
RARITY	Blue readily available, yellow rare
SOURCE	Mexico, Norway, Russia, United States

ATTRIBUTES Apatite has inspirational properties. The interface point between consciousness and matter, it is a stone of manifestation and promotes a humanitarian attitude, inclining toward service. Apatite is attuned to the future, yet connects to past lives. It develops psychic gifts and spiritual attunement, deepens meditation, raises the kundalini*, and aids communication and self-expression on all levels.

Psychologically, Apatite increases motivation and builds up energy reserves. It induces openness and social ease, encouraging extroversion, dissolving aloofness and alienation. It draws off negativity about oneself and others. It is helpful for hyperactive and autistic children.

Stimulating creativity and the intellect, Apatite clears confusion and helps to access information to be used personally and for the collective good. Apatite expands knowledge and truth and eases sorrow, apathy, and anger. It reduces irritability and overcomes emotional exhaustion. By releasing energy in the base chakra*, it clears frustration and endorses passion without guilt.

HEALING Apatite heals bones and encourages formation of new cells. It aids absorption of calcium and helps cartilage, bones, teeth, and motor skills and ameliorates arthritis, joint problems, and rickets. This stone suppresses hunger and raises the metabolic rate, encouraging healthy eating; heals the glands, meridians, and organs; and overcomes hypertension. It balances the physical, emotional, mental, and spiritual bodies, and the chakras, eliminating overactivity and stimulating underactivity. Used with other crystals, Apatite facilitates results.

POSITION Wear on skin over affected part, or place as appropriate.

SPECIFIC COLORS
In addition to the generic attributes, the following colors have additional properties:

Blue Apatite connects to a very high level of spiritual guidance. It facilitates public speaking, enhances group communication, opens the throat chakra, and heals the heart and emotional dis-ease.

Yellow Apatite is a great eliminator, especially of toxins. It activates the solar plexus and draws off stagnant energy. Yellow Apatite treats CFS*, lethargy, and depression, and overcomes lack of concentration, inefficient learning, and poor digestion. It removes cellulite and treats the liver, pancreas, gallbladder and spleen. At an emotional level, it neutralizes stored anger. Yellow Apatite elixir is an appetite suppressant.

Yellow Apatite

APOPHYLLITE

White cluster

COLOR	Clear, white, green, yellowish, peach
APPEARANCE	Cubic or pyramidal crystals, may be transparent or opaque, small single crystals to large clusters
RARITY	Readily available
SOURCE	Britain, Australia, India, Brazil, Czech Republic, Italy

ATTRIBUTES Apophyllite has a high water content which makes it a very efficient conductor of energy and a carrier of the Akashic Record* (the esoteric record of all that has occurred and will occur, including past-life information). Its presence in a room enhances the energies as it is a powerful vibrational transmitter. Apophyllite creates a conscious connection between the physical and the spiritual realms. During out-of-body journeys*, it keeps a strong connection with the physical body, allowing information to be transmitted from the spiritual realm into the physical. This spiritual stone enhances clear sight, stimulating intuition and enabling the future to be accessed. It is an excellent stone for scrying*.

Psychologically, Apophyllite promotes introspection into one's own behavior, and the correction of imbalances or flaws that are perceived. It abandons pretence and breaks down reserve. This is a stone of truth, bringing recognition of one's true self and allowing that to be shown to the world.

Mentally, Apophyllite has a calming effect. It is an effective stress reducer, releasing mental blockages and negative thought patterns. It has the effect of reducing desire. At a spiritual level, Apophyllite imbues universal love into analysis and the decision-making process so that the mind becomes attuned to the spirit.

Emotionally, Apophyllite releases suppressed emotions. It overcomes anxiety, worries, and fears. It calms apprehension and allows uncertainty to be tolerated.

Spiritually this stone calms and grounds the spirit. It has strong links to the spiritual realm, while at the same time allowing you to feel comfortable within your body. It facilitates journeys out of the body and spiritual vision. With its connection to the Akashic Record, it eases journeys into past lives.

HEALING Apophyllite is regarded as the stone *par excellence* to assist Reiki* healing. It facilitates taking the patient into a deeper state of relaxation and receptiveness, and, at the same time takes the healer out of the way so that the transmission of healing energy to the patient is purer.

Apophyllite works on the respiratory system and, when held to the chest, can stop asthma attacks. It neutralizes allergies and promotes the regeneration of the mucus membranes and the skin. Placing an Apophyllite crystal on each eye rejuvenates the eyes. Apophyllite is especially useful in healing matters of the spirit and in helping the spirit to come to terms with being in a physical body.

POSITION Place as appropriate. Single Apophyllite pyramids can be placed on the third eye* when channeling or meditating. When scrying*, look into the crystal from the corner of the eye.

SPECIFIC COLORS AND FORMS
In addition to the generic attributes, the following colors have additional properties:

Green Apophyllite

Green Apophyllite activates the heart chakra* and promotes a forthright heart, especially regarding decisions in matters of the heart. It absorbs and then transmits universal energy. This stone opens the heart chakra and allows absorption of universal energies. It helps those undertaking fire walking as it facilitates a meditative state and cools the feet after the walk. It releases hypnotic commands* and other control mechanisms from present or past lives.

Apophyllite Pyramid

Apophyllite Pyramids are powerful energizers. They enhance spiritual vision and open the third eye. Looking through the base of the pyramid toward the apex opens a "star gate."* Like all pyramids, they have powers of preservation and can be used to charge up objects or other crystals. Made into an elixir, Apophyllite pyramids bring light and energy into the heart.

66

AQUAMARINE

Clear, raw

COLOR	Green-blue
APPEARANCE	Clear to opaque crystal, often small and tumbled or faceted
RARITY	Readily available
SOURCE	United States, Mexico, Russia, Brazil, India, Ireland, Zimbabwe, Afghanistan, Pakistan

ATTRIBUTES Aquamarine is a stone of courage. Its calming energies reduce stress and quiet the mind. It harmonizes its surroundings and protects against pollutants. In ancient times it was believed to counteract the forces of darkness and procure favor from the spirits of light. It was carried by sailors as a talisman against drowning.

Psychologically, Aquamarine has an affinity with sensitive people. It has the power to invoke tolerance of others. It overcomes judgmentalism, gives support to anyone who is overwhelmed by responsibility, and encourages taking responsibility for oneself. It creates a personality that is upright, persistent, and dynamic. It can break old, self-defeating programs.

Aquamarine calms the mind, removing extraneous thought. It filters information reaching the brain and clarifies perception, sharpens the intellect, and clears up confusion. With its ability to bring unfinished business to a conclusion, Aquamarine is useful for closure on all levels. It clears blocked communication and promotes self-expression. This stone is helpful in understanding underlying emotional states and interpreting how you feel. It soothes fears and increases sensitivity.

Spiritually, Aquamarine sharpens intuition and opens clairvoyance. A wonderful stone for meditation, it invokes high states of consciousness and spiritual awareness and encourages service to humanity.

Aquamarine shields the aura* and aligns the chakras*, clearing the throat chakra and bringing communication from a higher plane. It also aligns the physical and spiritual bodies.

HEALING Aquamarine is useful for sore throats, swollen glands, and thyroid problems. It harmonizes the pituitary and the thyroid, regulating hormones and growth. This stone has a general tonic effect. It strengthens the body's cleansing organs and aids the eyes, jaw and teeth, and stomach. It is useful for counteracting short- or long-sightedness and calms overreactions of the immune system and autoimmune diseases such as hay fever.

POSITION Hold or place as appropriate. Can be placed on the eyes or used as an elixir.

ARAGONITE

Brown "sputnik" form

White "fan" form

White "coral" form

COLOR	White, yellow, gold, green, blue, brown
APPEARANCE	Several forms, usually small. Chalky and fibrous or translucent or transparent with distinct protrusions like little sputniks
RARITY	Easily obtained
SOURCE	Namibia, Britain, Spain

ATTRIBUTES Aragonite is a reliable earth-healer and grounding stone. Attuned to the Earth Goddess, it encourages conservation and recycling. This stone transforms geopathic stress* and clears blocked ley lines* even at a distance. With its ability to center and ground physical energies, it is useful in times of stress. Aragonite stabilizes the base and

69

earth chakras*, deepening connection with the earth. It gently takes you back into childhood or beyond to explore the past.

Psychologically, Aragonite teaches patience and acceptance. It combats oversensitivity. Good for people who push themselves too hard, it facilitates delegating. Its practical energy encourages discipline and reliability, and develops a pragmatic approach to life.

Mentally, this stone aids concentration on the matter at hand, and brings flexibility and tolerance to the mind. It gives insight into the causes of problems and situations. Emotionally, Aragonite combats anger and emotional stress. It provides strength and support.

Physically, Aragonite is a stone that makes you feel comfortable and well within your own body. It combats dis-ease*, especially the nervous twitching and spasms that come out of inner unrest. It is a stabilizing stone that grounds and centers within the body.

Spiritually, Aragonite stabilizes spiritual development that is out of control. Calming and centering, it restores balance and prepares for meditation by raising vibrations to a high spiritual level and bringing energy into the physical body.

HEALING Aragonite warms the extremities, bringing energy through the body. It treats Reynaud's Disease and chills. It heals bones, aids calcium absorption, and restores elasticity to discs. It also ameliorates pain. Aragonite stops night twitches and muscle spasms. It strengthens the immune system and regulates processes that are proceeding too fast. It is useful for grounding floaty people into their body. Aragonite can be placed on a map to heal stress lines in the earth.

POSITION Hold or place over affected part, or bathe with elixir. Place under pillow to combat restlessness at night. Makes a useful hand comforter. Can be worn as a pendant for grounding.

ATACAMITE

*Atacamite
on matrix*

COLOR	Deep turquoise
APPEARANCE	Tiny crystals on matrix—resembles Chrysocolla
RARITY	Quite rare but becoming more widely available
SOURCE	United States, Australia, Mexico, Chile

ATTRIBUTES Atacamite is a newly discovered crystal and its properties have not yet been fully explored. (If you meditate with an Atacamite crystal, it will tell you how it wants to work for you.) It is sometimes confused with gem Chrysocolla and may share some properties with this crystal.

What is known is that Atacamite forcefully opens the third eye*, creating powerful visual images and a strong spiritual connection.

71

Despite its forcefulness, it is a very safe crystal to use to stimulate spiritual vision and aid visualization. It is a stone of great clarity. Used in meditation, it takes the soul safely to the highest possible levels.

Atacamite restores lost spiritual trust and promotes a connection to higher guidance. It is a useful stone to hold when journeying out of the body, especially to the higher spiritual spheres.

Atacamite works willingly to open the higher heart chakra*, bringing more unconditional love into your life, and to stimulate the thymus gland and immune system functioning.

HEALING Atacamite purifies the kidneys, removing fear, and promotes elimination at all levels. It is a powerful cleanser for the etheric body and the brow chakra. It can be used to heal the genitals and is said to improve resistance to herpes and venereal disease. Placed on the throat, Atacamite heals the thyroid gland, opening the throat chakra and removing the blockages to self-expression that can lie behind hypothyroidism. With its calming green color, it is also beneficial for the nervous system, overcoming stress and frayed nerves at a subtle level.

POSITION Place on the third eye* to stimulate visualization or over organs as appropriate. Hold in hands for meditation or journeying.

AVENTURINE

Blue, raw

COLOR	Green, blue, red, brown, peach
APPEARANCE	Opaque, speckled with shiny particles, all sizes, often tumbled
RARITY	Readily available
SOURCE	Italy, Brazil, China, India, Russia, Tibet, Nepal

ATTRIBUTES Aventurine is a very positive stone of prosperity. It has a strong connection to the devic kingdom* and is used to grid* gardens or houses against geopathic stress*. Wearing Aventurine absorbs electromagnetic smog* and protects against environmental pollution. Taped to a cell phone, it acts as a protection against its emanations. This crystal defuses negative situations and turns them around.

Psychologically, Aventurine reinforces leadership qualities and decisiveness. It promotes compassion and empathy and encourages perseverance. It takes you back into the past to find sources of dis-ease*. This stone relieves stammers and severe neuroses, bringing understanding of what lies behind the conditions. Aventurine stabilizes one's state of mind, stimulates perception, and enhances creativity.

73

It sees alternatives and possibilities, especially those presented by other people. This stone brings together the intellectual and emotional bodies. Aventurine calms anger and irritation. It stimulates emotional recovery and enables living within one's own heart.

Physically, Aventurine promotes a feeling of well-being. It regulates growth from birth to seven years. It balances male–female energy and encourages regeneration of the heart. Spiritually, Aventurine protects the heart chakra*, guarding against psychic vampirism* of heart energy.

Peach Aventurine (raw)

HEALING Aventurine benefits the thymus gland, connective tissue, and nervous system; it balances blood pressure and stimulates the metabolism, lowering cholesterol and preventing arteriosclerosis and heart attacks. It has an anti-inflammatory effect and helps ease skin eruptions and allergies, relieves migraine headaches, and soothes the eyes. Aventurine heals the adrenals, lungs, sinuses, heart, and muscular and urogenital systems. As an elixir, it relieves skin problems.

Green Aventurine (tumbled)

POSITION Hold or place on appropriate point.

SPECIFIC COLORS
In addition to the generic attributes, the following colors have additional properties:

Blue Aventurine is a powerful mental healer.

Red Aventurine (raw)

Green Aventurine is a comforter and heart healer, and general harmonizer, protecting the heart. It brings things back into control and is useful in malignant conditions. It settles nausea and dissolves negative emotions and thoughts. An all-round healer, bringing in well-being and emotional calm.

AZEZTULITE

Raw, opaque

COLOR	Colorless or white
APPEARANCE	Clear or opaque quartz with striations, usually small
RARITY	Rare and expensive
SOURCE	North Carolina (one seam, mined out)

ATTRIBUTES A rare and light-bearing crystal, Azeztulite is a stone for the New Age. Its extremely pure vibration, one of the most refined in the mineral kingdom, is attuned to the highest frequencies. It brings higher frequencies down to the earth to aid spiritual evolution.

This crystal expands your consciousness. If you are ready, it can lift your awareness and vibrations to a higher level. As Azeztulite raises your vibrations, it helps you to give out a positive vibration to benefit others. Azeztulite never requires cleansing and is always energized.

This crystal should be handled with care if you are not used to working in the spiritual realms or at high frequencies. The vibrational shift it induces is powerful and can have unpleasant side effects until it has been fully assimilated. Using other spiritual crystals such as Ametrine and Aquamarine prepares the way. Old patterns should be dissolved and emotional cleansing completed before undertaking this shift. The opaque form of Azeztulite has a less fine vibration and can be a useful staging post on the way to working with the more transparent form of the crystal.

Spiritually, Azeztulite facilitates meditation, instantly inducing a state of "no mind" and providing a protective spiral around the physical body. It stimulates the kundalini* to rise up the spine. A stone of vision and inspiration, Azeztulite opens the third eye and the crown and higher crown chakras* reaching up to spiritual levels. It tunes into spiritual guidance from the future, assisting in making important decisions.

Azeztulite activates the ascension points at the base of the spine, middle of the abdomen, and center of the brain to shift to a higher vibration while still in the physical body. Used on the third eye*, it helps you to see the future.

HEALING At a physical level, this crystal treats cancer, cellular disorders, and inflammation. It aids the chronically sick by revitalizing purpose and restoring the will. Most of Azeztulite's healing work is at the spiritual vibration, working on the chakra connections to higher reality and facilitating a vibrational shift.

POSITION Third eye, crown, or as appropriate.

AZURITE

Raw

COLOR	Deep blue
APPEARANCE	Very small, shiny crystals (not visible when tumbled), often small tumbled stone
RARITY	Easily obtained, often in combination with Malachite
SOURCE	United States, Australia, Chile, Peru, France, Namibia, Russia, Egypt

ATTRIBUTES Azurite guides psychic and intuitive development. It urges the soul toward enlightenment. It cleanses and stimulates the third eye* and attunes to spiritual guidance. This crystal enables journeys out of the body to take place easily and safely. It raises consciousness to a higher level and gives greater control over spiritual unfoldment. It facilitates entering a meditative and channeling* state. Azurite is a powerful healing stone, facilitating psychosomatic understanding of the effect of the mind and emotions on the body.

Mentally, Azurite brings about clear understanding and new perspectives, and expands the mind. It releases long-standing blocks in communication and stimulates memory. Azurite challenges your view of reality and lets go of programmed belief systems to move into the unknown without fear, reaching deeper insights and a new reality. Old beliefs gently rise into the conscious mind to be tested against truth.

Emotionally, Azurite clears stress, worry, grief, and sadness, allowing more light into the emotions. It transmutes fear and phobias, and brings in understanding of why they occurred in the first place. It calms someone who talks too much out of nervousness, or encourages someone who holds back from self-expression.

HEALING Azurite treats throat problems, arthritis and joint problems, aligns the spine, and works at a cellular level to restore any blockage or damage to the brain. It heals kidney, gallbladder, and liver problems, and treats the spleen, thyroid, bones, teeth, and skin and aids detoxification. It encourages the development of the embryo in the womb. Azurite has a special resonance with the mind and mental processes, mental healing, and stress relief. It can energize and realign the subtle bodies* with the physical, clearing the chakras*. Azurite elixir ameliorates a healing crisis* where symptoms temporarily get worse before improving.

POSITION Wear touching the skin on the right hand or place as appropriate directly on the body, especially on the third eye. May induce palpitations. If so, remove immediately.

COMBINATION STONE
Azurite with Malachite combines the qualities of the two crystals and is a powerful conductor of energy. It unlocks spiritual vision, strengthens the ability to visualize, and opens the third eye. At an emotional level it brings deep healing, cleansing ancient blocks, miasms*, or thought patterns. It overcomes muscle cramps.

Azurite with Malachtite (tumbled)

BERYL

Blue

Golden

COLOR	Pink, golden, yellow, green, white, blue
APPEARANCE	Prismatic crystals, may be transparent and pyramidal, all sizes
RARITY	Readily available in most forms but may be expensive
SOURCE	United States, Russia, Australia, Brazil, Czech Republic, France, Norway

ATTRIBUTES Beryl teaches you how to do only that which you need to do. It is the stone *par excellence* for dealing with a stressful life and shedding unnecessary baggage. It aids in tuning into guidance as to what you should be doing. Representing purity of being, Beryl helps to actualize potential and is an excellent stone for scrying*, and is often used for crystal balls. It opens and activates the crown and solar plexus chakras*.

Psychologically, Beryl enhances courage, relieves stress, and calms the mind. Mentally, with its ability to filter out distractions and to reduce overstimulation, it encourages a positive view. It discourages overanalysis and anxiety. Emotionally, Beryl reawakens love in those who are married but jaded.

HEALING Beryl aids the organs of elimination, strengthens pulmonary and circulatory systems, and increases resistance to toxins and pollutants. It treats the liver, heart, stomach, and spine, and heals concussions. Beryl is a sedative stone. As an elixir it can be used to treat throat infections.

POSITION Place as appropriate or use for scrying*.

SPECIFIC COLORS
In addition to the generic attributes, the following colors have additional properties:

Golden Beryl is a seer's stone and is used for ritual magic. It aids scrying and magical workings. This crystal promotes purity of being. It teaches initiative and independence and stimulates the will to succeed and the ability to manifest potential into reality. It opens the crown and solar plexus chakras*.

Golden Beryl (polished)

Morganite (Pink Beryl) attracts love and maintains it. It encourages loving thoughts and actions, creating space to enjoy life and living. As a pink stone it activates and cleanses the heart chakra, calms a stressed life, and benefits the nervous system. This stone helps you to

Morganite (Pink Beryl)

recognize the escape routes, closed-mindedness, and egotism that block spiritual advancement. It assists in becoming aware of the disregarded needs of the soul. Morganite also aids in recognizing unfulfilled emotional needs and unexpressed feelings. Morganite is a powerful stone for dissolving conscious or unconscious resistance to healing and transformation, clearing the victim mentality and opening the heart to receive unconditional love and healing. It holds the emotional body stable while psychosomatic changes take place. Used in healing, Morganite treats stress and stress-related illness. Oxygenating cells and reorganizing them, it treats TB, asthma, emphysema, heart problems, vertigo, impotence, and lung blockages.

Bixbite (Red Beryl) opens and energizes the base chakras.

(*See also* Emerald, page 126.)

BERYL: **CHRYSOBERYL**

Raw   Faceted

COLOR	Golden yellow, yellow with brown, green with red
APPEARANCE	Tabular transparent crystals. Alexandrite appears green in natural light and red in artificial light. Cat's Eye or Cymophane is banded or eye-like
RARITY	Chrysoberyl readily available, Cat's Eye may be expensive, Alexandrite rare
SOURCE	Australia, Brazil, Myanmar, Canada, Ghana, Norway, Zimbabwe, Russia

ATTRIBUTES A form of Beryl, Chrysoberyl is a stone of new beginnings. It brings compassion and forgiveness, generosity and confidence. Aligning the solar plexus and crown chakras*, it incorporates the mind into spiritual endeavor and opens the crown chakra, increasing both spiritual and personal power, and is excellent for creativity.

Psychologically, Chrysoberyl strengthens self-worth and releases outworn energy patterns. Mentally, Chrysoberyl helps you to see both sides of a problem or situation and to use strategic planning. Emotionally, it encourages forgiveness for those who have perpetrated injustices.

HEALING Used with other crystals, Chrysoberyl highlights the cause of dis-ease. It supports self-healing, balances adrenaline and cholesterol, and fortifies the chest and liver.

SPECIFIC FORMS

In addition to the generic attributes, the following forms of Chrysoberyl have additional properties:

Alexandrite is a crystal of contrasts. It opens intuition and metaphysical abilities, creates a strong will and personal magnetism. Regenerative, it rebuilds self-respect, and supports rebirth of the inner and outer self. Alexandrite centers, reinforces, and realigns the mental, emotional, and spiritual bodies. It brings joy, expands creativity, expedites change, and enhances manifestation. An emotional soother, Alexandrite teaches how to expend less effort. It stimulates imagery, including dreams and the imagination. In healing it aids the nervous system, spleen, pancreas, and male reproductive organs and regenerates neurological tissue. Alexandrite treats nonassimilation of protein, side effects of leukemia, and relieves tension from neck muscles. It has a powerful detoxifying action and stimulates the liver.

Alexandrite

Cat's Eye has magical properties. It is a grounding stone but stimulates the intuition. It dispels negative energy from the aura* and provides protection. It brings confidence, happiness, serenity, and good luck. Cat's Eye treats eye disorders and improves night vision. It relieves headaches and facial pain. Wear on the right-hand side of the body.

Cat's Eye

Cymophane is a form of Cat's Eye. It stimulates and stabilizes the intellect and supports flexibility of mind. It enhances unconditional love.

Cymophane

BLOODSTONE

Also known as Heliotrope

Tumbled

Raw

COLOR	Red-green
APPEARANCE	Green quartz flecked with red or yellow jasper, often medium tumbled stone
RARITY	Readily available
SOURCE	Australia, Brazil, China, Czech Republic, Russia, India

ATTRIBUTES As its name suggests, Bloodstone is an excellent blood cleanser and a powerful healer. It is believed to have mystical and magical properties, controlling the weather and conferring the ability to banish evil and negativity and to direct spiritual energies. In ancient times Bloodstone was said to have been an "audible oracle,"* giving off sounds as a means of guidance. It heightens the intuition and increases creativity. An excellent grounding and protecting stone, Bloodstone keeps out undesirable influences. It stimulates dreaming and is a powerful revitalizer.

Psychologically, Bloodstone gives courage and teaches how to avoid dangerous situations by strategic withdrawal and flexibility. It encourages selflessness and idealism and aids the recognition that chaos precedes transformation. Bloodstone assists you in acting in the present moment.

Mentally, Bloodstone calms the mind, dispels confusion, and enhances the decision-making process. It can revitalize the mind if you are mentally exhausted. This stone assists in adjusting to unaccustomed circumstances.

Emotionally, Bloodstone helps in grounding the heart energy. It reduces irritability, aggressiveness, and impatience. Spiritually, Bloodstone assists in bringing spirituality into everyday life.

HEALING Bloodstone is an energy cleanser and immune stimulator for acute infections. It stimulates the flow of lymph and the metabolic processes, revitalizes and reenergizes when body and mind are exhausted, purifies blood, and detoxifies the liver, intestines, kidneys, spleen, and bladder. Bloodstone benefits blood-rich organs, regulates and supports blood-flow, and aids the circulation. It reduces the formation of pus and neutralizes overacidification. It is helpful in cases of leukemia as it supports the blood and removes toxins. The ancient Egyptians used it to shrink tumors. Bloodstone can be used to heal the ancestral line. It cleanses the lower chakras* and realigns their energies.

POSITION As appropriate. Wear continually for good health. Place in a bowl of water beside the bed to ensure peaceful sleep. As an immune stimulator, tape over the thymus.

BOJI STONE

Raw

(Male)   *(Female)*

COLOR	Brownish, some blue
APPEARANCE	Metallic looking, smooth (female) or with square protrusions (male), small to medium size
RARITY	True Boji Stones can be difficult to obtain
SOURCE	United States, Britain

ATTRIBUTES Boji Stones are one of the most effective grounding stones. They gently but firmly return you to earth and into your body, grounding you in the present, especially after work in other spiritual realities. They are extremely useful for people who find it difficult to have more than a toehold in incarnation. They have a strongly protective function and are very useful for overcoming blockages.

The smooth stones have feminine energy, the protruded ones masculine energy. Boji Stones are balancers and energizers and a pair

86

balances the male–female energy within the body and aligns the chakras and the subtle bodies*.

With their strong earth connection, Boji Stones are beneficial to plants and crops, but the stone may well disintegrate if left in the ground or exposed to the weather.

Psychologically, Boji Stones throw light on blockages at all levels. They clear blocked emotions and heal hurtful memories. They also reveal negative thought patterns and self-defeating behaviors for transformation. Going to the cause of psychosomatic disease, they dissolve blockages in the physical or subtle bodies. Holding a Boji Stone will align you to your shadow self, bringing up its repressed qualities so that you can gently release them and find the gift in them.

Physically, Boji Stones stimulate the flow of energy through the meridian systems of the body. Mentally, Boji Stones bring your attention to mental imprints and hypnotic commands from the past. Boji Stones can be emotionally stabilizing, but they tend to insist that any necessary work is done first.

HEALING Boji Stones heal energy blockages, relieve pain, and encourage tissue regeneration. They are useful when physical energy is low or when the condition is intractable. On a subtle level they realign the chakras* and repair and reenergize "holes" in the auric* body.

POSITION Hold a pair of Bojis in your hands for ten minutes or so, or place over a blocked or painful point. You can also grid* around your chair while meditating.

Blue Boji Stones have a high but grounded spiritual vibration. They are extremely useful when taking journeys out of the body as they facilitate traveling and guard the body until the soul returns.

CALCITE

Brown, point

Rhomboid, natural

Mangano, tumbled

COLOR	Green, blue, yellow, orange, clear, brown, pink gray, red
APPEARANCE	Translucent and waxy, often banded (may be acid-treated to enhance color), all sizes sometimes tumbled
RARITY	Common
SOURCE	United States, Britain, Belgium, Czech Republic, Slovakia, Peru, Iceland, Romania, Brazil

ATTRIBUTES Calcite is a powerful amplifier and cleanser of energy. Simply having Calcite in the room cleans negative energies from the environment and heightens your energy. Within the body, it removes stagnant energy. The spectrum of colors cleans the physical and subtle bodies. Calcite is an active crystal, speeding up development and growth. This is a spiritual stone linked to the higher consciousness that facilitates the opening of higher awareness and psychic abilities, channeling, and out-of-body experiences. It accelerates spiritual development and allows the soul to remember experiences when it returns to the body.

Psychologically, Calcite connects the emotions with the intellect, creating emotional intelligence. Calcite has a positive effect, especially where someone has lost hope or motivation. It combats laziness, aiding in becoming more energetic on all levels.

Mentally, Calcite calms the mind, teaches discernment and analysis, stimulates insights, and boosts memory. It facilitates knowing which information is important, and then retaining it. Calcite confers the ability to change ideas into action. It is a useful stone for study.

Calcite alleviates emotional stress and replaces it with serenity. It is a stabilizing stone, enhancing trust in oneself and strengthening the ability to overcome setbacks. On a subtle level, a layout of the appropriate colors of Calcite cleanses, balances, and energizes all the chakras*.

HEALING Calcite cleanses the organs of elimination. It encourages calcium uptake in bones but dissolves calcifications, strengthening the skeleton and joints. It alleviates intestinal and skin conditions. Calcite stimulates blood clotting and tissue healing. It fortifies the immune system and can encourage growth in small children. Calcite works quickly as an elixir and can be applied to the skin, ulcers, warts, and suppurating wounds. At a subtle level, Calcite cleans and reenergizes the chakras*.

POSITION Hold or place as appropriate. Wear as a pendant. Can be used to grid around a bed. Use as gem essence.

SPECIFIC COLORS

In addition to the generic attributes, the following colors have additional properties:

Black Calcite is a record-keeper stone for regression and regaining memories so that the past can be released. It returns the soul to the body after trauma or stress, alleviates depression, and is a useful companion during a dark night of the soul.

Black Calcite (raw)

Blue Calcite is a gentle stone for recuperation and relaxation. It lowers blood pressure and dissolves pain on all levels. Gently soothing the nerves and lifting anxieties, it releases negative emotions. Used on the throat chakra* it aids clear communication, especially where there is dissent. Blue Calcite can absorb energy, filter it, and return it to benefit the sender.

Blue Calcite

Clear Calcite is a "cure-all," especially as an elixir. It is a powerful detoxifier. At a physical level it acts as an antiseptic and at the subtle levels it cleanses and aligns all the chakras*, higher and lower. A clear Calcite with rainbows brings about

Clear Calcite

major change—it is a stone of new beginnings. Clear Calcite brings the gift of deep soul healing and revitalization of the subtle bodies*. It opens and clears the inner and outer eyes.

Gold Calcite (raw)

Gold Calcite is excellent for meditation and for attuning to the higher mental planes. It instills mental alertness as it grounds the higher mental energies into the physical realm. Place on the navel or crown chakras.

Green Calcite is a mental healer, dissolving rigid beliefs and old programs and restoring balance to the mind. It helps in letting go of what is familiar and comforting but which no longer serves, and aids communication and the transition from a stagnant to a positive situation. Green Calcite helps children to hold their own in debates. It is a powerful stimulator for the immune system and is especially useful in grids*. This stone absorbs negativity and rids the body of bacterial infections. It ameliorates arthritis and constrictions of the ligaments or muscles and is helpful in bone adjustments. Its green ray cools fevers, burns, and inflammation, calms the adrenals, and soothes anger-generated dis-ease*.

Green Calcite

Green Calcite placed regularly on the body absorbs dis-ease* and should be cleansed thoroughly after use.

Iceland Spar (Optical Calcite) amplifies images and heals the eyes. It can aid in seeing the double meaning hidden behind words. It reduces the tension that causes migraines. This form of Calcite is an excellent cleanser of the subtle bodies*.

Icelandic Calcite

Orange Calcite is a highly energizing and cleansing stone, especially for the lower chakras*. Orange Calcite balances the emotions, removes fear, and overcomes depression. It dissolves problems and maximizes potential. This stone heals the reproductive system, gallbladder, and intestinal disorders such as irritable bowel syndrome (IBS), and removes mucus from the system.

Orange Calcite

Pink Calcite (Mangano Calcite) is a heart crystal in contact with the angelic realm*. A stone of forgiveness, it releases fear and grief that keep the heart trapped in the past, bringing in unconditional love. It aids self-worth and self-acceptance, heals nervous conditions, and lifts tension and anxiety. This stone prevents nightmares. Pink Calcite's loving energy gently dissolves resistance. It is helpful for anyone who has suffered trauma or assault.

Red Calcite

Red Calcite increases energy, uplifts emotions, aids willpower, and opens the heart chakra. It removes stagnant energy, including constipation, and dissolves blockages. It resonates to the base chakras, which it energizes and heals. It alleviates fear, bringing understanding of the source. Red Calcite's vitality energizes a party. At a physical level, it heals hip and lower limb problems, loosening up joints, and on a subtle level it removes the blockages that prevent you from stepping forward in your life.

Rhomboid Calcite closes off mind chatter, bringing mental stillness. It is a powerful healer of the past.

Yellow Calcite

Yellow or Golden Calcite is a great eliminator and stimulates the will. Its energy, especially as an elixir, is uplifting. It enhances meditation, inducing a deep state of relaxation and spirituality and linking to the highest source of spiritual guidance. It stimulates the higher mind. Use at the crown and solar plexus chakras. Golden Calcite has an extremely expansive energy.

Green Calcite that has been acid-treated to enhance its color and texture

CARNELIAN

*Natural
formation*

COLOR	Red, orange, pink, brown
APPEARANCE	Small, translucent pebble, often water-worn or tumbled
RARITY	Common
SOURCE	Britain, India, Czech Republic, Slovakia, Peru, Iceland, Romania

ATTRIBUTES Carnelian grounds and anchors you in the present reality. A stabilizing stone with high energy, it is excellent for restoring vitality and motivation, and for stimulating creativity. It is useful for dramatic pursuits. Carnelian has the ability to cleanse other stones.

Psychologically, Carnelian imparts an acceptance of the cycle of life and removes fear of death. In ancient times it was used to protect the dead on their journey to the afterlife. It gives courage, promotes positive life choices, dispels apathy, and motivates for success in business and other matters. Carnelian is useful for overcoming abuse of any kind. This stone helps you to trust yourself and your perceptions. It gets to the bottom of what makes you tick, overcomes negative conditioning, and encourages steadfastness.

Mentally, Carnelian improves analytic abilities and clarifies perception. It removes extraneous thoughts in meditation and tunes daydreamers into everyday reality. It sharpens concentration and dispels mental lethargy. Emotionally, this stone is a powerful protector against envy, rage, and resentment, yours or other people's. It calms anger and banishes emotional negativity, replacing it with a love of life.

HEALING Carnelian is full of the life force and vitality. It stimulates the metabolism. Carnelian activates the base chakra*, influences the female reproductive organs, and increases fertility. This stone overcomes frigidity and impotence, heals lower back problems, rheumatism, arthritis, neuralgia, and depression, especially in those of advanced years. It regulates bodily fluids and the kidneys, accelerates healing in bones and ligaments, and stanches blood. Carnelian improves the absorption of vitamins and minerals and ensures a good supply of blood to organs and tissues.

POSITION Use as a pendant or belt buckle, or place in contact with the skin as appropriate. Carnelian near the front door invokes protection and invites abundance into the home.

SPECIFIC COLORS
In addition to the generic attributes, the following colors have additional properties:

Pink Carnelian

Pink Carnelian improves the parent–child relationship. It helps to restore love and trust after abuse or manipulation.

Red Carnelian warms and energizes. It is particularly useful for combating sluggishness and for invigorating the mind and body.

Orange Carnelian

CELESTITE

Blue geode

Blue point

COLOR	Blue, yellow, red, white
APPEARANCE	Transparent, pyramidal crystals as medium to large cluster or geode, or platelike piece
RARITY	Easily obtained but quite expensive
SOURCE	Britain, Egypt, Mexico, Peru, Poland, Libya, Madagascar

ATTRIBUTES Celestite has a high vibration and is a teacher for the New Age. It is imbued with divine energies. It takes you into the infinite peace of the spiritual and contacts the angelic realms*. It jump-starts spiritual development and urges you toward enlightenment. It is a useful stone for stimulating clairvoyant* communication, dream recall, and journeys out of the body*. This beautiful crystal promotes purity of the heart and attracts good fortune. It heals the aura* and reveals truth. It is a stone that brings balance and alignment. The deep peace it holds assists in conflict resolution and in maintaining a harmonious atmosphere in times of stress. Celestite can improve dysfunctional relationships by opening a space for peaceful negotiation.

Celestite is a creative stone, especially useful for the arts.

Psychologically, Celestite imparts gentle strength and enormous inner peace despite urging toward greater openness to new experiences. It is a teacher of trust in the infinite wisdom of the divine. With its calming effect, Celestite can cool fiery emotions.

Mentally, Celestite calms and sharpens the mind, dispersing worries and promoting mental clarity and fluent communication. It aids the analysis of complex ideas. This stone synthesizes intellect with instinct and promotes mental balance.

Placed on the third eye*, Celestite opens a connection to the universal energies. It brings a vision of peaceful coexistence with the whole of creation and holds the possibility of total harmony.

HEALING Celestite is an excellent healing stone, dissolving pain and bringing in love. It treats disorders of the eyes and ears, eliminates toxins, and brings cellular order. Its soothing influence relaxes muscle tension and calms mental torment. As with all blue crystals, Celestite is an effective opener and healer of the throat chakra* and its associated physical conditions.

POSITION Place as appropriate or use for meditation and scrying*. A large piece of Celestite placed within a room heightens the vibrations in that room. Do not place in direct sunlight as color will fade.

CERUSSITE

*Record-keeper
(note chevrons)*

COLOR	White, gray, gray-black, yellow
APPEARANCE	White and yellow translucent crystals, or gray and black granular, usually on a matrix
RARITY	Can be obtained from specialist stores
SOURCE	Namibia

ATTRIBUTES Cerussite is an excellent grounding stone that assists in feeling comfortable in the environment. It is extremely useful for people who feel that the earth is not their natural home, as it ameliorates "homesickness" and makes the soul feel at home wherever it finds itself. Cerussite may also form a star-shaped or record-keeper crystal. These precious stones attune to higher wisdom and karmic purpose*. Meditating reveals the unique secrets they hold for you. The star is said to assist in extraterrestrial contact. Cerussite helps to explore past lives that were not on earth and in recognizing people from past lives and the place they hold in the present. It explains why you chose to come to earth, the lessons you are learning, the task you have to do, and the gifts you bring to advance the evolution of humanity. This stone assists in letting go of the past and its effects.

Cerussite is beneficial for travel, whether on business or for pleasure, reducing jet lag and helping you to adjust to a different culture. This is a useful stone for making short-term compromises and adjusting to situations to which inner resistance is strong.

Cerussite is a pragmatic stone that promotes decision-making and stimulates growth. Teaching how to become flexible and how to take responsibility, it relieves tension and anxiety and shows how to adapt to necessary change. It instills the ability to be tactful in any situation and helps to promote extroversion rather than withdrawal.

Enhancing communication, Cerussite makes correspondence easy and imparts the ability to listen attentively. It balances the right- and left-brain hemispheres and encourages creativity. It is an excellent stone for anyone engaged in the arts.

Cerussite elixir has a useful insecticidal property. It can be sprayed onto house plants or into a room to protect from pests and diseases.

ATTRIBUTES Cerussite is a wonderful stone for imparting vitality and energy, especially where an illness has persisted for some time. It aligns the nervous system, treating involuntary movements, and strengthens muscles and bones. It is helpful for Parkinson's and Tourette's Syndrome. It overcomes insomnia and nightmares.

POSITION Place or hold as appropriate. Use as an elixir for pest control and for house plants.

CHALCEDONY

White geode

Blue (tumbled)

COLOR	White, pink, blue, red, grayish
APPEARANCE	Transparent or opaque, sometimes banded, all sizes, often seen as geode or small tumbled stone
RARITY	Common
SOURCE	United States, Austria, Czech Republic, Slovakia, Iceland, Mexico, Britain, Mexico, New Zealand, Turkey, Russia, Brazil, Morocco

ATTRIBUTES Chalcedony is a nurturing stone that promotes brotherhood and good will and enhances group stability. It can be used to assist thought transmission and telepathy. This stone absorbs negative energy and then dissipates it to prevent onward transmission.

In ancient times, chalices would be formed out of Chalcedony and lined with silver. They were said to prevent poisoning.

Chalcedony brings the mind, body, emotions, and spirit into harmony.

Instilling feelings of benevolence and generosity, Chalcedony removes hostility and transforms melancholy into joy. Psychologically, Chalcedony eases self-doubt and facilitates constructive inward reflection. It creates an open and enthusiastic persona. It absorbs and dissipates negative thoughts, emotions, and bad dreams.

HEALING Chalcedony is a powerful cleanser, including open sores. It fosters the maternal instinct and increases lactation, improves mineral assimilation, and combats mineral buildup in veins. Chalcedony lessens the effects of dementia and senility. This stone increases physical energy. It balances body, emotions, mind, and spirit and heals the eyes, gallbladder, bones, spleen, blood, and circulatory system.

POSITION Wear on fingers, around neck, on belt buckle, or place as appropriate, especially over organs and in contact with the skin.

SPECIFIC COLORS
In addition to the generic attributes, the following colors and forms have additional properties:

Blue Chalcedony (raw)

Blue Chalcedony is a creative stone. It opens the mind to assimilate new ideas and helps acceptance of new situations. Blue Chalcedony imparts mental flexibility and verbal dexterity, enhancing listening skills and communication. It stimulates the ability to learn new languages and improves memory. Blue Chalcedony gives a feeling of light-heartedness and the ability to look forward optimistically. It improves self-perception. This stone was traditionally used in weather magic and for clearing illnesses associated with changes in the weather.

Physically, Blue Chalcedony aids regeneration of mucus membranes and ameliorates dis-ease* caused by weather sensitivity or pressure, such as glaucoma. Blue Chalcedony enhances the immune system. It stimulates the flow of lymph and banishes edema, has an anti-inflammatory effect, and lowers temperature and blood pressure. It heals the lungs and clears the respiratory system of the effects of smoking.

Dendritic Chalcedony promotes clear and precise thought. This stone is useful when you are under pressure or attack as it facilitates calm communication while remaining relaxed. It encourages living in the present moment and helps you to face up to unpleasant matters. Dendritic Chalcedony helps in processing memories and brings joy to life. This stone supports an easy, friendly approach to other people. It promotes tolerant interaction without judgment.

Dendritic Chalcedony is a useful stone for chronic illness, for which it should be worn for long periods, and problems associated with smoking, strengthening the immune system. It enhances the assimilation of copper into the body, detoxifies the liver, removes inflammations of the female sexual organs, and treats thrush.

Pink Chalcedony encourages kindness and all good qualities. It brings out a sense of childlike wonder and

Pink Chalcedony (raw)

102

willingness to learn new things. It encourages storytelling as a form of creativity. This is a spiritual stone that encourages empathy and inner peace. It creates a deep sense of trust.

This stone is particularly useful for treating psychosomatic dis-eases*. Pink Chalcedony fortifies the heart and supports the immune system. It eases breastfeeding problems and the flow of lymphatic fluids.

Red Chalcedony bestows strength and persistence in reaching goals. It advises when to fight and when to give in gracefully. A confident stone, it helps to manifest dreams, devising strategies to bring these into being in the most positive way. As a healing stone, Red Chalcedony stimulates the circulation without raising blood pressure and encourages clotting of the blood. It reduces hunger pangs but should not be used for long periods, as it inhibits the absorption of nutrients and may cause temporary nausea.

NOTE Chalcedony geodes that have been painted silver or various colors are sold in Morocco and other places. The paint runs when wet to reveal white or gray Chalcedony underneath. The attributes are as generic Chalcedony.

CHAROITE

Polished

COLOR	Purple
APPEARANCE	Mottled, swirled and veined, often small to medium, tumbled or polished
RARITY	Becoming more easily obtainable
SOURCE	Russia

ATTRIBUTES Charoite is a stone of transformation. It is the soul stone that overcomes fear. Charoite stimulates inner vision and spiritual insight and aids in coping with enormous change at a spiritual level. To facilitate this, it synthesizes the heart and crown chakras*, cleanses the aura*, and stimulates unconditional love. Charoite encourages vibrational change and links to higher realities. At the same time, it provides deep physical and emotional healing. It helps you to accept the present moment as perfect.

104

Psychologically, Charoite integrates "negative qualities" and facilitates acceptance of others. It releases deep fears and is particularly useful for overcoming resistance or putting things into perspective. It bestows drive, vigor, and spontaneity and is able to reduce stress and worry, bringing about a relaxed attitude. Charoite can be used to overcome compulsions and obsessions. By balancing the crown chakra, it assists in overcoming a sense of alienation or frustration.

Mentally, Charoite stimulates perceptive observations and analysis and applies these to facilitate a fast decision. It helps anyone who is driven by other people's thoughts and programs rather than their own.

Spiritually, Charoite grounds the spiritual self into everyday reality. It encourages a path of service to humanity. This stone opens and balances the crown chakra. It can bring insightful visions of past lives and suggests ways to redress karma on a personal and collective level.

HEALING Charoite transmutes negative energy into healing and converts dis-ease into wellness. It reenergizes the body when exhausted, heals and integrates dualities, and regulates blood pressure. Charoite treats the eyes, heart, liver, and pancreas. It reverses liver damage due to alcohol, and alleviates cramps, aches, and pains. Charoite bestows deep sleep with powerful dreams, overcomes insomnia, and gives children calm sleep. It is helpful where dysfunction of the autonomic nervous system is affecting the heart. Charoite heals autism and bipolar disorders.

POSITION Over heart or placed as appropriate in contact with the skin. Gridding with Charoite is highly effective. Gem elixir is an excellent cleanser for the physical body and stabilizer for emotional turmoil.

CHIASTOLITE

ALSO KNOWN AS CROSS STONE, ANDALUSITE

Andalusite

Green

Brown

COLOR	Brown-gray, rose, gray, reddish-brown, olive green
APPEARANCE	Distinctive cross in center of stone, often small and tumbled
RARITY	Easily obtained
SOURCE	Chile, Russia, Spain

ATTRIBUTES Chiastolite is a powerfully protective stone. In ancient times it was used to ward off ill wishing and curses. It has the property of transmuting dissension into harmony. This is a creative stone with the power to dispel negative thoughts and feelings. It transmutes conflict into harmony and aids problem-solving and change.

Chiastolite is a gateway into mysteries and facilitates journeys out of the body. It facilitates understanding and exploration of immortality. Linked to death and rebirth, it is helpful for those making the transition beyond death. This stone can provide the answer to mysterious events.

Psychologically, Chiastolite dissolves illusions and calms fears, enabling you to face reality, and is particularly helpful in overcoming the fear of going mad. It aids in the transition between one situation and another, especially at the psychological level, and releases worn-out patterns and conditioning.

Mentally, Chiastolite aids problem-solving by strengthening analytic capabilities. Emotionally, Chiastolite clears feelings of guilt and stabilizes the emotions. Chiastolite maintains spirituality during illness or trauma, invoking protective forces. It assists in attuning to the soul's purpose.

HEALING Chiastolite lessens fevers, stanches blood flow, and alleviates overacidification, healing rheumatism and gout. It stimulates lactation in nursing mothers. This stone repairs chromosome damage and balances the immune system. It can cure paralysis and is a nerve fortifier.

POSITION Place as appropriate or wear around neck.

Green Andalusite is a heart cleanser and balancing stone. It releases emotional and chakra* blockages caused by pent-up anger and old emotional trauma, and is very helpful in psycho- or crystal therapy.

CHLORITE

Chlorite Phantom

COLOR	Green
APPEARANCE	Several forms, usually opaque, may be occluded in Quartz (generic name for a group)
RARITY	Easily obtained
SOURCE	Russia, Germany, United States

ATTRIBUTES A powerful, positive healing stone, beneficial for the environment or personal energy field. With Amethyst, it removes energy implants* and wards off psychic attack*. With Carnelian and Ruby, it protects against psychic attack and assists earthbound spirits to move on.

HEALING Chlorite assists in the elimination of toxins and the assimilation of Vitamins A and E, iron, magnesium, and calcium. It is a useful painkiller and removes skin growths and liver spots. This stone encourages the proliferation of helpful bacteria.

POSITION Hold or place as appropriate. Grid* an area against negative energies or entities.

(*See also* Chlorite Phantom, pages 233–234, and Seraphinite, page 262.)

CHRYSANTHEMUM STONE

Natural

COLOR	Brown, gray with white
APPEARANCE	Resembles the flower of a chrysanthemum, medium stone
RARITY	Readily available
SOURCE	China, Japan, Canada, United States

ATTRIBUTES Chrysanthemum Stone drifts gently through time, facilitating time travel. It exudes calm confidence and enhances any environment with its gentle presence. Radiating harmony, it synthesizes change with equilibrium and shows how the two can work together. This stone helps you to enjoy being centered in the present moment and encourages the self to bloom. It inspires and energizes, and brings endeavors to fruition. Chrysanthemum Stone teaches how to remain childlike, fun-loving, and innocent while on the spiritual path, and provides an impetuousity to self-development. Strengthening character, it overcomes bigotry, ignorance, narrow-mindedness, self-righteousness, and jealousy and encourages showing more love to the world, which in turn brings more love into your life.

Mentally, Chrysanthemum Stone counteracts superficiality. It adds depth to thought and guards against distractions. With Chrysanthemum Stone, the bigger picture can be perceived. Emotionally, Chrysanthemum Stone brings stability and trust, eliminating resentment and animosity.

HEALING Chrysanthemum Stone promotes physical maturation and transition. It treats the skin, skeleton, and eyes. It is a useful stone for dispersing toxins and dissolving growths.

POSITION Wear, carry, or place in the environment. Use as an elixir, but make by the indirect method of placing the stone in a glass bowl within the bowl of water as otherwise the "flower" is affected.

CHRYSOCOLLA

Raw

Polished

COLOR	Green, blue, turquoise
APPEARANCE	Opaque, often bands or inclusions, all sizes, frequently tumbled or polished
RARITY	Common
SOURCE	United States, Britain, Mexico, Chile, Peru, Zaire, Russia

ATTRIBUTES Chrysocolla is a tranquil and sustaining stone. It helps meditation and communication. Within the home, Chrysocolla draws off negative energies of all kinds. It can help you to accept with serenity situations that are constantly changing, invoking great inner strength. It is beneficial to relationships that have become rocky, stabilizing and healing both the home and personal interaction.

Chrysocolla calms, cleanses, and reenergizes all the chakras* and aligns them with the divine. At the solar plexus chakra, it draws out negative

111

emotions such as guilt, and reverses destructive emotional programming. At the heart chakra, it heals heartache and increases the capacity to love. At the throat, it improves communication but helps you to discern when to keep silent. At the third eye*, it opens psychic vision.

Psychologically, Chrysocolla encourages self-awareness and inner balance, and imparts confidence and sensitivity. It enhances personal power and inspires creativity. Overcoming phobias, it draws out negativity and supplies motivation for those who lack it.

Mentally, Chrysocolla reduces mental tensions and helps you to keep a cool head. It promotes truth-telling and impartiality. Emotionally, Chrysocolla alleviates guilt and brings in joy.

HEALING Chrysocolla treats arthritis, bone disease, muscle spasms, the digestive tract, ulcers, blood disorders, and lung problems. It detoxifies the liver, kidneys, and intestines. It reoxygenates the blood and the cellular structure of the lungs, giving greater lung and breathing capacity, and regenerates the pancreas, regulates insulin, and balances blood. This stone strengthens muscles and alleviates muscle cramps. With its cooling action, it heals infections, especially in the throat and tonsils, lowers blood pressure, and soothes burns. It relieves arthritic pain, strengthens the thyroid and is beneficial to the metabolism. An excellent stone for women, Chrysocolla treats PMS and menstrual cramps. On a subtle level, Chrysocolla dissolves miasms*.

POSITION Place as appropriate on skin or third eye.

COMBINATION STONE

Drusy Chrysocolla

Drusy Chrysocolla combines the properties of Chrysocolla with those of Quartz. This stone has great clarity and works extremely fast.

CHRYSOPRASE

*Lemon
(tumbled)*

Tumbled

Raw

COLOR	Apple green, lemon
APPEARANCE	Opaque, flecked, often small and tumbled
RARITY	Common
SOURCE	United States, Russia, Brazil, Australia, Poland, Tanzania

ATTRIBUTES Chrysoprase imparts a sense of being a part of the divine whole. It induces deep meditative states. Said by the ancients to promote love of truth, Chrysoprase also promotes hope and gives personal insights. It draws out talents and stimulates creativity. It encourages fidelity in business and personal relationships. This crystal energizes the heart and sacral chakras* and brings universal energy into the physical body.

Psychologically, Chrysoprase is calming and nonegotistical, creating openness to new situations. It assists in looking at egotistical motives in the past and the effect they have had on your development, and it aligns your ideals with your behavior. Overcoming compulsive or impulsive thoughts and actions, it turns your attention to positive events. This stone opposes judgmentalism, stimulating acceptance of oneself and others. It is useful for forgiveness and compassion.

Mentally, Chrysoprase stimulates fluent speech and mental dexterity. It prevents you from speaking out unthinkingly in anger. It lifts oppressive and recurrent images, preventing nightmares, especially in children. Emotionally, Chrysoprase brings a sense of security and trust. It is useful in healing codependence, supporting independence and yet encouraging commitment.

Physically, Chyrosprase has a strong detoxifying action. It can mobilize heavy metals out of the body, and it stimulates liver function.

HEALING Chrysoprase is excellent for relaxation and peaceful sleep. Resonating with the sacral chakra*, it enhances fertility, reverses infertility caused by infection, and guards against sexually transmitted diseases. This stone aids gout, eye problems, and mental illness. It treats skin diseases, heart problems, and goiters, balances the hormones, and soothes the digestive system. Chrysoprase ameliorates infirmity and brings universal energy into the body. It increases absorption of Vitamin C. Combined with Smoky Quartz, it treats fungal infections. The elixir calms stomach problems caused by stress. Chrysoprase heals the inner child*, releasing emotions locked in since childhood. It reduces claustrophobia and nightmares.

POSITION Wear or place as appropriate. In acute cases, use as an elixir. Carrying Chrysoprase for long periods attunes to the devic realm*.

CINNABAR

ALSO KNOWN AS DRAGON'S BLOOD

*Raw crystals
on matrix*

COLOR	Red, brown-red, gray
APPEARANCE	Small, crystalline or granular mass on matrix
RARITY	Readily available but expensive
SOURCE	China, United States

ATTRIBUTES Cinnabar attracts abundance. It increases persuasiveness and assertiveness in selling, and aids in prospering in one's endeavors without inciting aggression. It also assists organization and community work, business, and finance. Cinnabar is helpful when you want to enhance your persona or change your image as it invests a person with dignity and power. It makes the outward demeanor aesthetically pleasing and elegant. Mentally, Cinnabar imparts fluency to the mind and to speech. At a spiritual level, it connects to the acceptance of everything being perfect exactly as it is. It releases energy blockages and aligns the energy centers.

HEALING Cinnabar heals and purifies blood. It imparts strength and flexibility to the physical body, stabilizes weight, and enhances fertility.

POSITION Hold or place as appropriate. Keep in cash box.

CITRINE

Also known as Cairngorm

Point

Geode

COLOR	Yellow to yellowish brown or smoky gray-brown
APPEARANCE	Transparent crystals, all sizes, often as geode, point, or cluster
RARITY	Natural Citrine is comparatively rare; heat-treated Amethyst is often sold as Citrine
SOURCE	Brazil, Russia, France, Madagascar, Britain, United States

Cluster

ATTRIBUTES Citrine is a powerful cleanser and regenerator. Carrying the power of the sun, this is an exceedingly beneficial stone. It is warming, energizing, and highly creative. This is one of the crystals that never needs cleansing. It absorbs, transmutes, dissipates, and grounds negative energy and is therefore extremely protective for the environment. Citrine energizes every level of life. As an aura* protector, it acts as an early warning system so that action can be taken to protect oneself. It has the ability to cleanse the chakras*, especially the solar plexus and navel chakras. It activates the crown chakra and opens the intuition. Citrine cleanses and balances the subtle bodies*, aligning them with the physical.

Citrine is one of the stones of abundance. This dynamic stone teaches how to manifest and attracts wealth and prosperity, success, and all good things. Citrine is a happy, generous stone and encourages sharing what you have and yet helps you to hold on to your wealth. It has the power to impart joy to all who behold it. Gloom and negativity have no place around Citrine. It is a useful stone for smoothing group or family discord.

Psychologically, Citrine raises self-esteem and self-confidence, and removes destructive tendencies. It enhances individuality, improves motivation, activates creativity, and encourages self-expression. It makes you less sensitive, especially to criticism, and encourages acting on constructive criticism. It helps you develop a positive attitude and to look forward optimistically, going with the flow instead of hanging on to the past. This stone promotes enjoyment of new experiences and encourages exploring every possible avenue until you find the best solution.

Mentally, Citrine enhances concentration and revitalizes the mind. It is excellent for overcoming depression, fears, and phobias. Citrine promotes inner calm so that wisdom can emerge. It helps in digesting information, analyzing situations and steering them in a positive direction. This stone awakens the higher mind. Wearing a Citrine pendant overcomes difficulty in verbalizing thoughts and feelings.

Emotionally, Citrine promotes joy in life. It releases negative traits, fears, and feelings at the deepest of levels. It overcomes fear of responsibility and stops anger. This stone helps you move into the flow of feelings and become emotionally balanced.

Physically, Citrine imparts energy and invigoration to the physical body. It is useful for people who are particularly sensitive to environmental and other outside influences.

HEALING Citrine is an excellent stone for energizing and recharging. It is highly beneficial for CFS* and reverses degenerative disease. Citrine stimulates digestion, the spleen, and the pancreas. It negates infections in the kidney and bladder, helps eye problems, increases blood circulation, detoxifies the blood, activates the thymus, and balances the thyroid. It has a warming effect and fortifies the nerves. Citrine is an eliminator—it relieves constipation and removes cellulite. As an elixir, it is helpful for menstrual problems and menopausal symptoms such as hot flashes, balancing the hormones and alleviating fatigue.

POSITION Wear on fingers or throat in contact with the skin. Wearing a Citrine pointdown brings the golden ray of spirit into the physical realm. Position as appropriate for healing. Use a sphere for meditation. Place in the wealth corner of your home or business, or in your cash box. Citrine fades in sunlight.

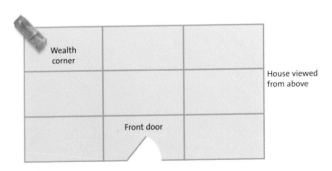

Wealth corner

House viewed from above

Front door

The wealth corner is the farthest back left point from your front door or the door into an individual room

DANBURITE

Pink

COLOR	Pink, yellow, white, lilac
APPEARANCE	Clear with striations, all sizes
RARITY	Readily available
SOURCE	United States, Czech Republic, Russia, Switzerland, Japan, Mexico, Myanmar

ATTRIBUTES Danburite is a highly spiritual stone carrying a very pure vibration and working on the heart energy. It activates both the intellect and higher consciousness, linking into the angelic realms*. Its brilliance comes from cosmic light and Danburite is sometimes found with a Buddha formation within the crystal that draws enlightenment and spiritual light. It smoothes the path ahead.

Wearing Danburite provides a link to serenity and eternal wisdom. Used in meditation, it takes you to a high state of consciousness and accesses inner guidance.

120

Danburite is an excellent stone for facilitating deep change and for leaving the past behind. It can act as a karmic cleanser, releasing miasms* and mental imperatives that have been carried forward. It starts the soul off on a new direction. Placed by the bedside, this crystal can accompany the dying on their journey beyond death, enabling a conscious spiritual transition to take place.

Spiritually, Danburite stimulates the third eye*, the crown, and the higher crown chakras*, opening these up to the fourteenth level. It aligns the heart chakra to these higher crown chakras (see pages 364–365, Crystals and the Chakras). Danburite clarifies the aura*. It promotes lucid dreaming.

Psychologically, Danburite promotes ease and changes recalcitrant attitudes, bringing patience and peace of mind.

HEALING Danburite is a very powerful healing stone. It clears allergies and chronic conditions and has a strong detoxifying action. It treats the liver and gallbladder. It adds weight to the body where required. It aids muscular and motor function.

POSITION Place as appropriate, especially over heart. Place Danburite under the pillow to promote lucid dreams.

SPECIFIC COLOR
In addition to the generic attributes, the following color has additional properties:

Pink Danburite opens the heart and encourages loving oneself.

Lilac Danburite

121

DIAMOND

Faceted

Raw

COLOR	Clear white, yellow, blue, brown, pink
APPEARANCE	Small, clear, transparent gemstone when cut and polished
RARITY	Expensive
SOURCE	Africa, Australia, Brazil, India, Russia, United States

ATTRIBUTES The Diamond is a symbol of purity. Its pure white light can help you to bring your life into a cohesive whole. It bonds relationships, bringing love and clarity into a partnership. Said to enhance the love of a husband for his wife, it is seen as a sign of commitment and fidelity. Diamond has been a symbol of wealth for thousands of years and is one of the stones of manifestation, attracting abundance. The larger the Diamond, the more abundance there is. A large Diamond is also excellent for blocking geopathic* or electromagnetic stress* and for protection against cell phones.

Diamond is an amplifier of energy. It is one of the few stones that never needs recharging. It increases the energy of whatever it comes into contact with and is very effective when used with other crystals for healing as it enhances their power. However, it can increase negative energy as well as positive. On a subtle level, it fills "holes" in the aura*, reenergizing it.

Psychologically, the qualities that Diamond imparts include fearlessness, invincibility, and fortitude. However, the merciless light of Diamond will pinpoint anything that is negative and requires transformation. Diamond clears emotional and mental pain, reduces fear, and brings about new beginnings. It is a highly creative stone, stimulating imagination and inventiveness.

Mentally, Diamond provides a link between the intellect and the higher mind. It brings clarity of mind and aids enlightenment.

At a spiritual level, Diamond cleanses the aura of anything shrouding a person's inner light, allowing the soul light to shine out. It reminds you of your soul's aspirations and aids spiritual evolution. It activates the crown chakra*, linking it to divine light.

HEALING Diamond treats glaucoma, clears sight, and benefits the brain. It treats allergies and chronic conditions and rebalances the metabolism. Traditionally, it was used to counteract poisons.

POSITION Wear next to the skin, hold, or place on the appropriate place. Particularly effective worn as earrings, especially against cell phone emanations.

DIOPTASE

Blue-Green
(non-crystalline)

Crystalline

COLOR	Deep blue-green or emerald green
APPEARANCE	Brilliant small crystals, usually on a matrix, or non-crystalline mass
RARITY	Quite rare and expensive
SOURCE	Iran, Russia, Namibia, Democratic Republic of the Congo, North Africa, Chile, Peru

ATTRIBUTES Dioptase is a powerful healer for the heart and opener for the higher heart chakra*. Its wonderful blue-green color brings all the chakras up to a greater level of functioning and facilitates spiritual attunement, reaching the highest levels of consciousness. It has a dramatic effect on the human energy field.

Psychologically, Dioptase promotes living in the present moment and, paradoxically, activates past-life memories. It supports a positive attitude to life and instills the ability to tune into one's own resources. Working in all areas of life to turn negative into positive, it overcomes any sense of lack and enables fulfilling potential. It is especially helpful when you do not know what to do next, as it indicates your direction.

Mentally, Dioptase is a strong mental cleanser and detoxifier. It releases the need to control others. Emotionally, Dioptase can act as a bridge to emotional healing, especially for the child within. Its green ray reaches deep within the heart to absorb festering wounds and forgotten hurts. It dissolves grief, betrayal, and sorrow and is extremely effective for healing heartache and the pain of abandonment.

Dioptase teaches that ultimately pain and difficulty in a relationship is a mirroring of an inner separation from the self. Repairing that link and drawing in love at all levels, it can heal an emotional black hole that is desperate for love. This stone clears away perceptions as to how love ought to be and brings in a new vibration of love.

Spiritually, Dioptase placed on the third eye* activates spiritual attunement and psychic vision*. It brings awareness of inner riches.

HEALING Dioptase regulates cell disorders, activates T-cells and the thymus, relieves Ménière's disease, eases high blood pressure, and alleviates pain and migraines. It prevents heart attacks and heals heart conditions. Dioptase lessens fatigue and overcomes shock. It is a detoxifier, lessening nausea and regenerating the liver. It is particularly effective for overcoming addictions and stress. Use as an elixir for headaches and pain.

POSITION Over the higher heart chakra. Excellent as a gem essence.

EMERALD

Raw

COLOR	Green
APPEARANCE	Small bright gemstone or larger cloudy crystal
RARITY	Gem quality is expensive but unpolished emerald readily available
SOURCE	India, Zimbabwe, Tanzania, Brazil, Egypt, Austria

ATTRIBUTES Emerald is a stone of inspiration and infinite patience. It is a life-affirming stone with great integrity. Known as the "stone of successful love," it brings domestic bliss and loyalty. It enhances unity, unconditional love, and partnership and promotes friendship. Emerald keeps a partnership in balance. If it changes color, it is said to signal unfaithfulness. Emerald opens the heart chakra* and has a calming effect on the emotions.

This stone ensures physical, emotional, and mental equilibrium. It eliminates negativity and brings in positive actions. Focusing intention and raising consciousness, it brings about positive action. It enhances psychic abilities, opens clairvoyance*, and stimulates gathering wisdom from the mental planes. Traditionally, emerald was said to protect from enchantment and the ploys of magicians, and to foretell the future.

Psychologically, Emerald gives the strength of character to overcome the misfortunes of life. It is a stone of regeneration and recovery and can heal negative emotions. It enhances the ability to enjoy life to the fullest. It is helpful in cases of claustrophobia.

Emerald imparts mental clarity, strengthens memory, inspires a deep inner knowing, and broadens vision. It is a wisdom stone, promoting discernment and truth, and aiding eloquent expression. It helps bring to the surface what is unconsciously known. Emerald is extremely beneficial to mutual understanding within a group of people, stimulating cooperation.

HEALING Emerald aids recovery after infectious illness. It treats sinuses, lungs, heart, spine, and muscles, and soothes the eyes. It improves vision and has a detoxifying effect on the liver. Emerald alleviates rheumatism and diabetes. It has been used as an antidote to poisons. Worn around the neck, Emerald was believed to ward off epilepsy. Its green ray can assist healing of malignant conditions.

POSITION Wear on the little finger, ring finger, over the heart, or on the right arm. Position as appropriate for healing. Do not wear constantly as it can trigger negative emotions. Opaque Emeralds are not suitable for mental attunement.

FLUORITE

Clear

Green

Brown

Purple

Purple

COLOR	Clear, blue, green, purple, yellow, brown
APPEARANCE	Transparent, cubic or octahedral crystals, all sizes
RARITY	Common
SOURCE	United States, Britain, Australia, Germany, Norway, China, Peru, Mexico, Brazil

ATTRIBUTES Fluorite is highly protective, especially on a psychic level.
It helps you to discern when outside influences are at work within
yourself and shuts off psychic manipulation and undue mental

128

influence. This stone cleanses and stabilizes the aura*. It is extremely effective against computer and electromagnetic stress. Appropriately positioned, it blocks geopathic stress*. Used in healing, Fluorite draws off negative energies and stress of all kinds. It cleanses, purifies, dispels, and reorganizes anything within the body that is not in perfect order. This is the best crystal to use to overcome any form of disorganization.

Fluorite grounds and integrates spiritual energies. It promotes unbiased impartiality and heightens intuitive powers; makes you more aware of higher spiritual realities and can quicken spiritual awakening; and focuses the mind and links it into the universal mind. Fluorite brings stability to groups, linking them into a common purpose.

Fluorite is associated with progress on many levels, incorporating structure into daily life. This stone can overcome chaos and reorganize the physical, emotional, and mental bodies.

Psychologically, Fluorite dissolves fixed patterns of behavior and gently opens the door to the subconscious, bringing suppressed feelings to the surface for resolution. It increases self-confidence and dexterity.

Fluorite improves physical and mental coordination and counteracts mental disorders. Dissolving fixed ideas, it helps to move beyond narrow-mindedness to the bigger picture. This stone dissolves illusions and reveals truth. It is very helpful when you need to act impartially and objectively.

Fluorite is an excellent learning aid—it organizes and processes information, linking what is already known into what is being learned, and increases concentration. It helps you to absorb new information and promotes quick thinking.

Emotionally, Fluorite has a stabilizing effect. It helps you to understand the effect of the mind and emotions on the body. In relationships, it teaches the importance of balance. Physically, Fluorite assists balance and coordination.

HEALING Fluorite is a powerful healing tool, dealing with infections and disorders. It benefits teeth, cells, and bones and repairs DNA damage. It is powerful against viruses, especially as an elixir. Fluorite regenerates the skin and mucus membranes, particularly in the respiratory tract, and heals ulcers and wounds. It is beneficial for colds, flu, and sinusitis. Dissolving adhesions and mobilizing joints, Fluorite alleviates arthritis, rheumatism, and spinal injuries. Stroked across the body toward the heart, Fluorite provides pain relief. It ameliorates the discomfort of shingles and other nerve-related pain, and heals the skin, removing blemishes and wrinkles. It can be used during dental work. Fluorite rekindles sexual libido.

POSITION Wear at earlobes or place in your environment. Position as appropriate for healing. Fluorite draws off negative energy and stress and needs cleansing after each application. Place on computer or between yourself and source of electromagnetic smog*. Spray the gem essence into the environment. Palm stones are useful soothers.

SPECIFIC COLORS
In addition to the generic attributes, the following colors have additional properties:

Blue Fluorite enhances creative, orderly thought and clear communication. A dual-action stone, it calms or revitalizes energy as needed for the physical or the biomagnetic bodies*. Blue Fluorite is effective for eye, nose, ear, and throat problems. It amplifies your healing potential by tightly focusing brain activity, and can invoke spiritual awakening.

Blue Fluorite

Clear Fluorite stimulates the crown chakra*, energizes the aura*, and harmonizes the intellect with the spirit. It aligns all the chakras, bringing universal energy into the physical body. This stone enhances the effect of other crystals during healing and can clear obscured vision.

Clear Fluorite on matrix

Green Fluorite grounds excess energy, dissipates emotional trauma, and clears infections. It is particularly effective at absorbing negative energies within the environment. It brings information up from the subconscious mind and accesses intuition. It is an effective auric, chakra, and mental cleanser, dissipating obsolete conditioning. It relieves stomach disorders and cramp in the intestines.

Violet and Purple Fluorite stimulates the third eye and imparts common sense to psychic communication. It is an excellent meditation stone. It is useful in the treatment of bones and bone marrow disorders.

Green Fluorite

Violet Fluorite

Yellow Fluorite enhances creativity and stabilizes group energy. It is particularly helpful for cooperative endeavors. It supports intellectual activities. At a physical level, it releases toxins. It treats cholesterol and aids the liver.

Yttrian Fluorite takes a slightly different form from other Fluorites and does not correct disorganization. It is, nevertheless, an effective healer of other conditions associated with Fluorite. This is a service-orientated stone. It attracts wealth and abundance, teaching the principles of manifestation. It heightens mental activity.

Yellow Fluorite

131

FUCHSITE

ALSO KNOWN AS GREEN MUSCOVITE

Raw

COLOR	Green
APPEARANCE	Plate-like and layered (form of mica), all sizes
RARITY	Available from specialist stores
SOURCE	Brazil

ATTRIBUTES Fuchsite accesses knowledge with great practical value. It can channel information regarding herbal treatment and holistic remedies. It suggests the most holistic action to take and receives guidance on health matters and well-being. Fuchsite helps you to understand your interaction with other people and relates to basic concerns about life.

Psychologically, Fuchsite deals with issues of servitude from past or present lives. It reverses a tendency toward martyrdom. It is excellent for those who instantly fall into savior or rescuer mode, whether it be to save one person or a group, and who then quickly become victims. It shows how to be of service without becoming embroiled in power struggles or false humility. Many people who serve do so out of a feeling of "not being good enough," and Fuchsite teaches true self-worth.

Fuchsite shows you how to do only what is appropriate and necessary for someone else's soul growth and assists you to stand by placidly while they learn their own lessons. It combines unconditional love with the tough love that says "no more." It is useful for combating a situation in which you appear to be "helping" and yet are actually gaining great psychological satisfaction from keeping the other person dependent. Fuchsite releases both souls to their own unique pathway.

It is particularly helpful for "the identified patient" within a family or group situation on whom dis-ease and tension is projected. The identified patient becomes ill or addicted on behalf of the family. When they want to become well, the family often puts pressure on the patient to remain "ill" or dependent. Fuchsite gives the identified patient the strength to find wellness and to withdraw from the family conflict. Fuchsite overcomes codependency and emotional blackmail. It imparts resilience after trauma or emotional tension.

HEALING Fuchsite amplifies the energy of crystals and facilitates their transfer. It moves energy to the lowest point, redressing the balance. It releases blockages caused by excess energy, shifting the energy into positive channels. It balances the red and white blood cell ratio, treats carpal tunnel syndrome and repetitive strain injury, and realigns the spine. Fuchsite increases flexibility in the musculoskeletal system.

POSITION Place as appropriate or hold during meditation.

(*See also* Muscovite, page 192.)

GALENA

Raw

COLOR	Metallic gray-lilac
APPEARANCE	Small shiny mass or larger granular and knobbly
RARITY	Available from specialist outlets
SOURCE	United States, Britain, Russia

ATTRIBUTES Galena is a "stone of harmony," bringing balance on all levels and harmonizing the physical, etheric, and spiritual planes. It is a grounding stone, anchoring and centering. It aids holistic healing. It is excellent for doctors, homeopaths, and herbalists. It encourages further investigation and experimental trials. Galena opens up the mind, expanding ideas and dissolving self-limiting assumptions from the past.

HEALING Galena reduces inflammation and eruptions, stimulates circulation and benefits veins, and increases assimilation of selenium and zinc. It is beneficial for the hair.

POSITION Place as appropriate. As Galena is lead-based, elixirs should be made by the indirect method only (see page 371) and applied externally to unbroken skin.

GARNET

Raw

Polished

Garnet crystal

Garnet pebble

COLOR	Red, pink, green, orange, yellow, brown, black
APPEARANCE	Transparent or translucent crystal, often small and faceted or larger opaque piece
RARITY	Common
SOURCE	Worldwide

ATTRIBUTES Garnet is a powerfully energizing and regenerating stone. It cleanses and reenergizes the chakras*. It revitalizes, purifies, and balances energy, bringing serenity or passion as appropriate. It is said to be able to warn of approaching danger and was long ago carried as a protective talisman. Garnet is one of the most plentiful stones. It has several forms according to its mineral base, each of which have different properties in addition to the generic attributes.

Garnet inspires love and devotion. It balances the sex drive and alleviates emotional disharmony. Red Garnet in particular stimulates the controlled rise of kundalini* energy and aids sexual potency. This is a stone of commitment.

Garnet is a useful crystal to have in a crisis. It is particularly helpful in situations where there seems to be no way out or where life has fragmented or is traumatic. It fortifies, activates, and strengthens the survival instinct, bringing courage and hope into seemingly hopeless situations. Crisis is turned into challenge under Garnet's influence. It also promotes mutual assistance in times of trouble.

Garnet has a strong link with the pituitary gland and can stimulate expanded awareness and past-life recall. Garnet activates other crystals, amplifying their effect. It clears negative chakra energy.

Square-cut garnets are said to bring success in business matters.

Psychologically, Garnets sharpen your perceptions of yourself and other people. It dissolves ingrained behavior patterns that are no longer serving you and bypasses resistance or self-induced unconscious sabotage. Mentally, Garnet helps you to let go of useless or old or obsolete ideas. Emotionally, Garnet removes inhibitions and taboos. It opens up the heart and bestows self-confidence.

HEALING Garnet regenerates the body. It stimulates the metabolism. Garnet treats spinal and cellular disorders, purifies and reenergizes the blood, heart, and lungs, and regenerates DNA. It assists assimilation of minerals and vitamins.

POSITION Earlobes, finger, or over heart. Wear in contact with the skin. Place on the skin as appropriate in healing. Past-life recall: place on the third eye*.

VARIETIES OF GARNET
In addition to the generic attributes, the following forms and colors have additional properties:

Almandine Garnet is a strongly regenerative healing stone bringing strength and stamina. It is supportive in taking time for yourself, bringing deep love, and aids in integrating truth and an affinity with the higher self. It opens the higher mind and initiates charity and compassion. Almandine opens the pathway between the base and crown chakras, channeling and grounding spiritual energies into the physical body, and anchoring the subtle body into physical incarnation. Almandine helps you to absorb iron in the intestines. It stimulates the eyes, and treats the liver and pancreas.

Almandine Garnet

Andradite is dynamic and flexible. It stimulates creativity and attracts into your relationships what you most need for your development. It dissolves feelings of isolation or alienation and attracts intimate encounters with others. Andradite supports male qualities such as courage, stamina, and strength. It realigns the magnetic fields of the body. It cleanses and expands the aura*, opening psychic vision. Andradite encourages the formation of blood and energizes the liver. It aids assimilation of calcium, magnesium, and iron.

Grossularite is a useful stone to have during challenges and lawsuits. It teaches relaxation and going with the flow, and inspires service and cooperation. This stone enhances fertility and aids assimilation of Vitamin A. It is excellent for arthritis and rheumatism and fortifies the kidneys. It is beneficial for the mucus membranes and skin.

Hessonite imparts self-respect, eliminating feelings of guilt and inferiority, and encourages service. It supports in seeking out new challenges. This stone opens the intuition and psychic abilities. Used for out-of-body journeys*, it carries you to your destination. It regulates hormone production; reduces infertility and impotence; heals the olfactory system, and draws off negative influences that cause ill health.

Melanite strengthens resistance and promotes honesty. It releases blockages from the heart and throat chakras*, enabling the speaking of truth. It overcomes lack of love in any situation, dispelling anger, envy, jealousy, and mistrust. It moves a partnership on to the next stage, no matter what that might be. Melanite strengthens bones and helps the body to adjust to medication. It treats cancer, strokes, rheumatism, and arthritis.

Pyrope bestows vitality and charisma and promotes an excellent quality of life. It unites the creative forces within oneself. This stone protects the base and crown chakras, aligning them with the subtle bodies, and linking the groundedness of the base with the wisdom of the crown. Pyrope is a stabilizing stone. It fortifies circulation and treats the digestive tract. It neutralizes heartburn and soothes a sore throat.

Rhodolite is a warm, trusting, and sincere stone. It stimulates contemplation, intuition, and inspiration. Rhodolite protects the base

chakra and enhances healthy sexuality, overcoming frigidity.
It stimulates the metabolism and treats heart, lungs, and hips.

Spessartite vibrates at a high rate. It imparts a willingness to help others and strengthens the heart. It enhances analytical processes and the rational mind. It is an antidepressant and it suppresses nightmares. Spessartite relieves sexual problems and treats lactose intolerance and calcium imbalances.

Uvarovite promotes individuality without egocentricity, and at the same time links the soul into its universal nature. It stimulates the heart chakra and enhances spiritual relationships. This is a calm and peaceful stone, helpful in experiencing solitude without loneliness. It is a detoxifier, reduces inflammation, and lowers fever. It treats acidosis, leukemia, and frigidity.

Red Garnet represents love. Attuned to the heart energy, it revitalizes feelings and enhances sexuality. Red Garnet controls anger, especially toward the self.

HEMATITE

Raw (crystalline)

Tumbled

Raw

COLOR	Silver, red
APPEARANCE	"Brain-like," red or gray when unpolished. Shiny when polished. Heavy. All sizes
RARITY	Common
SOURCE	Britain, Italy, Brazil, Sweden, Canada, Switzerland

ATTRIBUTES Hematite is particularly effective at grounding and protecting. It harmonizes mind, body, and spirit. Used during out-of-body journeying, it protects the soul and grounds it back into the body. This stone has a strong yang element and balances the meridians*, redressing yin imbalances. It dissolves negativity and prevents negative energies from entering the aura*, restoring peace and harmony to the body.

Hematite is said to be beneficial for legal situations.

Psychologically, Hematite is strong. It supports timid women, boosts self-esteem and survivability, enhances willpower and reliability, and imparts confidence. This stone removes self-limitations and aids expansion. It is a useful stone for overcoming compulsions and addictions. Hematite brings attention to the unfulfilled desires that are driving life. It treats overeating, smoking, and any form of overindulgence. Hematite helps you to come to terms with mistakes and to accept them as learning experiences rather than disasters.

Mentally, Hematite stimulates concentration and focus. It enhances memory and original thought. It brings the mind's attention to basic survival needs and helps to sort out problems of all kinds. This is a useful stone for the study of mathematics and technical subjects.

Physically, Hematite has a powerful connection with blood. It restores, strengthens, and regulates the blood supply. It can draw heat from the body.

HEALING Hematite aids circulatory problems such as Reynaud's Disease and blood conditions such as anemia. It supports the kidneys in cleansing blood and it regenerates tissue. Hematite stimulates the absorption of iron and the formation of red blood cells. It treats leg cramps, anxiety, and insomnia, and aids spinal alignment and fractures. Use as an elixir for fevers.

POSITION Base and top of spine to facilitate spinal manipulation. Hold or place as appropriate for healing or calming. Hematite should not be used where inflammation is present or for long periods of time.

HERKIMER DIAMOND

Small   *Large, with smoky occlusions*

COLOR	Clear
APPEARANCE	Clear, oily, inner rainbows, usually double terminated, small to large
RARITY	Expensive but readily available
SOURCE	United States, Mexico, Spain, Tanzania

ATTRIBUTES This stone energizes, enlivens, and promotes creativity. A powerful attunement crystal, especially the smaller, exceptionally clear stone. It stimulates psychic abilities, such as clairvoyance*, spiritual vision, and telepathy, linking into guidance from higher dimensions, and promotes dream recall and understanding. This stone stimulates conscious attunement to the highest spiritual levels and to your own potential. It clears the chakras* and opens channels for spiritual energy to flow. It can be used to access past-life information so that you recognize blockages or resistance to your spiritual growth. Herkimer then facilitates gentle release and transformation, bringing your soul's purpose forward. It activates the light body*.

Herkimer attunes people and links them together when they have to be parted: each person should retain one stone. It enhances telepathy, especially in the initial practice stages and attunes healer and patient. Herkimer has a crystal memory into which can be poured information for later retrieval. It can be programmed for other people to draw on. Herkimer Diamonds are one of the strongest crystals for clearing electromagnetic pollution or radioactivity. They block geopathic stress* and are excellent when gridded around a house or bed, for which the larger stones should be used.

HEALING Herkimer Diamond is a detoxificant. It protects against radioactivity and treats disease caused by contact; relieves insomnia caused by geopathic stress or electromagnetic pollution; corrects DNA, cellular disorders, and metabolic imbalances; and eliminates stress and tension from the body. It promotes past-life recall of injuries and disease that still affect the present life. Herkimer Diamond makes an excellent environmental spray or gem elixir.

POSITION Wear as pendant or earrings (short periods only). Place at base of spine or as appropriate. Position between yourself and source of electromagnetic smog*, or spray a room.

Smoky Herkimer has a particularly strong grounding energy that heals the earth chakra and the environment, clearing electromagnetic pollution and geopathic stress. It can be gridded* around a bed to help you overcome feeling wired.

Herkimer with Citrine is an excellent antidote to fatigue caused by negative energies.

HOWLITE

Tumbled

COLOR	Green, white, blue—often artificially colored
APPEARANCE	Marbled stone, often tumbled. All sizes
RARITY	Easily obtained
SOURCE	United States

ATTRIBUTES Howlite is an extremely calming stone. Placed under the pillow, it is an excellent antidote to insomnia, especially when this is caused by an overactive mind. It can also be used as an elixir and sipped for an hour or so before going to bed.

Howlite links into the spiritual dimensions, opening attunement and preparing the mind to receive wisdom and insights. It assists journeys out of the body and accessing past lives. Focusing your sight into a piece of Howlite can transport you to another time or dimension. Placed on the third eye*, it opens memories of other lives, including those in the "between-life"* state and the spiritual dimensions.

Howlite formulates ambitions, both spiritual and material, and aids in achieving them.

Psychologically, Howlite teaches patience and helps to eliminate rage and uncontrolled anger. A piece placed in the pocket absorbs your own anger and any that is directed toward you. It also helps to overcome a tendency to criticalness and selfishness, strengthening positive character traits.

Howlite stills the mind and is excellent for sleep or meditation. It allows for calm and reasoned communication to take place. This stone strengthens memory and stimulates a desire for knowledge.

Howlite can calm turbulent emotions, especially those that have past-life causes. It releases the strings that tie old emotions to present-life triggers.

HEALING Howlite relieves insomnia. It balances the calcium levels within the body and aids teeth, bones, and soft tissue. Howlite makes a useful gem essence.

POSITION Place as appropriate or hold during meditation or to mitigate anger. Grid* around bed to aid insomnia. Keep in pocket to absorb negativity.

SPECIFIC COLOR
In addition to the generic attributes, the following color has additional properties:

Blue Howlite aids dream recall, accessing the insights dreams bring.

Blue Howlite (artificially colored)

145

IDOCRASE

Tumbled

COLOR	Green, brown, yellow, pale blue, red
APPEARANCE	Resinous, small transparent crystal with flecks
RARITY	Available from specialist shops
SOURCE	United States

ATTRIBUTES Idocrase provides a link to the higher self and the information it offers to the soul in incarnation. Psychologically, it releases feelings of imprisonment and restraint. It is helpful for healing past-life experiences of being a prisoner, of extreme danger, or of mental or emotional restraint; it gently dissolves anger and alleviates fear, creating inner security. Idocrase has powerful mental connections. It opens the mind and clears negative thought patterns so that the mind can function more clearly. It stimulates inventiveness and the urge to discover, linking this into creativity.

HEALING Idocrase strengthens the enamel on teeth and restores the sense of smell. It assists in assimilating nutrients from food. Idocrase banishes depression.

POSITION as appropriate.

IOLITE

Raw

COLOR	Gray, violet, blue, yellow
APPEARANCE	Small, translucent, color changes with angle of view
RARITY	Obtainable from specialist shops
SOURCE	United States

ATTRIBUTES Iolite is a vision stone. It activates the third eye* and facilitates visualization and intuitive insight when all the chakras* are in alignment. It stimulates connection to inner knowing. It is used in shamanic ceremonies and assists in journeys out of the body. In contact with the auric field, Iolite gives off an electrical charge that reenergizes the field and aligns with the subtle bodies*.

Psychologically, Iolite aids in understanding and releasing the causes of addiction and helps you to express your true self, freed from the expectations of those around you. At a mental level, Iolite clears thought forms*.

Emotionally, Iolite releases discord within relationships. As it encourages taking responsibility for yourself, it can overcome codependency within your partnership.

HEALING Iolite creates a strong constitution. It reduces fatty deposits in the body, mitigates the effect of alcohol, and supports detoxification and regeneration of the liver. This stone treats malaria and fevers, aids the pituitary, the sinuses, and the respiratory system, and alleviates migraine headaches. It also kills bacteria.

POSITION As appropriate, and on the third eye* if all chakras* are already aligned.

IRON PYRITE

ALSO KNOWN AS FOOL'S GOLD

Pyrite flower

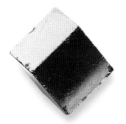

Cubic Pyrite

COLOR	Gold or brownish
APPEARANCE	Metallic, may be cubic, small to medium
RARITY	Readily available
SOURCE	Britain, North America, Chile, Peru

ATTRIBUTES Iron Pyrite is an excellent energy shield. It blocks out negative energy and pollutants at all levels including infectious diseases. Worn around the neck, it protects all the subtle* and physical bodies*, deflecting harm and danger.

Iron Pyrite is a very positive stone. It overcomes inertia and feelings of inadequacy. It facilitates tapping into abilities and potential, stimulating the flow of ideas. A piece of Iron Pyrite placed on a desk energizes the area around it. It is helpful when planning large business concepts. This stone teaches how to see behind a façade to what is, and promotes diplomacy.

149

Psychologically, Iron Pyrite relieves anxiety and frustration and boosts self-worth and confidence. It is helpful for men who feel inferior as it strengthens confidence in themselves and their masculinity, but it may be too powerful for "macho" men, initiating aggression. It helps women to overcome servitude and inferiority complexes.

Mental activity is accelerated by Iron Pyrite as it increases blood flow to the brain. It improves memory and recall. Cubic Pyrite in particular expands and structures mental capabilities, balancing instinct with intuition, creativity with analysis.

Emotionally, Iron Pyrite is helpful for melancholy and deep despair. Physically, Iron Pyrite increases energy and overcomes fatigue. It blocks energy leaks from the physical body and the aura*. Iron Pyrite increases the oxygen supply to the blood and strengthens the circulatory system. It is a stone that holds the ideal of perfect health and well-being. In healing it is extremely fast acting, bringing up the cause of the dis-ease* to be examined. It is particularly helpful for getting to the root of karmic and psychosomatic dis-ease.

HEALING Iron Pyrite treats bones and stimulates cellular formation, repairs DNA damage, aligns the meridians, and aids sleep disturbed by gastric upset. It strengthens the digestive tract and neutralizes ingested toxins, benefits the circulatory and respiratory systems, and boosts oxygen in the bloodstream. Iron Pyrite is beneficial for the lungs, alleviating asthma and bronchitis.

POSITION Place at throat in a pouch, or under pillow.

JADE

ALSO KNOWN AS JADEITE, NEPHRITE

Green (tumbled)

Green (polished)

Blue

COLOR	Green, orange, brown, blue, blue-green, cream, lavender, red, white
APPEARANCE	Translucent (Jadeite) or creamy (Nephrite), somewhat soapy feel. All sizes
RARITY	Most colors are available but some are rare. Nephrite is more easily obtained than Jadeite
SOURCE	United States, China, Italy, Myanmar, Russia, Middle East

ATTRIBUTES Jade is a symbol of purity and serenity. Much prized in the East, it signifies wisdom gathered in tranquility. Jade is associated with the heart chakra* and increases love and nurturing. It is a protective stone, which keeps the wearer from harm and brings harmony. It is believed to attract good luck and friendship.

Psychologically, Jade stabilizes the personality and integrates the mind with the body. It promotes self-sufficiency. Mentally, Jade releases negative thoughts and soothes the mind. It stimulates ideas and makes tasks seem less complex so that they can be acted upon immediately.

Emotionally, Jade is a "dream stone." Placed on the forehead, it brings insightful dreams. It aids emotional release, especially of irritability.

Spiritually, Jade encourages you to become who you really are. It assists in recognizing yourself as a spiritual being on a human journey and awakens hidden knowledge.

Physically, Jade is a cleansing stone, aiding the body's filtration and elimination organs. It is the stone par excellence for the kidneys. Jadeite and Nephrite have the same healing properties but individual colors have specific attributes.

HEALING Jade treats the kidneys and supra-adrenal glands, removes toxins, rebinds cellular and skeletal systems, and heals stitches. It assists fertility and childbirth. It works on the hips and spleen. Jade balances the fluids within the body and the water–salt/acid–alkaline ratios.

POSITION Place or wear as appropriate. The Chinese believe that holding Jade transfers its virtues into the body.

SPECIFIC COLORS
In addition to the generic attributes, the following colors have additional properties:

Blue/Blue-Green Jade symbolizes peace and reflection. It brings inner serenity and patience. It is the stone for slow but steady progress. It helps people who feel overwhelmed by situations beyond their control.

Brown Jade is strongly grounding. It connects to the earth and brings comfort and reliability. It aids in adjusting to a new environment.

Blue-Green Jade

Green Jade is the most common Jade. It calms the nervous system and channels passion in constructive ways. Green Jade can be used to harmonize dysfunctional relationships.

Lavender Jade alleviates emotional hurt and trauma and bestows inner peace. It teaches subtlety and restraint in emotional matters and sets clear boundaries.

Orange Jade is energetic and quietly stimulating. It brings joy and teaches the interconnectedness of all beings.

Lavender Jade

Red Jade is the most passionate and stimulating Jade. It is associated with love and letting off steam. It accesses anger, releasing tension in such a way that it can be constructive.

White Jade directs energy in the most constructive way. It filters distractions, emphasizing the best possible result, and aids decision-making as it pulls in relevant information.

Multicolored Jade

Yellow Jade is energetic and stimulating but with a mellowness to it, bringing joy and happiness. It teaches the interconnectedness of all beings. It aids the digestive and elimination systems of the body.

JASPER

Tumbled

Red, raw

Brecciated, raw

COLOR	Red, brown, yellow, green, blue, purple
APPEARANCE	Opaque, patterned, often water-worn or small and tumbled
RARITY	Common
SOURCE	Worldwide

ATTRIBUTES Jasper is known as the "supreme nurturer." It sustains and supports during times of stress, and brings tranquility and wholeness. Used in healing, it unifies all aspects of your life. Jasper reminds people to help each other.

Jasper aligns the chakras and can be used in chakra* layouts. Each color is appropriate to a specific chakra. This stone facilitates shamanic journeys and dream recall. It provides protection and grounds energies and the body. It absorbs negative energy and cleanses and aligns the chakras and the aura*. Jasper balances yin and yang and aligns the physical, emotional, and mental bodies with the etheric realm. It clears electromagnetic and environmental pollution, including radiation, and aids dowsing.

Psychologically, Jasper imparts determination to all pursuits. It brings the courage to get to grips with problems assertively, and encourages honesty with yourself. It supports during necessary conflict.

Mentally, Jasper aids quick thinking, and promotes organizational abilities and seeing projects through. It stimulates the imagination and transforms ideas into action.

Physically, Jasper prolongs sexual pleasure. It supports during prolonged illness or hospitalization and reenergizes the body.

HEALING Jasper supports the circulatory, digestive, and sexual organs. It balances the mineral content of the body. It is particularly useful as a gem elixir because it does not overstimulate the body.

POSITION As appropriate in contact with the skin. Specific placements are shown under each color. Use for long periods of time as Jasper works slowly. Place a large piece of decorative Brown Jasper in a room to absorb negative energy.

SPECIFIC COLORS AND FORMS

In addition to the generic attributes, the following colors have additional properties:

Blue Jasper (tumbled)

Blue Jasper connects you to the spiritual world. It stimulates the throat chakra*, balances yin–yang energy, and stabilizes the aura*. This stone sustains energy during a fast, heals degenerative diseases, and balances mineral deficiency. *Position* Navel and heart chakras for astral travel.

Brown Jasper (including Picture Jasper) is connected to the earth and encourages ecological awareness. As a result, it brings stability and balance. It is particularly useful for alleviating geopathic* and environmental stress*. It facilitates deep meditation, centering, and regression to past lives, revealing karmic causes. This stone improves night vision, encourages astral travel*, and stimulates the earth chakra. It boosts the immune system, clears pollutants and toxins from the body, and stimulates the cleansing organs. It heals the skin. Brown Jasper strengthens the resolve to give up smoking. *Position* Forehead, or as appropriate.

Green Jasper (raw)

Green Jasper heals and releases dis-ease* and obsession. It balances out parts of your life that have become all-important to the detriment of others. This stone stimulates the heart chakra. Green Jasper treats skin disorders and dispels bloating. It heals ailments of the upper torso, the digestive tract, and the purifying organs. It reduces toxicity and inflammation.

Purple Jasper stimulates the crown chakra. It eliminates contradictions. *Position* Crown.

Red Jasper (including Brecciated Jasper) is gently stimulating. It grounds energy and rectifies unjust situations. Red Jasper brings problems to light before they become too big and provides insights into the most difficult situations. It makes an excellent "worry bead," calming the emotions when played with. Placed under the pillow, it helps dream recall. Red Jasper stimulates the base chakras and assists rebirthing. It cleans and stabilizes the aura, and strengthens your boundaries. This is a stone of health, strengthening and detoxifying the circulatory system, the blood, and liver. It dissolves blockages in the liver or bile ducts. *Position* Base chakra or as appropriate.

Yellow Jasper protects during spiritual work and physical travel. It channels positive energy, making you feel physically better, and energizes the endocrine system. Yellow Jasper stimulates the solar plexus chakra. It releases toxins and heals digestion and the stomach. *Position* Forehead, chest, throat, wrist, or place over pain until it eases.

Yellow Jasper (tumbled)

Basanite (Black Jasper) is a useful scrying* stone. It takes you deep into an altered state of consciousness and brings prophetic dreams and visions.

Mookaite (Australian Jasper) provides a useful balance between inner and outer experiences*. It imparts both a desire for new experiences and a deep calm with which to face them. Flexible Mookaite encourages versatility. It points out all possibilities and assists in choosing the right one. Mookaite is a physically stabilizing stone that fortifies the immune system, heals wounds, and purifies the blood.

Mookaite (tumbled)

Picture Jasper (see Brown Jasper) is said to be the Earth Mother speaking to her children. It contains a message from the past within its pictures for those who can read it. It brings to the surface hidden feelings of guilt, envy, hatred, and love, and thoughts that are normally pushed aside, whether from the present or past lives. Once the repression is released, they are seen as lessons along the way. This stone

157

Tiger Iron (raw)

instills a sense of proportion and harmony. Picture Jasper brings comfort and alleviates fear. It stimulates the immune system and cleanses the kidneys.

Orbicular Jasper supports service, assists in accepting responsibility and instilling patience. Its circular markings resonate with circular breathing, which it facilitates. It eliminates the toxins that cause unpleasant body odor.

Royal Plume Jasper opens the crown chakra* and aligns the spiritual energies to personal purpose, bringing status and power. This stone eliminates contradictions and supports preserving one's dignity. It brings emotional and mental stability.

Orbicular Jasper

158

Brecciated Jasper (Jasper veined with Hematite) is an excellent aid to keeping your feet on the ground and attaining emotional stability. It draws excess energy away from the head, promoting mental clarity.

(*See also* Rhyolite, pages 248–249.)

COMBINATION STONE

Tiger Iron is a combination of Jasper, Hematite, and Tiger's Eye. It promotes vitality and helps in passing through change, pointing to a place of refuge when danger threatens. It is extremely helpful for people who are deeply exhausted at any level, especially those suffering from emotional or mental burn-out or family stress. It promotes change by opening a space to contemplate what is needed and then supplying the energy necessary for action. Tiger Iron's solutions are usually pragmatic and simple. Tiger Iron is a creative and artistic stone that brings out inherent talents.

Tiger Iron (tumbled)

Tiger Iron works on the blood, balancing the red-white cell count, eliminates toxins, and heals the hips, lower limbs, and feet, strengthening muscles. It aids assimilation of B vitamins and produces natural steroids. Keep Tiger Iron in contact with the skin.

JET

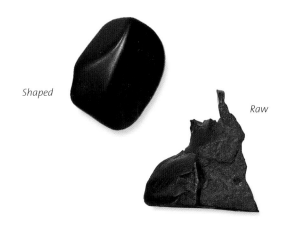

Shaped

Raw

COLOR	Black
APPEARANCE	Coal-like, usually polished and small
RARITY	Readily available
SOURCE	Worldwide, especially United States

ATTRIBUTES Jet is actually formed from fossilized wood but looks like coal. It has been used as a talisman since Stone Age times. Jet draws out negative energy and alleviates unreasonable fears. Worn around the neck, it is a stone of protection. It guards against violence and illness and provides protection during spiritual journeying. It was used in olden times to protect from "entities of darkness."

160

It is said that those who are attracted to this stone are "old souls" who have a long experience of being incarnated on the earth.

Jet can also be used to open to psychic experiences and to assist the quest for spiritual enlightenment.

Traditionally, Jet jewelry was said to become part of the body of the wearer. This suggests that Jet jewelry that is inherited or purchased should be cleansed with particular care. Jet used in healing should be thoroughly cleansed after each application.

Jet is said to stabilize finances and to protect businesses. It can be placed in a cash box or the wealth corner of the house (far left rear corner) or business premises.

Psychologically, Jet promotes taking control of life. It balances mood swings and alleviates depression, bringing stability and balance.

Jet cleanses the base chakra* and stimulates the rise of the kundalini* force. Placed at the chest, it directs the kundalini force toward the crown chakra.

HEALING Jet treats migraines, epilepsy, and colds. It diminishes glandular and lymphatic swellings and heals stomach pain. It was traditionally used for menstrual cramps.

POSITION Anywhere. As jewelry, Jet should be set in silver.

KUNZITE

Green (Hiddenite)

Pink

COLOR	Pink, green, yellow, lilac, clear
APPEARANCE	Transparent or translucent, striated crystal, all sizes
RARITY	Becoming more readily available
SOURCE	United States, Madagascar, Brazil, Myanmar, Afghanistan

ATTRIBUTES Tranquil Kunzite is an extremely spiritual stone with a high vibration. It awakens the heart center and unconditional love, producing loving thoughts and communication. It radiates peace and connects you to universal love. Kunzite induces a deep and centered meditative state and is beneficial for those who find it hard to enter into meditation. It also enhances creativity. Kunzite encourages humility and the willingness to serve.

Kunzite is a protective stone, working on the individual and the environment. It has the power to dispel negativity. This stone shields the aura* from unwanted energies, providing a protective sheath around it, and dispelling attached entities* and mental influences* from it. It imparts the ability to be self-contained, even within a crowd. Kunzite strengthens the energy field around the body.

Psychologically, Kunzite encourages self-expression and allows free expression of feelings. It removes obstacles from your path and helps you to adjust to the pressure of life. It can aid in recovering memories that have been blocked. It is a useful healer for people who had to grow up too fast, bringing back lost trust and innocence. It promotes the quality of tolerance for the self and others. Kunzite is helpful in reducing stress-related anxiety.

Mentally, Kunzite facilitates introspection and the ability to act on constructive criticism. It has the power to combine intellect, intuition, and inspiration.

Kunzite can be used to clear emotional debris and to free up the emotions, healing heartache, especially that carried forward from other lives. It clears resistance and assists in effecting compromises between personal needs and those of others. Kunzite's mood-lifting effect is helpful in depression arising from emotional causes. It is excellent for alleviating panic attacks.

Spiritually, Kunzite activates the heart chakra* and aligns it with the throat and third eye.

Physically, Kunzite can be used to block geopathic stress*. It is most effective when worn as a pendant or taped to a cell phone or other electromagnetic device.

HEALING This stone strengthens the circulatory system and the heart muscle. It is helpful for conditions affecting the nerves of the body, such as neuralgia. It calms epilepsy and soothes joint pain. It neutralizes the effects of anesthesia and stimulates the immune system. Kunzite contains lithium and is beneficial for psychiatric disorders and depression, especially when taken as an elixir. Kunzite helps the physical body to recover from the effects of emotional stress. It can be used by radionic* practitioners to represent the patient during treatment given at a distance.

POSITION Hold or place as appropriate or use as an elixir. (Sunlight causes Kunzite to fade.) Wear as a pendant or tape to a mobile phone or computer. Holding Kunzite or placing on solar plexus alleviates panic.

SPECIFIC COLORS
In addition to the generic attributes, the following colors have additional properties:

Clear Kunzite assists soul retrieval* work. It facilitates the journey back to the site of the soul loss and can be used as the receptacle for the soul until it is reintegrated into the body.

Clear Kunzite

Yellow Kunzite clears environmental smog* and deflects radiation and microwaves from the auric field. It aligns the chakras*, restructures DNA, stabilizes the cellular blueprint and the calcium–magnesium balance in the body.

Lilac Kunzite is a Celestial Doorway* and a symbol of infinity. It facilitates transition for the dying, imparting the knowledge that the departing soul requires, helping it to move over into enlightenment. Lilac Kunzite breaks through the barriers of time into the infinite.

Lilac Kunzite

164

Hiddenite (Green Kunzite) varies in color from yellow to emerald green. It connects to other worlds to assist the transfer of knowledge from the higher realms. Hiddenite benefits intellectual and emotional experiences. It will gently release feelings of failure and helps people who "put a brave face" on things to accept comfort and support from other people and the universe. It has the power to link the intellect with love to give birth to the unknown. Green Kunzite grounds spiritual love. This is a stone that supports new beginnings. In healing, Hiddenite facilitates diagnosis when gently "combed" over the body, showing areas of weakness, coldness, and dis-ease*. It supports the thymus and the chest area of the body. To stimulate spiritual insight, it is best placed on the third eye*.

Hiddenite

KYANITE

Also known as Disthene

*Blue
(pearlized blades)*

COLOR	Blue-white, pink, green, yellow, gray, black
APPEARANCE	Striated, bladed crystal, may be transparent or opaque and "pearlized," all sizes
RARITY	Readily available
SOURCE	Brazil

166

ATTRIBUTES Kyanite is excellent for attunement and meditation. It is tranquilizing and a powerful transmitter and amplifier of high frequency energies, stimulating psychic abilities and the intuition. With its ability to tune into the causal level, this stone can help spiritual energy to manifest in thought. This crystal connects to spirit guides* and instills compassion. Grounding spiritual vibrations, it brings spiritual integrity and maturation. It facilitates dream recall and promotes healing dreams. Kyanite is helpful for those making the transition through death.

Kyanite instantly aligns the chakras* and subtle bodies*, clearing the pathways and meridians. It restores Qi* to the physical body and its organs. In healing, it stabilizes the biomagnetic field* after clearing and transformation.

As Kyanite does not hold negativity, it never requires cleaning.

Psychologically, Kyanite encourages speaking one's truth, cutting through fears and blockages. Opening the throat chakra, this stone encourages self-expression and communication. It cuts through ignorance and opens to spiritual and psychological truth.

Kyanite slices through confusion and dispels blockages, illusion, anger, frustration, and stress. It increases the capacity for logical and linear thought, stimulates the higher mind, and links into the causal level.

Spiritually, Kyanite assists in detaching from the idea of blind fate or implacable karma*. It shows the part played by the self in creating causes and the measures required to balance the past. Kyanite facilitates the ascension process by drawing the light body* down into the physical realm and connecting the higher mind to the highest frequencies.

HEALING Kyanite treats muscular disorders, fevers, the urogenital system, thyroid and parathyroid, adrenal glands, throat, and brain. A natural pain reliever, it lowers blood pressure and heals infections.

It releases excess weight, supports the cerebellum and the motor responses of the body. Kyanite helps to balance yin–yang energy.

POSITION As appropriate, particularly between navel and heart. Wear as pendant.

SPECIFIC COLORS
In addition to the generic attributes, the following colors have additional properties:

Blue Kyanite strengthens the voice and heals the throat and the larynx. Useful for performers and public speakers.

Black Kyanite grounds the body when aligning the chakras* and during or after meditation.

LABRADORITE

ALSO KNOWN AS SPECTROLITE

Polished

COLOR	Grayish to black with blue, yellow
APPEARANCE	All sizes, usually polished: dark until catches light, then iridescent blue or gold flashes. Yellow form is transparent, usually small and tumbled
RARITY	Readily available
SOURCE	Italy, Greenland, Finland, Russia, Canada, Scandinavia

ATTRIBUTES Iridescent Labradorite is a highly mystical and protective stone, a bringer of light. It raises consciousness and connects with universal energies. Labradorite deflects unwanted energies from the aura and prevents energy leakage. It forms a barrier to negative

169

energies shed during therapy. It can take you into another world or into other lives. A stone of esoteric knowledge, it facilitates initiation into the mysteries.

Labradorite aligns the physical and etheric bodies* and accesses spiritual purpose. It raises consciousness and grounds spiritual energies into the physical body. This stone stimulates intuition and psychic gifts, including the art of "right timing," bringing messages from the unconscious mind to the surface and facilitating their understanding.

Psychologically, Labradorite banishes fears and insecurities and the psychic debris from previous disappointments, including those experienced in past lives. It strengthens faith in the self and trust in the universe. It removes other people's projections, including thought forms that have hooked into the aura*.

Labradorite calms an overactive mind and energizes the imagination, bringing up new ideas. Analysis and rationality are balanced with the inner sight. Labradorite brings contemplation and introspection. Synthesizing intellectual thought with intuitive wisdom, it is an excellent dispeller of illusions, going to the root of a matter and showing the real intention behind thoughts and actions. This stone brings up suppressed memories from the past.

Labradorite is a useful companion through change, imparting strength and perseverance. A stone of transformation, it prepares body and soul for the ascension process.

HEALING Labradorite treats disorders of the eyes and brain, relieves stress, and regulates metabolism. It treats colds, gout, and rheumatism, balances hormones and relieves menstrual tension, and lowers blood pressure. Labradorite can be used as a witness during radionic* treatment, pinpointing the cause of the dis-ease*.

POSITION Wear over the higher heart chakra*, hold or place as appropriate.

SPECIFIC COLOR

In addition to the generic attributes, the following color has additional properties:

Yellow Labradorite

Yellow Labradorite accesses the highest levels of consciousness, enhances visualization, trance, clairvoyance*, and channeling*. It is beneficial for the solar plexus chakra and expands the mental body, bringing in higher wisdom. It heals the stomach, spleen, liver, gallbladder, and adrenal glands.

Position: Place on third eye*, solar plexus, or hold.

LAPIS LAZULI

Raw   *Polished*

COLOR	Deep blue flecked with gold
APPEARANCE	Dense, veined, Lapis Lazuli looks like the night sky. All sizes, sometimes tumbled
RARITY	Easily obtained but expensive
SOURCE	Russia, Afghanistan, Chile, Italy, United States, Egypt, Middle East

ATTRIBUTES Lapis Lazuli opens the third eye* and balances the throat chakra*. It stimulates enlightenment and enhances dream work and psychic abilities, facilitating spiritual journeying and stimulating personal and spiritual power. This stone quickly releases stress, bringing deep peace. It possesses enormous serenity and is the key to spiritual attainment.

Lapis Lazuli is a protective stone that contacts spirit guardians. This stone recognizes psychic attack*, blocks it, and returns the energy to its source. It teaches the power of the spoken word, and can reverse curses or dis-ease caused by not speaking out in the past.

This stone harmonizes the physical, emotional, mental, and spiritual levels. Imbalances between these levels can result in depression, dis-ease*, and lack of purpose. In balance, the harmony brings deep inner self-knowledge.

Lapis Lazuli encourages taking charge of life. It reveals inner truth, encourages self-awareness, and allows self-expression without holding back or compromising. If repressed anger is causing difficulties in the throat or in communication, Lapis Lazuli releases these. This stone brings the enduring qualities of honesty, compassion, and uprightness to the personality.

Lapis Lazuli is a powerful thought amplifier. It stimulates the higher faculties of the mind, bringing objectivity and clarity. It encourages creativity through attunement to the source. Lapis Lazuli helps you to confront truth, wherever you find it, and to accept what it teaches. It aids in expressing your own opinions and harmonizes conflict. It teaches the value of active listening.

Lapis Lazuli bonds relationships in love and friendship and aids expressing feelings and emotions. It dissolves martyrdom, cruelty, and suffering. As a gem essence, it dissolves emotional bondage.

HEALING Lapis Lazuli alleviates pain, especially that of migraine headaches. It overcomes depression, benefits the respiratory and nervous systems and the throat, larynx, and thyroid, cleanses organs, bone marrow, thymus, and the immune system. Lapis Lazuli overcomes hearing loss, purifies blood, and boosts the immune system. It alleviates insomnia and vertigo, and lowers blood pressure.

POSITION Wear or place at the throat or third eye*. Lapis Lazuli should be positioned above the diaphragm, anywhere between the sternum and the top of the head.

LARIMAR

ALSO KNOWN AS DOLPHIN STONE, BLUE PECTOLITE

Tumbled

COLOR	Blue, blue-green, gray, or red, with white
APPEARANCE	Translucent, smooth, with whorls of color or white veins showing through the base color. Often small to medium, tumbled
RARITY	Easily obtained
SOURCE	Dominican Republic, Bahamas

ATTRIBUTES Recently discovered, ethereal Larimar is one of the "spiritual stones" that open to new dimensions, stimulating evolution of the earth. It radiates love and peace and promotes tranquility. Larimar effortlessly induces a deeply meditative state. It naturally raises consciousness and harmonizes body and soul to new vibrations. Spiritually, it is empowering, dissolving spurious boundaries that constrain the spiritual self, and guiding the soul onto its true pathway in life. Larimar facilitates angelic contact and communication with other realms. It is an excellent stone for those seeking a soulmate, and it facilitates the healing of past-life relationships or heart trauma.

Psychologically, Larimar removes self-imposed blockages and constraints. It dissolves self-sabotaging behavior, especially a tendency toward martyrdom, and assists taking control of life. It is particularly useful for alleviating guilt and removing fear. When moving through periods of stress and inevitable change, it enables challenges to be met with equanimity.

Mentally, Larimar brings serenity and clarity, and constructive thought. It stimulates creativity and encourages "going with the flow."

Emotionally, Larimar brings calmness and equilibrium. It is an antidote to emotional extremes and ameliorates bipolar disorders. It heals trauma to the heart and reconnects to natural playfulness and joyful childlike energy.

An earth-healing stone, Larimar connects to the energy of the earth goddess, helping women to reattune to their innate femininity and restoring their connection with nature. Placed on the earth, it will counteract earth energy imbalances and geopathic stress*.

HEALING Positioned over the heart, third eye*, or solar plexus, or gently stroked over the body, Larimar removes attached entities*. It stimulates third eye, heart, crown, and throat chakras*, and promotes self-healing. It is particularly helpful for cartilage and throat conditions, dissolving energy blockages in the chest, head, and neck. It can also be laid on constricted joints or blocked arteries. Placed on a painful spot, it will quietly draw out the pain. Used as a reflexology tool, Larimar pinpoints the site of dis-ease* and clears the meridians* of the body.

POSITION Hold or wear for prolonged periods; use on feet.

LEPIDOLITE

Raw (mica form)

Polished

COLOR	Purple, pink
APPEARANCE	Plate-like layers, slightly shiny, or grainy mass, all sizes
RARITY	Easily obtained
SOURCE	United States, Czech Republic, Brazil, Madagascar, Dominican Republic

ATTRIBUTES Lepidolite clears electromagnetic pollution and should be placed on computers to absorb their emanations. When Lepidolite takes mica-like form its properties are greatly amplified, and this is the most efficient "mopping up" tool. Lepidolite insists on being used for the highest good. It dissipates negativity. It activates and opens the throat, heart, third eye*, and crown chakras*, clearing blockages and bringing cosmic awareness. This stone aids in shamanic or spiritual journeying and accesses the Akashic Record*. It tunes you in to thoughts and feelings from other lives that are creating a blockage in your life now. It can take you forward into the future.

Lepidolite is extremely useful in the reduction of stress and depression. It halts obsessive thoughts, relieves despondency, and overcomes insomnia. Lepidolite contains lithium and is helpful in stabilizing mood swings and bipolar disorders. It is excellent for overcoming any kind of emotional or mental dependency, supportive in releasing from addictions and complaints of all kinds, including anorexia. As a "stone of transition," it releases and reorganizes old psychological and behavioral patterns, inducing change. Lepidolite encourages independence and achieving goals without outside help.

Mentally, Lepidolite stimulates the intellect and analytic qualities. With its power of objectivity and concentration, it speeds up decision-making. Lepidolite focuses on what is important, filtering out extraneous distractions.

Emotionally, Lepidolite enhances standing in your own space, free from the influences of others. It is a calming stone that soothes sleep disturbances and emotional stress, bringing deep emotional healing.

HEALING Lepidolite locates the site of dis-ease*. Placed on the body over an area of dis-ease, it vibrates gently. Lepidolite relieves allergies, strengthens the immune system, restructures DNA, and enhances the generation of negative ions. It relieves exhaustion, epilepsy, and Alzheimers. It numbs sciatica and neuralgia, and overcomes joint problems. It is a detoxifier for the skin and connective tissue. Lepidolite is excellent for the menopause, especially as a gem elixir. It treats illnesses caused by "sick-building syndrome"* or computer stress.

POSITION Place or wear as appropriate. Place under pillow for relief from sleep disturbances.

MAGNESITE

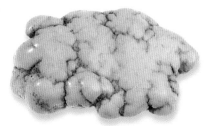

"Brain-like" form (raw)

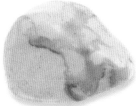

Marbled form (tumbled)

COLOR	White, gray, brown, yellow
APPEARANCE	Size and form varies widely, may be "brain-like," chalky and marbled, or crystalline
RARITY	Readily available, crystalline is rare
SOURCE	Brazil, United States

ATTRIBUTES Magnesite brings a deep peace to meditation and relaxation. Placed on the third eye*, this stone enhances visualization and imagery. It opens the heart chakra* and stimulates heartfelt love, including love for the self, which is necessary before you can embrace love from other people.

Magnesite can be very helpful in the practice of unconditional love in situations where relationships with other people are difficult because of their behavior or addictions. It helps you to feel centered, standing by placidly and allowing the other person to be totally who they are without requiring them to change or being affected yourself in any way by their difficulties.

Psychologically, Magnesite brings to the surface all forms of self-deceit. It helps to recognize unconscious thoughts and feelings and to explore the reason for these, taking you back into the past if necessary. It induces a positive attitude to life. Magnesite helps egotistical people to take a back seat and teaches how to listen attentively to others.

The brain-like form of Magnesite has a powerful effect on the mind, bringing the hemispheres into harmony and stimulating ideas and their application.

Magnesite brings a calming effect to the emotions, promoting tolerance for emotional stress. It supports people who are nervous and fearful and helps them to overcome irritability and intolerance.

HEALING Magnesite contains a high level of magnesium and aids its absorption in the body. It detoxifies and neutralizes body odor, acts as an antispasmodic and muscle relaxant, and treats menstrual, stomach, intestinal, and vascular cramps and the pain from gallbladder and kidney stones. Magnesite treats bone and teeth disorders and prevents epilepsy. It relieves headaches, especially migraines, and slows blood clotting. Magnesite speeds up fat metabolism and disperses cholesterol, preventing arteriosclerosis and angina. It is a useful preventative for heart disease. It balances body temperature, lessening fevers and chills.

POSITION Place as appropriate in contact with the skin. Can be used as a gem essence for internal or external application.

MAGNETITE

Also known as Lodestone

Raw

COLOR	Black, brownish-gray
APPEARANCE	Dark and grainy, magnetic (iron ore), all sizes
RARITY	Easily obtained
SOURCE	United States, Canada, India, Mexico, Romania, Italy, Finland, Austria

ATTRIBUTES Magnetite is magnetic and has a powerful positive–negative polarity. It can be used as magnetic therapy, working with the body's own biomagnetic field* and meridians*, and with that of the planet in earth healing. It acts as a grounding stone. When used by an experienced healer, it realigns reversed and retroverted energy flows in the body or the earth.

Magnetite will attract and repel, energize and sedate. There are times when the body tries too hard to heal itself, in which case a meridian is overenergized. If an organ or meridian is overactive, then Magnetite will calm it with its negative charge. If it is sluggish, Magnetite will activate it with its positive charge. It is extremely useful for sports injuries as it relieves aches and pains in muscles.

Magnetite temporarily aligns the chakras* and the meridians of the subtle* and etheric bodies*. It connects the base and earth chakras* to the nurturing energies of the earth, which sustains the life force and vitality in the physical body.

Magnetite aids telepathy, meditation, and visualization. It provides for a balanced perspective and trust in your own intuitions.

As Magnetite is magnetic, it attracts love, commitment, and loyalty.

Psychologically, Magnetite can be used to alleviate negative emotions such as fear, anger, grief, and overattachment, and bring in positive qualities such as tenacity and endurance. It points out how to remove yourself from detrimental situations and promotes objectivity. This stone balances the intellect with the emotions to bring inner stability.

HEALING Magnetite provides the healing energy necessary for recovery. It is beneficial for asthma, blood and the circulatory system, skin, and hair. It stimulates sluggish organs and sedates overactive ones. It is anti-inflammatory, healing muscle strains and cramps. It is useful for stopping nosebleeds.

POSITION Place on back of neck and base of spine, or on an aching joint. Put at the end of the bed to end night cramps.

MALACHITE

Tumbled

Raw

COLOR	Green
APPEARANCE	Concentric light and dark bands and rosettes. All sizes, often tumbled or polished
RARITY	Easily obtained
SOURCE	Romania, Zambia, Democratic Republic of the Congo, Russia, Middle East

ATTRIBUTES Malachite is a powerful stone but one that needs to be handled with caution. It is best used under the supervision of a qualified crystal therapist. It is toxic and should be used only in its polished form. Avoid breathing its dust. If used as a gem elixir, apply externally only or make by the indirect method of placing the stone in a glass container and standing this within spring water so that the stone does not touch the water.

Malachite amplifies both positive and negative energies. It grounds spiritual energies onto the planet. It is believed by some people that Malachite is still evolving and will be one of the most important healing stones of the new millennium.

Malachite is already an important protection stone. It absorbs negative energies and pollutants easily, picking them up from the atmosphere and from the body. It should be cleansed before and after use by placing it on a quartz cluster in the sun (do not use salt, which will damage the surface).

Malachite soaks up plutonium pollution, and guards against radiation of all kinds. It should be placed in the home of anyone who lives near a nuclear or natural radiation source. It also clears electromagnetic pollution and heals earth energies. It has a strong affinity with nature and with the devic* forces.

This stone clears and activates the chakras and attunes to spiritual guidance. Placed on the third eye*, it activates visualization and psychic vision. On the heart, it brings balance and harmony. It opens the heart to unconditional love.

Malachite can be used for scrying* or to access other worlds, inner or outer*. Journeying through its convoluted patterns releases the mind and stimulates pictures. It can assist in receiving insights from the subconscious or messages from the future.

Psychologically, Malachite is a stone of transformation. Life is lived more intensely under the influence of this adventurous stone, which encourages risk-taking and change. It mercilessly shows what is blocking your spiritual growth. Malachite draws out deep feelings and psychosomatic causes, breaks unwanted ties and outworn patterns, and teaches how to take responsibility for one's actions, thoughts, and feelings. It releases inhibitions and encourages expressing feeling. This stone develops empathy with other people, showing how it would feel to be in their place. It alleviates shyness, and supports friendships. Malachite is useful for psycho-sexual problems, especially when these have been caused by traumatic past-life sexual experiences. It assists the rebirthing process.

Mentally, Malachite goes to the core of a problem, enhancing intuition and insight. It helps alleviate mental disturbances, including psychiatric illness, and combats dyslexia. It strengthens the ability to absorb and process information, makes you more observant, and helps in understanding difficult concepts.

Placed on the solar plexus, Malachite facilitates deep emotional healing. It releases negative experiences and old traumas, bringing suppressed feelings to the surface and restoring the ability to breathe deeply. At this point, it balances the heart and navel chakras*, revealing insights. At an emotional level, it may make moods more intense but quick to change. Malachite can be used for inner exploration. It stimulates dreams and brings memories vividly to life. However, Malachite may need to be supported in the healing and transformation process by other stones.

HEALING Malachite is an extremely versatile healing stone. It is particularly useful for cramps, including menstrual cramps, and facilitates childbirth—it has been called the midwife stone. It resonates with the female sexual organs and treats any sexual dis-ease*. This stone lowers blood pressure, treats asthma, arthritis, epilepsy, fractures, swollen joints, growths, travel sickness, vertigo, tumors, the optic nerve, pancreas, spleen, and the parathyroid. It aligns DNA and cellular structure, and enhances the immune system. Malachite stimulates the liver to release toxins, reducing acidification of tissues. It treats diabetes when worn around the waist.

POSITION Wear on left hand or place on third eye. Position as appropriate for healing. Place on solar plexus to absorb negative emotions. Use polished malachite and indirect method for elixir preparation. Apply externally.
Note: Malachite may cause slight heart palpitations, in which case remove immediately and replace with Rose Quartz or Rhodonite.

Malachite with Chrysocolla (raw)

COMBINATION STONE
Malachite with Chrysocolla may manifest as a clear, gem crystal with a very high healing vibration. This combination symbolizes wholeness and peace. Placed on an area of imbalance, it gently restores equilibrium. If one stone is placed on the third eye and another on the solar plexus, mind, body, and emotions are balanced.

(*See also* Azurite with Malachite, page 78.)

Malachite with Chrysocolla (polished)

MERLINITE

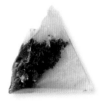

Shaped and polished

COLOR	Black and white
APPEARANCE	Two distinct opaque colors, usually small
RARITY	Becoming more readily available
SOURCE	New Mexico

ATTRIBUTES Merlinite is a magical stone that holds the imprint of the combined knowledge of shamans, alchemists, magician–priests, and other workers of magic. Its dual coloring blends the spiritual and earthly vibrations together, giving access to the spiritual and shamanic realms. This stone supports shamanic practices or magical ritual. It facilitates reading the Akashic Record*, inducing travel into past or future lives to gain insight on how to live life in the future. Merlinite can bring magic into your life.

HEALING Merlinite can be used for past-life healing and to bring harmony into the present life. It balances yin–yang and masculine and feminine energies, conscious and subconscious, intellect and intuition.

POSITION Wear around the neck or place behind the ears to access past lives.

MOLDAVITE

Crystalline

COLOR	Dark green
APPEARANCE	Small, transparent, folded mass, often glassy
RARITY	Rare but readily available, although increasingly expensive as source is used up
SOURCE	Czech Republic, Germany, Moldova

ATTRIBUTES Moldavite is another of the stones for the New Age. It is a form of Tektite, said to have extraterrestrial origin, formed when a giant meteorite struck the earth. The heat of impact metamorphosed surrounding rocks, creating a "strew field" by flinging the resulting crystals over a vast area. Moldavite is therefore a fusion of extraterrestrial energies with mother earth. This is a rare stone. It is now found along the banks of the river Moldau and is unlikely to be discovered anywhere else in the world. The crystal will become extinct.

Moldavite has been used since Stone Age times as a talisman and amulet for good fortune and fertility. Many people believe that it came to aid in earth's transition and healing and that the time has come to use Moldavite's energies wisely. It can greatly enhance the effect of other crystals, taking them to their highest vibration.

Moldavite brings you into communication with the higher self and with extraterrestrials. Moldavite has its own cosmic oversoul*, which can put you in touch with the Ascended Masters* and cosmic messengers. Holding the stone up to the light and gazing into it shifts your consciousness. This stone takes you into the highest spiritual dimensions and facilitates the ascension process. It needs to be grounded or else it can leave you spaced-out and rootless. Holding a pair of Boji Stones gently grounds after spiritual experiences with Moldavite, and the energies of clear Quartz stabilize its effects.

Moldavite has an extremely high vibration, which opens, clears blockages from, and aligns the chakras*. It integrates the divine blueprint and accelerates spiritual growth. Moldavite resonates with the crown chakra, opening it to receive the highest spiritual guidance. Placed on the throat, Moldavite communicates interplanetary messages especially with regard to the state of the ecology of the earth and its need for healing.

This is a stone that transcends time. Placed on the third eye*, Moldavite can enable you to go forward into the future or back into the past. It facilitates journeys to other lives if this is appropriate. Rather than going back into the past to relive a life, except to regain spiritual wisdom, or journeying to the before-incarnation state to access purpose, Moldavite shows you future potentials. Under the influence of Moldavite you can go forward to a future life to see the results of actions taken in the present life, or to learn what is needed in the present life in order to prevent destruction in the future.

Moldavite is a useful stone for sensitive people who find it difficult being in incarnation on the earth and who cannot adjust to suffering and deep emotions. Many such people are star children* who have come to aid the earth in its time of transition to a new vibration. They are unused to the heavy energies of earth and find it difficult to integrate the spiritual bodies into the physical, and need to ground. Moldavite, used in conjunction with grounding stones such as Hematite and Smoky Quartz, aids this process. Placed on the heart, Moldavite eases "homesickness" for those whose origin is not Earth. Moldavite has no crystalline structure and so it takes you way beyond your limits and boundaries. Psychologically, it assists in developing detachment from mundane, earthbound security issues such as money and worries for the future. Moldavite provides an overview of reasons for incarnating and contacts your spiritual purpose, integrating this into earthly life. It supports qualities such as empathy and compassion.

At a mental level, Moldavite is unconventional and inspiring, bringing the unexpected solution forward. It can awaken latent memories and access spiritual information through the intellect. It releases fixed ideas and archaic belief systems and can neutralize hypnotic commands*.

Physically, holding Moldavite may trigger a huge rush of energy through the body that has powerful metaphysical effects. It "downloads" information from the Akashic Record* and the light body*, which then has to be processed and made conscious. This process may take some time but the process accelerates spiritual growth and the raising of personal vibrations.

HEALING Rather than healing individual conditions, Moldavite makes one aware of the cause and source of dis-ease* and then supports the releasing and healing process. It also brings the gift contained within the illness to your attention. Moldavite can be used as a tool for diagnosis. People who dislike its deep green color often have an aversion to emotion and need to experience unconditional love and wholeness. They may also have hidden emotional trauma that needs to surface and heal, for which other crystals are required.

POSITION Place on forehead, throat, or crown. Note: Moldavite is fragile and should not be cleaned with salt as it scratches the surface.

MOONSTONE

Cream (natural state)   White   Clear (polished)

COLOR	White, cream, yellow, blue, green
APPEARANCE	Milky, translucent, all sizes
RARITY	Easily obtained
SOURCE	India, Sri Lanka, Australia

ATTRIBUTES Moonstone is a "stone of new beginnings." As its name suggests, it is strongly connected to moon and to the intuition. Like the moon, the stone is reflective and reminds us that, as the moon waxes and wanes, so everything is part of a cycle of change. Its most powerful effect is that of calming the emotions.

Moonstone makes conscious the unconscious and promotes intuition and empathy. It encourages lucid dreaming, especially at the time of the full moon.

Moonstone has traditionally been used to enhance psychic abilities and to develop clairvoyance*. It can be worn as a pendant to encourage acceptance of your psychic gifts.

190

Psychologically, Moonstone calms overreactions to situations and to emotional triggers. Moonstone is filled with receptive, passive, feminine energy. It balances male–female energies and aids men who want to get in touch with their feminine side. It is the perfect antidote for the excessively macho man or overly aggressive female.

Mentally, Moonstone opens the mind to sudden and irrational impulses, serendipity, and synchronicity. Care has to be taken that it does not induce illusions in response to wishful thinking.

Emotionally, Moonstone soothes emotional instability and stress, and stabilizes the emotions. It improves emotional intelligence. Placed on the solar plexus, it draws out old emotional patterning so that it can be understood and then dissolved. Moonstone provides deep emotional healing and heals disorders of the upper digestive tract that are related to emotional stress.

Physically, Moonstone powerfully affects the female reproductive cycle and alleviates menstrual-related dis-ease* and tension. It is linked to the pineal gland and balances the hormonal system, stabilizes fluid imbalances, and attunes to the biorhythmic clock. It is helpful in cases of shock and can be used to calm hyperactive children.

HEALING Moonstone helps the digestive and reproductive systems, assimilates nutrients, eliminates toxins and fluid retention, and alleviates degenerative conditions of skin, hair, eyes, and fleshy organs such as the liver and pancreas. It is excellent for PMS, conception, pregnancy, childbirth, and breast-feeding. A Moonstone elixir was traditionally used for insomnia and the stone can prevent sleepwalking.

POSITION Wear as a ring or place on the appropriate body part— forehead for spiritual experiences, and solar plexus or heart for emotions. Women may need to remove Moonstone at full moon.

MUSCOVITE

ALSO KNOWN AS MICA

Raw

COLOR	Pink, gray, brown, green, violet, yellow, red, white
APPEARANCE	Pearl-like mica in layers, all sizes
RARITY	Easily obtained
SOURCE	Switzerland, Russia, Austria, Czech Republic, Brazil, New Mexico, United States

ATTRIBUTES Muscovite is the commonest form of mica. It is a mystical stone with a strong angelic contact, stimulating awareness of the higher self. Used in scrying*, this visionary stone links to the highest spiritual realms. Muscovite stimulates the heart chakra*, facilitates astral travel*, and opens the intuition and psychic vision.

192

Muscovite has the ability to allow recognition of the flaws in humanity and at the same time stimulates unconditional love and acceptance. It is a reflective stone, mirroring back and allowing you to recognize your projections—the parts of yourself that you do not recognize and therefore see "out there." It helps you to see that the things you do not like in another are really the characteristics you cannot accept in yourself. Muscovite then aids in the integration and transformation of these qualities.

Muscovite can be used to grid* earthquake areas as it gently and safely relieves tensions within the earth. It also releases tension within the physical body and aligns the subtle bodies* and meridians* with the physical body, bringing about balance.

Psychologically, Muscovite disperses insecurity, self-doubt, and clumsiness. It is useful for those who suffer from dyspraxia* and left–right confusion. Muscovite eliminates anger and nervous stress, to bring flexibility at all levels of being. It assists in looking forward joyfully to the future and back to the past to appreciate all the lessons that have been learned. By allowing you to see yourself as others see you, Muscovite aids in changing the image presented to the outside world. It supports during the exploration of painful feelings.

Mentally, Muscovite aids problem-solving and stimulates quick-wittedness. It facilitates the clear expression of thoughts and feelings. Physically, Muscovite improves your appearance. It imparts sheen to the hair and a sparkle to the eyes. It helps the body to achieve its most appropriate weight.

HEALING Muscovite controls blood sugar, balances pancreatic secretions, alleviates dehydration, and prevents hunger while fasting. It regulates the kidneys. Muscovite relieves insomnia and allergies and heals any condition resulting from dis-ease* or distress.

POSITION Carry or hold. Stroke over the skin.

SPECIFIC COLORS

In addition to the generic attributes, the following colors have additional properties:

Pink Muscovite is the most effective color for making angelic contact.

Violet Muscovite opens the higher crown chakras* and facilitates raising consciousness to a very fine vibration.

(*See also* Fuchsite [Green Muscovite], page 132.)

NEBULA STONE

Polished

COLOR	Black with green spots
APPEARANCE	Dense stone with distinct patches, usually small and tumbled
RARITY	A new stone recently appearing on the market
SOURCE	Southwestern United States, Mexico

ATTRIBUTES Composed of four minerals, Nebula Stone is said to have unique metaphysical properties, which are still being explored. It is known to blend the vibration of light carried in its Quartz component into the physical body, enlightening the cells and activating their consciousness. This raises overall conscious-awareness, bringing remembrance of the soul's spiritual roots.

Gazing into a Nebula Stone takes you outward into infinity and inward into the smallest particle of being. Ultimately, the two become one. This is a stone of nonduality and oneness.

HEALING Nebula Stone can bring about profound healing at the cellular level of being.

POSITION Hold in the hands or place on the third eye*.

OBSIDIAN

Raw

COLOR	Brown, black, blue, green, rainbow, red-black, silver, gold-sheen
APPEARANCE	Shiny, opaque, glass-like, all sizes, sometimes tumbled
RARITY	Some colors are readily available, others are rare, and some blue-green colors are manufactured glass
SOURCE	Mexico and worldwide

ATTRIBUTES Obsidian is molten lava that cooled so quickly it had no time to crystallize. Obsidian is a stone without boundaries or limitations. As a result, it works extremely fast and with great power. Its truth-enhancing, reflective qualities are merciless in exposing flaws, weaknesses, and blockages. Nothing can be hidden from Obsidian. Pointing out how to ameliorate all destructive and disempowering conditions, Obsidian impels us to grow and lends solid support while we do so. It needs careful handling and is best used under the guidance

of a qualified therapist as it can bring negative emotions and unpleasant truths rushing to the surface. Under skilled guidance, its cathartic qualities are exceedingly valuable. It provides deep soul healing. Obsidian can facilitate in going back to past lives to heal festering emotions or trauma that has carried forward into the present.

Obsidian is a strongly protective stone, forming a shield against negativity. It provides a grounding cord* from the base chakra* to the center of the earth, absorbs negative energies from the environment, and strengthens in times of need. It is helpful for highly sensitive people. It blocks psychic attack* and removes negative spiritual influences.

A large piece of Obsidian can be extremely efficient at blocking geopathic stress* or soaking up environmental pollution, but its propensity for exploding the truth into the open has to be taken into account. Many people find its powerful effects overwhelming and prefer to choose a gentler stone for this task. But it is extremely helpful for therapists and counselors as it not only facilitates getting to the core of the problem, but also mops up energies released as a result. Black or Mahogany Obsidian are the most suitable types for this purpose, Mahogany being the gentler.

In the same way, placing Obsidian by the bed or under the pillow can draw out mental stress and tension, and may have a calming effect, but it can also bring up the reasons for that stress. These reasons then have to be confronted before peace can return; this resolves the problem permanently rather than having a palliative effect. One of the gentler forms of Obsidian, such as an Apache Tear or Snowflake, would be best for this. As Obsidian is so effective in soaking up negative energies, it is essential to clean the stone under running water each time it has been used in this way.

Spiritually, Obsidian vitalizes soul purpose. It eliminates energy blockages and relieves tension, integrating the psychological shadow into the whole to bring spiritual integrity. It anchors the spirit into the body. This stone stimulates growth on all levels. It urges exploration of the unknown, opening new horizons.

Mentally, Obsidian brings clarity to the mind and clears confusion and constricting beliefs. However, it may well do this by making it absolutely clear what lies behind mental distress or dis-ease*. Once this has been cleared, Obsidian expands consciousness, entering the realm of the unknown with confidence and ease.

Psychologically, Obsidian helps you to know who you truly are. It brings you face to face with your shadow side and teaches you how to integrate it. This stone also helps you to identify behavioral patterning that is now outdated. Obsidian dissolves emotional blockages and ancient traumas, bringing a depth and clarity to emotions. It promotes qualities of compassion and strength.

HEALING Obsidian's greatest gift is insight into the cause of dis-ease. It aids the digestion of anything that is hard to accept and promotes physical digestion. It detoxifies, dissolving blockages and tension in the physical and subtle bodies*, including hardened arteries. It reduces the pain of arthritis, joint problems, cramps, and injuries. An elixir is beneficial for shock. It alleviates pain and stanches bleeding, benefiting the circulation. This stone warms the extremities. It can be used to shrink an enlarged prostate.

POSITION Place as appropriate. Use as a ball or mirror for scrying*.

SPECIFIC COLORS
In addition to the generic attributes, the following colors have additional properties:

Black Obsidian is a very powerful and creative stone. It grounds the soul and spiritual forces into the physical plane, bringing them under the direction of the conscious will and making it possible to manifest spiritual energies on earth. Self-control is increased by the use of this stone.

Black Obsidian (raw)

Black Obsidian forces facing up to one's true self, taking you deep into the subconscious mind in the process. It brings imbalances and shadow qualities to the surface for release, highlighting hidden factors. It magnifies all negative energies so that they can be fully experienced and then released. This healing effect goes back into past lives, and can work on the ancestral and family line*. Black Obsidian composts the past to make fertile energy for growth of the soul. It reverses previous misuse of power and addresses power issues on all levels, teaching that to be empowered is not to wield personal power but rather to channel power for the good of all.

Black Obsidian is protective. It repels negativity and disperses unloving thoughts. It facilitates the release of old loves and provides support during change.

Used in shamanic ceremonies to remove physical disorders, Black Obsidian also has the gift of prophesy. Black Obsidian balls are powerful meditation and scrying aids but should be used only by those who can consciously process what they see and use it for the highest good of all. Clear Quartz helps to ground and articulate what is revealed.

In healing, a Black Obsidian placed on the navel grounds spiritual energy into the body. Held briefly above the third eye* it breaks through mental barriers and dissolves mental conditioning. Used with care, it can draw together scattered energy and promote emotional release.

Blue Obsidian aids astral travel, facilitates divination, and enhances telepathy. It activates the throat chakra* and supports communication skills. In healing, Blue Obsidian opens the aura* to receive healing energy. It treats speech defects, eye disorders, Alzheimer's, schizophrenia, and multiple personality disorder. Placed over the spot, it alleviates pain.

Blue-Green Obsidian opens the heart and throat chakras, facilitates speaking one's truth and understanding from the heart. It aids Reiki* healing; balances the mind, body, and spirit. Blue-Green Obsidian improves the assimilation of Vitamins A and E, and enhances night vision.

Electric-Blue Obsidian is an intuitive stone. It facilitates divination, trance states, shamanic journeying, psychic communication, and past-life regression. This stone opens the third eye, and assists inner journeys. As with all obsidians, it accesses the roots of difficulties, and balances energy fields. The stone enhances radionic* treatment and is effective as a pendulum for dowsing. It makes a patient more receptive. It treats spinal misalignment and impacted vertebrae, circulatory disorders, growths, and spasmodic conditions. As an elixir, it heals the eyes.

Gold-Sheen Obsidian

Gold-Sheen Obsidian is particularly effective for scrying. It takes you into the future and the past and deep into the core of a problem. It shows what is needed for healing, but other crystals will be needed to achieve healing. Psychologically, Gold-Sheen Obsidian eliminates any sense of futility or ego conflict. Releasing ego involvement, it imparts knowledge of spiritual direction. Used in healing, Gold-Sheen Obsidian balances energy fields.

Green Obsidian opens and purifies the heart and throat chakras. It removes hooks and ties from other people and protects against repetition. In healing, it treats the gallbladder and the heart. Ensure that the crystal you have is actually Obsidian and not glass

Mahogany Obsidian has a gentler energy than black. Resonating with the earth, it grounds and protects, gives strength in times of need, vitalizes purpose, eliminates energy blockages, and stimulates growth on all levels. It is a stabilizing stone that strengthens a weak aura and restores the correct spin to the sacral and solar plexus chakras. Worn on the body, Mahogany Obsidian relieves pain and improves circulation.

Mahogany Obsidian

Rainbow Obsidian is one of the gentler obsidians but with strong protective properties. It teaches you about your spiritual nature. This stone cuts the cords of old love and gently releases hooks that others have left in the heart, replenishing the heart energy. Worn as a pendant, Rainbow Obsidian absorbs negative energy from the aura and draws off stress from the body.

Rainbow Obsidian

Red-Black Obsidian raises the kundalini* energy. It promotes vitality, virility, and brotherhood. In healing, Red-Black Obsidian treats fevers and chills.

Silver-Sheen Obsidian enhances meditation and is the perfect crystal for crystal gazing. As with all Obsidians, it provides a mirror of inner being. It brings advantages throughout life and imparts patience and perseverance when required. It is helpful stone when journeying out of the body, as it connects the astral body with the physical body and so brings the soul back into physical incarnation.

Red-Black Obsidian

OBSIDIAN: **APACHE TEAR**

*Natural
formation*

COLOR	Black
APPEARANCE	Small, often smooth and water-worn. Translucent when held to the light
RARITY	Common
SOURCE	United States

ADDITIONAL PROPERTIES Apache Tear is a form of Black Obsidian but it is much gentler in its effect. It still brings up negativity but does so slowly so that it can be transmuted. An Apache Tear is excellent for absorbing negative energy and for protecting the aura*. It grounds and cleanses the earth chakra*. Apache Tear is so named because it is believed to shed tears in times of sorrow. It comforts grief, provides insight into the source of distress, and relieves long-held grievances. This stone stimulates analytical capabilities and promotes forgiveness. An Apache Tear will remove self-limitations and increase spontaneity.

HEALING It enhances assimilation of Vitamins C and D, removes toxins from the body, and calms muscle spasms.

POSITION Men at abdomen, women at breast.

OBSIDIAN: **SNOWFLAKE OBSIDIAN**

Tumbled

COLOR	Black and white
APPEARANCE	Mottled black-white, as though snowflakes were on the surface, often small and tumbled
RARITY	Easily obtained
SOURCE	Worldwide

ADDITIONAL PROPERTIES Placed on the sacral chakra, Snowflake Obsidian calms and soothes, putting you in the right frame of mind to be receptive before bringing to your attention ingrained patterns of behavior. It teaches you to value mistakes as well as successes.

It is a stone of purity, providing balance for body, mind, and spirit. Snowflake Obsidian helps you to recognize and release "wrong thinking" and stressful mental patterns. It promotes dispassion and inner centering. With the aid of Snowflake Obsidian, isolation and loneliness become empowering, aiding surrender in meditation.

HEALING Snowflake Obsidian treats veins and the skeleton, and improves circulation. The elixir is good for the skin and eyes.

POSITION Place as appropriate or use as elixir.

OKENITE

*Okenite ball
on matrix*

COLOR	White
APPEARANCE	Long and fibrous, looks like a small furry snowball
RARITY	Easily obtained from specialist shops
SOURCE	India

ATTRIBUTES Okenite has a soft and furry energy and is one of the stones for the New Age. People usually want to stroke it but this mats the fibers together or breaks them. Okenite links to the higher self and supports the conscious manifestation of its energies on the earth plane. Okenite clears obstacles from your path and promotes the stamina to finish your life tasks.

This crystal helps you to come to terms with being in incarnation and brings your attention to the reasons for your current experiences.

It pinpoints karmic* debts and opportunities that help you to grow. Assisting in understanding how the karmic past has produced the present, and how the present will create the future, Okenite facilitates deep karmic healing on all levels.

Okenite can be used to prepare for channeling*. It purifies the chakras* and the physical and subtle bodies*, uniting their energies.

This crystal has a dual action. A stone of truth, it instills truthfulness in yourself and others, and protects from the harshness that can arise when others speak their truth. It helps you to accept with love the verbal jibes of other people, showing whether there is any truth there to be accepted.

Psychologically, Okenite brings deep self-forgiveness. It promotes completion of karmic cycles, going back into past lives to forgive yourself for your mistakes and easing karmic guilt. This is a stone of karmic grace. It teaches that everything is part of the cycle of learning the soul's lessons and, growing from that knowledge, that nothing has to be endured forever. When you have done all you can, you can step out of a situation without incurring further karmic debt.

Mentally, Okenite facilitates in changing your mental set. It releases old patterns and brings in new, more appropriate beliefs. It is helpful for anyone suffering from prudishness, especially where this is linked to past-life vows of chastity.

HEALING Okenite encourages the flow of blood and milk, a boon for nursing mothers, and stimulates the circulation in the upper body. It lowers fevers and relieves nervous disorders. As an elixir, it treats skin eruptions.

POSITION As appropriate.

ONYX

Polished

COLOR	Black, gray, white, blue, brown, yellow, red
APPEARANCE	Banded, marble-like, often polished. All sizes
RARITY	Readily available
SOURCE	Italy, Mexico, United States, Russia, Brazil, South Africa

ATTRIBUTES Onyx is strength-giving. It provides support in difficult or confusing circumstances and during times of enormous mental or physical stress. Centering your energy and aligning it with a higher power, accessing higher guidance, is facilitated by Onyx as is connection with the whole. It can take you forward to view the future and, with its capacity to impart personal strength, facilitates being master of one's destiny. This stone promotes vigor, steadfastness, and stamina. It aids learning lessons, imparting self-confidence and helping you to be at ease in your surroundings.

Onyx is a secretive stone that assists in keeping your own counsel. However, Onyx is said to hold the memories of things that have happened to the wearer. It can be used for psychometry, telling the story to those who are sensitive to its vibrations.

This property of holding physical memories makes Onyx useful in past-life work for healing old injuries and physical trauma that are affecting the present life. Holding a piece of Onyx takes your attention to the site of the previous injury, which can then be released through body work, reframing*, or crystal therapy. Onyx can also be used to heal old grief and sorrows.

Psychologically, Onyx recognizes and integrates dualities within the self. It anchors the flighty into a more stable way of life and generally imparts self-control. Onyx is a mental tonic that alleviates overwhelming fears and worries. Onyx conveys the invaluable gift of wise decisions.

Physically, Onyx assists in absorbing from the universe energies that are required for healing or other purposes. It balances the yin and yang energies within the body.

HEALING Onyx is beneficial for teeth, bones, bone marrow, blood disorders, and the feet.

POSITION Wear on left side of body. Place or hold as appropriate. Traditionally, Onyx worn around the neck was said to cool lust and support chastity.

OPAL

Polished

Raw

Common Opal

Dark Opal

COLOR	White, pink, black, beige, blue, yellow, brown, orange, red, green, purple
APPEARANCE	Clear or milky, iridescent and fiery, or vitreous without fire, often small and polished
RARITY	Easily obtained, although gem Opals are expensive
SOURCE	Australia, Mexico, Peru, South America, Britain, Canada, United States, Honduras, Slovakia

ATTRIBUTES Opal is a delicate stone with a fine vibration. It enhances cosmic consciousness and induces psychic and mystical visions. Stimulating originality and dynamic creativity, it aids in accessing and expressing one's true self. Opal is absorbent and reflective. It picks up thoughts and feelings, amplifies them, and returns them to source. It is a karmic* stone, teaching that what you put out comes back. Opal is a protective stone in that, when properly programmed, it makes you unnoticeable or invisible. It can be used when venturing into dangerous places, and in shamanic work where stealth is required.

Psychologically, Opal amplifies traits and brings characteristics to the surface for transformation. Enhancing self-worth, it helps you to understand your full potential. Mentally, Opal brings lightness and spontaneity. It encourages an interest in the arts.

Emotionally, Opal has always been associated with love and passion, desire and eroticism. It is a seductive stone that intensifies emotional states and releases inhibitions. It can act as an emotional stabilizer, but the stone may scatter energy and the user needs to be well-centered before using Opal to explore or induce feelings, or to have other stones standing by to aid integration. Opal shows you what your emotional state has been in the past, especially in other lives, and teaches how to take responsibility for how you feel. It encourages putting out positive emotions. Wearing Opal is said to bring loyalty, faithfulness, and spontaneity, but may amplify fickleness where the propensity is already present. Opals can be used to send healing to the earth's energy field, repairing depletions and reenergizing and stabilizing the grid.

HEALING Opal strengthens the will to live. It treats Parkinson's disease, infections, and fevers and strengthens memory. Purifying the blood and kidneys, Opal regulates insulin, eases childbirth, and alleviates PMS (use dark colors). This stone is beneficial to the eyes, especially as an elixir.

209

POSITION Place as appropriate, especially on the heart and solar plexus. Wear on little finger.

SPECIFIC TYPES AND COLORS
In addition to the generic attributes, the following colors have additional properties:

Black-Brown-Gray Opal resonates with the sacral chakra* and the reproductive organs. It is particularly useful for releasing sexual tension that arises from an emotional cause, and for processing and integrating newly released emotions.

Blue Opal is an emotional soother that realigns to spiritual purpose. It resonates with the throat chakra and can enhance communication, especially of that which has been suppressed through lack of confidence. It is useful when past-life experiences or injuries are affecting the present life, as these can be healed through the etheric blueprint*.

Cherry Opal aids in cleansing and activating the base and sacral chakras. It promotes a feeling of being centered. At a spiritual level, this stone activates clairvoyance* and clairsentience*. It is particularly helpful for healing headaches that arise from a blocked and unopened third eye. It promotes tissue regeneration and heals blood disorders, muscle tension, and spinal disorders, and ameliorates menopausal symptoms.

Cherry Opal

Chrysopal (Blue-Green) opens to new impressions and encourages openness to others. It helps you to observe the world with new eyes. A mood-enhancing stone, it alleviates emotional burdens, often through crying, and liberates feelings. It detoxifies and regenerates the liver and relieves feelings of constriction from heart and chest.

210

Fire Opal (Orange-Red) is an enhancer of personal power, awakening inner fire, and a protector against danger. It is a symbol of hope, excellent for business, and an energy amplifier. This stone facilitates change and progress. Used in situations of injustice and mistreatment, Fire Opal supports through the resulting emotional turmoil. Fire Opal is said to magnify thoughts and feelings, returning them threefold, and can release deep-seated feelings of grief even when these stem from other lives. It is a wonderful stone for letting go of the past, although it can be explosive in its action when bottled-up emotions are suddenly released.

Fire Opal

Fire Opal resonates with the abdomen and lower back and the triple burner meridian. It heals the intestines and the kidneys, balancing the adrenal glands and preventing burn-out, and stimulates the sexual organs. This is an excellent stone for reenergizing and warming.

Green Opal is a cleansing and rejuvenating stone that promotes emotional recovery and aids relationships. With the ability to filter information and reorient the mind, it gives meaning to everyday life and brings about a spiritual perspective. In healing, Green Opal strengthens the immune system and alleviates colds and flu.

Hyalite (Water Opal) is a wonderful stone for scrying. Its watery depths stimulate connection with the spiritual realms. A mood stabilizer, it connects the base chakras with the crown, enhancing meditative experience. Hyalite helps those making the transition out of the body. It teaches that the body is a temporary vehicle for the soul.

Green Hyalite

PERIDOT

ALSO KNOWN AS CHYRYSOLITE, OLIVINE

Raw

Faceted

Polished

COLOR	Olive green, yellowish-green, honey, red, brownish
APPEARANCE	Opaque. Clear crystal when faceted and polished. Usually quite small
RARITY	Easily obtained but good crystals rare
SOURCE	United States, Brazil, Egypt, Ireland, Russia, Sri Lanka, Canary Islands

ATTRIBUTES In ancient times, Peridot was believed to keep away evil spirits. It is still a protective stone for the aura*.

This stone is a powerful cleanser. Releasing and neutralizing toxins on all levels, it purifies the subtle and physical bodies, and the mind. It opens, cleanses, and activates the heart and solar plexus chakras* and releases "old baggage." Burdens, guilt, or obsessions are cleared. Peridot teaches that holding on to people, or the past, is counterproductive. Peridot shows you how to detach yourself from outside influences and to look to your own higher energies for guidance.

This stone releases negative patterns and old vibrations so that a new frequency can be accessed. If you have done the psychological work, Peridot assists you to move forward rapidly. This visionary crystal helps you to understand your destiny and your spiritual purpose. It is particularly helpful to healers.

Psychologically, Peridot alleviates jealousy, resentment, spite and anger, and reduces stress. It enhances confidence and assertion without aggression. Motivating growth, Peridot helps to bring about necessary change. It assists in looking back to the past to find the gift in your experiences, and shows how to forgive yourself. This stone promotes psychological clarity and well-being. It is attuned to the attainment of spiritual truth, and regulates the cycles of life.

Mentally, Peridot sharpens the mind and opens it to new levels of awareness. It banishes lethargy, bringing to your attention all the things you have neglected consciously or unconsciously. With Peridot's aid, you can admit mistakes and move on. It helps you to take responsibility for your own life, especially when you believe it is all "someone else's fault." The influence of Peridot can greatly improve difficult relationships.

HEALING Peridot has a tonic effect. It heals and regenerates tissues. It strengthens the metabolism and benefits the skin. Peridot aids the heart, thymus, lungs, gallbladder, spleen, intestinal tract, and ulcers, and strengthens eyes. Placed on the abdomen, it aids giving birth by strengthening the muscle contractions but lessening pain. Its energy balances bipolar disorders and overcomes hypochondria.

POSITION Wear at the throat. Place as appropriate, especially over the liver in contact with the skin.

PETALITE

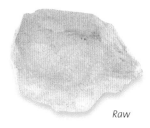

Raw

COLOR	Clear, white, pink, gray, reddish-white, greenish-white
APPEARANCE	Quartz-like, striated, slightly iridescent, usually small
RARITY	Rare and expensive
SOURCE	Brazil, Madagascar

ATTRIBUTES Petalite is another stone for the New Age. It is sometimes known as the Angel Stone because it enhances angelic connection. With a high, pure vibration, Petalite opens to cosmic consciousness. It aids in spiritual purification. This is a protective stone that enhances meditation and attunement. It takes you to a very calm and clear spiritual dimension from which causes can be ascertained and transmuted. It is particularly useful for ancestral and family healing, as it reaches back to a time before the dysfunction arose.

Petalite is a shamanic stone. It provides a safe environment for spiritual contact or for a vision quest*. It activates and energizes the process, and at the same time grounds during spiritual activity.

This stone calms the aura* and opens the throat and higher crown chakras*, linking to high spiritual vibrations. It moves you beyond your present metaphysical abilities, linking you to the highest levels of spiritual knowing, and facilitates speaking of what you see during spiritual visions.

Even a small piece of Petalite is extremely potent as an elixir. It can be used to release negative karma and to clear entities from the aura or the mental body. It is extremely helpful during tie-cutting as it brings the higher selves of each person into the process and neutralizes manipulation at any level.

Carried on the body, Petalite constantly energizes and activates all the energy centers of the body at every level. It enhances and energizes the environment in which it finds itself.

HEALING Petalite harmonizes the endocrine system and activates the triple-burner meridian. This stone is useful in the treatment of AIDS and cancer. It benefits cells, eyes, lungs, muscular spasms, and the intestines.

POSITION Wear as pendant or earrings, or place as appropriate, especially on the third eye.

SPECIFIC COLORS
In addition to the generic attributes, the following colors have additional properties:

Pink Petalite clears the heart meridian and emotional baggage. It strengthens the emotional body, and releases fear and worry. A stone of compassion, it promotes flexibility while maintaining gentle strength.

Clear Petalite renders negative energies impotent. It clears implants, miasms*, and negative karma at any level.

PHENACITE

Raw

COLOR	Colorless, may be tinted yellow, yellow-red, red, pink, brown
APPEARANCE	Glassy, quartz-like, with small crystals
RARITY	Fairly rare and usually expensive
SOURCE	Madagascar, Russia, Zimbabwe, Colorado, Brazil

ATTRIBUTES Phenacite has one of the highest crystal vibrations yet discovered. It connects personal consciousness to a high frequency, enabling information from that space to be translated to the earth. It contacts the angelic realms* and the Ascended Masters*.

Phenacite is purifying and integrating, bringing the spiritual vibrations down to earth. It resonates with the etheric body, activates the light body*, and aids the ascension process. This crystal heals the soul and purifies the subtle* and physical bodies* to provide a suitable vehicle for it. Its energies are only available to those who have prepared themselves by shifting their personal vibration to a higher level.

Phenacite has a strong connection with all the chakras* and imparts knowledge on how to heal and activate them all. It stimulates the third eye* and activates the higher crown chakra, enhancing inner knowing.

This crystal appears to have different properties, depending on where it was mined. Madagascan Phenacite is interdimensional and has been experienced as intergalactic. Phenacite from Brazil often has its own "crystal guardian."

HEALING Phenacite works at a subtle level, purifying the body and clearing energy pathways. It downloads information from the Akashic Record* via the etheric blueprint* so that dis-ease* from any source can be identified and released. Phenacite activates healing from the etheric body* to the physical, healing the etheric blueprint when necessary as a prerequisite for physical healing. Phenacite has the power to amplify the energy of other healing crystals.

POSITION Wear as faceted stone or place as appropriate, especially above head.

SPECIFIC COLORS
In addition to the generic attributes, the following colors have additional properties:

Clear Phenacite aids interdimensional travel. It facilitates moving through vibratory spiritual states that would not normally be accessed from earth. It activates memories of earlier spiritual initiations and teaches that "like attracts like," urging you to raise your vibrations, purify your thoughts, and put out only positive energy.

Yellow Phenacite has a particular aptitude for extraterrestrial contact. This is a stone of manifestation, bringing what is desired into being on the physical plane provided it is for the highest good of all.

PIETERSITE

ALSO KNOWN AS TEMPEST STONE

Tumbled

COLOR	Golden-brown to gray-blue
APPEARANCE	Mottled, iridescent, often small, tumbled
RARITY	Easily obtained
SOURCE	Namibia

ATTRIBUTES Known as the Tempest Stone because of its connection to the storm element, Pietersite is a fairly recent discovery. It is said to hold "the keys to the kingdom of heaven." It links everyday consciousness to the spiritual, reminding you that you are a spiritual being on a human journey. Centering in the spiritual being, Pietersite has the ability to ground you not to the earth but to the etheric body*. This facilitates spiritual journeying, especially to read the Akashic Record* and the insights on your incarnations that are to be found there.

Pietersite is a stone of vision and can be used for a vision quest* or shamanic journey. It works strongly with the body during moving meditations, quickly accessing a very high state of altered awareness.

218

It stimulates the third eye* and the pineal gland, accessing the intuition and promoting profound spiritual visions and precognition. It links into a very loving level of guidance.

Pietersite is said to dispel the illusion of separateness and to remove beliefs and conditioning imposed by other people. It links you to the source of your own inner guidance and helps you to recognize the truth or falsehood of other people's words. It dissolves stubborn blockages and clears confusion. Used in past-life healing, Pietersite removes dis-ease* caused by not following your own truth. It releases mental and verbal conditioning—beliefs imposed in the past by authority figures such as parents and rule-makers—and dispels spiritual illusions. It can release you from vows and promises made in other lives that have carried over into the present life, and supports your own willpower.

Psychologically, Pietersite promotes walking your own truth. It is an extremely supportive and strengthening stone, aiding in speaking out and exploring anything that is blocking your access to truth. It assists in processing ancient conflicts and suppressed feelings.

HEALING Pietersite stimulates the pituitary gland, balancing the endocrine system and the production of hormones that govern metabolism, blood pressure, growth, sex, and temperature. It helps the lungs, liver, intestines, feet, and legs and promotes absorption of nutrients from food. At a subtle level, it clears and energizes the meridian* pathways of the body. This stone clears dis-ease* caused by exhaustion in those who have no time to rest.

POSITION Place or hold as appropriate.

PREHNITE

Raw

COLOR	Green, yellow, white, brown
APPEARANCE	Bubbles on matrix, small to medium pieces
RARITY	Easily obtained from specialist stores
SOURCE	South Africa

ATTRIBUTES Serene Prehnite is a stone of unconditional love and the crystal to heal the healer. It enhances the visualization process and induces deep meditation in which the higher self is contacted. When meditating with this crystal, you are put in touch with the universe's energy grid. It is said to connect to the archangel Raphael and to other spiritual and extraterrestrial beings. Prehnite enhances precognition and inner knowing. It is a stone that enables you always to be prepared, no matter what. Attuning to divine energies, Prehnite enhances prophecy and shows you the way forward for your spiritual growth.

This crystal seals the auric field in a protective shield of divine energy. It is a useful stone for gridding* as it calms the environment and brings peace and protection. It is an excellent stone for placing in the garden and Prehnite helps you to make your home into a healing sanctuary for yourself. This stone teaches how to be in harmony with nature and the elemental forces, revitalizing and renewing your surroundings.

A good Feng Shui stone, Prehnite is helpful for "decluttering," helping you to let go of possessions you no longer need, and to organize what you keep in an appropriate way. It aids those who hoard possessions, or love, because of an inner lack. This may well come from past-life experiences of deprivation and poverty or lack of love. With Prehnite's assistance, trust in the universe is restored and the soul once again believes in divine manifestation.

Psychologically, Prehnite alleviates nightmares, phobias, and deep fears, uncovering and healing the dis-ease* that creates them. It is beneficial for hyperactive children and the karmic* causes that underlie the condition.

HEALING Prehnite is useful for diagnosis, going to the root cause. It is healing for the kidneys and bladder, thymus gland, shoulders, chest, and lungs. It treats gout and blood disorders, repairs the connective tissue in the body and can stabilize malignancy.

POSITION Place or hold as appropriate. For prophecy, visualization, and guidance, place on the third eye*.

PYROLUSITE

Natural

COLOR	Silver, black, blue, dark gray
APPEARANCE	Large, shiny, fan-like on brown matrix or granular mass
RARITY	Readily available from specialist shops
SOURCE	United States, Britain, Brazil, India

ATTRIBUTES Pyrolusite has the ability to transform and restructure energies. At its most beneficial, and when consciously directed, it can restructure life. This stone heals energetic disturbances and transmutes dis-ease* in the physical, emotional, and mental bodies.

Pyrolusite is an extremely useful stone to place in your immediate environment or meditation space. It repels negative energy and dispels psychic interference from any source, strengthening the aura* in the process. It can prevent undue mental influence from someone with a strong mind, dissolve emotional manipulation, and provide a barrier to the attentions of those who inhabit the lower astral worlds.

If you have to be in the presence of someone in authority with a specific agenda to which you do not subscribe, keep a piece of Pyrolusite close beside you. It will enable you to stay true to your own beliefs. Because of its delicate construction, some Pyrolusite is not suitable for wearing or keeping on your person, but it can be held whenever its protective energies are required.

Psychologically, Pyrolusite promotes confidence, optimism, and determination. This tenacious stone gets to the bottom of problems and offers a means of transformation. It can give support during deep emotional healing, including past-life or body work to release emotional dis-ease* and blockages in the emotional body.

Emotionally, Pyrolusite has the power to change and stabilize relationships. It can help in transmuting negative expectations into positive ones.

HEALING Pyrolusite treats bronchitis, regulates the metabolism, reinforces blood vessels, and stimulates sexuality. It is also useful for strengthening eyesight.

POSITION Place or hold as appropriate. As Pyrolusite is quite delicate and heavy to place on the body, it can be made into an elixir by the indirect method and applied topically or taken internally.

QUARTZ

Cluster with point

Pillar (shaped)

COLOR	Clear
APPEARANCE	Long, pointed crystals, transparent, milky or striated, often in clusters, all sizes
RARITY	Most types of Quartz are easily obtained
SOURCE	Worldwide

ATTRIBUTES Quartz is the most powerful healing and energy amplifier on the planet because of its unique helical spiral crystalline form. Found worldwide, it absorbs, stores, releases, and regulates energy and is excellent for unblocking it. When acupuncture needles are coated in Quartz, the effects increase by ten percent. As demonstrated by a Kirlian camera*, holding a Quartz crystal in your hand doubles your biomagnetic field. It enhances muscle testing and protects against radiation. Quartz generates electromagnetism and dispels static electricity.

This crystal works at a vibrational level attuned to the specific energy requirements of the person needing healing or undertaking spiritual work. It takes the energy to the most perfect state possible, going back to before the dis-ease set in. It cleanses and enhances the organs and subtle bodies and acts as a deep soul cleanser, connecting the physical dimension with the mind.

At a spiritual level, this crystal raises energy to the highest possible level. Containing every color possible, Clear Quartz works on all levels of being. Storing information like a natural computer, these crystals are a spiritual library waiting to be accessed. Quartz has the ability to dissolve karmic seeds*. It enhances psychic abilities and attunes you to your spiritual purpose. Used in meditation, Quartz filters out distractions. Quartz is the most efficient receptor for programming.

At a mental level, Quartz aids concentration and unlocks memory.

Quartz is a great energy saver. Attached to a fuel line in a car, a Quartz point reduces fuel consumption.

Quartz points have different facet shapes according to how fast they formed. These shapes are deeply significant. (See the Crystal Shapes section starting on page 324.)

HEALING Quartz is a master healer and can be used for any condition. It stimulates the immune system and brings the body into balance.

It is excellent for soothing burns. Quartz harmonizes all the chakras* and aligns the subtle bodies*.

POSITION Place as appropriate.

SPECIFIC COLORS AND TYPES OF QUARTZ
In addition to the generic attributes, specific colors and types of Quartz have additional properties:

Blue Quartz assists in reaching out to others and assuages fear. Calming the mind, it aids in understanding your spiritual nature and inspires hope. In healing, it is beneficial for the organs in the upper body. Blue Quartz purifies the bloodstream and strengthens the immune system.

Blue Quartz

Golden Healer (naturally coated, transparent yellow) facilitates spiritual communication over a long distance, including between worlds, and empowers healing at all levels.

Green Quartz opens and stabilizes the heart chakra. It transmutes negative energy, inspires creativity, and balances the endocrine system.

Harlequin Quartz has strings of red dots dancing within it. It links the base and heart chakras with the crown chakra, drawing physical and spiritual vitality into the body. Balancing the polarities and meridians in the body, this crystal anchors them to the etheric, harmonizing the subtle and physical nervous systems. Harlequin Quartz aids in the expression of universal love and acts as a bridge between the spiritual and physical worlds. In healing, Harlequin Quartz strengthens veins, memory, and the thyroid, and overcomes thyroid deficiencies.

Golden Healer (double terminated)

It activates the will to recover from illness and dis-ease* and helps to relieve despondency.

Lithium Quartz (naturally coated, spotted lilac-reddish purple) is a natural antidepressant. Its powerful healing energies gently lift the conditions underlying the depression to the surface, neutralizing ancient anger and grief. It can reach back into past lives to dissolve the roots of the emotional dis-ease that is pervading the present life. Lithium Quartz is an excellent cleanser for the chakras and will purify water. It is extremely useful as a healer for plants and animals.

Lithium Quartz

Natural Titanium is "spotted" onto Quartz Crystals that have the same powers as Rainbow Aura Quartz (see page 230) and is often occluded in Quartz as Rutilated Quartz (see page 237).

Titanium Quartz

Natural Rainbow, found within many Quartz crystals, stimulates an awareness of universal love, draws off negativity, and disperses healing energy to the body and to the environment.

Tangerine Quartz (naturally coated transparent orange) is an excellent stone to use after shock or trauma, especially at the soul level. It can be used for soul retrieval* and integration, and to

Natural Rainbow in Quartz point

227

Tibetan Quartz with black spot occlusions*

heal after psychic attack. Tangerine Quartz can be used in past-life healing and is beneficial where the soul feels it has made a mistake for which it must pay. The soul learns to find the gift in the experience. Tangerine Quartz activates and harmonizes the sacral chakra*, stimulating the flow of creative energy. Tangerine Quartz can take you beyond your limited belief system and into a more positive vibration. It demonstrates that like attracts like.

Tibetan Quartz occurs in single and double terminators and may have "black spot" occlusions within it. It carries the resonance of Tibet and the esoteric knowledge that has existed there for so long. This knowledge can be attuned to when meditating with Tibetan Quartz. This knowledge can then be used instinctively in healing and in spiritual practices. It accesses the Akashic Record*. This rarefied and yet grounded Quartz has a strongly centered energy that passes into the body and the personal self, bringing about deep healing and energizing of the subtle bodies*. Used on the physical body, it purifies and energizes all the meridians.

(*See also* pages 229–243 for more types of Quartz and pages 336–337 for the uniquely shaped Cathedral Quartz.)

Natural Siberian Quartz with phantom

QUARTZ: AQUA AURA AND LABORATORY-MADE SPECIALIST QUARTZES

Aqua Aura

COLOR	Blue (Siberian), red (Rose or Ruby Aura), yellow (Sunshine Aura), rainbow
APPEARANCE	Quartz crystals artificially bonded with gold, producing intense color, small points or clusters
RARITY	Readily available
SOURCE	Manufactured coating on quartz crystal

ADDITIONAL PROPERTIES Despite being artificially created, Aqua Aura has an intense energy reflecting the alchemical process that bonds gold onto pure Quartz. Aqua Aura frees you from limitation and creates space for something new. This crystal heals, cleanses, and calms the aura*, releasing any stress and healing "holes." It then activates the chakras, especially at the throat where it encourages communication from the heart. Aqua Aura releases negativity from the subtle energetic* bodies and from the connections the spiritual body makes to universal energies. The expression of soul energy is then activated, fulfilling your highest potential.

Aqua Aura stimulates channeling* and self-expression, and deepens spiritual attunement and communication. It is a protective stone that safeguards against psychic or psychological attack*. It bestows profound peace during meditation. Used in conjunction with other crystals, Aqua Aura enhances their healing properties.

HEALING Aqua Aura strengthes the thymus gland and the immune system.

POSITION Hold, wear, or place as appropriate.

SPECIFIC AURA QUARTZES

Each Aura Quartz has its own specific properties related to its color but shares many properties because of the gold alchemized onto its surface.

Rainbow Aura is formed through the bonding of gold and titanium onto pure Quartz. Activating all the energy centers in the body, this crystal clears a path for the life force to manifest through the various bodies, bringing in vibrant energy and zest for life. Rainbow Aura is beneficial for dysfunctional relationships as it shows projections and helps release negative emotions such as resentment or old grief from the past, bringing deep insights into relationships at all levels. It aids in releasing karmic* ties that are hindering relationships in the present life. The transformed relationship is vital and harmonious.

Opal Aura Quartz has a much paler rainbow color that is produced from platinum. In the same way that a rainbow in the sky stimulates hope and optimism, Opal Aura is a crystal of joy. It purifies and balances all the chakras and integrates the light body into the physical dimensions. Opal Aura opens to a deep state of meditative awareness, grounding the information received in the physical body. It brings about a state of total union with the divine through cosmic consciousness.

Rose Aura is formed through the bonding of Quartz and platinum, producing a dynamic energy that works on the pineal gland and the heart chakra, transmuting deeply held doubts about self-worth. It bestows the gift of unconditional love of the self and connection to universal love. This form of Aura Quartz imbues the whole body with love, restoring the cells to perfect balance.

Ruby Aura is also formed from Quartz and platinum, but produces a much deeper color. Ruby Aura cleanses the base chakra* of old survival issues and abuse, bringing in passion and vitality, and activates the wisdom of the heart. Spiritually uplifting, it opens to Christ consciousness*.

Ruby Aura

This is a protective crystal against aggression and violence. In healing, Ruby Aura benefits the endocrine system and is a natural antibiotic for fungal infections and parasites.

Sunshine Aura is a garish yellow crystal formed from gold and platinum. Its energies are powerful and extremely active. It activates and cleanses the solar plexus, releasing old emotional trauma and hurt. At a spiritual level, Sunshine Aura is expansive and protective. It relieves constipation on all levels and releases toxins.

Siberian Blue Quartz is a brilliant blue laboratory-regrown crystal created from Quartz and cobalt. It is a powerful antidepressant, lifting the spirit and bringing deep peace. Siberian Blue Quartz activates the throat and third eye chakras*, stimulating psychic vision and telepathy and enhancing communication. It brings about intense visionary experiences and opens to cosmic consciousness. This stone helps you to speak your truth and facilitates being heard. As an elixir it treats throat infections, stomach ulcers, and stress. Applied externally, it relieves inflammation, sunburn, and stiff neck or muscles.

QUARTZ: **PHANTOM QUARTZ**

Amethyst

Chlorite

COLOR	Varies according to mineral
APPEARANCE	Ghost-like crystal within main crystal
RARITY	Easily obtained
SOURCE	Worldwide

APPEARANCE Smallish white or colored "ghost" crystal encompassed within the main clear Quartz crystal.

ADDITIONAL PROPERTIES A phantom crystal symbolizes universal awareness. Its purpose is to stimulate healing for the planet and to activate healing abilities in individuals. For this purpose, it connects to a spiritual guide* and enhances meditation. A Phantom Quartz facilitates accessing the Akashic Record*, reading past lives and recovering repressed memories to put the past into context. It can also take you

233

into the between-lives state*. In healing, a Phantom Quartz treats hearing disorders and opens clairaudience*.

Amethyst Phantom accesses the prebirth state* and the plan for the present lifetime. It aids evaluation of progress made with spiritual lessons during the current incarnation.

Chlorite Phantom (Green) helps in self-realization and the removal of energy implants but should be used for this purpose under the guidance of a qualified crystal therapist. (*See also* Chlorite, page 108.)

Smoky Phantom takes you back to a time before you left your soul group* and links you into the purpose of the group incarnation. It can also help you to identify and attract members of your soul group. If negative energies have intervened in the group purpose, a Smoky Phantom will remove these, taking the group back to the original purity of intention.

QUARTZ: **ROSE QUARTZ**

Raw

Polished

COLOR	Pink
APPEARANCE	Usually translucent, may be transparent, all sizes, sometimes tumbled
RARITY	Easily obtained
SOURCE	South Africa, United States, Brazil, Japan, India, Madagascar

ADDITIONAL PROPERTIES Rose Quartz is the stone of unconditional love and infinite peace. It is the most important crystal for the heart and the heart chakra*, teaching the true essence of love. It purifies and opens the heart at all levels, and brings deep inner healing and self-love. It is calming, reassuring, and excellent for use in trauma or crisis.

If you want to attract love, look no further than romantic Rose Quartz. Placed by your bed or in the relationship corner of your home, it is so effective in drawing love and relationships toward you that it often needs Amethyst to calm things down. In existing relationships, it will restore trust and harmony, and encourage unconditional love.

Rose Quartz gently draws off negative energy and replaces it with loving vibes. It strengthens empathy and sensitivity and aids the acceptance of necessary change. It is an excellent stone for mid-life crisis. Holding Rose Quartz enhances positive affirmations. The stone can then remind you of your intention. This beautiful stone promotes receptivity to beauty of all kinds.

Emotionally, Rose Quartz is the finest healer. Releasing unexpressed emotions and heartache and transmuting emotional conditioning that no longer serves, it soothes internalized pain and heals deprivation. If you have never received love, Rose Quartz opens your heart so that you become receptive. If you have loved and lost, it comforts your grief. Rose Quartz teaches you how to love yourself, vital if you have thought yourself unlovable. You cannot accept love from others nor love them unless you love yourself. This stone encourages self-forgiveness and acceptance, and invokes self-trust and self-worth.

HEALING Rose Quartz strengthens the physical heart and circulatory system and releases impurities from body fluids. Placed on the thymus, Rose Quartz aids chest and lung problems. It heals the kidneys and adrenals and alleviates vertigo. Rose Quartz is said to increase fertility. The stone or elixir soothes burns and blistering and smoothes the complexion. It is helpful in Alzheimer's, Parkinson's, and senile dementia.

POSITION Wear, especially over the heart. Place on the heart, thymus, or in relationship corner of room.

QUARTZ: **RUTILATED QUARTZ**

ALSO KNOWN AS ANGEL HAIR

Tumbled

COLOR	Colorless or smoky with golden brown, reddish, or black strands
APPEARANCE	Long thin "threads" in clear crystal, all sizes
RARITY	Readily available
SOURCE	Worldwide

ADDITIONAL PROPERTIES Rutilated Quartz is an effective integrator of energy at any level. It heightens the energetic impulse of Quartz and is a very efficient vibrational healer.

Spiritually, Rutilated Quartz is said to have a perfect balance of cosmic light and to be an illuminator for the soul, promoting spiritual growth. It cleanses and energizes the aura*. This stone aids astral travel*, scrying*, and channeling*. It facilitates contact with the highest spiritual guidance. It draws off negative energy and breaks down the barriers to spiritual progress, letting go of the past.

237

Rutilated Quartz is helpful for therapists and counselors as it filters negative energy from a client, and at the same time supports their energy field during emotional release and confrontation with the darker aspects of the psyche. It gives protection against psychic attack*.

Rutilated Quartz can be used in past-life healing to draw off dis-ease* from the past and to promote insights into the events in past lives that affect the present. It assists in moving to a core life to access causes and to understand the results of previous actions. It connects to soul lessons and the plan for the present life.

Psychologically, Rutilated Quartz reaches the root of problems and facilitates transitions and a change of direction. Emotionally, Rutilated Quartz soothes dark moods and acts as an antidepressant. It relieves fears, phobias, and anxiety, releasing constrictions and countering self-hatred. This stone promotes forgiveness at all levels.

Rutilated Quartz opens the aura to allow healing. At a physical level, it absorbs mercury poisoning from nerves, muscles, blood, and the intestinal tract.

HEALING Rutilated Quartz has a vitality that is helpful for chronic conditions and for impotence and infertility. It is excellent for exhaustion and energy depletion. This crystal treats the respiratory tract and bronchitis, stimulates and balances the thyroid, repels parasites. It stimulates growth and regeneration in cells and repairs torn tissues. It is said to encourage an upright posture.

POSITION Neck for thyroid; heart for thymus; solar plexus for energy; ears to balance and align; sweep over aura to draw off negativity.

QUARTZ: **SMOKY QUARTZ**

Tumbled

Natural point

COLOR	Brownish to blackish hue, sometimes yellowish
APPEARANCE	Translucent, long, pointed crystals with darker ends. All sizes. (Note: very dark quartz may be artificially irradiated and is not transparent.)
RARITY	Easily obtained but ensure that it is natural Smoky Quartz
SOURCE	Worldwide

ADDITIONAL PROPERTIES Smoky Quartz is one of the most efficient grounding and anchoring stones and at the same time raises vibrations during meditation. This protective stone has a strong link with the earth and the base chakras*, promoting a concern for the environment and ecological solutions. This stone is a superb antidote to stress. It assists in tolerating difficult times with equanimity, fortifying resolve.

Grounding spiritual energy and gently neutralizing negative vibrations, Smoky Quartz blocks geopathic stress*, absorbs electromagnetic smog*, and assists elimination and detoxification on all levels. It brings in a positive vibration to fill the space. Smoky Quartz teaches you how to leave behind anything that no longer serves you. It can be used to protect the earth chakra below the feet and its grounding cord* when in an area of disturbed earth energy.

Psychologically, Smoky Quartz relieves fear, lifts depression, and brings emotional calmness. It alleviates suicidal tendencies and ambivalence about being in incarnation. Smoky Quartz aids acceptance of the physical body and the sexual nature, enhancing virility and cleansing the base chakra so that passion can flow naturally. This crystal alleviates nightmares and manifests your dreams. When it comes into contact with negative emotions, it gently dissolves them.

Mentally, Smoky Quartz promotes positive, pragmatic thought and can be used in scrying to give clear insight and to neutralize fear of failure. It dissolves contradictions, promotes concentration, and alleviates communication difficulties. Smoky Quartz facilitates moving between alpha and beta states of mind and aids clearing the mind for meditation.

Physically, because Smoky Quartz is often naturally irradiated, it is excellent for treating radiation-related illness or chemotherapy. However, care should be taken to select naturally formed stones with minuscule radiation rather than ones that have been artificially treated with radiation (these stones are usually very black and nontransparent). Tolerance of stress is much improved with the assistance of relaxing Smoky Quartz and this stone provides pain relief. In healing, a layout of slow-release Smoky Quartz pointing out from the body can prevent a healing crisis from occurring.

HEALING Smoky Quartz is particularly effective for ailments of the abdomen, hips, and legs. It relieves pain, including headaches, and benefits the reproductive system, muscle and nerve tissue, and the heart. Smoky Quartz dissolves cramps, strengthens the back, and fortifies the nerves. This stone aids assimilation of minerals and regulates liquids within the body.

POSITION Anywhere, especially base chakra. Under pillow, by a telephone, or on geopathic stress lines. Wear as a pendant for long periods. To dispel stress, place a stone in each hand and sit quietly for a few moments. Place over painful point to dissolve pain. Place point away from body to draw off negative energies, point toward to energize.

Smoky Quartz: the one on the left has been artificially irradiated

241

QUARTZ: **SNOW QUARTZ**

ALSO KNOWN AS MILK QUARTZ, QUARTZITE

Tumbled

COLOR	White
APPEARANCE	Firmly compacted, milky, often water-worn pebble or large boulder
RARITY	Easily obtained
SOURCE	Worldwide

ADDITIONAL PROPERTIES Snow Quartz supports you while learning lessons and helps you to let go of overwhelming responsibilities and limitations. It is perfect for people who feel put upon whilst actually creating that situation because they need to be needed. It can overcome martyrdom and victimhood.

Mentally, this stone enhances tact and cooperation. It helps you to think before you speak. When used in meditation, it links to deep inner wisdom previously denied in yourself and society.

HEALING Snow Quartz is appropriate wherever Clear Quartz would be used. Its effect is slower and gentler but nevertheless effective.

POSITION Use anywhere as appropriate.

QUARTZ: **TOURMALINATED QUARTZ**

Tumbled

COLOR	Clear with dark strands
APPEARANCE	Long, thick, dark "threads" in clear crystal, all sizes
RARITY	Easily obtained
SOURCE	Worldwide

ADDITIONAL PROPERTIES Tourmalinated Quartz brings together the properties of Quartz and Tourmaline. An effective grounding stone, it strengthens the body's energy field against external invasion and deflects detrimental environmental influences. It dissolves crystallized patterns and releases tensions at any level. This stone harmonizes disparate and opposite elements and polarities, and turns negative thoughts and energies into positive ones. Psychologically, it helps to integrate and heal the shadow energies, alleviating self-sabotage. It is an effective problem solver.

HEALING Tourmalinated Quartz harmonizes the meridians*, the subtle bodies*, and the chakras*.

POSITION Place as appropriate.

RHODOCHROSITE

Polished   Raw   Tumbled

COLOR	Pink to orange
APPEARANCE	Banded, all sizes, often polished or tumbled
RARITY	Easily obtained
SOURCE	United States, South Africa, Russia, Argentina, Uruguay

ATTRIBUTES Rhodochrosite represents selfless love and compassion. It expands consciousness and integrates the spiritual with material energies. This stone imparts a dynamic and positive attitude.

Rhodochrosite is an excellent stone for the heart and relationships, especially for people who feel unloved. It is the stone *par excellence* for healing sexual abuse. Rhodochrosite attracts a soulmate but this may not be the blissful experience you're hoping for. Soulmates are the people who help us to learn our lessons in life, and although this is not always pleasant, it is for our higher good. Rhodochrosite teaches the heart to assimilate painful feelings without shutting down, and removes denial.

This stone clears the solar plexus and base chakras*. Gently bringing painful and repressed feelings to the surface, it allows them to be acknowledged and then dissipated through emotional release. Rhodochrosite then helps to identify ongoing patterns and shows the purpose behind the experience. This is a stone that insists you face the truth, about yourself and other people, without excuses or evasion but with loving awareness.

Rhodochrosite is useful for diagnosis at the psychological level. People who have an aversion to the stone are repressing something in themselves they do not want to look at. The stone urges that they confront irrational fears and paranoia, and reveals that the emotions they have been taught to believe are unacceptable are natural. They then see things less negatively. Psychologically, Rhodochrosite improves self-worth and soothes emotional stress.

Rhodochrosite is mentally enlivening. It encourages a positive attitude and enhances dream states and creativity. This stone links you into the higher mind and helps you integrate new information.

Emotionally, Rhodochrosite encourages spontaneous expression of feelings, including passionate and erotic urges. It lifts a depressed mood and brings lightness into life.

HEALING Rhodochrosite acts as an irritant filter and relieves asthma and respiratory problems. It purifies the circulatory system and kidneys and restores poor eyesight, normalizes blood pressure and stabilizes the heartbeat, and invigorates the sexual organs. As it dilates blood vessels, it relieves migraines. The elixir relieves infections, improves the skin, and balances the thyroid.

POSITION Wear on the wrist or place over the heart or solar plexus. For migraines, place on the top part of the spine.

RHODONITE

Tumbled   Raw

COLOR	Pink or red
APPEARANCE	Mottled, often flecked with black, often small and tumbled
RARITY	Easily obtained
SOURCE	Spain, Russia, Sweden, Germany, Mexico, Brazil

ATTRIBUTES Rhodonite is an emotional balancer that nurtures love and encourages the brotherhood of humanity. It has the ability to show both sides of an issue. This stone stimulates, clears, and activates the heart and the heart chakra*. It grounds energy, balances yin–yang, and aids in achieving one's highest potential. It is said to enhance mantra-based meditation, aligning the soul more closely to the vibration.

A useful "first aid stone," Rhodonite heals emotional shock and panic,

246

lending a supportive energy to the soul during the process. It is extremely beneficial in cases of emotional self-destruction, codependency, and abuse. Rhodonite clears away emotional wounds and scars from the past—whenever that might be—and brings up for transmutation painful emotions such as festering resentment or anger. This stone has a strong resonance with forgiveness and assists in reconciliation after long-term pain and abuse. It can be used in past-life healing to deal with betrayal and abandonment. With its ability to promote unselfish self-love and forgiveness, it helps in taking back projections that blame the partner for what is really inside the self.

Rhodonite is a useful stone to turn back insults and to prevent retaliation. It recognizes that revenge is self-destructive and promotes remaining calm in dangerous or upsetting situations.

Rhodonite balances and integrates physical and mental energies. It builds up confidence and alleviates confusion.

HEALING Rhodonite is an excellent wound healer that also relieves insect bites. It can reduce scarring. It beneficially affects bone growth and the hearing organs, fine-tuning auditory vibrations, and stimulates fertility. This stone treats emphysema, inflammation of joints and arthritis, autoimmune diseases, stomach ulcers, and multiple sclerosis. Use the elixir as a rescue remedy for shock or trauma.

POSITION As appropriate. Place over the heart for emotional wounds, on the skin for external or internal wounds.

GEM RHODONITE activates the pineal gland and brings intuitive guidance. It aligns the chakras and removes blockages to clear chakra energy flow. Its gentle pink ray is particularly appropriate for assisting emotional healing.

247

RHYOLITE

Raw

Polished and shaped

COLOR	White, green, light gray, red
APPEARANCE	Banded or spotted with crystal inclusions, all sizes, often tumbled
RARITY	Available from specialist stores, often shaped and polished
SOURCE	Australia, Mexico, United States

ATTRIBUTES Rhyolite ignites the potential and creativity of the soul. It facilitates change without enforcing it, assists in fulfilling quests and facilitates knowing from a soul level. It can access karmic* wisdom. Strengthening soul, body, and mind, Rhyolite is immensely helpful when exploring the full extent of the self.

This stone facilitates a deep state of meditation in which inner and outer journeys may be made.

A useful stone for past-life healing, Rhyolite processes the past and integrates it with the present. It brings things to a resolution, no matter where the source of difficulties may have been, and actively encourages moving forward. This is an excellent stone to keep you anchored in the present moment rather than harking back to the past.

Psychologically, Rhyolite enhances self-esteem and self-worth. It imparts a sense of self-respect and acceptance of your true self.

Mentally, Rhyolite imparts the strength to deal calmly with challenging life circumstances and brings awareness of one's own strength.

Emotionally, Rhyolite has a balancing effect, gently facilitating emotional release where this is appropriate.

HEALING Rhyolite fortifies the body's natural resistance. It treats veins, rashes, skin disorders, and infections, and improves assimilation of B vitamins. It can dissolve kidney stones and hardened tissue. As an elixir, Rhyolite gives strength and improves muscle tone.

POSITION Wear or position as appropriate. Place on the forehead for past-life regression (under the direction of a skilled therapist) and on the solar plexus for emotional release.

RUBY

Raw   *Polished*

COLOR	Red
APPEARANCE	Bright, transparent when polished, opaque when not. Small faceted crystal or larger cloudy piece
RARITY	Uncut Ruby is readily available, polished gemstone is expensive
SOURCE	India, Madagascar, Russia, Sri Lanka, Cambodia, Kenya, Mexico

ATTRIBUTES Ruby is an excellent stone for energy. Imparting vigor to life, it energizes and balances but may sometimes overstimulate in delicate or irritable people. Ruby encourages passion for life but never in a self-destructive way. It improves motivation and setting of realistic goals.

Ruby stimulates the heart chakra* and balances the heart. It encourages "following your bliss." This stone is a powerful shield against psychic attack* and vampirism of heart energy. It promotes positive dreams and clear visualization, and stimulates the pineal gland. Ruby is one of the stones of abundance and aids retaining wealth and passion.

Psychologically, Ruby brings up anger or negative energy for transmutation and encourages removal of anything negative from your path. It promotes dynamic leadership.

Mentally, Ruby brings about a positive and courageous state of mind. Under the influence of Ruby, the mind is sharp with heightened awareness and excellent concentration. Given this stone's protective effect, it makes you stronger during disputes or controversy.

Emotionally, Ruby is dynamic. It charges up passion and fires the enthusiasm. Ruby is a sociable stone that attracts sexual activity.

Physically, Ruby overcomes exhaustion and lethargy and imparts potency and vigor. Conversely, it calms hyperactivity.

HEALING Ruby detoxifies the body, blood, and lymph, and treats fevers, infectious disease, and restricted blood flow. It is extremely beneficial for the heart and circulatory system. It stimulates the adrenals, kidneys, reproductive organs, and spleen.

POSITION Heart, finger, ankle.

COMBINATION STONE
Ruby in Zoisite (Anyolite) activates the crown chakra, creates an altered state of consciousness and facilitates access to soul memory and spiritual learning. It can be extremely helpful in soul healing and in past-life work. This stone has the unusual property of promoting individuality while at the same time retaining interconnectedness with the rest of humanity. It powerfully amplifies the biomagnetic field* around the body.

Ruby in Zoisite

SAPPHIRE

Black, polished

Black, raw

COLOR	Blue, yellow, green, black, purple
APPEARANCE	Bright, transparent when polished, often small or larger cloudy piece
RARITY	Some sapphire colors are rare but most are easily obtained as uncut stones
SOURCE	Myanmar, Czech Republic, Brazil, Kenya, India Australia, Sri Lanka

ATTRIBUTES Sapphire is known as the wisdom stone, each color having its own particular wisdom. It focuses and calms the mind and releases unwanted thoughts and mental tension. Bringing in peace of mind and serenity, Sapphire aligns the physical, mental, and spiritual planes and restores balance within the body.

This stone releases depression and spiritual confusion and stimulates concentration. It brings prosperity and attracts gifts of all kinds. Placed on the throat, Sapphire releases frustration and facilitates self-expression.

HEALING Sapphire calms overactive body systems and regulates the glands. It heals the eyes, removing impurities and stress. It treats blood disorders and alleviates excessive bleeding, strengthens veins, and improves their elasticity.

POSITION Touching the body. Wear on the finger or place as appropriate.

SPECIFIC COLORS
Each color of Sapphire has its own unique attributes in addition to the generic qualities:

Black Sapphire is protective and centering. It imparts confidence in one's own intuition. This stone heightens employment prospects and helps in retaining a job.

Blue Sapphire is a seeker after spiritual truth, traditionally associated with love and purity. It is extremely effective for earth and chakra* healing. This tranquil stone helps you to stay on the spiritual path and is used in shamanic ceremonies to transmute negative energies. It opens and heals the throat chakra and the thyroid, and facilitates self-expression and speaking your truth.

Blue Sapphire

253

Green Sapphire

Green Sapphire improves vision, both inner and outer, and improves dream recall. It stimulates the heart chakra, bringing loyalty, fidelity, and integrity. This stone enhances compassion and an understanding of the frailties and unique qualities of others. It honors trust and respect for other people's belief systems.

Pink Sapphire acts as a magnet to draw into your life all that you need in order to evolve. It is a fast-acting stone that teaches you how to master emotions, clearing emotional blockages and integrating the transmuted energies.

Purple Sapphire awakens. It is helpful for meditation, stimulating the kundalini* rise and the crown chakra and opening spirituality. This stone activates the pineal gland with its link to psychic abilities, and stimulates visionary qualities. It is extremely calming for the emotionally unstable.

Royal Sapphire eliminates negative energies from chakras, and stimulates the third eye* to access information for growth. This stone teaches responsibility for your own thoughts and feelings. It treats brain disorders, including dyslexia.

Star Sapphire has a five-pointed star-shaped formation in its depths. This rare stone draws you into its depths and opens intuition. It brings about centering of your thoughts and aids in anticipating the intentions of other people. It is said to contact extraterrestrial beings.

White Sapphire has an extremely pure energy. Opening the crown chakra, it takes spiritual awareness to a very high space, opening cosmic consciousness*. This is an extremely protective stone that removes obstacles to the spiritual path. It is helpful in accessing your potential and life purpose.

Yellow Sapphire attracts wealth to the home and can be placed in cash boxes to increase prosperity and earnings. If worn, it should touch the body. Yellow Sapphire stimulates the intellect and improves overall focus so that the bigger picture is seen. As an elixir, it removes toxins from the body.

Yellow Sapphire

SARDONYX

Black, tumbled

Black and Reddish-Brown, tumbled

COLOR	Black, red, brown, clear
APPEARANCE	Banded, opaque, may be large or small, often tumbled
RARITY	Easily obtained from specialist stores
SOURCE	Brazil, India, Russia, Asia Minor

ATTRIBUTES Sardonyx is a stone of strength and protection. It invokes the search for a meaningful existence and promotes integrity and virtuous conduct.

Bringing lasting happiness and stability to marriage and partnerships, Sardonyx attracts friends and good fortune. It can be gridded around the house and garden to prevent crime. (A stone can be placed at each corner, and at doors and windows, but it is more effective to dowse for exactly the right place (see page 374).)

256

Psychologically, Sardonyx supplements willpower and strengthens character. It increases stamina, vigor, and self-control. This stone alleviates depression and overcomes hesitancy. Mentally, Sardonyx improves perception and aids the process of osmosis and processing of information.

HEALING Sardonyx heals lungs and bones and resensitizes the sensory organs. It regulates fluids and cell metabolism, strengthens the immune system, and aids the absorption of nutrients and elimination of waste products.

POSITION Anywhere, especially laid on the stomach.

SPECIFIC COLORS
In addition to the generic properties, specific colors have additional attributes:

Black Sardonyx absorbs negativity.

Brown Sardonyx grounds energy.

Clear Sardonyx purifies.

Red Sardonyx stimulates.

Red Sardonyx

SELENITE

ALSO KNOWN AS SATIN SPAR, DESERT ROSE

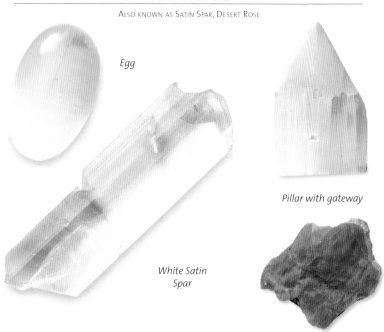

Egg

Pillar with gateway

White Satin Spar

Orange-Brown

COLOR	Pure white, orange, blue, brown, green
APPEARANCE	Translucent with fine ribbing (Satin Spar) or coarser ribbing, fishtail, or petal-like (Desert Rose). All sizes
RARITY	Easily obtained
SOURCE	United States, Mexico, Russia, Austria, Greece, Poland, Germany, France, England

ATTRIBUTES Translucent Selenite has a very fine vibration and brings clarity of mind, opening the crown and higher crown chakras* and accessing angelic consciousness and higher guidance. Pure Selenite is a link to the light body*, helping to anchor it in the earth vibration.

Selenite is a calm stone that instills deep peace and is excellent for meditation or spiritual work. Telepathy is enhanced by each person holding a piece of pure-vibration Selenite. The purest translucent white Selenite has an ethereal quality and is said to inhabit the place between light and matter. An ancient stone, it is nevertheless one of the most powerful crystals for the new vibration on earth.

Selenite can be used to form a protective grid* around a house, creating a safe and quiet space that does not allow outside influences in—use internally in the corners of the house. A large piece of Selenite placed in the house ensures a peaceful atmosphere. Selenite wands can be used to detach entities from the aura* or for preventing anything external from influencing the mind.

Carrying the imprint of all that has happened in the world, Selenite reaches other lives and is very useful for checking on progress made and for accessing the plan for the present life from the between-lives state*. It pinpoints lessons and issues that are still being worked upon, and shows how they can best be resolved. It can be used for scrying*, to see the future or to ascertain what has happened in the past.

Psychologically, Selenite assists judgment and insight. Mentally, it clears confusion and aids in seeing the deeper picture. It brings about a conscious understanding of what has been occurring at the subconscious level. This is a powerful disperser and stabilizer for erratic emotions.

HEALING Selenite aligns the spinal column and promotes flexibility. It guards against epileptic seizures. This stone neutralizes mercury

poisoning from dental amalgam and reverses the effects of "free radicals." It is an excellent crystal for breastfeeding and nurturing a child. Its finest healing occurs at the energetic levels.

POSITION Hold, or place in or around house. (Note: Selenite dissolves when wet.)

SPECIFIC COLORS AND FORMS
In addition to the generic properties, different colored Selenites have specific properties:

Orange-Brown Selenite earths angelic energies and aids earth healing.

Blue Selenite placed on the third eye quiets the intellect, facilitates shutting off mind chatter during meditation, and quickly reveals the core of a problem.

Blue Selenite

Green Selenite assists in working toward the highest good. It makes you feel good about yourself and helps to overcome the effects of aging on the skin and skeleton.

Green Selenite

260

*Fishtail
Selenite*

Fishtail Selenite provides deep healing for the nerves. It is extremely calming, stabilizing emotions and defusing tension. This form of Selenite is often called Angel's Wing Selenite, as it facilitates angelic contact.

*Desert Rose
Selenite*

Desert Rose Selenite helps to dissolve self-imposed programs that have been running for too long. It releases the program and assists in finding an appropriate replacement. It can be used to strengthen affirmations of purpose.

261

SERAPHINITE

ALSO KNOWN AS SERAFINA

Polished slice

COLOR	Green
APPEARANCE	Silvery feathers within the darker stone, often small and polished
RARITY	Available in specialist stores
SOURCE	Siberia

ATTRIBUTES Placed on the third eye* or meditated with, Seraphinite is a stone of spiritual enlightenment and is excellent for accessing self-healing. It is one of the crystals for making angelic connection and for opening the crown and higher crown chakras*. This stone promotes living from the heart and has a gently cleansing effect on the heart chakra, opening to love.

Its feathery wings whisk you up to a high spiritual vibration and it is excellent for making journeys out of the body, protecting the physical body while you are gone. It can assist with reviewing the progress of life and with identifying the changes needed to put you on the path to peace and fulfillment.

HEALING Seraphinite works best at a subtle level. It activates the spinal cord and its links to the etheric body*, especially behind the heart, and can release muscle tension up into the neck. It is useful for overcoming chills and for promoting weight loss.

POSITION Place on third eye or heart, or under pillow, or wear around the neck.

(*See also* Chlorite, page 108.)

SERPENTINE

Raw

COLOR	Red, green, brown-red, brown-yellow, black-green, white
APPEARANCE	Mottled, dual appearance, can be water-worn and often polished. All sizes
RARITY	Easily obtained from specialist stores
SOURCE	Britain (Cornwall), Norway, Russia, Zimbabwe, Italy, United States

ATTRIBUTES Serpentine is an earthing stone that aids meditation and spiritual exploration. Clearing the chakras* and stimulating the crown chakra, it opens psychic abilities and helps you to understand the spiritual basis of life. This stone opens new pathways for the kundalini* energy to rise. It assists the retrieval of wisdom, and regains memory of past lives.

Psychologically, Serpentine helps you to feel more in control of your life. It corrects mental and emotional imbalances and assists the conscious direction of healing energy toward problem areas.

Physically, Serpentine is extremely cleansing and detoxifying for the body and blood. It is said to ensure longevity.

HEALING Serpentine eliminates parasites, aids calcium and magnesium absorption, and treats hypoglycemia and diabetes.

POSITION Hold or place on appropriate spot.

INFINITE STONE (Light-Green Serpentine) is a gentle, tender-natured stone that brings you into contact with angelic guidance. It accesses and integrates the past, present, and future and is excellent for past-life exploration, as it promotes compassion and forgiveness for yourself and what you went through. Holding this stone takes you into the healing realms that exist in the between-lives state* so that healing that was not undertaken after a former life ended can be completed.

Infinite Stone

This stone heals imbalances from past lives and clears emotional baggage from previous relationships. Placed on the throat, it aids speaking of the past and resolves issues that have been carried over into the present. Use Infinite Stone if you want to confront anyone from your past, as it brings a gentle touch to the meeting.

Light Green Serpentine is excellent for pain relief, especially menstrual and muscular aches and pains.

SHATTUCKITE

Tumbled

COLOR	Dark and light blue, turquoise
APPEARANCE	Mottled, often small and tumbled
RARITY	Obtainable from specialist stores
SOURCE	United States

ATTRIBUTES Shattuckite is a highly spiritual stone that heightens vibration. It stimulates the third eye* and the throat chakra*, bringing them into harmony and alignment. It brings clear psychic vision and aids in understanding and communicating what is seen. Particularly useful in cases where past-life experience has closed down metaphysical abilities, Shattuckite removes hypnotic commands and edicts against using psychic vision. It can clear past-life curses and commands to secrecy.

Shattuckite is helpful during channeling*, as it is strongly protective, ensuring that the entity does not take over the physical body. It reaches a high vibration, ensuring that the purest source is contacted. It can be used to develop pyschic abilities such as automatic writing* and telepathy and to facilitate clear communication with extraterrestrials.

HEALING Shattuckite is beneficial for all minor health complaints, bringing the body gently back into balance. The elixir is useful as a general tonic, especially in the spring. The stone treats tonsillitis, increases the clotting properties of blood, and clears blockages from intercellular structures.

POSITION Place as appropriate.

SMITHSONITE

Pink

Blue-Green

COLOR	Pink, lavender, green, blue-green, purple, brown, yellow, white-gray, blue
APPEARANCE	Pearly, lustrous, like layers of silky bubbles, all sizes
RARITY	Easily obtained
SOURCE	United States, Australia, Greece, Italy, Mexico, Namibia

ATTRIBUTES Smithsonite is a stone of tranquility, charm, kindness, and favorable outcomes. It has an extremely gentle presence and forms a buffer against life's problems. It is the perfect stone for releasing stress that is almost at breaking point and for alleviating mental breakdown.

This stone is ideal for anyone who has had a difficult childhood and who felt unloved or unwanted. Smithsonite heals the inner child* and alleviates the effects of emotional abuse and misuse. It is gentle, dissolving emotional hurt subtly. Its effects are noticed in feeling better rather than in traumatic emotional release. It may need the support of other crystals to bring things into conscious awareness. This is an excellent crystal for birth and rebirth and can treat infertility.

Smithsonite aligns the chakras* and strengthens psychic abilities. Holding Smithsonite during psychic communication makes you intuitively aware of its validity, or otherwise. Placed on the crown chakra, it connects to the angelic realm*.

Psychologically, Smithsonite supports leadership qualities, especially where tact is required. Emotionally, Smithsonite aids difficult relationships. An excellent stone for a secure and balanced life, this stone imparts harmony and diplomacy and remedies unpleasant situations. Physically, as Smithsonite is excellent for the immune system, it can be gridded around the four corners of your bed, with a piece under the pillow or on a bedside table. It is particularly effective combined with Bloodstone or Green Tourmaline taped over the thymus.

HEALING Smithsonite heals a dysfunctional immune system, sinus and digestive disorders, osteoporosis, and alcoholism. It restores elasticity to veins and muscles.

POSITION Place as appropriate or carry always. Place at crown to align chakras. Place Pink Smithsonite over the heart or thymus. Grid* around the bed or body.

SPECIFIC COLORS
In addition to the generic attributes, specific colors of Smithsonite have additional properties:

Blue-Green Smithsonite heals emotional and other wounds by bringing in universal love. Gently releasing anger, fear, and pain, it balances the energy field between the etheric and emotional bodies, and eases panic attacks, assists in attaining the heart's desire, promotes friendship, and is auspicious in midwifery and for nurturing babies.

Lavender-Violet Smithsonite has a very gentle vibration. It clears negative energy, and encourages joyful spiritual service and higher states of consciousness, giving guidance and protection. It is an excellent stone for meditation and soul retrieval* and facilitates going back into past lives to regain soul energy that did not make the transition away from a past-life death. In this respect, it can heal past-life death trauma and point the way to soul healing. Physically, it soothes neuralgia and inflammation.

Lavender-Pink Smithsonite has a very loving vibration. It heals the heart, and experiences of abandonment and abuse, rebuilding trust and security. Assisting in feeling loved and supported by the universe, it is helpful in convalescence and soothes pain. Lavender-Pink Smithsonite helps ameliorate drug and alcohol problems and the emotions that lie behind them.

Yellow Smithsonite balances the solar plexus chakra* and the mental body. It releases old hurts and outgrown emotional patterning. In healing, this stone aids digestion and assimilation of nutrients, and relieves skin problems.

SODALITE

Raw

Tumbled

COLOR	Blue
APPEARANCE	Mottled dark and light blue-white, often tumbled. All sizes
RARITY	Easily obtained
SOURCE	North America, France, Brazil, Greenland, Russia, Myanmar, Romania

ATTRIBUTES Sodalite unites logic with intuition and opens spiritual perception, bringing information from the higher mind down to the physical level. This stone stimulates the pineal gland and the third eye and deepens meditation. When in Sodalite-enhanced meditation, the mind can be used to understand the circumstances in which you find yourself. This stone instills a drive for truth and an urge toward idealism, making it possible to remain true to yourself and stand up for your beliefs.

271

Sodalite clears electromagnetic pollution and can be placed on computers to block their emanations. It is helpful for people who are sensitive to "sick-building syndrome"* or to electromagnetic smog*.

This is a particularly useful stone for group work, as it brings harmony and solidarity of purpose. It stimulates trust and companionship between members of the group, encouraging interdependence.

An excellent stone for the mind, Sodalite eliminates mental confusion and intellectual bondage. It encourages rational thought, objectivity, truth, and intuitive perception, together with the verbalization of feelings. As it calms the mind, it allows new information to be received. Sodalite stimulates the release of old mental conditioning and rigid mind-sets, creating space to put new insights in practice.

Psychologically, this stone brings about emotional balance and calms panic attacks. It can transform a defensive or oversensitive personality, releasing the core fears, phobias, guilt, and control mechanisms that hold you back from being who you truly are. It enhances self-esteem, self-acceptance, and self-trust. Sodalite is one of the stones that bring shadow qualities up to the surface to be accepted without being judged.

HEALING Sodalite balances the metabolism, overcomes calcium deficiencies, and cleanses the lymphatic system and organs, boosting the immune system. This stone combats radiation damage and insomnia. It treats the throat, vocal cords, and larynx and is helpful for hoarseness and digestive disorders. It cools fevers, lowers blood pressure, and stimulates absorption of fluid in the body.

POSITION Place as appropriate or wear for long periods of time.

SPINEL

Red Spinel on matrix

COLOR	Colorless, white, red, blue, violet, black, green, yellow, orange, brown
APPEARANCE	Small, crystalline with terminations, or tumbled pebbles
RARITY	Readily available
SOURCE	India, Canada, Sri Lanka, Myanmar

ATTRIBUTES Spinel is a beautiful crystal connected with energy renewal, encouragement in difficult circumstances, and rejuvenation. It opens the chakras* and facilitates movement of kundalini* energy up the spine. Different colors of Spinel relate to the whole chakras spectrum.

Psychologically, Spinel enhances positive aspects of the personality. It aids in achieving and accepting success with humility.

POSITION May be laid out on the chakras, or worn as appropriate.

SPECIFIC COLORS
In addition to the generic attributes, specific colors of Spinel have additional properties:

Black Spinel offers insights into material problems and gives you the stamina to continue. This color is protective and earths energy to balance the rise of the kundalini.

Blue Spinel stimulates communication and channeling. It calms sexual desire and opens and aligns the throat chakra*.

Brown Spinel cleanses the aura* and opens connections to the physical body. It opens the earth chakra and grounds you.

Colorless Spinel stimulates mysticism and higher communication. Linking the chakras on the physical body with the crown chakra of the etheric body, it facilitates visions and enlightenment.

Green Spinel stimulates love, compassion, and kindness. It opens and aligns the heart chakra.

Orange Spinel stimulates creativity and intuition, balances emotions, and treats infertility. It opens and aligns the navel chakra.

Red Spinel stimulates physical vitality and strength. It arouses the kundalini* and opens and aligns the base chakra.

Violet Spinel stimulates spiritual development and astral travel. It opens and aligns the crown chakra.

Yellow Spinel stimulates the intellect and personal power. It opens and aligns the solar plexus chakra.

STAUROLITE

*Natural cross removed
from matrix*

COLOR	Brown, yellow-brown, reddish-brown
APPEARANCE	Resembles Chiastolite, may crystallize as a cruciform or exhibit a cross
RARITY	Available from specialist shops
SOURCE	United States, Russia, Middle East

ATTRIBUTES Staurolite is known as the Fairy Cross. It was believed to be formed from tears the fairies shed when they heard the news of Christ's death. Traditionally, this protective stone is a talisman for good luck.

Staurolite enhances and strengthens rituals and is used in white-magic ceremonies. It is said to access the ancient wisdom of the Middle East. This stone connects the physical, etheric, and spiritual planes, promoting communication between them.

Psychologically, Staurolite is exceptionally useful in relieving stress. It alleviates depression and addictions, and negates a tendency to overwork and to overcommit energy.

Physically, Staurolite is an excellent stone for those wishing to stop smoking and to mitigate and heal its effects. It assists in understanding the hidden reasons behind the addiction to nicotine and provides a grounding energy for airy people who have used nicotine to anchor them to the earth.

HEALING Staurolite treats cellular disorders and growths, increases assimilation of carbohydrates, and reduces depression. It was traditionally used for fever.

POSITION Hold or place as appropriate.

STILLBITE

Plate form

COLOR	White, yellow, pink, orange, red, brown
APPEARANCE	Small crystalline plates or pyramids as a cluster
RARITY	Easily obtained from specialist stores
SOURCE	United States

ATTRIBUTES Stillbite is a highly creative stone that opens the intuition and carries a loving and supportive vibration in any endeavor. It is very helpful in metaphysical working at all levels. It grounds spiritual energy and helps to manifest intuitive thought into action on the physical plane.

Stillbite aids spiritual journeying, protecting and maintaining physical contact while traveling. The stone gives guidance and direction throughout the journey, no matter where the destination may lie. Used at its highest vibration, it aids traveling into the upper spiritual realms and bringing back the conscious memory of one's experiences there. Stillbite crystal clusters can be used as a scrying* tool.

HEALING Stillbite treats brain disorders, strengthens ligaments, treats laryngitis and loss of taste. It can increase pigmentation in the skin. It was used traditionally to counteract poisoning as it is a very potent detoxifier.

POSITION Hold or position as appropriate. Place on third eye* to facilitate journeying or intuition.

Pyramid form

SUGILITE

ALSO KNOWN AS LUVULITE

Polished

Tumbled

COLOR	Purple, violet-pink
APPEARANCE	Opaque, lightly banded or, rarely, translucent, all sizes, often tumbled
RARITY	Available from specialist stores
SOURCE	Japan, South Africa

ATTRIBUTES Sugilite is one of the major "love stones," bringing the purple ray energy to earth. It represents spiritual love and wisdom and opens all the chakras* to the flow of that love, bringing them into alignment. Sugilite inspires spiritual awareness and promotes channeling* ability.

Sugilite teaches you how to live from your truth and reminds the soul of its reasons for incarnating. It accompanies moving into past lives or the between-lives state* to retrieve the cause of dis-ease*. This stone finds answers to all the great questions of life such as "Why am I here?", "Where did I come from?", "Who am I?", and "What else do I need to understand?" It is a useful accompaniment to spiritual quests of all kinds. This loving stone protects the soul from shocks, trauma and disappointments and relieves spiritual tension. It helps sensitive people and light workers to adapt to the earth vibration without becoming mired or despondent. Sugulite can help to bring light and love into the darkest situations.

Aiding forgiveness and eliminating hostility, Sugilite is a useful stone for work with groups as it resolves group difficulties and encourages loving communication.

Psychologically, Sugilite is beneficial for misfits of any kind, people who do not feel the earth is their home, and those who suffer from paranoia and schizophrenia. It is excellent for autism, helping to ground the soul more into the present reality, and overcomes learning difficulties. Sugilite promotes understanding of the effect of the mind on the body and its place in dis-ease*. Emotionally, Sugilite imparts the ability to face up to unpleasant matters. It alleviates sorrow, grief, and fear, and promotes self-forgiveness.

Mentally, Sugilite encourages positive thoughts and reorganizes brain patterns that underlie learning difficulties such as dyslexia. It supports the overcoming of conflict without compromise.

Physically, Sugilite benefits cancer sufferers, as it gently releases emotional turmoil and can alleviate despair. It draws off negative energy and lends loving support, channeling healing energy into body, mind, and spirit.

HEALING An exceptionally good pain reliever, the manganese in Sugilite clears headaches and discomfort at all levels. It treats epilepsy and motor disturbances and brings the nerves and brain into alignment. Light-colored Sugilite purifies lymph and blood.

POSITION As appropriate, especially over the heart and lymph glands. Hold to the forehead for headaches. Place on third eye* to alleviate despair.

SULPHUR

Natural crystalline form

COLOR	Yellow
APPEARANCE	Powdery or smallish translucent crystals on matrix
RARITY	Obtainable from specialist shops
SOURCE	Italy, Greece, South America, volcanic regions

ATTRIBUTES Sulphur has a negative electrical charge and is extremely useful for absorbing negative energies, emanations, and emotions. Placed in the environment, it absorbs negativity of any kind and removes barriers to progress.

Volcanically produced, this is an excellent stone for anything that erupts: feelings, violence, skin conditions, and fevers. It can also be useful for bringing latent psychic abilities to the surface.

Psychologically, Sulphur ameliorates willfulness and aids in identifying negative traits within the personality. It reaches the rebellious, stubborn, or obstreperous part of a personality that willfully disobeys instructions and tends automatically to do the opposite of whatever is suggested, especially when this is "for your own good." Sulphur softens this position and assists the recognition of the effect, opening the way to conscious change.

Mentally, Sulphur blocks repetitive and distracting thought patterns. Inspiring the imagination, it aids reasoning and grounds thought processes in the practical here and now.

Physically, Sulphur is helpful in reenergizing after exhaustion or serious illness and can enhance creativity.

Sulphur is toxic and should not be taken internally. The gem elixir is best made with the crystalline form by the indirect method and applied externally only.

HEALING Sulphur is extremely useful for conditions that flare up, such as infections and fevers. Placed over the site of the swelling, it reduces fibrous and tissue growths. Placed in the bathwater, or as an essence, Sulphur alleviates painful swellings and joint problems. It can be applied externally to heal skin conditions. Powdered sulphur can be used as a natural insecticide fumigant, but it is toxic to humans and a mask should be worn to avoid breathing the fumes. Ventilate the area thoroughly afterward.

POSITION Place or hold as appropriate (the crystalline form is better for this, as the powdery form is messy and best kept for bathwater or environmental use.) It is traditional that Sulphur that has been placed over growths be buried afterward. If not, thoroughly cleanse before reusing. Burn powdered Sulphur to fumigate (wear a mask.) Make the elixir by the indirect method (see page 371) and use externally only.

SUNSTONE

Raw

Polished

COLOR	Yellow, orange, red-brown
APPEARANCE	Clear transparent or opaque crystal with iridescent reflections, often small, tumbled
RARITY	Easily obtained from specialist shops
SOURCE	Canada, United States, Norway, Greece, India

ATTRIBUTES Sunstone is a joyful, light-inspiring stone. It instills *joie de vivre* and good nature and heightens intuition. If life has lost its sweetness, Sunstone will restore it and help you to nurture yourself. Clearing all the chakras* and bringing in light and energy, this stone allows the real self to shine through happily. Traditionally it linked to benevolent gods and to luck and good fortune. This is an alchemical stone that brings about a profound connection to light and the regenerative power of the sun during meditation and in everyday life.

Sunstone is extremely useful for removing "hooks" from other people,

283

whether located in the chakras or the aura*. These hooks can be at the mental or emotional level and may come from possessive parents, children, or lovers. They have the effect of draining your energy. Sunstone lovingly returns the contact to the other person and is extremely beneficial for tie-cutting. Keep Sunstone with you at all times if you have difficulty saying "No" and continually make sacrifices for others. Removing codependency, it facilitates self-empowerment, independence, and vitality. If procrastination is holding you back, Sunstone will overcome it.

Emotionally, Sunstone acts as an antidepressant and lifts dark moods. It is particularly effective for seasonal affective disorder, lightening the darkness of winter. It detaches from feelings of being discriminated against, disadvantaged, and abandoned. Removing inhibitions and hang-ups, Sunstone reverses feelings of failure and increases self-worth and confidence. Encouraging optimism and enthusiasm, Sunstone switches to a positive take on events. Even the most incorrigible pessimist responds to Sunstone. Placed on the solar plexus, Sunstone lifts out heavy or repressed emotions and transmutes them.

HEALING Sunstone stimulates self-healing powers, regulates the autonomic nervous system, and harmonizes all the organs. It treats chronic sore throats and relieves stomach ulcers. Exceptionally good for seasonal affective disorder, Sunstone lifts any depression. Sunstone can be gridded around the body and relieves cartilage problems, rheumatism, and general aches and pains.

POSITION Place, wear, or hold as appropriate. Sunstone is particularly beneficial when used in the sun.

(*See also* Yellow Labradorite, page 171.)

TEKTITE

Raw

COLOR	Black or dark brown, green (Moldavite)
APPEARANCE	Small, glassy, densely translucent
RARITY	Because Tektite is a meteorite, it is quite rare but available from specialist shops
SOURCE	Middle and Far East, Philippines, Polynesia, can occur worldwide

ATTRIBUTES Because of its extraterrestrial origin, Tektite is believed to enhance communication with other worlds and to encourage spiritual growth through absorption and retention of higher knowledge. It forms a link between the creative energy and matter. Tektite helps you to release undesirable experiences, remembering lessons learned and concentrating on those things that are conducive to spiritual growth. It takes you deep into the heart of a matter, promoting insight into the true cause and necessary action.

Placed on the chakras*, Tektite balances the energy flow and may reverse a chakra that is spinning the wrong way. Helpful for telepathy and clairvoyance*, if Tektite is placed on the third eye* it opens

285

communication with other dimensions. This stone strengthens the biomagnetic sheath* around the body.

Traditionally, Tektites have been worn as talismans for fertility on all levels. This stone balances male–female energies within the personality.

HEALING Tektite reduces fevers, aids the capillaries and circulation. It prevents the transmission of diseases. Certain types of Tektites have been used for psychic surgery.

POSITION Place or hold as appropriate.

(*See also* Moldavite, page 187.)

THULITE

ALSO KNOWN AS PINK THULITE

Raw

COLOR	Pink, rose, white, red, gray
APPEARANCE	Granulated mass, often large
RARITY	Obtained from specialist stores
SOURCE	Norway

ATTRIBUTES A dramatic stone with a powerful link to the life force, stimulating healing and regeneration, Thulite is helpful wherever there is resistance to be overcome. It assists in bringing out the extrovert, promoting eloquence and showmanship. Mentally, it encourages curiosity and inventiveness in solving problems and explores the dualities of the human condition, combining love with logic.

Emotionally, Thulite encourages expression of passion and sexual feelings. It teaches that lust, sensuality, and sexuality are normal parts of life and encourages their constructive and positive expression.

HEALING Thulite treats calcium deficiencies and gastric upsets. It enhances fertility and treats disease of the reproductive organs. A strengthening and regenerating stone, useful in cases of extreme weakness and nervous exhaustion.

POSITION Place on skin or pubic bone as appropriate.

TIGER'S EYE

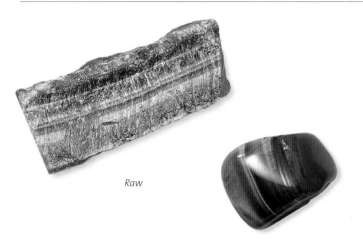

Raw

Tumbled

COLOR	Brown-yellow, pink, blue, red
APPEARANCE	Banded, slightly shiny, often small and tumbled
RARITY	Easily obtained
SOURCE	United States, Mexico, India, Australia, South Africa

ATTRIBUTES Tiger's Eye combines the earth energy with the energies of the sun to create a high vibrational state that is nevertheless grounded, drawing the spiritual energies to earth. Placed on the third eye*, it enhances psychic abilities in earthy people and balances the lower chakras*, stimulating the rise of the kundalini* energy.

Tiger's Eye is a protective stone that was traditionally carried as a talisman against ill wishing and curses. It shows the correct use of power and brings out integrity. It assists in accomplishing goals, recognizing inner resources and promoting clarity of intention. Placed on the navel chakra, Tiger's Eye is excellent for people who are spaced out or uncommitted. It grounds and facilitates manifestation of the will. Tiger's Eye anchors change into the physical body.

This stone is useful for recognizing both your needs and those of other people. It differentiates between wishful thinking about what you want and what you really need.

Mentally, Tiger's Eye integrates the hemispheres of the brain and enhances practical perception. It aids in collecting scattered information to make a coherent whole. It is helpful for resolving dilemmas and internal conflicts, especially those brought about by pride and willfulness. Tiger's Eye is particularly useful for healing mental dis-ease* and personality disorders.

Psychologically, Tiger's Eye heals issues of self-worth, self-criticism, and blocked creativity. It aids in recognizing one's talents and abilities and, conversely, faults that need to be overcome. It supports an addictive personality in making changes.

Emotionally, Tiger's Eye balances yin–yang and energizes the emotional body. It alleviates depression and lifts moods.

HEALING Tiger's Eye treats the eyes and aids night visions, heals the throat and reproductive organs, and dissolves constrictions. It is helpful for repairing broken bones.

POSITION Wear on the right arm or as a pendant for short periods. Position on the body as appropriate in healing. Place on the navel chakra for spiritual grounding.

SPECIFIC COLORS

In addition to the generic attributes, specific colors of Tiger's Eye have specific properties:

Blue Tiger's Eye

Blue Tiger's Eye is calming and releases stress. It aids the overanxious, quick-tempered, and phobic. In healing, Blue Tiger's Eye slows the metabolism, cools an overactive sex drive, and dissolves sexual frustrations.

Gold Tiger's Eye aids in paying attention to detail, warning against complacency. It assists in taking action from a place of reason rather than emotion. Gold Tiger's Eye is an excellent companion for tests and important meetings.

Red Tiger's Eye

Red Tiger's Eye is a stimulating stone that overcomes lethargy and provides motivation. In healing it speeds up a slow metabolism and increases a low sex drive.

SPECIFIC FORM

In addition to the generic properties, a type of Tiger's Eye has the following properties.

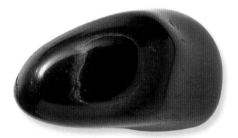

Hawk's Eye

Hawk's Eye

ADDITIONAL PROPERTIES A banded "hawk-like" form of Tiger's Eye, Hawk's Eye is an excellent stone for healing the earth's energy and for grounding energy. It stimulates and invigorates the physical body. Soaring above the world, Hawk's Eye aids vision and insight, and increases psychic abilities such as clairvoyance*. Hawk's Eye clears and energizes the base chakra*.

Placed in the wealth corner of a room, Hawk's Eye attracts abundance.

Hawk's Eye is particularly good for dissolving restrictive and negative thought patterns and ingrained behavior. It brings issues into perspective, ameliorates pessimism and the desire to blame others for problems of your own making. This stone will also bring to the surface locked-in emotions and dis-ease from the present or past lives. Placed on the third eye*, Hawk's Eye aids in traveling back to the source of an emotional blockage, whenever that might be.

HEALING Hawk's Eye improves the circulatory system, bowels, and legs. It can bring to the surface the psychosomatic reasons behind a frozen shoulder or stiff neck.

POSITION Hold or place on appropriate spot.

TOPAZ

Blue Topaz (polished)

Golden-Yellow Topaz (raw)

COLOR	Golden-yellow, brown, blue, clear, red-pink, green
APPEARANCE	Transparent, pointed crystals, often small and faceted or large piece
RARITY	Easily obtained from specialist stores, red-pink is rare
SOURCE	United States, Mexico, India, Australia, South Africa, Sri Lanka, Pakistan

ATTRIBUTES Topaz is a mellow, empathetic stone that directs energy to where it is needed most. It soothes, heals, stimulates, recharges, remotivates, and aligns the meridians of the body. Topaz promotes truth and forgiveness. It helps shed light on the path, highlights goals, and taps into inner resources. This crystal brings about a trust in the universe that enables you to "be" rather than to "do." It cuts through doubt and uncertainty.

Topaz's vibrant energy brings joy, generosity, abundance, and good health. It has traditionally been known as a stone of love and good fortune, bringing successful attainment of goals. It is extremely supportive for affirmations and manifestation, and for visualization. It is said that the facets and ends of a Topaz crystal have both positive and negative energies through which a request to the universe can be focused and then manifested on the earth plane.

Excellent for cleaning the aura* and for inducing relaxation, Topaz releases tension at any level and can speed up spiritual development where it has been laborious.

Psychologically, Topaz helps you to discover your own inner riches. It makes you feel confident and philanthropic, wanting to share your good fortune and spread sunshine all around. Negativity does not survive around joyful Topaz. This stone promotes openness and honesty, self-realization, self-control, and the urge to develop inner wisdom.

Mentally, Topaz aids problem-solving and is particularly useful for those engaged in the arts. It helps you to become aware of the influence you have and of the knowledge you have gained through hard work and life experiences. This stone has the capacity to see both the bigger picture and the minute detail, recognizing how they interrelate. Topaz assists in expressing ideas and confers astuteness.

Topaz is an excellent emotional support—it stabilizes the emotions and makes you receptive to love from every source.

HEALING Topaz can be used to manifest health. It aids digestion and combats anorexia, restores the sense of taste, fortifies the nerves, and stimulates the metabolism. Saint Hildegard of Bingen recommended an elixir of Topaz to correct dimness of vision.

POSITION Ring finger, solar plexus, and brow chakra*. Position or place as appropriate for healing. The elixir can be applied to the skin.

SPECIFIC COLORS

In addition to the generic properties, certain colors have additional attributes:

Blue Topaz, placed on the throat chakra or third eye*, aids those chakras and verbalization. It is an excellent color for meditation and attuning to the higher self, assisting in living according your own aspirations and views. This color attunes to the angels of truth and wisdom. It assists in seeing the scripts you have been living by and to recognize where you have strayed from your own truth.

Clear Topaz aids in becoming aware of thoughts and deeds, and the karmic* effect that these have. It assists in purifying emotions and actions, activating cosmic awareness. In healing, Clear Topaz removes stagnant or stuck energy.

Clear Topaz

Golden Topaz (Imperial Topaz) acts like a battery and recharges spiritually and physically, strengthening faith and optimism. It is an excellent stone for conscious attunement to the highest forces in the universe and can be used to store information received in this way.

Golden Topaz It reminds you of your divine origins.

Imperial Topaz assists in recognizing your own abilities, instills a drive toward recognition, and attracts helpful people. This stone is beneficial for those seeking fame as it bestows charisma and confidence with pride in your abilities while remaining generous and open-hearted. It assists in overcoming limitations and in setting great plans afoot. In healing, it regenerates cellular structures and strengthens the solar plexus, and is beneficial for nervous exhaustion and insufficient combustion of nutrients. It treats the liver, the gallbladder, and the endocrine glands.

Yellow Topaz

Pink Topaz is a stone of hope. It gently eases out old patterns of dis-ease* and dissolves resistance, opening the way to radiant health. This stone shows you the face of the divine.

COMBINATION STONE
Rutilated Topaz is rare but is extremely effective for visualization and manifestation. It is an excellent stone for scrying*, bringing deep insights when properly programmed and attracting love and light into one's life.

TOURMALINE

Blue Tourmaline

Light Blue Tourmaline

Blue Tourmaline wand

COLOR	Black, brown, green, pink, red, yellow, blue, watermelon, blue-green
APPEARANCE	Shiny, opaque, or transparent, long striated or hexagonal structure. All sizes
RARITY	Easily obtained from specialist stores
SOURCE	Sri Lanka, Brazil, Africa, United States, Western Australia, Afghanistan, Italy

ATTRIBUTES Tourmaline cleanses, purifies, and transforms dense energy into a lighter vibration. It grounds spiritual energy, clears and balances all the chakras*, and forms a protective shield around the body.

Tourmaline is a shamanic stone that brings protection during rituals. It can be used for scrying* and was traditionally used to point to the culprit or cause in times of trouble, and indicate a "good" direction in which to move.

Natural Tourmaline wands are useful healing tools. They clear the aura, remove blockages, disperse negative energy, and point to solutions for specific problems. They are excellent for balancing and connecting the chakras. At a physical level, they rebalance the meridians*.

Tourmaline has a strong affinity with the devic* energies and is extremely beneficial for the garden and plants. It can act as a natural insecticide, keeping pests at bay, and, buried in the soil, encourages the growth and health of all crops.

Psychologically, Tourmaline aids in understanding oneself and others, taking you deep into yourself, promoting self-confidence and diminishing fear. It banishes any feeling of being a victim and attracts inspiration, compassion, tolerance, and prosperity.

Tourmaline is a powerful mental healer, balancing the right–left hemispheres of the brain and transmuting negative thought patterns into positive ones. This stone brings the mental processes, the chakras, and the biomagnetic sheath* into alignment. It is helpful in treating paranoia, and for overcoming dyslexia, as it improves hand-to-eye coordination and the assimilation and translation of coded information.

Emotionally, Red, Yellow, and Brown Tourmalines are beneficial for sexuality and the emotional dysfunction that can lie behind loss of libido. Physically, Tourmaline releases tension, which makes it helpful in spinal adjustments. It balances male–female energy within the body.

HEALING The striations along the side of Tourmaline enhance energy flow, making it an excellent stone for healing, energy enhancement, and removal of blockages. Each of the different colors of Tourmaline has its own specific healing ability.

POSITION Place or wear as appropriate. To stimulate meridians*, place with the tip pointing in the same direction as the flow. Excellent for gem essences which work quickly and efficiently.

SPECIFIC COLORS AND FORMS
In addition to the generic properties, colored Tourmalines have specific additional properties:

Black Tourmaline (Schorl) protects against cell phones, electromagnetic smog*, radiation, psychic attack*, spells and ill-wishing, and negative energies of all kinds. Connecting with the base chakra*, it grounds energy and increases physical vitality, dispersing tension and stress.

Black Tourmaline

Clearing negative thoughts, Schorl promotes a laid-back attitude and objective neutrality with clear, rational thought processes. It encourages a positive attitude, no matter what the circumstances, and stimulates altruism and practical creativity.
In healing, Black Tourmalines placed point-out from

298

the body draw off negative energy. Black Tourmaline defends against debilitating disease, strengthens the immune system, treats dyslexia and arthritis, provides pain relief, and realigns the spinal column. Wear around your neck or place between yourself and the source of electromagnetics.

Blue Tourmaline (Indicolite) activates the throat and third eye chakra* and stimulates the urge for spiritual freedom and clarity of self-expression. This color aids psychic awareness, promotes visions, and opens the way for service to others, encouraging fidelity, ethics, tolerance, and a love of truth. It carries the ray of peace and dissolves sadness and blocked feelings, bringing them up gently to the surface to be healed and dissipated, and assists in developing an inner sense of responsibility. This stone promotes living in harmony with the environment. It is an excellent stone for healers, as it prevents negativity from sticking.

In healing, bright Blue Tourmaline is a useful diagnostic tool and helps in identifying underlying causes of dis-ease*. Blue Tourmaline benefits the pulmonary and immune systems and the brain, corrects fluid imbalances, treats kidney and bladder, thymus and thyroid, and chronic sore throat. It is helpful for insomnia, night sweats, sinusitis, and bacterial infections. It is traditionally used on the throat, larynx, lungs, esophagus, and eyes. It soothes burns and prevents scarring. Dark Blue Tourmaline is particularly helpful for the eyes and brain and can be made into an elixir. Blue Tourmaline can be placed anywhere there is dis-ease or congestion. It helps to overcome speech impediments.

Brown Tourmaline (Dravide) is an excellent grounding stone, clearing and opening the earth chakra and the grounding cord* holding the physical body in incarnation. It clears the aura, aligns the etheric body

and protects it. Encouraging community spirit and social commitment, Brown Tourmaline makes one feel comfortable in a large group. This stone heals dysfunctional family relationships and strengthens empathy. Brown Tourmaline is pragmatic and promotes creativity. In healing, Brown Tourmaline treats intestinal disorders and skin diseases, and stimulates regeneration in the whole body.

Brown Tourmaline

Colorless Tourmaline (Achroite) synthesizes all other colors and opens the crown chakra*. In healing, it aligns the meridians* of the physical* and etheric bodies*.

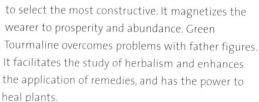

Green Tourmaline (Verdelite) is an excellent healer and is helpful for visualization. It opens the heart chakra, promotes compassion, tenderness, patience, and a sense of belonging. This nurturing stone brings balance and *joie de vivre*. Transforming negative to positive energy and dispelling fears, Green Tourmaline promotes openness and patience. It rejuvenates and inspires creativity. With this stone, one is able to see all possible solutions and to select the most constructive. It magnetizes the wearer to prosperity and abundance. Green Tourmaline overcomes problems with father figures. It facilitates the study of herbalism and enhances the application of remedies, and has the power to heal plants.

Colorless Tourmaline

In healing, as with all green stones, this color aids sleep and quiets the mind. It fortifies the nervous

Green Tourmaline

system and prepares it for a vibrational shift. Green Tourmaline treats eyes, heart, thymus, brain, and immune system; facilitates weight loss; and relieves CFS and exhaustion. It assists in realigning the spine and aids strained muscles. Green Tourmaline is a useful detoxifier and heels constipation and diarrhea. It can reduce claustrophobia and panic attacks. Green Tourmaline is beneficial for hyperactive children.

Multicolored Gem Tourmaline (Elbaite) contains all colors and, as a result, it brings the mind, body, spirit, and soul into wholeness. It is an excellent stone for imagery and promoting dreams, inspiring creativity and enhanced imagination. This stone provides a gateway into the inner self and the higher spiritual realms.

In healing, Multicolored Tourmaline stimulates the immune system and the metabolism.

Pink Tourmaline is an aphrodisiac that attracts love in the material and spiritual world. Providing assurance that it is safe to love, it inspires trust in love, and confirms that it is necessary to love yourself before you can hope to be loved by others. This stone assists in sharing physical pleasure. It disperses emotional pain and old destructive feelings through the heart chakra, which it cleanses, and synthesizes love with spirituality. Promoting peace and relaxation, Pink Tourmaline connects you to wisdom and compassion and stimulates receptivity to healing energies.

In healing, Pink Tourmaline balances a dysfunctional endocrine system and treats heart, lungs, and skin. Place on the heart.

Purple-Violet Tourmaline stimulates healing of the heart and produces loving consciousness.

Purple Tourmaline

It connects the base and heart chakras*, increasing devotion and loving aspiration. This stone stimulates creativity and intuition. It unblocks the third eye* chakra, stimulates the pineal gland, and strips away illusions. This is a useful stone for past-life healing, taking you to the heart of the problem and then dispersing it.

In healing, Purple Tourmaline reduces depression and releases obsessional thoughts. It treats sensitivity to pollutants, Alzheimer's, epilepsy, and CFS*.

Red Tourmaline
in matrix

Red Tourmaline (Rubellite) strengthens the ability to understand love, promotes tactfulness and flexibility, sociability and extroversion, balancing too much aggression or overpassivity. It heals and energizes the sacral chakra and increases creativity on all levels. This color offers stamina and endurance. In healing, Red Tourmaline gives vitality to the physical body and detoxifies. It heals the heart; it treats the digestive system, blood vessels, and the reproductive system; it stimulates blood circulation and spleen and liver function; and it repairs veins. It is useful for muscle spasms and chills.

Watermelon Tourmaline (pink enfolded in green) is the "super-activator" of the heart chakra, linking it to the higher self and fostering love, tenderness, and friendship. This stone instills patience and teaches tact and diplomacy. Alleviating depression and fear, it promotes inner security. Watermelon Tourmaline assists understanding of situations and expressing intentions clearly. It treats emotional dysfunction and releases old pain. Watermelon Tourmaline is beneficial for relationships and helps to find the joy in situations.

Watermelon Tourmaline

In healing, Watermelon Tourmaline dissolves any resistance to becoming whole once more. It encourages regeneration of the nerves, especially in paralysis or multiple sclerosis, and treats stress.

Yellow Tourmaline stimulates the solar plexus and enhances personal power. It opens up the spiritual pathway and benefits intellectual pursuits and business affairs.

Yellow Tourmaline

In healing, Yellow Tourmaline treats the stomach, liver, spleen, kidneys, and gallbladder.

COMBINATION STONES
Black Tourmaline with Mica
returns ill-wishing to its source
so the perpetrator learns from it.
This combination is particularly
efficient at nullifying
electromagnetic smog*.

Black Tourmaline rod in Quartz
Quartz containing chunky Black
Tourmaline rods, as opposed to the
strands in Tourmalinated Quartz,
is excellent for neutralizing
psychic or actual attack*,
strengthening the person on the

Black Tourmaline with Mica

303

receiving end and enhancing their well-being. It can be used to guard against terrorist attack and to heal the effects of such an attack. This stone has the ability to go beyond dualities and to integrate the shadow into the whole personality.

Tourmaline with Lepidolite on a matrix is excellent for giving up addictions of all kinds, for understanding the reasons behind addiction, and for accepting that denial has been present. It then helps you to live life without the spurious support of the addictive substance or behavior, replacing it with the love and protection of the universal energies and powerful self-healing potential.

Tourmaline rod in Quartz

(*See also* Tourmalinated Quartz, page 243.)

Tourmaline with Lepidolite

TURQUOISE

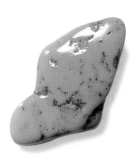

Polished

Tumbled

COLOR	Turquoise, green or blue
APPEARANCE	Opaque, often veined, all sizes often polished
RARITY	Easily obtained
SOURCE	United States, Egypt, Mexico, China, Iran, Peru, Poland, Russia, France, Tibet, Egypt, Afghanistan, Arabia

ATTRIBUTES Turquoise is a most efficient healer, providing solace for the spirit and well-being for the body. It is a protective stone and has been used for amulets since time immemorial. It is believed to change color to warn of danger of infidelity. Turquoise promotes spiritual attunement and enhances communication with the physical and spiritual worlds. Placed on the third eye*, it enhances intuition and meditation. On the throat chakra*, it releases old vows, inhibitions, and prohibitions, and allows the soul to express itself once more. It explores past lives and shows how the creation of your "fate" is ongoing and depends on what you do at each moment.

Turquoise is a purification stone. It dispels negative energy and clears electromagnetic smog*, providing protection against pollutants in the environment. It balances and aligns all the chakras with the subtle bodies and attunes the physical level to the spiritual. In traditional thought, Turquoise unites the earth and the sky, bringing together male and female energies. This stone is empathetic and balancing. A promoter of self-realization, it assists creative problem-solving and calms the nerves when speaking in public.

Psychologically, Turquoise is a strengthening stone. It dissolves a martyred attitude or self-sabotage. Mentally, Turquoise instills inner calm while remaining alert, and aids creative expression. Emotionally, Turquoise stabilizes mood swings and brings inner calm. It stimulates romantic love.

Physically, Turquoise is an excellent stone for exhaustion, depression, or panic attacks. One of its protective functions is against outside influences or pollutants in the atmosphere.

HEALING Turquoise strengthens the meridians of the body and the subtle energy fields. It enhances the physical and psychic immune systems and regenerates tissue, supports the assimilation of nutrients, alleviates pollution and viral infections, and heals the whole body, especially the eyes, including cataracts. It reduces excess acidity and benefits gout, rheumatism, and the stomach. This stone is anti-inflammatory and detoxifying and alleviates cramps and pain.

POSITION Anywhere but especially on the throat, third eye, and solar plexus. It makes an excellent elixir.

SPECIFIC TYPE

In addition to the generic properties, the following type has additional attributes:

Tibetan Turquoise is green and carries a slightly different vibration from the more vivid blue. It is especially useful for healing throat chakra blockages and suppressed self-expression back down the ancestral line until the source is cleared.

Tibetan Turquoise (raw)

ULEXITE

ALSO KNOWN AS TV STONE

Shaped

COLOR	Transparent
APPEARANCE	Clear, silky, squarish crystal, sometimes lightly striated. Magnifies.
RARITY	Easily obtained
SOURCE	United States

ATTRIBUTES Ulexite is best known for its ability to magnify anything placed under it. It is an extremely clear stone and brings things into focus on the inner and spiritual levels, lending much-needed objectivity and clarity. It is excellent for understanding the meaning of dreams and visions. It shows the path one should take at a spiritual level and takes you deep into the self.

At a more pragmatic level, Ulexite takes you to the core of a problem, pointing the way to resolution and activating solutions. Ulexite is a stone of revelation in the physical world. It gives you the ability to see into another's heart, knowing what they are thinking and feeling, so that decisions can be based on a complete knowing.

Ulexite's soft energy is beneficial for meditation and relaxation. Placed on the third eye*, it enhances visualization and dispels negative mental energy. Balancing the yin–yang energies, it aligns the subtle bodies*.

Mentally, Ulexite enhances the imagination and stimulates creativity, especially in business. If you are getting things out of proportion, Ulexite helps you to see them clearly.

HEALING Ulexite is used to bring clarity to the eyes. It is excellent as a skin elixir for smoothing wrinkles, but should not be left in water for too long, as it has a tendency to dissolve.

POSITION Wear or place as appropriate, especially on the eyes and third eye. Ulexite makes an excellent meditation stone if you gaze into its depths.

UNAKITE

Tumbled

Raw

COLOR	Green-pink
APPEARANCE	Mottled, often small tumbled stone
RARITY	Easily obtained
SOURCE	United States, South Africa

ATTRIBUTES Unakite is a stone of vision. It balances emotions with spirituality. Placed on the third eye*, it opens it and promotes visualization and psychic vision. This stone also provides grounding when it is needed and can be useful after meditation or psychic work.

Unakite can be used as a casting crystal for scrying*, signifying where compromise and integration are needed. The best way to use it is with ten or twelve other suitable stones (see pages 375–376). The tumbled stones should be kept together in a bag. One stone is then selected to answer a question, or a handful are cast onto a scrying wheel.

310

Placed in the environment, either as a large piece or as several tumbled stones in a bowl, Unakite brings a calm gentle energy and can negate the effects of electromagnetic pollution from television sets if placed on top or close by.

Unakite facilitates rebirthing, bringing to light and integrating insights from the past about the cause of blockages, and gently releasing conditions that inhibit spiritual and psychological growth. It is also helpful in past-life healing for going back to the source of a problem and reframing it. Unakite can be held or placed on the third eye for this purpose.

Whether dis-ease* arises in the far or near past, Unakite reaches the root cause of it at whatever level it occurs, bringing it to the surface so that it can be transformed.

HEALING Unakite is supportive in convalescence and recovery from a major illness. It treats the reproductive system, stimulates weight gain where required, and aids healthy pregnancy and the growth of skin tissue and hair.

POSITION Place as appropriate or apply as an elixir.

VANADINITE

Crystals on matrix

COLOR	Orange-brown, red-brown, yellow-brown, red, orange, yellow
APPEARANCE	Very small, bright transparent crystals on a matrix
RARITY	Obtainable from specialist stores
SOURCE	United States

ATTRIBUTES Vanadinite is an excellent stone for people who have problems accepting their physicality. It has a strong connection with the earth chakra* in the earth body beneath the feet. Grounding the soul into the physical body and assisting it being comfortable in the

312

earth environment, Vanadinite guards against squandering energy and teaches you how to conserve energy at the physical level.

Vanadinite is an aid to meditation. Shutting off mind chatter, it can facilitate a state of "no mind" or be used to direct awareness consciously for psychic vision and journeying. It has the power to open an internal channel within the body to receive an inflooding of universal energy. This energy aligns the chakras and brings the higher self into the physical body, facilitating a deep inner peace.

Mentally, Vanadinite fills the gap between thought and intellect. It assists in defining and pursuing goals and shuts off mind chatter, allowing insight and rational thought to combine in an inner voice of guidance.

This stone has the useful property of curbing overspending. Place in the wealth corner of the house or put a small piece in your purse to retain your money.

Vanadinite is poisonous and elixirs should be prepared by the indirect method (see page 371).

HEALING Vanadinite is useful for breathing difficulties such as asthma and congested lungs. It facilitates the practice of circular breathing. Vanadinite treats chronic exhaustion and bladder problems. If used as an elixir, only one made by the indirect method can be taken internally.

POSITION Place as appropriate or rub the elixir externally over the chest area. If using to aid acceptance of physicality, the indirect-method elixir should be taken for several weeks.

VARISCITE

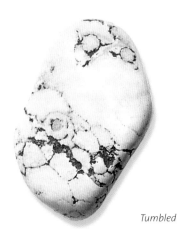

Tumbled

COLOR	Green, gray, and white
APPEARANCE	Opaque, sometimes veined, may appear as large mass or small encrustations on a matrix
RARITY	Obtainable from specialist stores
SOURCE	United States, Germany, Austria, Czech Republic, Bolivia

ATTRIBUTES Variscite is a stone of encouragement. Bringing hope and courage, it is extremely useful for illness and invalids. It supports and encourages an invalid to continue despite the illness and helps caregivers to deal with the dis-ease* an illness can create. Opening the heart chakra, it brings unconditional love into the situation.

Variscite is extremely helpful for past-life exploration. It facilitates visual images of the experience while going deeply into the feelings and experiences of appropriate lives. It stimulates insights into the cause of dis-ease or patterns that have been carried over, and aids reframing situations to bring about healing.

Psychologically, Variscite facilitates moving out of deep despair and into a position of hope and trust in the universe. This stone does away with pretence, enabling you to show yourself to the world exactly as you are. It calms nervousness and brings a peaceful heart. Variscite supports sobriety and yet has a lively energy that prevents you from becoming too serious. Placed under the pillow at night, it brings peaceful sleep and an untroubled mind.

Mentally, Variscite aids clear thinking and increases perception. It helps in self-expression and the communication of ideas.

Physically, Variscite is an energizer that helps to restore depleted energy reserves.

HEALING Variscite heals the nervous system, treats abdominal distension and constricted blood flow, and regenerates elasticity of veins and skin. It neutralizes overacidity and aids gout, gastritis, ulcers, rheumatism, and allied conditions. Helpful for male impotence, it also relieves cramps.

POSITION Place as appropriate and use for long periods of time. Position over third eye* for past-life recall. Wear as a pendant or hold in the left hand.

WULFENITE

Crystals on matrix

COLOR	Yellow, golden, orange, green, gray, yellow-gray, brown, white, colorless
APPEARANCE	Small crystals or blades on a matrix, or large transparent, squarish crystal
RARITY	Available from specialist stores
SOURCE	United States, Mexico

ATTRIBUTES Wulfenite is an extremely useful stone as it assists in accepting the less positive aspects of life and prevents despondency or inertia setting in when you're faced with negative situations or feelings. It is particularly useful for those people who have become unbalanced by focusing only on the positive, repressing negative traits and experiences so that they become "sugary sweet" and so nice that they are inauthentic and ungrounded. Wulfenite helps them to accept and integrate the shadow energies and to move beyond the duality of "positive" and "negative," accepting them as complementary and balancing forces.

At a spiritual level, Wulfenite facilitates moving easily and quickly from the physical level to the psychic, intuitive, or spiritual levels. It is said to access the past, present, and future and to aid communication with those states. It facilitates contact and communication with the spiritual world, opening a channel to bring spiritual vibrations down to earth.

If you have made an agreement with another soul that you will meet in the present life, Wulfenite facilitates recognition of that soul and attunement to the reasons why you arranged to meet. It bonds the souls together while the purpose or lesson is carried out and then releases when appropriate.

Wulfenite is a stone that can be used for white magic, supporting and enhancing ritual working and journeying, and regaining magical knowledge that one had in other lives. This knowledge can then be put into practice in the present. Such knowledge may come from the temples of ancient Egypt or Greece or from the more recent past. If someone has suffered at the hands of the Christian Church for beliefs connected with magic, then Wulfenite helps to heal the experience, making it feel safe to practice once again.

HEALING Wulfenite has the power to rejuvenate and preserve energy but has no specific healing attributes.

POSITION Hold or place as appropriate. A piece of Wulfenite can be programmed to bring you into contact with soul links* and then placed in the relationship corner of the house.

ZEOLITE

*Cluster containing
Stillbite, Apophyllite,
Prehnite, and Okenite*

COLOR	Colorless, white, blue, peach
APPEARANCE	Varied, all sizes, often as a cluster
RARITY	Available from specialist stores
SOURCE	Britain, Australia, India, Brazil, Czech Republic, Italy, United States

ATTRIBUTES Zeolite is the generic name for a group of crystals that are often found together on a matrix. They include Apophyllite, Okenite, Pectolite, Prehnite, and Stillbite (see pages 64, 204, 220, 277). The combination stone is very beautiful and can be used as a decorative feature to enhance the environment. Zeolite absorbs toxins and odors. Buried in the ground, or placed near crops, Zeolite benefits agriculture and gardening.

Zeolite is a Reiki* stone that aids attunement to the energies and enhances the response to the healing.

HEALING Zeolite can be used to treat goiters, to dispel bloating, and to release toxins from the physical body. It has a supportive effect in overcoming addictions, especially to alcohol, and can be made into an elixir for this purpose. However, cider vinegar should be used as the preservative rather than brandy or vodka.

POSITION Place as appropriate or use as an elixir.

ZINCITE

*Transparent,
reformed*

COLOR	Red, orange-yellow, green, colorless
APPEARANCE	Grainy mass, although some striking transparent crystals are available from Poland that formed as part of the smelting process at a mine
RARITY	Available from specialist stores
SOURCE	Poland, Italy, United States

ATTRIBUTES Zincite is a powerful stone that synthesizes physical energy and personal power with creativity. This fiery stone can aid the manifestation process and reenergize depleted energy systems. It removes energy blocks from the body and allows the life force to flow unhindered. This stone attracts abundance at a physical and spiritual level and Zincite can be used to anchor the light body securely into the physical realm.

Zincite resonates with the lower chakras*, reenergizing the whole body and stimulating creativity and fertility. It assists with the rise of the kundalini* energy and enhances gut instincts and intuition.

Zincite instills confidence and the ability to find your own strength. Psychologically, Zincite heals shock and trauma and instills the courage to deal with traumatic situations. It ameliorates depression and releases painful memories so that these can be laid to rest. If you suffer from lethargy or procrastination, Zincite has the power to push you forward into manifesting your full potential. It helps you to embrace necessary change.

Zincite is useful for phobias. It assists in getting to the root cause and gently releasing it, and then reprograms the mind into a more positive mode. It can also release hypnotic commands and mental imprints.

If you are a woman struggling with menopausal symptoms or the empty-nest syndrome, Zincite gently alleviates the symptoms and helps you to come to terms with the change of life.

Zincite promotes group activities, drawing together like-minded people and bringing them into a whole. It is also beneficial for physical relationships. If purification is required, Zincite can stimulate a healing crisis that provides catharsis and then reenergizes the system.

HEALING Zincite improves the skin and the hair. It is beneficial for the prostate gland and for menopausal symptoms, and boosts the immune system and the energy meridians* of the body. It treats CFS, AIDS and auto-immune diseases, alleviates candida, mucus conditions, and bronchitis, and helps to prevent epilepsy. Zincite stimulates the organs of elimination and assimilation and has been used to treat problems of infertility.

POSITION Place or hold as appropriate.

321

ZOISITE

Raw

COLOR	Colorless, white, yellow, brown, blue, green, red, pink (Thulite), lavender-blue
APPEARANCE	Solid mass, pleochroic*, all sizes
RARITY	Obtained from specialist shops, often with Ruby
SOURCE	Austria, Tanzania, India, Madagascar, Russia, Sri Lanka, Cambodia, Kenya

ATTRIBUTES Zoisite transmutes negative energies into positive ones and connects to the spiritual realms.

Psychologically, Zoisite assists in manifesting your own self rather than being influenced by others or trying to conform to the norm. It aids in realizing your own ideas and transforms destructive urges into constructive ones. This stone dispels lethargy and brings to the surface repressed feelings and emotions so that they can be expressed.

Mentally, Zoisite is a creative stone, bringing the mind back to its objectives after an interruption. Physically, Zoisite encourages recovery from severe illness or stress.

HEALING Zoisite is a detoxifier, neutralizing overacidification and reducing inflammation. It strengthens the immune system and regenerates cells and treats the heart, spleen, pancreas, and lungs. This stone stimulates fertility and heals diseases of the ovaries and testicles. When combined with Ruby, it increases potency.

POSITION Wear or place on the body in contact with the skin as appropriate. Wear for long periods of time, as it is a slow-acting stone.

ADDITIONAL COLOR
In addition to the generic properties, the following color has additional properties:

Tanzanite (Lavender-Blue Zoisite) is a heat-amended stone with a high vibration, facilitating altered states and a profoundly deep meditative state. It changes color when viewed from different directions. This shifting color facilitates raising consciousness. It links to the angelic realms*, spirit guides*, and the Ascended Masters*. Tanzanite downloads information from the Akashic Record* and facilitates inner and outer journeying. It activates a chakra* link from the base to the higher crown chakras, bringing the higher mind into contact with the physical realm. Stimulating the throat chakra, it facilitates communication of insights received from the higher levels. In healing, Tanzanite works on the head, throat, and chest. It makes an excellent gem essence and combines with stones such as Aquamarine and Moldavite. Added to Iolite and Danburite and applied during past-life healing, Tanzanite dissolves old patterns of karmic* dis-ease* and creates the space for new patterns to be integrated.

Tanzanite

(*See also* Thulite, page 287, and Ruby in Zoisite page 251.)

CRYSTAL SHAPES

Crystals come in all shapes and sizes. Some have natural facets and points, others are rounded and smooth. Some form clusters, others stand alone. There are crystals that are formed in layers and others that are formed in bubbles. Some occur naturally; others are artificially cut to a precise shape. Each shape has its own attributes and application. Knowing how to use these different shapes opens the way to magical possibilities. For example, you can use the ability of Quartz to store information rather as a computer does. Some shapes open a window into another world—past, present, or future, earthly or extraterrestrial. Others attract a soulmate or bring abundance into your life.

A geode with its cavelike center gathers and holds energy, releasing it slowly, while a cluster radiates it out rapidly in all directions. These shape-specific properties are relevant to how you choose and use your crystal. They can make all the difference between a crystal working brilliantly or not at all. A Citrine cluster attracts abundance but it may flow out again. However, the holding properties of a Citrine geode enable you to keep hold of your money, while a single point directs it in a specific direction.

CRYSTAL FORMS

Knowing the properties of different shapes of crystals, such as geodes and points, and being aware of the potential of particular facet shapes, helps you to harness the unique power of crystals, especially the myriad forms of Quartz. Certain forms are natural, while others have been cut to shape. Some of these artificial shapes mimic those found naturally—many large Clear or Smoky Quartz crystals are cut into tall pillar crystals for use as decorative items or healing tools, for instance, and special Quartz facets that occur very rarely in their natural states can be recreated so that they are more widely available.

Apophylite cluster

Crystals seldom occur as perfect balls, but for centuries Quartz, Obsidian, and Beryl have been carefully shaped by hand as scrying* tools. Seers gaze into their depths to ascertain the future. But balls have another function; they emit energy equally in all directions into the environment.

Quartz-based crystals in particular have naturally occurring facets at their tips. There are usually six facets, which equate to the six chakras* from the base to the third eye*, with the termination point representing the crown chakra and its link with the infinite.

How a crystal grows is significant in esoteric crystal lore. Quartz crystals that are cloudy at the base and become clearer as they reach the tip represent the potential for spiritual growth. A crystal pillar or large point with flaws or occlusions* can point to a traumatic or wounding period in life. The dross has to be cleared in order for consciousness to evolve. Quartz crystals that are totally clear are symbols of alignment with cosmic harmony. Keeping one of these crystals with you aligns your energies to the spiritual realm.

While specific facet shapes are most obvious on large crystals, even the smallest Quartz point may have a "window" formed out of the facets. A left-facing parallelogram window shape will take you back into the past. Facing the opposite way, the same shape will take you forward to the future. A differently contoured window will help you to channel or to transmit healing energy over long distances. There are record-keeper crystals that hold the wisdom of the ages engraved on their sides. Meditating with these venerable stones accesses universal knowledge. A soulmate crystal, on the other hand, attracts and holds on to true love.

If your crystal has rainbows in it, it is a sign of joy and happiness. Rainbows are caused by thin fractures within the stone. A rainbow crystal can be used to alleviate depression. Enhydros are crystals that contain bubbles of liquid that is millions of years old. They are a symbol of the collective unconscious that underlies and unites everything.

Each crystal shape has a specific use in healing. Wands sharply focus energy and may stimulate points on the body or draw off negativity. Crystals with terminations at both ends help to break old patterns, and can integrate spirit and matter. A crystal egg detects and corrects energy imbalances. A single point focuses energy into a beam, a square consolidates it, and a sphere emits energy in all directions. The following pages show you how different crystals, used wisely, can make excellent healing tools.

POINT

Many crystals have points, some large and some so small they can hardly be seen with the naked eye. Points may be natural or artificially shaped. A single crystal point has a definite faceted, pointed end and the other end tends to look ragged where it has been separated from a cluster base. A single crystal point is often used in healing. Pointed away from the body, it draws energy off. Pointed inward, it channels energy to the body.

Natural point

Natural point

DOUBLE TERMINATION

Double-terminated crystals have definite points at both ends. Some are natural and others artificially shaped. A double termination radiates or absorbs energy at both ends simultaneously, channeling it in two directions at once. A stone of balance, a double termination integrates spirit and matter and can provide a bridge between two energy points.

These crystals are useful in healing as they absorb negative energy and break old patterns, which can assist in overcoming addictions. They can also be used to integrate previously blocked parts of the self. Placed on the third eye*, double terminations can enhance telepathy.

*Artificially shaped double termination
(see page 350 for a natural double termination)*

328

CLUSTER

A cluster has many points bedded, but not necessarily fixed, into a base. The crystals may be small or large. Clusters radiate energy out to the surrounding environment and can also absorb detrimental energy. They can be programmed and left in place to do their work. They are especially useful for cleansing a room or other crystals, in which case the crystal should be left overnight on the cluster.

Cluster

GEODE

A geode is contained within an outer form. When opened, it is hollow with many crystals pointing inward. Geodes hold and amplify energy within themselves. Due to their rounded, cavelike shape and numerous terminations, they diffuse the amplified energy, softening the energy but not neutralizing it, allowing it to flow out slowly if required. They are useful for protection and aid spiritual growth. Geodes assist in breaking addictions and are beneficial for an addictive or overindulgent personality.

Geode

NATURALLY OCCURRING LONG POINT

This crystal focuses energy in a straight line. It is often mimicked in purpose-made crystal wands. It is used extensively in healing or ritual work. It will rapidly transmit energy if pointed toward the body, or draw it off if turned away. (See Wands on pages 354–359.)

PHANTOM

A phantom crystal appears ghostlike within the body of a larger crystal. Owing to the method of its formation, a phantom has absorbed learning over eons of time. Putting the past into perspective, it points the way toward growth and evolution and is helpful in overcoming stagnation. Each has a specific meaning, depending on the type of crystal. (See page 233.)

Long point

Phantom

BALL

Balls are usually shaped from a larger piece of crystal and may well have planes or flaws within them. They emit energy in all directions equally. Used as a window to the past or future, they move energy through time and provide a glimpse of what is to come or what has been, a practice called scrying*.

Ball

SQUARE

A square crystal consolidates energy within its form. It is useful for anchoring intention and for grounding. Naturally occurring square crystals such as Fluorite can also draw off negative energy and transform it into positive.

Square

PYRAMID

A pyramid-shaped crystal has four sides on a base, but the base itself may be squared off if the crystal is natural rather than artificially shaped. Naturally occurring pyramid-shaped crystals, such as Apophyllite, amplify and then tightly focus energy through the apex and are suitable for holding manifestation programs.

Pyramid

Pyramids can also be used to draw off negative energies and blockages from the chakras, replenishing with vibrant energy. Artificially shaped pyramids are available in an abundance of materials. They enhance and focus the inherent properties of the crystal.

EGG

Egg-shaped crystals confine and shape energy and can be used to detect and rebalance blockages in the body. The more pointed end is a useful reflexology or acupressure tool. They make excellent "hand comforters" to use in times of stress.

Egg

AMORPHOUS

Amorphous crystals, such as Obsidian, have no particular shape. Energy flows rapidly through an amorphous crystal as it has no rigid internal organization. They are strong-acting and instant in their effect.

Amorphous

LAYERED

Layered, or plate-like crystals, such as Lepidolite, are helpful for working on several levels at once as they spread energy out in layers. Their energy can assist in getting to the bottom of things.

Layered Lepidolite

TABULAR

A tabular crystal has two wide sides, resulting in a flat crystal which may be double terminated. Many tabular crystals have notches in them that can be rubbed to activate the information contained within the crystal. Energy flows freely through a tabular crystal, which offers little resistance. It removes confusion, misinterpretation, and misunderstanding and is an excellent aid to communication at all levels, both inner and outer. It is said that a tabular crystal is the finest tool for communication with other realms.

In healing, a tabular crystal links two points, bringing about perfect balance, and they can be used to enhance telepathy. This crystal activates other crystals.

Tabular

ELESTIAL

An elestial has many natural terminations and folds over a multilayered crystal. It has a gently flowing energy that removes blockages and fear, balancing the polarities and opening the way to necessary change. Sustaining and comforting, it is helpful in overcoming emotional burdens and in connecting to the eternal self. This crystal can take you into other lives to understand your karma or deep into yourself to give an insight into the spiritual processes at work.

Elestial

OCCLUSION*

An occlusion is usually formed from a deposit of another mineral within a Quartz crystal (see Chlorite, page 108). It is a cloudy spot or patch depending on the mineral. Minerals may also be deposited on an external face and show through when viewed from the other side. An occlusion radiates the energy of the mineral, focused and amplified by the Quartz surrounding it.

Tibetan Quartz with occlusions

ABUNDANCE

An abundance crystal consists of one long Quartz crystal with many small crystals clustered around its base. Its function is to attract wealth and abundance into your life. It is best positioned in the wealth corner of a house or business—the point at the farthest rear left of the front door.

Abundance

GENERATOR

A single generator crystal has six facets meeting equally in a sharp point. Large or small, this powerful crystal is the optimum shape for generating energy. A generator crystal optimizes healing energy. It aids focus and clarity of intention.

A generator cluster is very large with many long points, each of which can be programmed for a specific purpose. A generator cluster brings a group together in peaceful harmony—each person can have a point programmed specifically for them. It is extremely useful for generating healing energy and is often placed in the center of a healing group.

Large generator point

Generator cluster

MANIFESTATION

A manifestation crystal is a rare and precious thing. One or more small crystals are totally enclosed by a larger crystal. When you are absolutely clear as to what you want to manifest, this crystal will aid you, especially if it is carefully programmed. If you have any ambivalence or confusion over what you want, or are asking for purely selfish reasons, the crystal cannot work. The manifestation crystal can also be used to stimulate creativity and original thought, promote visualization, and invoke planetary healing. It is an excellent crystal for group work and functions to its highest purpose when programmed for the good of all.

Manifestation

*Large Cathedral
Quartz*

CATHEDRAL QUARTZ

Cathedral Quartz is a cosmic computer that contains the wisdom of the ages. It is a Light Library*, holding a record of all that has occurred on earth. Many of the Cathedral Quartzes are extremely large—the one pictured here is longer than a forearm. Even a small piece will give you the information you need, however. Parts of this book were written with the assistance of a palm-sized Cathedral Quartz natural generator studded with bridge crystals.

Cathedral Quartz may appear to be composed of several convoluted or separate pieces, but these are in fact all part of the main crystal which has multiple terminations with at least one point at the apex.

The Light Library can be accessed by meditating with a Cathedral Quartz. It aids attunement to the universal mind, and acts as a receptor and transmitter for group thought, which is raised to a higher vibration through contact with the pure energies of the crystal. It also provides access to the Akashic Record*.

It is believed that Cathedral Quartz makes itself known every two thousand years to aid the evolution of consciousness by raising thought to a higher vibration. Cathedral Quartz can be programmed to bring about a better world.

Placed over the site of pain, Cathedral Quartz has been found to bring significant relief.

RECORD KEEPER

A record-keeper crystal has clearly etched pyramid shapes on its side or sides. Sometimes these shapes are separated, so that the face is covered with triangles, others show only one, and some are grooved around each other in a chevron pattern. These crystals are often, but not necessarily, clear Quartz. They symbolize the perfect harmony of mind, body, emotions, and spirit and the all-seeing eye.

Record keepers hold the imprint of all that has gone before and are portals for spiritual wisdom. Discrimination and integrity are needed when working with a record keeper. Placed with a triangle on the third eye*, this crystal can be meditated with to access the personal or collective past or reattune to your own wisdom, and to facilitate insights for evolution. The crystal can be held and gently rubbed with a finger over the pyramid, which will "open the book."

Record keepers are an excellent way to explore your inner self. They can act as a catalyst for growth and aid in removing obstacles to progress. Reenergizing your whole being, they can prevent burn-out. (*See also* Record-Keeper Cerussite, page 98.)

Quartz record keeper

ETCHED

An etched crystal looks as though hieroglyphs or cuneiform writing have been inscribed on its faces. Used when meditating, this crystal takes you back to the ancient civilizations to access wisdom and knowledge of past lives. It can be extremely useful in attuning to spiritual training and initiations carried out at that time, reawakening inherent skills and healing abilities.

It is said that an etched crystal is a personal crystal and should be used by one person only but, appropriately cleansed and reprogrammed before and after use, it can skillfully guide another soul consciously to access their own past knowledge. It is especially helpful in past-life therapy when going to a time before dis-ease* or destructive emotional patterns set in, so that the regressee can feel what it was like to be without these heavy burdens, facilitating recovery of the state of inner perfection.

Quartz etched

SCEPTER QUARTZ

A scepter Quartz is a large central rod around one end of which another crystal formed. Scepter Quartz is also available in a smaller form in which the Quartz rod has a distinctive ridge and wider top, and as a reversed scepter in which a small crystal or opaque point emerges from a larger base stone.

Large scepter Quartz is a very special stone. Used as a meditation tool, it links into the wisdom of the ages and facilitates channeling high vibrations. Generating and amplifying energy, scepter Quartz is an excellent healing tool, as it directs healing to the core of a problem or to the center of the subtle bodies*. Dis-ease* is dissolved and the energies restructured at the physical, mental, emotional, or spiritual levels of being as appropriate. It is particularly useful where energy has to be transmitted in a specific direction.

Legend has it that these stones were used as a symbol of spiritual authority in Atlantis and Lemuria* and that they have reemerged to bring crystal power to the present day. A natural lingam, they can be used for fertility problems and to balance male and female energies.

Reversed Quartz scepters transmit healing energy, cleanse it, and then return it to the healer. They free the mind from false illusions and bring it to a point of stillness.

Other crystals may be found as scepters. Long and delicate natural Selenite wands are sometimes attached to another crystal to form a powerful healing tool that resonates at a high frequency and imparts deep wisdom and ancient knowledge. A Selenite scepter can be used to cut out dis-eased or damaged parts of the etheric blueprint* that carry the imprint of past-life wounds from the physical or emotional level and that have impinged on the present-life body.

Large scepter

Reversed scepter

TIME LINK (ACTIVATOR)

Time link or activator crystals can be found in two forms, right and left. From the unique helical atomic structure of Quartz, a small parallelogram forms a window that inclines to either right or left. This formation teaches that time is an illusion that we use to organize our experiences while on earth but that, in reality, there is no time as we know it. A left-inclined time link takes you into "the past" to explore other lives and the spiritual dimensions, and a right-inclined time link takes you to an apparent future or futures, showing that the future is what we make it. Some crystals display both.

A matched pair of activator crystals is an excellent tool for synthesizing the left and right hemispheres of the brain and can be used to heal disorders on different sides of the body, especially those caused by brain damage or dysfunction—a left-inclined activator treating problems on the right, and a right-inclined reversing dis-ease* on the left. Activators can also be used to align the chakras*, right-inclined treating the chakras from the back and left-inclined from the front of the body.

Time link (left)

Time link (right)

DIAMOND WINDOW

Flat faces at the top of a crystal are called windows. Windows may form in a diamond shape, some large, some small, which facilitate clarity of mind and the organization of information received from different levels of being. Gazing into a diamond window takes you deep inside yourself or enables you to read information for someone else.

A true diamond window is large and connected to the apex and the base, but even small diamond windows can assist the balance between the spiritual and the material worlds, facilitating living in everyday reality while at the same time being connected to a greater reality. Diamond windows provide a doorway into other levels of being and a deep connection with the self. They reflect the inner state of being and causes of dis-ease and can help to find a missing person's whereabouts or surroundings if a strong enough picture of the person is projected into the center of the diamond. (*See also* pages 352–353.)

Diamond window

SELF-HEALED

A self-healed crystal has many small terminations where it has been broken above its base and has then healed the break by laying down fresh crystals. A wound-healer, this crystal has an impressive knowledge of self-healing, which it is happy to share. It teaches how to heal and become whole again no matter how damaged and wounded one may have been.

ANCESTRAL TIME LINE

An ancestral time-line crystal has a very clear flat ledge going up from the base of the crystal toward the apex. It frequently has a fault line showing exactly where the family pain is located and how far back into the ancestral line it goes. Attuning to this crystal brings the source of the family dis-ease* to the surface so that it can be healed and the healing can then be sent back through the generations to a point before the dis-ease manifested. This transforms the whole family line, sending its benefits forward into future generations.

Self-healed

Time line

344

GATEWAY (APERTURE)

A gateway, or aperture, crystal has a cup-shaped depression within it that is large enough to hold liquid. Gazing into the liquid center provides a gateway to other worlds and enables one to travel through past, present, and future. It is an excellent stone for preparing a gem elixir that aids spiritual vision and psychic faculties.

KEY (APERTURE)

A key crystal has an indentation or aperture in one of its sides, which narrows as it penetrates the crystal. This indentation is usually, but not necessarily, three- or six-sided. It provides a doorway to unlock parts of the self that are normally kept hidden or to access hidden information of any kind. Meditating with one of these crystals reveals what is being hidden from you, especially by your subconscious mind, sweeping away illusion. It is an excellent tool for letting go of anything that holds the soul back and for tie-cutting.

Key

LIFE PATH

A life path crystal is a long, thin, clear Quartz crystal with one or more absolutely smooth sides. This crystal accesses your life purpose and helps you to go with the flow and follow your bliss, leading you to your spiritual destiny. This stone teaches you to follow what your soul, not your ego, wants.

SPIRAL QUARTZ

A spiral Quartz has a distinct twist down its axis and is beneficial for maintaining balance at any level. It draws universal energy into the body and anchors it during meditation. This crystal can stimulate the rise of kundalini* through the chakras*, clearing any energy blockages that impede the rise of kundalini energy.

Life Path

Spiral

SHEET QUARTZ

Sheet Quartz is laid down as a clear, flat layer, often between two crystals. It provides a window into other dimensions, facilitating communication, and it accesses the Akashic Record*. It can be used to contact relevant past lives and to go deep within the self. This crystal encourages the fullest use of psychic potential, stimulating the third eye* and enhancing visualization and spiritual vision. Used in meditation, it takes you to a place where answers can be found.

Sheet Quartz

COMPANION

A companion crystal has two crystals entwined and partly growing in each other, or a small crystal that grows out of the main crystal. Occasionally, one crystal will totally surround another. Companion crystals are nurturing and provide enormous support, particularly during difficult times. They can help you to understand a relationship better and to recognize how one partner can best support the other.

Companion

Tantric Twin

Soulmate

SOULMATE (TANTRIC TWIN)

A soulmate crystal does exactly what its name suggests—draws a soulmate to your side—although this soulmate may not be a sexual partner. Soulmate crystals, or tantric twins, are a pair of crystals approximately the same size growing from a common base, joined together along one side but with distinct and separate terminations. Tantric means "union of energies." Soulmate crystals are beneficial for all kinds of relationships. The closer they are in size, the more harmonious will be the partnership.

These stones have a powerful message concerning the bonding of two people into a close and intimate relationship. They teach how to be unique and separate, while united in equal partnership. To be in a

348

successful union, you need to be comfortable with yourself. If not, you will project your unresolved issues onto your partner. Tantric twins help you truly to know and accept yourself. As a result, interdependence and deep intimacy with another person are possible.

A twin crystal of unequal-sized sections is useful when working on a relationship such as mother–daughter, father–son, employer–employee. It helps more unconditional love to manifest in the situation and brings the two people into greater harmony.

If you are fortunate enough to find a soulmate or tantric twin Quartz crystal that has vivid rainbows across the intersection, then your relationship will be particularly harmonious. You will find a true soulmate. Place your soulmate crystal in the relationship corner of your house or bedroom—the farthest right from the door.

A true tantric twin crystal has two absolutely identical crystals aligned side by side. It is an excellent stone for two people working together as equals, whether spiritually or materially. They can also be used to harmonize and integrate the different levels of the self. A double-terminated tantric twin is the perfect stone for ascension— raising your vibration, it brings the higher self into line with the soul's purpose.

The relationship corner is the farthest back right point from your front door or the door into an individual room

349

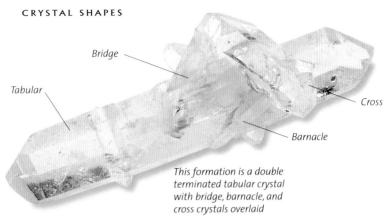

Bridge

Tabular

Cross

Barnacle

This formation is a double terminated tabular crystal with bridge, barnacle, and cross crystals overlaid

BARNACLE

A barnacle crystal has many small crystals covering or partially covering a larger crystal. The large crystal is said to be the "old soul" whose wisdom attracts the younger crystals. It is a useful crystal for meditating on family or community problems and for people who are employed in service industries. It provides a cohesive group energy that enhances common purpose and promotes working together. It is said to be an extremely comforting crystal after the loss of a loved one.

BRIDGE

A bridge crystal grows out of another, larger crystal. As its name suggests, it bridges gaps and brings things together. It can be used to join the inner and outer world, the higher self with the ego, or yourself with another. It is helpful for public speaking, especially when trying to communicate new ideas.

CROSS

A cross formation has one crystal at right angles to another, usually larger crystal. Stabilizing you within yourself, it opens to the multiplicity of worlds and facilitates spiritual study. This formation removes energy implants* and clears and activates any chakra.

BUDDHA

A Buddha crystal is distinguished by a formation closely resembling a Buddha sitting in the crystal's upper quadrant. It occurs in clear crystals such as Quartz and Danburite and is an excellent crystal for enlightenment and deep meditation, especially by a group taking it to the highest levels of awareness. A Buddha crystal assists in treading your path and acts as a guide in the physical, mental, and spiritual worlds. This crystal facilitates the transfer of ancient wisdom from the East into the pineal gland and from there into consciousness.

Buddha

CHANNELING

A channeling* crystal has a seven-sided facet at the front of the termination and a triangular face on the opposite side. As its name suggests, it channels healing energy or information from higher sources and then assists in expressing what is learned. Channeling crystals can facilitate trance channeling but should only be used by those who are experienced in such matters.

TRANSMITTER

A transmitter crystal has two seven-sided facets with two perfect triangles between them. They can be used to send long-distance healing or for energy or thought transmissions. Linking to the purest possible vibrations, they open the intuition and attract wisdom and communication from higher realms.

Transmitter

TRANS-CHANNELING

A trans-channeling crystal combines the channeling and transmitter crystal. It has a rare formation of three seven-sided facets, between each of which is a perfect triangular face. This is said to be a highly creative crystal, which is dedicated to the service of humankind and which can access the highest personal and collective wisdom, bringing intuitive awareness into any situation.

Trans-channeling

352

SEER STONE

A seer stone is a natural, water-polished stone that is cut to reveal an inner world.

This is an excellent aid to scrying* as it shows past, present, and future and can take you deep into your own inner self. It is also said that you can program a seer stone to take you back to a specific time frame to access its knowledge.

Seer Stone

ISIS (GODDESS)

The Isis crystal has a dominant face which is five-sided, with a tall sharp point rather like an arrowhead. This crystal is extremely useful for healing anything that is broken—body, mind, emotions, or spirit. It can be used to integrate spiritual energies into the emotional body, bringing in more balanced and joyful emotions, and to ameliorate overidentification with the suffering of others. This crystal can take you deep into your own heart for healing, insights, and acceptance. Helpful for men who want to get more in touch with their feeling nature, it can also assist sensitive children to stabilize their nature. An Isis crystal is beneficial for anyone who is facing transition, especially to the next world.

Isis

353

Artificially shaped wand

WANDS

Wands are the traditional healing tools of shamans, healers, and metaphysicians. The magic wands of myth and legend, they are believed to have been used by the highly evolved crystal healers of Atlantis, and many practitioners today believe that wands from those far-off times are surfacing once again, complete with their powerful programming.

Wands have the ability to focus energy tightly through their tip. Most wands are artificially shaped but naturally formed. Long pointed crystals such as the powerful laser Quartz are excellent healing tools.

The healing ability of wands is vastly expanded when programmed with intent (see page 29). When using a wand, it is important consciously to allow universal healing energy to flow in through your crown chakra*, down your arm to the hand holding the wand, and then into the wand where it is amplified and passed into the patient. Using your own energy for this purpose is shortsighted and inefficient, as you will become weak and depleted and need healing yourself.

QUARTZ WAND

A long, clear Quartz wand, whether natural or shaped, emits both positive and negative energy. It strongly amplifies energy and focuses this where it is needed, or draws it off and dissipates it as appropriate. Quartz can be used to reach the underlying cause of dis-ease* and to transform it. It points to, and then treats, areas of blockage or weakness in the physical body or the aura*.

LASER QUARTZ

Laser Quartz is a naturally formed, long, slender Quartz crystal that tapers toward the termination, which has very small faces. Its sides are often slightly curved. This is an extremely powerful instrument that should be used with caution. It should never be randomly pointed at anyone else and must be used only with clarity of intention. If this advice is followed, it is an amazing healing tool.

A laser Quartz focuses, concentrates, and accelerates the energy passing through it into a tight beam that acts like a laser. Suitable for psychic surgery, it stimulates acupuncture points and can reach tiny structures deep within the body, such as the pineal or pituitary gland, or perform precision work on the physical or subtle bodies. This wand can detach entities or attachments and ties to other people, and cuts away negativity of all kinds. It provides powerful protection for the aura and physical body. At a mental or emotional level, it removes inappropriate attitudes, outmoded thought patterns, and energy blockages.

Laser Quartz

TOURMALINATED QUARTZ

A Quartz wand with strands of Tourmaline running through it is extremely effective for anyone who is "buttoned down tight," whether from stress or trauma. It gently creates an opening for healing energy to flow into the body, realigning and reenergizing the meridians* and the organs. It cleanses and replenishes the chakras* and the aura*, providing excellent protection. Tourmalinated Quartz dissolves destructive patterns and behavior that has been carried forward from other lives, and alleviates negativity from the present life that is becoming fixed and will pass on to future lives. It fills the gap with self-confidence and a sense of self-worth that prevents the negativity from returning.

TOURMALINE WAND

Natural Tourmaline wands are useful healing tools. They clear the aura, remove blockages, disperse negative energy, and point to solutions for specific problems. They are excellent for balancing and connecting the chakras. At a physical level, they rebalance the energy meridians.

Natural Tourmaline wands

356

VOGEL WAND

Vogel (and vogel-type) wands have a
very precise vibratory signature. They
have specially created, indented facets
with specific angles down the sides of
a Quartz wand to create a superbly
efficient healing tool that has a very
high and pure vibration. The powers and
properties of Vogel wands vary with the
number of faces. The shorter, "fatter" end is
female and draws pranic energy which is amplified
as it spirals through the facets. The longer, thinner end is
male and transmits energy out in a strongly focused laser-like beam.
Vogels are excellent for connecting the chakras, removing attached
entities*, and removing negativity. They detect and rectify energy
blockages and strongly cohere the energy fields around and within
the body.

*Vogel-type
wands*

Vogels need to be programmed and employed in a very precise
manner and they are best used after appropriate training.

FLUORITE WAND

Fluorite wands are artificially shaped, most often from a mixture of
Green and Purple Fluorite. They have a wonderfully soothing energy
and can be stroked over the skin to relieve pain and inflammation.
Even a small wand will absorb an enormous amount of stress and,
if not cleansed, may crack under the strain. It is often suggested that
the wand be immersed in water to cleanse it, the water then being
returned to the earth for transmutation of the pain.

OBSIDIAN WAND

An Obsidian wand is ideal in cases where there are negative energies within the emotional body that require removal and the patient is ready for these to surface. Once they have been released, the Obsidian wand then protects the aura* and connects to the earth, pointing the way forward. Obsidian wands can also be used for diagnosis and location of blockages.

AMETHYST WAND

An Amethyst wand is the perfect tool for opening the brow chakra* and activating the pineal gland to stimulate intuitive vision. It will also remove blockages from the sacral chakra and from the aura. It can be used to heal a weak aura and to provide protection.

Specially formed crystal wands

ROSE QUARTZ WAND

A Rose Quartz wand is imbued with wonderful peace. It is excellent for calming emotional distress and for healing a broken heart, but it works equally well for any state of agitation or anxiety. A racing pulse is quickly normalized and raised blood pressure returned to normal under this stone's gentle influence. If the chakras are spinning erratically, Rose Quartz will instantly stabilize the energy and bring things into harmony.

SMOKY QUARTZ WAND

Smoky Quartz is an excellent crystal for grounding negative energy and providing protection. A Smoky Quartz wand grounds the energy of the base chakra by linking it to the earth chakra beneath your feet. It purifies this chakra* in the etheric body and neutralizes the effect of any geopathic stress*. It can be used anywhere on the body where negative energy needs to be removed.

Natural Smoky Quartz wand

SELENITE WAND

Selenite wands have a very pure vibration. They can be used to detach entities from the aura or to prevent anything external from influencing the mind.

Natural Selenite wand

QUICK REFERENCE

In the pages that follow, you will find quick reference guides to the correspondences between crystals and the zodiac and crystals and the body, their links with the chakras* and the aura*, suggested layouts and grids, and how to make gem remedies. These are designed to help in your selection of crystals and to show you some general principles.

The healing and protection layouts, for instance, can easily be adapted to your purpose. Find the layout closest to your intention, look in the body correspondences or the Index, and find the crystals you need. Checking their properties in the Directory will help you to refine your choice. Place as shown in the layout, or vary slightly according to your specific need. If you are looking for love, for example, you could adapt the heart chakra* healing layout with crystals such as Rose Quartz, Rhodochrosite, Rhodonite, and Kunzite. If you are of mature years, you could add Green Aventurine as this encourages love in later life. If it is passion you are after, Red Jasper and Green Tourmaline stimulate this. You will quickly learn to use your intuition to select exactly the right combination of crystals for your needs.

CRYSTALS AND THE ZODIAC

Birthstones ground and amplify celestial energies. Each of the twelve signs of the zodiac has traditional crystal affinities. Some arise from a month of birth, others from the planets connected to a sign. As new crystals are found they are assigned to a sign. Use the chart below.

Garnet

ARIES March 21 – April 19	Ruby, Diamond, Amethyst, Aquamarine, Aventurine, Bloodstone, Carnelian, Citrine, Diamond, Fire Agate, Garnet, Jadeite, Jasper, Kunzite, Magnetite, Pink Tourmaline, Orange Spinel, Ruby, Spinel, Topaz
TAURUS April 20 – May 20	Emerald, Topaz, Aquamarine, Azurite, Black Spinel, Boji Stone, Diamond, Emerald, Kyanite, Kunzite, Lapis Lazuli, Malachite, Rose Quartz, Rhodonite, Sapphire, Selenite, Tiger's Eye, Topaz, Tourmaline, Variscite
GEMINI May 21 – June 20	Tourmaline, Agate, Apatite, Apophyllite, Aquamarine, Blue Spinel, Calcite, Chrysocolla, Chrysoprase, Citrine, Dendritic Agate, Green Obsidian, Green Tourmaline, Sapphire, Serpentine, Tourmalinated and Rutilated Quartz, Tiger's Eye, Topaz, Variscite, Zoisite, Ulexite
CANCER June 21 – July 22	Moonstone, Pearl, Amber, Beryl, Brown Spinel, Carnelian, Calcite, Chalcedony, Chrysoprase, Emerald, Moonstone, Opal, Pink Tourmaline, Rhodonite, Ruby, Moss Agate, Fire Agate, Dendritic Agate
LEO July 23 – Aug 22	Cat's or Tiger's Eye, Ruby, Amber, Boji Stone, Carnelian, Chrysocolla, Citrine, Danburite, Emerald, Fire Agate, Garnet, Golden Beryl, Green and Pink Tourmaline, Kunzite, Larimar, Muscovite, Onyx, Orange Calcite, Petalite, Pyrolusite, Quartz, Red Obsidian, Rhodochrosite, Ruby, Topaz, Turquoise, Yellow Spinel
VIRGO Aug 23 – Sept 22	Peridot, Sardonyx, Amazonite, Amber, Blue Topaz, Dioptase, Carnelian, Chrysocolla, Citrine, Garnet, Magnetite, Moonstone, Moss Agate, Opal, Peridot, Purple Obsidian, Rubellite, Rutilated Quartz, Sapphire, Sardonyx, Sodalite, Sugilite, Smithsonite, Okenite

LIBRA Sept 23 – Oct 22	Sapphire, Opal, Ametrine, Apophyllite, Aquamarine, Aventurine, Bloodstone, Chiastolite, Chrysolite, Emerald, Green Spinel, Green Tourmaline, Jade, Kunzite, Lapis Lazuli, Lepidolite, Mahogany Obsidian, Moonstone, Opal, Peridot, Sapphire, Topaz, Prehnite, Sunstone
SCORPIO Oct 23 – Nov 21	Topaz, Malachite, Apache Tear, Aquamarine, Beryl, Boji Stone, Charoite, Dioptase, Emerald, Garnet, Green Tourmaline, Herkimer Diamond, Kunzite, Malachite, Moonstone, Obsidian, Red Spinel, Rhodochrosite, Ruby, Topaz, Turquoise, Hiddenite, Variscite
SAGITTARIUS Nov 22 – Dec 21	Topaz, Turquoise, Amethyst, Azurite, Blue Lace Agate, Chalcedony, Charoite, Dark Blue Spinel, Dioptase, Garnet, Gold Sheen Obsidian, Labradorite, Lapis Lazuli, Malachite, Snowflake Obsidian, Pink Tourmaline, Ruby, Smoky Quartz, Spinel, Sodalite, Sugilite, Turquoise, Wulfenite, Okenite
CAPRICORN Dec 22 – Jan 19	Jet, Onyx, Amber, Azurite, Carnelian, Fluorite, Garnet, Green and Black Tourmaline, Jet, Labradorite, Magnetite, Malachite, Onyx, Peridot, Quartz, Ruby, Smoky Quartz, Turquoise, Aragonite, Galena
AQUARIUS Jan 20 – Feb 18	Aquamarine, Amethyst, Amber, Angelite, Blue Celestite, Blue Obsidian, Boji Stone, Chrysoprase, Fluorite, Labradorite, Magnetite, Moonstone, Atacamite
PISCES Feb 19 – March 20	Moonstone, Amethyst, Aquamarine, Beryl, Bloodstone, Blue Lace Agate, Calcite, Chrysoprase, Fluorite, Labradorite, Moonstone, Turquoise, Smithsonite, Sunstone

Smoky Quartz

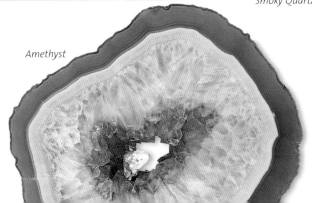

Amethyst

Citrine

CRYSTALS AND THE CHAKRAS

When healing and balancing the chakras*, an appropriate stone is placed on the chakra—on the front or back of the body, whichever is more comfortable. Leave for 15 minutes. Stones can be placed on all the chakras, or above the head and below the feet to perform certain tasks.

Pink Kunzite

GROUNDING ENERGY FROM CROWN TO BASE: Smoky Quartz
OPENING AND CLEANSING ALL: Amber, Dendritic Agate, Malachite
CLEANSING AND PROTECTING ALL: Tourmaline, Garnet
ALIGNING: Boji Stone, Yellow Kunzite, Kyanite
ELEVATING: Turquoise
CLEANSING LOWER CHAKRAS: Bloodstone

HIGHER CROWN	Kunzite, Apophyllite, Celestite, Muscovite, Selenite, Petalite, Azeztulite, Phenacite
CROWN	Moldavite, Citrine, Quartz, Red Serpentine, Purple Jasper, Clear Tourmaline, Golden Beryl, Lepidolite, Purple Sapphire
BROW/THIRD EYE	Apophyllite, Sodalite, Moldavite, Azurite, Herkimer Diamond, Lapis Lazuli, Garnet, Purple Fluorite, Kunzite, Lepidolite, Malachite with Azurite, Royal Sapphire, Electric Blue Obsidian, Azeztulite, Atacamite
THROAT	Azurite, Turquoise, Amethyst, Aquamarine, Blue Topaz, Blue Tourmaline, Amber, Kunzite, Amethyst, Lepidolite, Blue Obsidian, Petalite
HIGHER HEART	Dioptase, Kunzite
HEART	Rose Quartz, Green Quartz, Aventurine, Kunzite, Variscite, Muscovite, Red Calcite, Rhodonite, Watermelon Tourmaline, Pink Tourmaline, Green Tourmaline, Peridot, Apophyllite, Lepidolite, Morganite, Green Quartz, Pink Danburite, Ruby, Chrysocolla, Green Sapphire
SOLAR PLEXUS	Malachite, Jasper, Tiger's Eye, Citrine, Yellow Tourmaline, Golden Beryl, Rhodochrosite, Smithsonite

SACRAL	Blue Jasper, Red Jasper, Orange Carnelian, Topaz, Orange Calcite, Citrine
BASE	Azurite, Bloodstone, Chrysocolla, Obsidian, Golden Yellow Topaz, Black Tourmaline, Carnelian, Citrine, Red Jasper, Smoky Quartz
EARTH	Boji Stone, Fire Agate, Brown Jasper, Smoky Quartz, Cuprite, Hematite, Mahogany Obsidian, Tourmaline, Rhodonite,

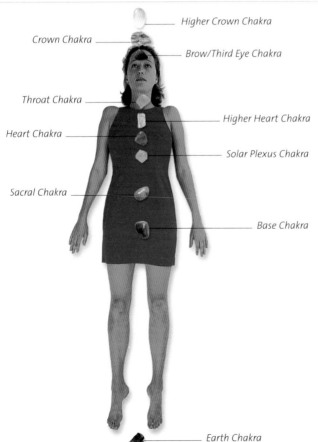

Higher Crown Chakra

Crown Chakra

Brow/Third Eye Chakra

Throat Chakra

Higher Heart Chakra

Heart Chakra

Solar Plexus Chakra

Sacral Chakra

Base Chakra

Earth Chakra

CRYSTALS AND THE AURA

Wear or place the following crystals around your body about
a handspan away to perform the functions listed.

Apache Tear

Bloodstone

AMBER	An ancient protector. It aligns the aura* with the physical body, mind, and spirit. It draws off negative energy and so cleans the aura.
AMETHYST	Gently cleanses the aura, heals holes, and protects it, drawing in divine energy.
APACHE TEAR (CLEAR BLACK OBSIDIAN)	Gently protects the aura from absorbing negative energies.
BLACK JADE	Guards the aura against negativity.
BLOODSTONE	Etheric cleanser that greatly benefits the aura.
CITRINE	Cleanses and aligns the aura, filling in gaps.
FLUORITE AND TOURMALINE	Provide a psychic shield.
GREEN TOURMALINE	Heals holes in the aura.
JET	Protects the aura against other people's negative thoughts.
LABRADORITE	Prevents energy leakage. It provides protection by aligning to spiritual energy.
MAGNETITE	Strengthens the aura.
QUARTZ	Cleanses, protects, and increases the auric field, sealing any holes.
KUNZITE AND SELENITE	Detach mental influences from the aura.
PETALITE	Highest vibration. Releases negative karma and entities from the aura.
SMOKY QUARTZ	Grounds energy and dissolves negative patterns encased in the aura.

THE BIOMAGNETIC SHEATH

The aura and its etheric bodies with the chakra linkage points
(see page 364).

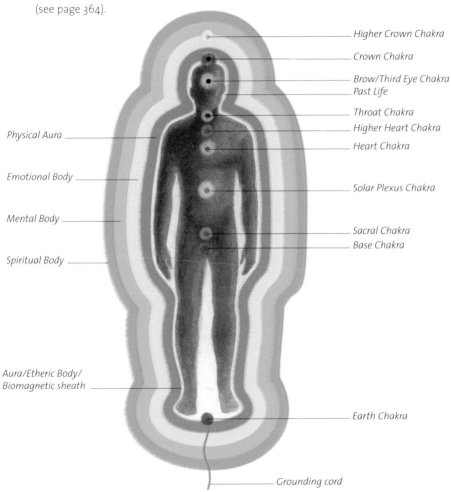

Higher Crown Chakra

Crown Chakra

Brow/Third Eye Chakra
Past Life

Throat Chakra
Higher Heart Chakra

Heart Chakra

Solar Plexus Chakra

Sacral Chakra
Base Chakra

Physical Aura

Emotional Body

Mental Body

Spiritual Body

Aura/Etheric Body/
Biomagnetic sheath

Earth Chakra

Grounding cord

367

CRYSTAL CORRESPONDENCES

Place an appropriate crystal over the organ to bring it back into balance or to stimulate or sedate it as required.

Red-Black Obsidian

Peridot

BRAIN	Amber, Green Tourmaline, Dark Blue Tourmaline, Beryl, Blue Lace Agate
EAR	Amber, Red-black and Snowflake Obsidian, Celestite, Rhodonite, Orange Calcite
EYES	Aquamarine, Beryl, Chalcedony, Chrysoprase, Sapphire, Charoite, Dark Blue Tourmaline, Celestite, Blue Fluorite, Fire Agate, Cat's Eye, Orange Calcite
TEETH	Aquamarine, Rutilated Quartz, Fluorite
NECK	Aquamarine, Quartz
SHOULDERS	Selenite
MUSCLE TISSUE	Cuprite, Magnetite, Danburite
LUNGS	Beryl, Pink Tourmaline, Peridot, Rhodonite, Amber, Dioptase, Kunzite, Lapis Lazuli, Turquoise, Rhodochrosite, Sardonyx, Blue Tourmaline, Chrysocolla, Emerald, Morganite
SPLEEN	Amber, Aquamarine, Azurite, Bloodstone, Chalcedony, Red Obsidian
STOMACH	Green Fluorite, Fire Agate, Beryl
INTESTINES	Beryl, Peridot, Celestite, Green Fluorite
APPENDIX	Chrysolite
ARMS	Malachite, Jadeite
PROSTATE GLAND	Chrysoprase
TESTES	Jadeite, Topaz, Carnelian, Variscite
HANDS	Moldavite, Aquamarine, Moonstone
SKELETAL SYSTEM	Amazonite, Azurite, Chrysocolla, Calcite, Cuprite, Fluorite, Dendritic Agate, Purple Fluorite, Sardonyx, Iron Pyrite
NERVOUS SYSTEM/ NEUROLOGICAL TISSUE	Amber, Green Jade, Lapis Lazuli, Green Tourmaline, Dendritic Agate

BONE MARROW	Purple Fluorite
PINEAL GLAND	Gem Rhodonite
PITUITARY GLAND	Pietersite
JAW	Aquamarine
THROAT	Aquamarine, Beryl, Lapis Lazuli, Blue Tourmaline, Amber, Green Jasper
THYROID	Amber, Aquamarine, Azurite, Blue Tourmaline, Citrine
THYMUS	Aventurine, Blue Tourmaline
HEART	Cuprite, Rose Quartz, Charoite, Rhodonite, Garnet, Dioptase
LIVER	Aquamarine, Beryl, Bloodstone, Carnelian, Red Jasper, Charoite, Danburite
GALLBLADDER	Carnelian, Jasper, Topaz, Calcite, Citrine, Yellow Quartz, Tiger's Eye, Chalcedony, Danburite
KIDNEYS	Aquamarine, Beryl, Bloodstone, Hematite, Jadeite, Nephrite, Rose Quartz, Citrine, Orange Calcite, Smoky Quartz, Amber, Muscovite
PANCREAS	Red Tourmaline, Blue Lace Agate, Chrysocolla
SPINE	Garnet, Tourmaline, Labradorite, Beryl
FALLOPIAN TUBES	Chrysoprase
FEMALE REPRODUCTIVE SYSTEM	Carnelian, Moonstone, Chrysoprase, Amber, Topaz, Unakite
BLADDER	Topaz, Jasper, Amber, Orange Calcite
CIRCULATORY SYSTEM AND BLOOD	Amethyst, Bloodstone, Chalcedony, Cuprite, Hematite, Red Jasper
VEINS	Variscite, Pyrolusite, Snowflake Obsidian
KNEES	Azurite, Jadeite
JOINTS	Calcite, Azurite, Rhodonite, Magnetite
SKIN	Azurite, Brown Jasper, Green Jasper
FEET	Onyx, Smoky Quartz, Apophyllite

Beryl

Red Carnelian

369

Fire Agate

ENDOCRINE SYSTEM	Amber, Amethyst, Yellow Jasper, Pink Tourmaline, Fire Agate
IMMUNE SYSTEM	Amethyst, Black Tourmaline, Lapis Lazuli, Malachite, Turquoise
DIGESTIVE TRACT	Chrysocolla, Red Jade, Green Jasper
METABOLISM	Amethyst, Sodalite, Pyrolusite
BACK	Malachite, Sapphire, Lapis Lazuli
LOWER BACK	Carnelian
CAPILLARIES	Dendritic Agate

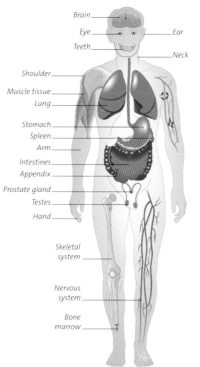

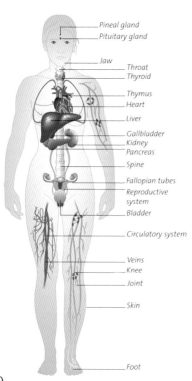

GEM REMEDIES

As crystals have powerful vibrations, it is easy to transfer these vibrations to water. Gem remedies, also known as elixirs or essences, can be taken internally—unless the stone is toxic. They can also be applied to the skin or put into bathwater. Remedies such as Black Tourmaline can be put into a mister in water and sprayed into the room.

TO MAKE A GEM ELIXIR

Place a cleansed, nonfriable crystal in a glass bowl with spring water. (Place friable or toxic stones in a small glass jar and then in the glass bowl. This is the indirect method.) Stand the bowl in sunlight for twelve hours. Remove the crystal and bottle the mother tincture in a glass bottle with an airtight stopper. To keep for more than a week, add fifty percent brandy or vodka as a preservative. Store in a cool, dark place. Add to bathwater or make a dosage bottle (see page 372).

Direct method of gem remedy preparation

Bottling the elixir

TO MAKE A DOSAGE BOTTLE

Add seven drops of the mother tincture to a glass dropper bottle. Fill with one-third brandy to two-thirds water if taking by mouth or putting on the skin. If using as an eye drop, do not add alcohol. Take seven drops three times a day. (Note: Certain remedies should be used externally only.)

BLUE LACE AGATE	Treats eye infections.
BLACK TOURMALINE	Provides psychic protection and screens from electro-magnetic smog*. Relieves jet lag. releases toxic energy from emotions, mind, and body.
MALACHITE	Harmonizes physical, mental, emotional, and spiritual; grounds the body. Use tumbled stone only.
FLUORITE	Breaks up blockages in the etheric body. Anti-viral.
JADEITE	Heals eye conditions, brings peace.
AMAZONITE	Balances the metabolism.
GREEN JASPER	Restores biorhythms and natural sexuality.
HEMATITE	Strengthens boundaries.
KUNZITE	Opens the heart.
AMBER	Acts as an antibiotic, heals throat problems.
GOLDEN BERYL	A gargle for sore throats.
BLOODSTONE	Releases constipation and emotional stagnation.
CHAROITE	An excellent cleanser for the body.
HERKIMER DIAMOND	Aids psychic vision and dream recall.
MOSS AGATE	Treats fungal infections.

Moss Agate

Black Tourmaline

CRYSTAL LAYOUTS AND GRIDS

Laying crystals on or around your body quickly brings relief from dis-ease*. You can also grid crystals around your bed or to protect your house. You can use crystals to stimulate the immune system or to alleviate stress. You can protect yourself from geopathic stress* or electromagnetic smog* or sharpen your memory. Remember to program your crystals before use.

ALLEVIATING STRESS

Relaxation is the best antidote to stress. Take eight Amethyst points and lay them around your body about a handspan away, point inward. Place one between and slightly below your feet, one above your head, two level with your neck, two at your hips, and two at your ankles. Close your eyes and relax for at least ten minutes—twenty would be better. You can leave them in place overnight, or position around your bed.

STIMULATING THE IMMUNE SYSTEM

Short treatment Place Pink Smithsonite over your heart, Green Tourmaline over the thymus above the heart, and a Quartz point-up above your head. Place eight Malachites around your body. Leave for fifteen to twenty minutes.

Long treatment During sleep tape Green Tourmaline over your thymus. Place Pink Smithsonite at each corner of your bed and a piece under your pillow.

Pink Smithsonite

CHAKRA LAYOUT

Place a brown stone between and slightly beneath your feet, a red stone on base chakra, an orange stone below navel, a yellow stone on solar plexus, pink stone on heart, Kunzite on higher heart, blue stone on throat, indigo stone on third eye, purple stone at crown, and white high-vibration stone above head.

Green Tourmaline

GRIDDING THE HOUSE
Place Black Tourmaline (for protection, geopathic stress*, or electromagnetic smog*), Selenite (for protection and angelic guidance), or Sardonyx (guards against crime) at each corner of the house, or room. Where possible, place a large piece outside the front door.

MEMORY LAYOUT
You will need two Citrine or Yellow Fluorite to strengthen memory, Green Calcite for mental clarity, Azurite for insight. Place yellow crystals either side of your head at ear level. Place Green Calcite on top of your head and Azurite over the third eye*. Leave in place for twenty minutes.

HEALING THE HEART
Place seven Rose Quartz, one Dioptase, and one Watermelon Tourmaline as shown and leave in place for twenty minutes. Four Amethyst points can be added, point facing outward, to draw off any emotional imbalances that may be blocking the heart.

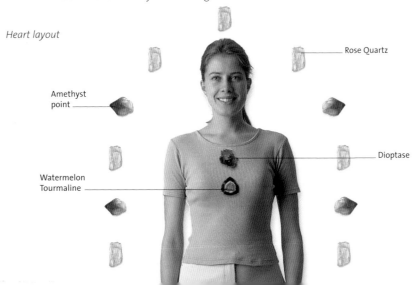

Heart layout

Rose Quartz

Amethyst point

Dioptase

Watermelon Tourmaline

DIVINATORY MEANINGS

Crystals have traditional meanings associated with them. For a quick answer to a question, place a selection of the crystals listed below in a bag. Concentrate on your question. Pick out a crystal at random; look at the meanings associated with that crystal to find your answer. If two or three crystals fall into your hand, read all the meanings.

AMETHYST	A life change and shift in consciousness. Faithfulness in love, freedom from jealousy.
AGATE	Worldly success or a pleasant surprise. Good health, wealth, and long life. Particularly lucky for people connected with the land.
BLUE LACE AGATE	Healing is needed.
BLACK AGATE	Needs and will find courage and prosperity.
RED AGATE	Health and longevity are yours.
BLOODSTONE	Unpleasant surprise, unlikely to be an illness.
RED JASPER	Pay attention to earthly affairs.
AVENTURINE	Future growth and expansion are possible.
GARNET	A letter is on its way.
CITRINE	Celestial wisdom is advising you.
DIAMOND OR CLEAR QUARTZ	Permanence. Business advancement. If the crystal loses its sparkle, betrayal.
EMERALD	Fertility or a secret admirer. If color pales, love is fading.
HEMATITE	New opportunities await.
JADE	Needs and will find immortality and perfection.
LAPIS LAZULI	Divine favor is yours.
QUARTZ	Be sure to clarify issues you asked about and those that arise.
ROSE QUARTZ	Love and self-healing are needed and will come.

Moss Agate

Opal

SNOW QUARTZ	Profound changes are coming.
RUBY	Power and passion, good fortune and friendship, but beware of strangers.
SAPPHIRE	Truth and chastity and the past will catch up with you.
SNOWFLAKE OBSIDIAN	End of challenging time.
TIGER'S EYE	All is not as it appears to be.
UNAKITE	Compromise and integration.
OPAL	Death or endings. If the crystal loses its brilliance, an unfaithful lover.
SARDONYX	A wedding may be in the offing.
TOPAZ	Exercise caution.
TURQUOISE	A journey is imminent.

Snowflake
Obsidian

INVOKING LOVE

Crystals can be used in ritual; here is an example using Rose Quartz to invoke love. You need four pieces of Rose Quartz and a large Amethyst. You also need candles and candleholders—which could be fashioned from Rose Quartz.

1 Place your crystals and four candles on a table covered with a silk cloth. Place one candle to the north, welcoming the spirits of that direction as you light it. Then place the others to the south, east, and west, again welcoming the spirits of each direction as you light each candle. Ask that these spirits act as guardians and keep you safe.

2 Take your Rose Quartz crystals into your hands and sit facing your table (if the crystals are large, do one at a time.) Close your eyes and quietly attune to the crystals. Let their energy flow through your hands, up your arms, and into your heart. As the energy reaches your heart, feel it open and expand. Touch the crystals to your heart. Rose Quartz is a powerful heart cleanser and healer, so allow your heart to be purified by the energies of the crystals.

3 Then say, out loud: "I am a magnet for love. I welcome love into my heart." Place the crystals around the Amethyst on the table and say out loud: "And love into my life." Sit quietly for a few moments with your eyes focused on the crystals. When you are ready to complete the ritual, get up and blow out each candle in turn, saying: "I send your light and love into the world." Either leave the crystals on the table or place them around your bed.

GLOSSARY

AKASHIC RECORD In ESOTERIC THOUGHT, a storehouse that exists beyond time and space that contains information on all that has occurred, and all that will occur, in the universe.

ANCESTRAL LINE The means by which family patterns and beliefs are inherited from previous generations.

ANGELIC REALM The energetic level where angels are said to live.

ASCENDED MASTERS Highly evolved spiritual beings who may or may not previously have been incarnated, who guide the spiritual evolution of the earth. People on earth who seek to raise their spiritual and physical vibrations are embarking on the ASCENSION PROCESS.

ASTRAL TRAVEL The soul is able to leave the physical body behind and travel to distant locations. Also known as OUT OF BODY EXPERIENCE or SOUL JOURNEYING.

ATTACHED ENTITIES Spirit forms can become attached to the aura of a living person.

AUDIBLE ORACLE An oracle that conveys its prophecies through sounds such as cracking.

AURA The subtle biomagnetic sheath that surrounds the physical body, providing a protective zone that extends for about eighteen inches to three feet from the body and contains information about a person's physical, mental, emotional, and spiritual state of being. This traditional name for the human energy field comes from the Greek *avra*, meaning "breeze." The intuitive eye can see dis-ease in the aura. *See also* ETHERIC BODY.

AUTOMATIC WRITING A type of writing that occurs when a loosely-held pen moves across the page of its own accord, or when the person holding the pen is impelled to write by thoughts passing through the mind into the pen.

BIOMAGNETIC FIELD/SHEATH The energy field that surrounds all living things.

BETWEEN-LIVES STATE In esoteric thought, the state into which the soul moves out of a physical incarnation (i.e. has died on earth). The soul exists in this state in a subtle energy body, which carries the imprint of what happened to it in former lives. Here the soul formulates its plan for the next life. The between-lives state can also be accessed by the soul during a physical incarnation. While in this state it is possible to heal the past and to access the purpose and plan for the present life.

BLISSED OUT Describes a sensation of heightened awareness in which the subject is excessively joyful, ungrounded, and light-headed, unable to function properly in the physical, everyday world.

BLOWN CHAKRA A chakra that has been damaged by drugs, unwise psychic practices, or meditating for too long a period of time. The chakra remains open and cannot perform its functions of energy filtration and mediation.

CELESTIAL DOORWAY The means of access to the higher, spiritual realms. *See also* CELESTIAL REALM.

CELESTIAL REALM In New Age thinking, the abode of the higher beings.

CHAKRA A spinning vortex of subtle energy. The term comes from the Sanskrit word *chakram*, which means "wheel," because these centers appear to clairvoyants and yogis as whirling disks of light. The system of subtle energy channels and centers is the basis for the MERIDIANS and energy points used in acupuncture, yoga practice, and energy healing. There are eight main chakras, located in a line aligned with the spine. These centers connect the energy of the physical body with that of the SUBTLE BODY. The eight chakras are located in the crown of the head, the center of the forehead (third eye), the throat, the solar plexus, the base of the spine, the genitals, and beneath the feet (earth) (*see pages* 364–365). When the chakras are functioning properly, the body's physical and subtle energies are in balance and harmony. Malfunctions can lead to physical, mental, emotional, or spiritual disturbances. Many energy workers believe that the chakras can be healed by the interaction between the vibrations of crystals and the energies of the body's BIOMAGNETIC or subtle energy FIELD. *See also* BLOWN CHAKRA.

CHANNELING The process whereby information is passed from a discarnate being (souls not in physical incarnation) via the voice and mind of an incarnate being.

CHRIST CONSCIOUSNESS In Christian thought, a belief in our own divinity (similar to that manifested by Christ) that links us with all life forms of the universe. In esoteric thought, the highest awareness and manifestation of divine energy. *See also* COSMIC CONSCIOUSNESS.

CHRONIC FATIGUE SYNDROME (CFS) A debilitating, virus-associated disorder, characterized by extreme fatigue, muscular pain, lack of concentration, memory loss, and depression, for which there is no known conventional medical cure at present.

CLAIRAUDIENCE Clear psychic hearing—the ability to hear things that are inaudible to the physical sense of hearing.

CLAIRSENTIENCE Clear psychic feeling—the ability to feel things that are physically intangible.

CLAIRVOYANCE Clear psychic vision—the ability to see things that are not visible in the physical world.

COSMIC CONSCIOUSNESS A very high state of awareness in which the subject is part of nonphysical, divine energies.

DEVIC KINGDOM The home of the devas, or nature spirits, believed in esoteric thinking to inhabit or rule over natural objects such as trees, rivers, or mountains. Though devas are generally invisible, people with clairvoyance can sometimes see or communicate with them or gain intuitive access to the devic kingdom, the energetic level at which these spirits exist.

DIS-EASE The state that results from physical imbalances, blocked feelings, suppressed emotions, and negative thinking.

DYSPRAXIA A condition characterized by clumsiness, lack of coordination, and the inability to distinguish left from right. Often occurs in combination with dyslexia.

EARTH CHAKRA The chakra located between and slightly below the feet which holds the soul into incarnation and links the physical body to the earth. *See also* GROUNDING and GROUNDING CORD.

EARTH HEALING The attempt to rectify the distortion of the earth's energies caused by pollution and the destruction of its resources.

ELECTROMAGNETIC SMOG A subtle but detectable electromagnetic field that can have an adverse effect on sensitive people. The smog is given off by electrical power lines and items such as computers, cell phones, and televisions.

ENERGY IMPLANT Thoughts or negative emotions that are implanted in the SUBTLE BODIES from an external, alien source.

ESOTERIC THOUGHT Nonscientific, nonmaterial thought based on a belief

in the existence of metaphysics rather than any one school of thought.

ETHERIC BLUEPRINT The subtle program from which a physical body is constructed. It carries imprints of past-life dis-ease or injury from which present-life illness or disability can result.

ETHERIC BODY The subtle biomagnetic sheath surrounding the body, also known as the AURA. *See also* AURA; BIOMAGNETIC FIELD.

FAULT LINE An inner flaw or break in a crystal that refracts light and appears to divide the crystal into sections.

GEOPATHIC STRESS Stress that is created by subtle emanations and energy disturbances from undergound water, power lines, and negative earth energy lines (LEY LINES). Geopathic stress runs through the earth and can affect or pollute people and buildings. It contributes to dis-ease of all kinds. *See also* LEY LINES.

GRIDDING The placing of crystals around a building, person, or room for protection or enhancement of energies.

GROUNDING Creating a sound connection between oneself and the planet Earth that allows excess and out-of-balance energies to flow from the body.

GROUNDING CORD A vibratory energetic cord that hooks into the earth and holds the etheric bodies and the soul in incarnation.

HEALING CRISIS A positive sign that symptoms will soon disappear, marked by a brief intensifying of those same symptoms

HOMEOPATHY A system of healing, first practiced by the Greek physician Hippocrates (c. 460–377 B.C.E.), that stimulates the body's healing power by introducing minute, diluted amounts of a substance that can cause the symptoms of a particular illness or disease. German doctor Samuel Hahnemann (1755–1843) was the modern founder of homeopathy.

HYPNOTIC COMMANDS Unconscious programs instilled by an external source can "run" a person, causing them to act in automatic mode.

INNER CHILD The part of the personality that remains childlike and innocent, or that can be the repository of abuse and trauma and may therefore need healing.

INNER LEVELS The levels of being that encompass intuition, psychic awareness, emotions, feelings, and subtle energies. *See also* OUTER LEVELS and SUBTLE BODIES.

KARMIC Arising from or appertaining to a past incarnation. Debts, beliefs, and emotions such as guilt can be carried over into the present life.

KARMIC SEEDS The residue of past-life trauma, attitude, or illness that lodges in the etheric body and has the potential to develop into dis-ease or illness in the present life.

KIRLIAN CAMERA A Russian invention that takes photographs of the BIOMAGNETIC SHEATH or AURA surrounding the body. This method of photography was discovered in 1939 by Semyon Kirlian.

KUNDALINI An inner spiritual and sexual energy that resides at the base of the spine but can be stimulated to rise to the crown chakra.

LEMURIA In esoteric thought, an ancient civilization believed to predate Atlantis.

LEY LINES Subtle energy lines, straight or spiral, that connect ancient sites or prominent points in the landscape.

LIGHT BODY A subtle energy body vibrating at a very high frequency. It is the vehicle for the soul and higher consciousness.

LIGHT LIBRARY An energetic repository of healing and knowledge.

MATRIX The bedrock on which crystals are laid down in their natural state.

MENTAL INFLUENCES The sometimes powerful effect other people's thoughts and opinions can have on some minds.

MERIDIAN In Chinese Medicine, a subtle energy channel that runs close to the surface of the skin and contains the acupressure points.

MIASM The subtle imprint of an infectious dis-ease from the past, such as TB or syphilis, that has been passed down through a family or place. The term was coined by Samuel

Hahnemann, the founder of homeopathy. *See also* HOMEOPATHY.

NEGATIVE EMOTIONAL PROGRAMMING "Oughts" and "shoulds," along with guilt, that are instilled in childhood or in past lives and remain in the subconscious mind to influence present behavior. They sabotage efforts to evolve unless released or reprogrammed.

OCCLUSION A mineral deposit within a crystal, which usually shows up as cloudy patches, spots, or a ghostlike image, depending on the color of the material. *See* Tibetan Quartz, page 228.

OUTER LEVELS The levels of being that are physically and environmentally orientated. *See also* INNER LEVELS.

OVERSOUL The part of a SOUL GROUP that resonates at a higher frequency and directs the spiritual progress of the group. *See also* SOUL GROUP.

PRANIC ENERGY The energy that permeates everything. It is particularly useful in healing work as it revitalizes and reenergizes. From the Sanskrit word *prana*, meaning "breath."

PLEOCHROIC In a crystal, appearing to have two or more different colors, or shades of color, depending on the angle from which it is viewed.

PRE-BIRTH STATE The dimension inhabited by human beings before birth. *See also* BETWEEN-LIVES STATE.

PSYCHIC ATTACK The direction of malevolent thoughts or feelings toward another person, whether consciously or unconsciously, that can create illness or disruption in that person's life.

PSYCHIC VAMPIRISM A person's ability to draw or "feed off" the energy of others.

PSYCHIC GIFTS Abilities such as clairvoyance, telepathy, and healing.

QI (OR KI) The life force that energizes the physical and subtle bodies. Chinese, pronounced "chee."

RADIONICS A method of diagnosis and treatment at a distance, using specially designed instruments, based on the premise that all dis-ease is a distortion of the electromagnetic field surrounding the body. The method originated in the research of the nineteenth-century U.S. physician Dr. Albert Abrams.

REFRAMING Returning to see a past event in a different light so that the situation it is creating in the present life can be healed.

REIKI A natural, hands-on healing technique that feels like a flow of a high frequency of energy trasmitted to the patient through the hands of the practitioner. The word REIKI comes from *rei*, meaning "a supernatural force or spiritual intelligence," and *ki* (*qi*), meaning "life energy." The technique was first used in Japan in 1922 by Mikao Usui.

SCRYING Discerning images in a crystal that reveal the future or the secrets of the past or present.

SICK-BUILDING SYNDROME The set of symptoms, including headaches, dizziness, nausea, chest problems, and general fatigue, associated with buildings with actual air pollution or inadequate ventilation, or negative environmental energies.

SMUDGING A method of purification, used by Native Americans, for the preparation of oneself and one's sacred place for spiritual practice. The process involves wafting about the smoke of slowburning herbs.

SOUL GROUP A cluster of souls who are in incarnation.

SOUL LINKS The connections between the members of a SOUL GROUP.

SOUL RETRIEVAL Trauma, shock, or abuse can cause a part of the soul energy to leave and remain "stuck." A soul retrieval practitioner or shaman retrieves the soul, bringing it back to the physical body or, temporarily, to a crystal.

SPIRIT GUIDES Discarnate souls who work from the between-lives state to provide assistance to those on earth. *See also* BETWEEN-LIVES STATE.

STAR CHILDREN Evolved beings from other planetary systems who have incarnated on the earth to help its spiritual evolution.

STAR GATE The access point through which extraterrestrial contact can be made.

SUBTLE BODIES The layers of the BIOMAGNETIC SHEATH that relate to the physical, emotional, mental, and spiritual levels of being. *See also* BIOMAGNETIC SHEATH.

SUBTLE ENERGY FIELD The invisible but detectable energy field that surrounds all living beings.

THIRD EYE The chakra located between and slightly above the eyebrows. Also known as the brow chakra, it is the site of inner vision and intuition. *See also* CHAKRA.

THOUGHT FORMS Forms created by strong positive or negative thoughts that can exist on the etheric or spiritual level that can affect a person's mental functioning.

TRIPLE-BURNER MERIDIAN One of the body meridians used in Traditional Chinese Medicine. *See also* MERIDIAN.

TUMBLED The term used to refer to stones that have been polished in a large drum with grit, resulting in a smooth and often shiny stone.

VISION QUEST A Native American shamanic practice, involving isolation in a wild, natural environment, in order to commune with nature and confront fears. It should not be undertaken without proper guidance.

INDEX

USEFUL INFORMATION

BIBLIOGRAPHY
Gienger, Michael *Crystal Power, Crystal Healing* Cassell & Co., London, 1998

Hall, Judy *The Illustrated Guide to Crystals* Godsfield Press, Alresford, 2000

Hall, Judy *Crystal User's Handbook* Godsfield Press, Alresford, 2002

Hall, Judy *The Art of Psychic Protection* Samuel Weiser, Maine, 1997

Melody *Love Is In The Earth* Earth Love Publishing House, Colorado, 1995

Raphaell, Katrina *Crystal Healing Vols I, II, III* Aurora Press, Sante Fe, 1987

Raven, Hazel *Crystal Healing The Complete Practitioner's Guide* Raven & Co., Manchester, 2000

TRAINING ORGANIZATIONS

UNITED STATES
The Association of Melody Crystal Healing Instructors (TAOMCHI)
http://www.taomchi.com

UNITED KINGDOM
Institute of Crystal and Gem Therapists
MCS
PO Box 6
Exeter EX6 8YE
Tel: 01392 832005
Email: cgt@greenmantrees.demon.co.uk
http://www.greenmantrees.demon.co.uk/found.html

International Association of Crystal
Healing Therapists (founder Hazel Raven)
IACHT
PO Box 344
Manchester M60 2EZ
Tel: 01200 426061
Fax: 01200 444776
Email: info@aicht.co.uk
http://www.iacht.co.uk

AUTHOR ACKNOWLEDGMENTS
My knowledge of crystals has been acquired over thirty years, much of it from intuitive use. However, the books in the bibliography provided additional material for this directory. I would also like to thank Pat Goodenough, Trudi Green, and Dawn Robins for practical, hands-on teaching and crystal contact. As always, the assistance of Steve, Jackie, and the rest of the staff at Earthworks, Poole, has been invaluable in compiling this book and sourcing appropriate crystals. Clive at Earth Design, Broadwindsor, introduced me to some remarkable crystals, as did Mike at The Dorset Pedlar, Bridport. And finally, I could not work with crystals and much else besides without Crystal Clear, for which I thank David Eastoe.

PICTURE ACKNOWLEDGMENTS
Grahame Baker Smith p367
Kate Nardoni of MTG p370